Netscape® Communicator 4

6 in 1

by Ed Guilford and Joe Kraynak

A Division of Macmillan Computer Publishing
201 West 103rd Street, Indianapolis, Indiana 46290 USA

President
Roland Elgey

Senior Vice President/Publishing
Don Fowley

Publisher
Joseph B. Wikert

Publishing Manager
Jim Minatel

General Manager
Joe Muldoon

Editorial Services Director
Elizabeth Keaffaber

Managing Editor
Thomas F. Hayes

Acquisitions Editors
Jill Byus
Martha O'Sullivan

Product Development Specialists
John Gosney
Henly Wolin

Production Editor
Audra Gable

Webmaster
Thomas H. Bennett

Product Marketing Manager
Kristine R. Ankney

**Assistant Product Marketing Manager/
Design**
Christy M. Miller

Assistant Product Marketing Manager/Sales
Karen Hagen

Technical Editors
Christy Gleeson
Sunil Hazari
Troy Holwerda
Roy Laudenslager
Tony Schafer
Mark Totleben

Media Development Specialist
David Garratt

Technical Support Specialist
Nadeem Muhammed

Acquisitions Coordinator
Michelle R. Newcomb

Software Relations Coordinator
Susan D. Gallagher

Editorial Assistant
Virginia Stoller

Book Designer
Barbara Kordesh

Cover Designer
Nathan Clement

Production Team
Marcia Deboy
Maribeth Echard
Tim Neville
Sossity Smith

Indexer
Chris Barrick

Acknowledgments

The authors want to thank these hard-working people at Que for their contributions in the construction of this book: Martha O'Sullivan, Lorna Gentry, John Gosney, Henly Wolin, all the technical editors, Audra Gable, and the production team. Special thanks to Martha O'Sullivan for expertly expediting this project.

Special thanks to my wife Karen and our children: Elizabeth, Eric, Katherine, and Abigail. Without their love and support, this book would not have been possible. —E.G.

Trademark Acknowledgments

All terms mentioned in this book that are known to be or are suspected of being trademarks or service marks have been appropriately capitalized. Que Corporation cannot attest to the accuracy of this information. Use of a term in this book should not be regarded as affecting the validity of any trademark or service mark.

We'd Like to Hear from You!

QUE Corporation has a long-standing reputation for high-quality books and products. To ensure your continued satisfaction, we also understand the importance of customer service and support.

Tech Support

If you need assistance with the information in this book or with a CD or disk accompanying the book, please access Macmillan Computer Publishing's online Knowledge Base at **http://www.superlibrary.com/general/support**. If you do not find the answer to your questions on our Web site, you may contact Macmillan Technical Support by phone at **317/581-3833** or via e-mail at **support@mcp.com**.

Also be sure to visit QUE's Web resource center for all the latest information, enhancements, errata, downloads, and more. It's located at **http://www.quecorp.com/**.

Orders, Catalogs, and Customer Service

To order other QUE or Macmillan Computer Publishing books, catalogs, or products, please contact our Customer Service Department at **800/428-5331** or fax us at **800/835-3202** (International Fax: **317/228-4400**). Or visit our online bookstore at **http://www.mcp.com/**.

Comments and Suggestions

We want you to let us know what you like or dislike most about this book or other QUE products. Your comments will help us to continue publishing the best books available on computer topics in today's market.

Henly Wolin
Product Development Specialist
QUE Corporation
201 West 103rd Street, 4B
Indianapolis, Indiana 46290 USA
Fax: 317/581-4663 E-mail: **hwolin@que.mcp.com**

Please be sure to include the book's title and author as well as your name and your phone or fax number. We will carefully review your comments and share them with the author. Please note that due to the high volume of mail we receive, we may not be able to reply to every message.

Thank you for choosing QUE!

Contents

Part 2: Netscape Netcaster

Part 3: Netscape Messenger

Part 4: Netscape Collabra

Part 5: Netscape Conference

Part 6: Designing and Publishing Web Pages with Netscape Composer

Part 7: Appendixes

Introduction

Congratulations! You've just selected Netscape Communicator, the world's most powerful Internet suite, to harness the power of the Internet. The only problem now is, you need to figure out how to use it. Of course, you're not looking forward to having to deal with manuals and Help systems that never tell you what you really want to know—at least, not without making you waste a lot of time searching. No, with a schedule as busy as yours, what you really need is a straightforward guide that'll teach you what you need to know in the shortest amount of time.

Welcome to *Netscape Communicator 4 6 in 1*, a book designed for busy people like you. Nobody has the luxury of sitting down uninterrupted for hours at a time just to learn Communicator. That's why *Netscape Communicator 4 6 in 1* doesn't attempt to teach you everything at once. Instead, each feature of Communicator is presented in a single self-contained lesson, designed to take only a short time to complete. So whenever you have a few minutes to spare in your busy day, you can easily complete a lesson on navigating the Web, using Web search tools, exchanging e-mail, or reading and posting messages in newsgroups.

Whom This Book Is For

Granted, *Netscape Communicator 4 6 in 1* might not be the right book for everyone. But if you can slide your way around Windows without too much help, it is the book for you. If you know a little bit about the Internet but you don't know anything at all about Netscape Navigator, e-mail, newsgroups, HTML, and all those other funny-sounding Internet names, this is *definitely* the book for you.

Netscape Communicator 4 6 in 1 is perfect for people who have busy schedules, a need to get up and running quickly, and a few ten-minute segments every day in which to learn. If this description fits you, *Netscape Communicator 4 6 in 1* is your book.

How This Book Is Organized

Netscape Communicator 4 6 in 1 is divided into six parts:

- **Part 1: Browsing with Netscape Navigator**   This part teaches you the basics of using Netscape Navigator to navigate the World Wide Web and download files. You'll also learn how to download and install *plug-ins* and *helper applications*, special programs that extend the capabilities of Netscape so it can play video clips, audio recordings, interactive presentations, virtual worlds, and other media files.

- **Part 2: Netscape Netcaster**   In this part, you'll learn how to tune in to Web pages with Netcaster. The lessons in this part show you how to use Netcaster to subscribe to Web sites and have updated pages delivered to your Windows desktop. You'll also learn how to quickly tune in to Web pages by flipping channels!

- **Part 3: Netscape Messenger**   This part shows you how to send and receive electronic messages (e-mail) with Netscape Messenger (formerly called Netscape Mail).

- **Part 4: Netscape Collabra**   In this part, you'll learn how to use Netscape's newsreader (formerly called Netscape News) to view and post messages to Internet newsgroups and carry on discussions with colleagues on an intranet.

- **Part 5: Netscape Conference**   This part provides instructions on how to use Netscape Conference to place free long-distance phone calls, carry on virtual meetings with its chat tool and whiteboard, browse the Web with your colleagues, share files, and leave voice mail messages.

- **Part 6: Designing and Publishing Web Pages with Netscape Composer**   Designing Web pages using HTML commands can be a daunting task. In this part, you'll learn how to use the Communicator's Web page editor to create your own Web pages, insert HTML commands, and publish your pages on the Web.

Hey, Slow Down! I'm New to This!   If you're new to the Internet and the World Wide Web, be sure to read the sections "What Is the Internet?" and "What, Then, Is the World Wide Web?" later in this introduction.

Each part is divided into several lessons. Because each of the lessons takes only 10 minutes or less to complete, you'll quickly master the skills you need. In addition, the straightforward, easy-to-understand explanations and numbered lists within each lesson guide you quickly and easily to your goal of mastering Netscape Communicator.

Conventions Used in This Book

The following icons are included throughout the text to help you quickly identify particular types of information.

Tip icons mark shortcuts and hints for saving time and using Netscape Communicator more efficiently.

Term icons point out easy-to-follow definitions that you'll need to know in order to understand Netscape Communicator and how it fits into the scheme of the Internet.

Caution icons mark information that's intended to help you avoid making mistakes.

In addition to the special icons, you'll find these conventions used throughout the text:

On-screen text	On-screen text appears in bold type.
What you type	Information you need to type also appears in bold.
Items you select	Items you need to select or keys you need to press also appear in bold type.
`Computer output`	Long sections of computer text appear in a monospace font.

What Is the Internet?

The Internet is simply a collection of interconnected networks. These networks are located within many universities, businesses, libraries, government offices, and research facilities all over the world. The Internet links these various networks so that people all over the world can share their information. When you connect to the Internet, you can access the information on such computers and view it, save it, or print it.

Even just a few years ago, if you connected to the Internet, what you saw wasn't very pretty. Typically, you connected to an Internet provider, typed in a series of very weird UNIX commands (as shown in Figure I.1), and eventually got to something useful.

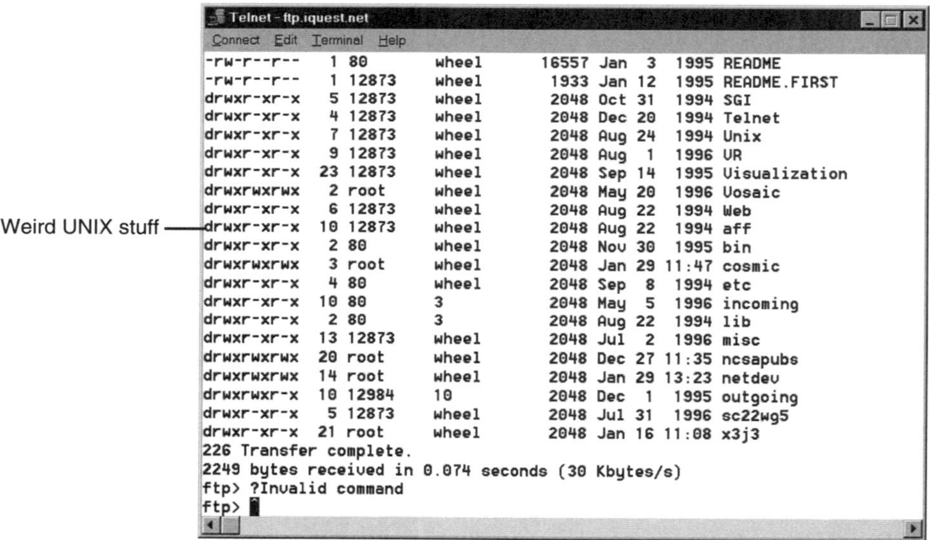

Weird UNIX stuff

Figure I.1   Under UNIX, the Internet is a scary place.

UNIX   UNIX is the language of the Internet, just as DOS used to be the language of most PCs. UNIX, like DOS, is an operating system. To use it, you type commands at a prompt (a reminder from the operating system that it's waiting for a command) to instruct the operating system what to do (to list the files in the current directory, for example).

Although you can still deal with the Internet by entering UNIX commands, you can avoid this cryptic language for the most part. Instead, you can use specialized programs to take advantage of Internet features. For example, you can use an e-mail program to send and receive messages electronically, a newsgroup reader to take part in discussion groups, a Web browser to open pages full of text, graphics, video clips, and other media, a chat tool to carry on live conversations by typing and transmitting messages, an Internet phone program for placing toll-free phone calls, and so on.

How Does Netscape Communicator Fit In?

Netscape Communicator is a suite of specialized Internet programs that work together to help you take advantage of most of what the Internet has to offer. Netscape Communicator consists of the following six programs:

- **Netscape Netcaster** allows you to subscribe to your favorite Web sites and have updated information sent directly to your computer at a scheduled time (typically during off hours when Internet traffic is light). You can then read the pages from your hard drive, where Netscape Navigator can access them much more quickly. Netcaster also transforms Netscape into TV control for the Web, allowing you to channel surf.

- **Netscape Navigator**, Netscape's award-winning Web browser, is the core program, which enables you to navigate the World Wide Web, copy files, search for specific information, display text and pictures, and much more. See "Understanding Web Browsers" (later in this introduction) for details.

- **Netscape Messenger** enables you to send e-mail messages postage free, with same-day delivery. It also allows you to read and respond to the messages you receive.

- **Netscape Collabra** allows you to post messages in electronic message areas called *newsgroups*, read messages posted by other people, and respond to messages. There are more than 15,000 newsgroups on the Internet covering politics, gardening, tattoos, dog training, and every topic in between.

- **Netscape Conference** is a tool with which you can place voice phone calls across the Internet or on an intranet. It also enables you to hold meetings during which everyone in the group can send pictures and messages back and forth and transmit notes. This tool is perfect for telecommuters.

- **Netscape Composer** is a Web page desktop publishing tool. It enables you to create your own Web pages and then place them on the World Wide Web for all to see. With Composer, you create and format a Web page just as if you were working with a word processor or desktop publishing program. Composer inserts the HTML codes that make up the Web page behind the scenes, so you don't have to deal with them.

Push Content   Netcaster takes advantage of a new Internet innovation called "push content." With push content, Web sites *push* updated pages to your computer rather than your having to *pull* them with your Web browser. This speeds up Internet access by allowing sites to deliver information while you are working on something else (or sleeping).

What, Then, Is the World Wide Web?

Except for e-mail, the World Wide Web (the Web, for short) is the most important and popular feature of the Internet. The World Wide Web (known as simply WWW) is a subset of the Internet. You can think of the Web as a large book whose pages are located on various parts of the Internet. You start on one page of this vast "book," and instead of turning from one page to another with your fingers, you click some text or a fancy picture, and you're taken to a different Web page.

Home Page   Your starting point when you connect to the Web through your Web browser. With Netscape Navigator, for example, you usually start on the Netscape home page. A home page is filled with links to other Web pages. The Netscape home page contains links to the pages Netscape deems important.

Home Sweet Home   You can create your own home page and fill it with links to your favorite Web pages. See Part 6, "Designing and Publishing Web Pages with Netscape Composer," for more information.

The pages of this "book" are actually a set of interconnected documents containing information on an array of topics. There's no telling what you might find on a Web document (Web page). You'll probably find text and graphics, but you might also find sound and video clips that you can play just by clicking them. You might even find fancy animations, such as a live stock ticker. Figure I.2 shows a Web page that contains many of these elements.

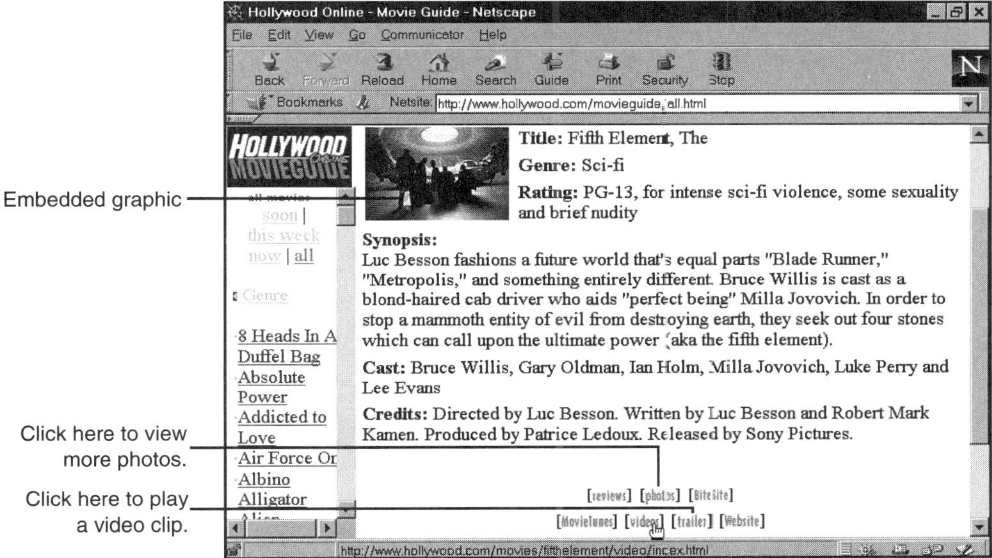

Figure I.2   A Web page often contains many elements.

The pages of the World Wide Web are connected like the threads of a large spider web. This enables you to jump from one Web page to another simply by following its "thread."

The documents or *pages* that make up the Web are connected through *links* that are sometimes called hypertext or hypermedia links. To jump from the current Web page to some other related page on the Web, you simply click a link. A link, by the way, is usually some highlighted text or a colorful graphic (see Figure I.3).

This is how a link works: Imagine that you're connected to the Web and you're currently looking at a Web page that contains current news headlines. You click one of the headlines (which is actually a link), and you jump to a Web page detailing a recent plane crash.

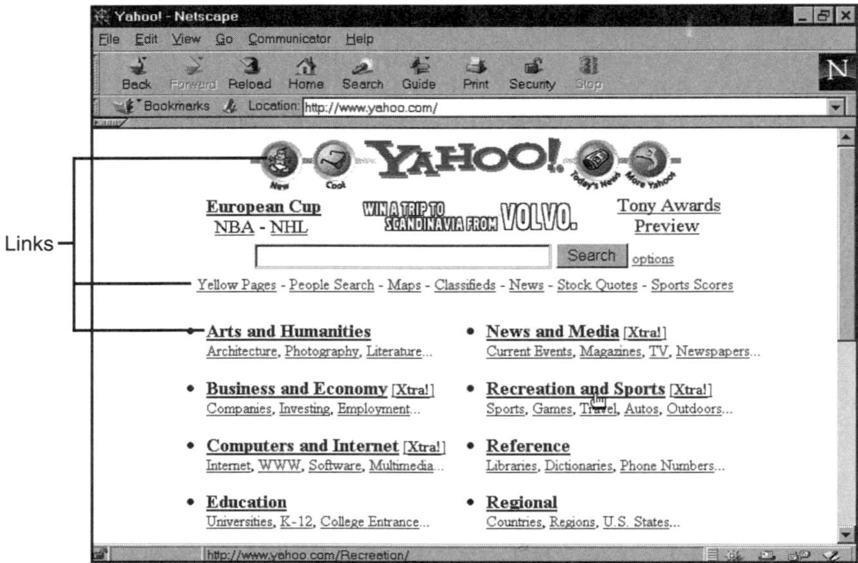

Figure I.3 Links can connect you to a related Web page.

Link Highlighted text or a graphic that, when clicked, takes the user to a related Web page.

Understanding Web Browsers

A Web browser is a program that connects you to the World Wide Web, a subsection of the larger Internet. As you learned earlier, the Web is like a large book whose "pages" you can read in whatever order you choose. With your Web browser, you can jump from page to page on the Web, download files, view graphics, and create bookmarks of your favorite Web pages. Netscape Navigator is one of the more popular Web browsers (commanding about eighty percent of the browser market), but there are others, including NCSA Mosaic, the Internet Explorer, and the Web browsers that are built into online services such as America Online and CompuServe.

Netscape Navigator (formerly known simply as "Netscape") was Netscape's first and—for a brief time—only product. When Netscape started to diversify its product line by offering an e-mail program, a newsreader, and other specialized software, Netscape changed its browser's name to "Navigator" to distinguish it from the other products. Netscape's newest product, Communicator (shown in Figure I.4), is made up of Netscape's most popular programs. Those component programs work together to provide some powerful features:

- Netscape Netcaster works along with the other components to deliver the latest information to your destop.
- The Component bar appears in front of all the other program windows, allowing you to quickly change to Navigator, Messenger, Collabra, or Composer.
- Navigator allows you to open a Web page, which you can then edit and save with Composer (assuming you have authority to edit the page).
- Composer works with Messenger, so you can use its powerful Web page editing tools to add graphics, links, sounds, and other items to your e-mail messages.
- Composer works with Collabra, allowing you to add pictures, links, sounds, and other items to the messages you post in newsgroups.
- Navigator works with Conference, allowing you to browse the Internet with a group of friends or colleagues.

The Component bar lets you quickly change to Navigator, Messenger, Collabra, or Composer.

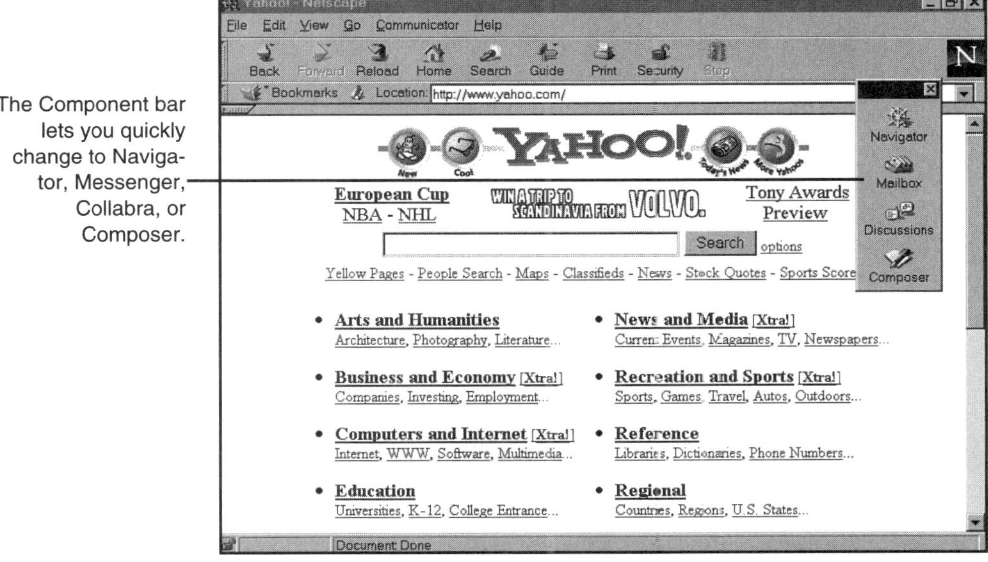

Figure I.4   Netscape Navigator sits at the center of the Communicator suite.

In this introduction, you learned the basics of Netscape Communicator and the Web. If you have not yet obtained or installed the program and you need instructions for doing so, flip to Appendix A, "Obtaining and Installing Netscape Communicator." Once you have the program installed, you're ready to get started. In Part 1, "Browsing with Netscape Navigator," you will learn how to use Communicator's award-winning Web browser, Netscape Navigator, to navigate the World Wide Web.

Browsing with Netscape Navigator

Navigating Netscape

In this lesson, you learn how to move from page to page on the Web.

Starting Netscape Navigator

Before you can start Navigator, you need to connect to your Internet service provider. If you use Windows 95, you should already have an Internet icon. You created it using the Dial-Up Networking program when you set up your Internet account. Follow these steps to connect to the Internet and start Navigator:

1. Click **Start**, select **Programs**, select **Accessories**, and click **Dial-Up Networking**.

2. Double-click the icon you created for connecting to the Internet, and the Connect To dialog box appears.

3. If you don't use a terminal window to connect to your service provider, enter your logon name and password now and click **Connect**. Then skip to step 7.

   If you normally enter your logon name and password through a terminal window after connecting to your service provider, don't enter them in the Connect To dialog box. Instead, click **Connect**.

Terminal Window   A window that pops up on your screen when you connect to your service provider's computer, prompting you for input. A terminal window is very similar to a screen you might use to log on to a network.

4. If a terminal window appears, enter your user name and password, as shown in Figure 1.1. (The password will not appear on-screen.) If you are using a SLIP or CSLIP connection, continue to step 5. If not, click **Continue** and skip to step 7.

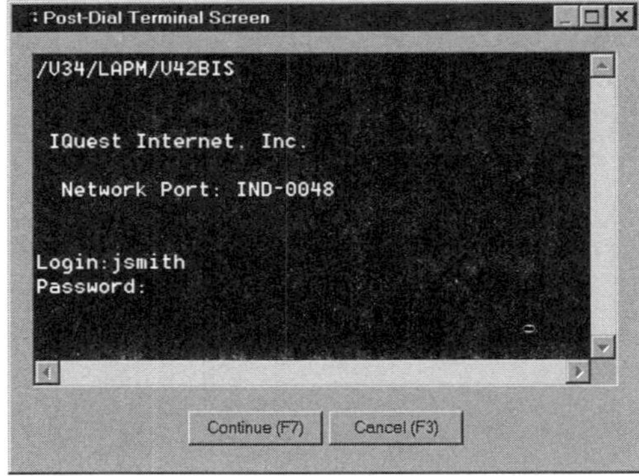

Figure 1.1   A terminal window prompts you to enter your username or login name and password.

SLIP/CSLIP   SLIP (short for serial line Internet protocol) is a set of rules that govern the communications transactions between a computer and the Internet through a serial (typically a modem) connection. CSLIP stands for compressed SLIP, a streamlined version of SLIP.

5. Use the scroll bars if necessary to see the IP address to which you've been assigned. Write this number down and click **Continue**.

6. Enter the IP address you wrote down and click **OK**.

7. You are connected to the Internet. To start Navigator, click **Start, Programs, Netscape Communicator, Netscape Navigator**.

Save Some Time   In Windows 95, you can start Navigator by double-clicking the Netscape Communicator icon on the Windows desktop. In addition, you may not have to establish your Internet connection before running Navigator. When you start Navigator, the Connect To dialog box should automatically appear, prompting you to establish the connection. Click the **Connect** button.

If you use Windows 3.1, follow these steps to connect to the Internet and start
Navigator:

1. Double-click the **Trumpet Winsock** icon.

Trumpet Winsock A Winsock is a software interface that acts as a middleman standing between the Internet and your other Internet applications (such
as Netscape Navigator and Netscape Messenger). The Winsock connects your
computer to the Internet and provides several sockets (sort of like outlets) into
which you "plug" your other Internet applications.

2. Open the **Dialler** menu and select **Login.**

3. If necessary, enter the phone number of your service provider and press
Enter.

4. Enter your user name and your password. After connecting, you should
see the message **Script completed.** Underneath, you'll see **SLIP
ENABLED**. Minimize the Trumpet Winsock window if you want.

5. To start Navigator, double-click the **Netscape Communicator** icon.

Understanding Navigator's Screen

When you start Navigator, you go directly to the Netscape home page. From the
home page, you can go anywhere you want (as you'll see in a moment). Figure
1.2 shows the Netscape home page and points out some of the important
elements in the Navigator window.

Your home page is your starting point. As you gain more experience with the
Internet, you may want to change your home page to some favorite Web page,
or you may want to create your own Web page, filled with links to your favorite
places on the Web. (A *link*, as you may recall, is a graphic or some highlighted
text that you click to go to the associated Web page.) You'll learn how to change
your home page in Lesson 5; you'll learn how to create Web pages in Part 6.

The Navigator window contains the following elements:

Component bar This bar appears in the upper-right or lower-right corner
of the screen and contains buttons for switching to Netscape Navigator
(Navigator button), Netscape Messenger (Mailbox), Collabra (Discussions),
and Composer. See "Working with Navigator's Toolbars," later in this
lesson for details.

Menu bar   Like other Windows programs, Navigator provides a number of menus from which you can select commands.

Toolbars   Navigator also provides three toolbars for quick access to frequently entered commands. The *Navigation* toolbar helps you move from one page to the next, stop loading the current page, and reload a page. The *Location* toolbar lets you go to a specific page by entering the address of the page or selecting it from the Bookmarks menu. The *Personal* toolbar lets you create buttons for the pages you visit often.

Location box   This text box displays the address of the current Web page. You can enter an address (a *Uniform Resource Locator*, or URL) in this box to jump directly to the associated Web page. (See Lesson 2 for more information on URLs.)

Bookmarks icon   This opens a menu of Web pages that you have marked with bookmarks. You can create a bookmark for the current page by dragging the Location icon over the Bookmarks icon. See Lesson 4, "Revisiting Your Favorite Sites," for details.

N logo   In the upper-right corner of the window is an N logo that displays flying comets when Navigator is in the process of loading a page. A little-known secret is that you can click this N icon to quickly return to Netscape's home page.

Links   Not part of Navigator's window, links appear on Web pages that Navigator displays. Links, which may appear as highlighted text, icons, buttons, or graphical maps, connect the current Web page to other Web pages and files. When you move the mouse pointer over a link, the pointer turns into a hand.

Status bar   At the bottom of the window is the status bar, which displays messages to indicate what's going on. For example, when you move the mouse pointer over a link, the status bar displays the address to which the link points.

Location/Netsite/Go to Box   The name of the Location box changes depending on what you are currently doing in Navigator. When you're viewing and working in a Web page, it is called either "Location" or "Netsite" and shows the address of the current page. If you click in the text box and begin typing an URL, the name changes to "Go to."

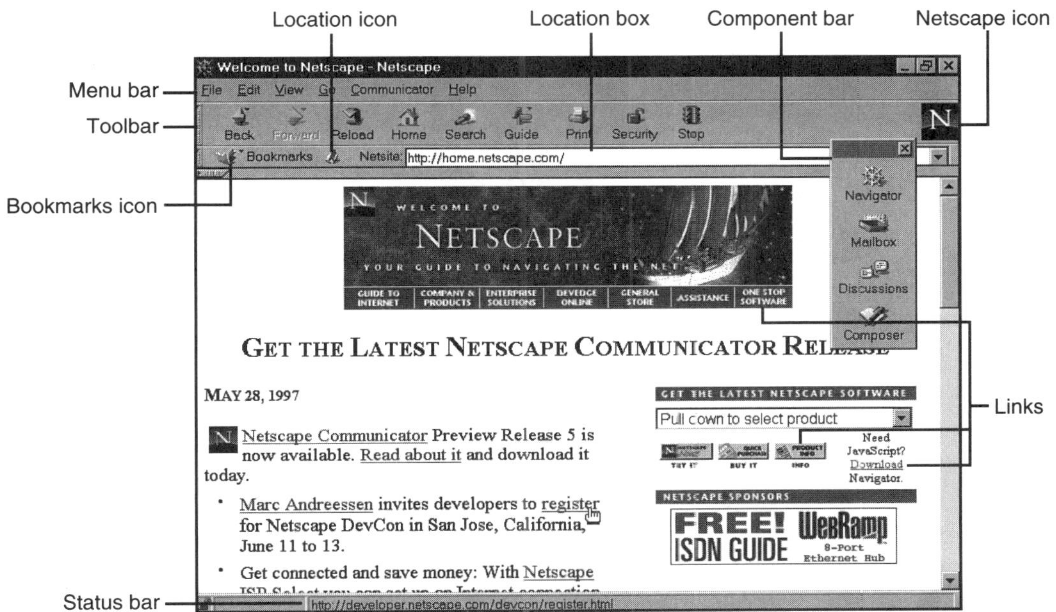

Figure 1.2 When you start Navigator, you immediately see the Netscape home page.

Working with Navigator's Toolbars

Like most Windows programs, Navigator displays several toolbars that you can use to bypass the pull-down menus and save yourself some time. For example, if you click a link to move to another page, and then you decide you want to look at the previous page, you can click the **Back** button instead of opening the **Go** menu and selecting **Back**.

The following list explains the purpose of each button on the Navigation toolbar:

Back takes you back to the previous page. If you point to the Back button and hold down the mouse button, a menu appears, showing the names of pages you've recently visited. You can select a page from the menu to go back to it.

Forward takes you to the next page, assuming you backed up from it. Like the Back button, the Forward button doubles as a menu.

Reload refreshes the current page if the transfer was interrupted before the page was completely loaded (for instance, if you clicked the Stop button).

Home displays Netscape's home page.

Search displays a search page at Netscape that contains links to various tools you can use to search for specific information on the Web. (See Lesson 7, "Searching for Information on the Web.")

Guide opens a menu that contains links to important places on the Web, including "cool" sites (sites that Netscape deems cool), new sites, and sites from which you can download useful software and search for people.

Print displays a dialog box that allows you to print the current Web page.

Security displays a dialog box indicating whether you can safely transmit information at a site. See Lesson 13, "Digital Passport, Cookies, and Other Security Topics," for details.

Stop tells Navigator to stop loading the page. You might stop loading a page if the process is taking too long or if you change your mind and decide that you don't want to see that page.

Smart Buttons   In this new release of Communicator, Netscape has introduced *Smart buttons*, which appear only under certain conditions. For example, the Images button appears only if you enter a preference telling Navigator not to load images (in order to increase the speed at which Navigator loads pages). You can turn off the pictures by selecting **Edit**, **Preferences**, **Advanced**, **Automatically Load Images**.

Navigator actually has three toolbars: the Navigation, Location, and Personal toolbars. You can turn any of these toolbars on or off to provide more space for viewing Web pages. Open the **View** menu and select the **Hide** or **Show** option for the toolbar you want to turn on or off (for instance, **Hide Location Toolbar**). Each toolbar also has a tab that you can click to hide the toolbar or bring it back into view (see Figure 1.3).

You can drag a toolbar's tab to change the toolbar's relative position on the screen. In addition, you can drag links from a Web page up to the Personal toolbar to create buttons for the pages you most frequently visit.

Although the Component bar is not exactly a Navigator toolbar, you can take control of it in Navigator by performing any of the following tasks:

- Click the **Close** (X) button in the upper-right corner of the Component bar to embed the bar in the status bar; this is called "docking" the bar. If the Component bar is already docked, click the button at the left end of the Component bar to return it to its normal size.

- If the Component bar is big and floating, drag its title bar to move it.

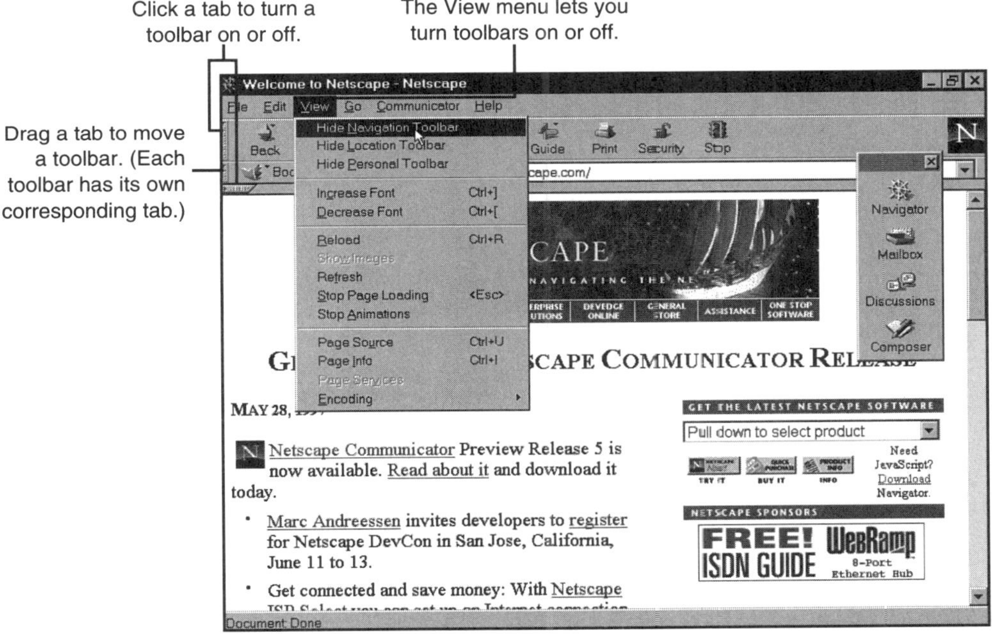

Figure 1.3   You can control Navigator's toolbars.

- If the Component bar is big, right-click its title bar to display the menu shown in Figure 1.4. This menu allows you to control whether the bar stays on top of other windows, change the orientation of the bar (horizontal or vertical), and turn off the text descriptions of the buttons (Hide Text).

- In Navigator (and in the other Communicator component windows), if the Component toolbar is docked, open the **Communicator** menu and select **Show Component Bar** to undock the bar. To dock the Component bar, open the **Communicator** menu and select **Dock Component Bar**.

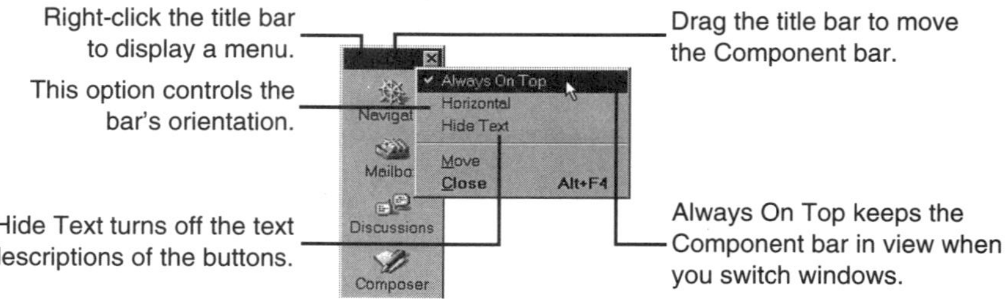

Figure 1.4   The undocked ("floating") Component bar.

Using Links to Jump to a Page

A link often appears as a bit of highlighted text or as a graphic. To use a link, simply click it. When you do, Navigator opens the Web page whose address the link points to.

Before you click a link, you might want to know where it will take you. To find out, point to the link; the address of the associated Web page appears in the status bar (see Figure 1.5).

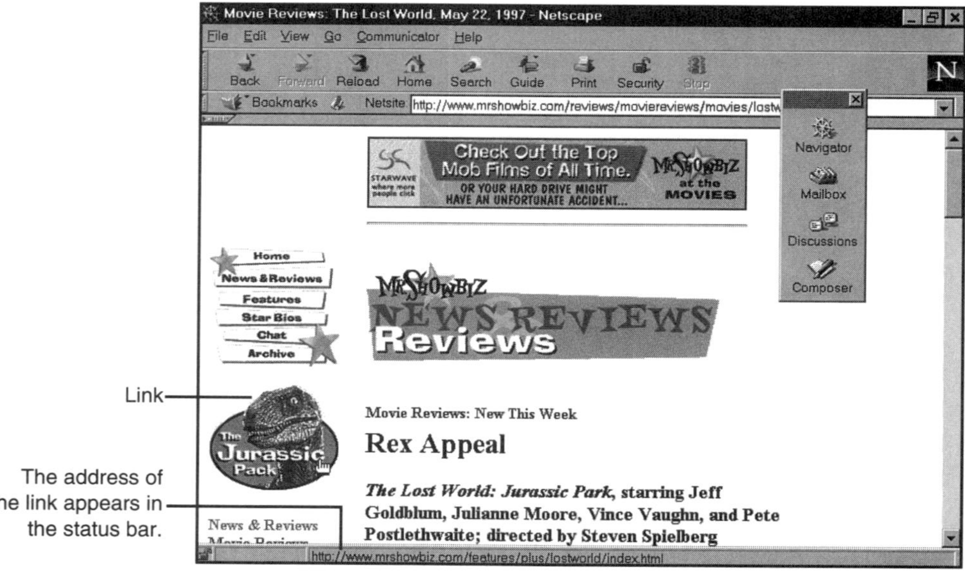

Figure 1.5   Click a link to load the page it points to.

Most links appear as blue text to begin with. However, once you click a link, it changes to purple. Navigator does this so that if you return to the original page later, you can easily see which links you've followed. (Sometimes, you may run into colors other than blue and purple, but you get the idea.)

Quick URL Primer

The beauty of the Web is that you don't need to know much to navigate. You click links and follow meandering trails to find the pages and resources you need. However, as you navigate, it's helpful to know a little bit about page addresses (URLs) just in case your Web browser has trouble finding a particular address. The following list explains the various parts of an URL. For more details, see Lesson 2, "Using Addresses (URLs)."

http:// All Web page addresses start with **http://**. HTTP stands for HyperText Transfer Protocol, the set of rules that govern the way data is transmitted over the Web. Sometimes, you'll see https; the "s" stands for secure. If you see an address that starts with something else (ftp://, gopher://, news:), Navigator is accessing a different Internet feature (not the Web).

domain.name.com The second part of the URL is the domain name of the computer that is serving up Web pages. For example, www.whitehouse.gov is the domain name for the computer that serves up Web pages for the White House. The domain name for most Web servers starts with www (World Wide Web). The end of the domain name provides some indication of the type of organization you are connected to (gov for government, com for commercial, edu for education, and so on).

directory/subdirectory/subsub/ Following most domain names is a path to the directory in which the desired Web page file is stored. These directory paths can be quite long.

webpage.html The last part of the URL provides the file name of the Web page. Web page names use the extension htm or html, which stands for HyperText Markup Language (the programming language used to create Web pages). If no file name is provided, the file's name is probably index.html.

What to Do When a Link Fails

If the link you click points to a Web page that has moved, you'll get an error message saying **File not found.** If that happens, you can try deleting the last part of the address (in the Location text box) and pressing Enter again to retry it. For example, if you clicked a link that pointed to the address http://www.movies.com/actors/gibson.html, and it didn't work, try erasing gibson.html. If that doesn't work, try deleting actors/, too. If you can connect to www.movies.com, you may be able to pick up the trail to your favorite actor's Web page.

If you get the error message **Document contains no data**, it's usually because the address to which the link refers is incomplete or has a typo. For example, a normal link will look something like http://www.news.com/current/headlines/clinton.html. If the link's address is http://www.news.com/current/headlines/, there's no document to which Navigator can connect. Try connecting to just http://www.news.com. From there, you can probably find a link with the complete address of the page you want.

Sometimes a Page Just Won't Load   One way to know if Navigator is stuck is to watch the status bar; Navigator displays its progress there. If nothing happens, or if it just plain takes too long, you may want to try reloading the page. To do so, click the **Stop** button, and then click the **Reload** button.

CAUTION

If you click a link to a type of file that Navigator doesn't recognize (such as a unique video or sound format), it probably won't play. Instead, you'll see a message telling you that you don't yet have a viewer configured to handle the file. If Navigator "knows" which viewer you need, Navigator might prompt you to get the viewer and install it. See Lesson 18, "Using Plug-Ins and Helper Applications," for details.

Unknown File Types   In Lessons 14 through 24, you'll learn how to download and install the proper in-line plug-ins and helper apps that enable Navigator to handle unknown file types. In many cases, Navigator can tell which plug-in you need to play a particular file type, and it prompts you to get the plug-in right away. Follow the on-screen instructions, or see one of the lessons later in this part for details.

CAUTION

You might click a link and get the error message **Netscape is unable to locate the server: xxxx. The server does not have a DNS entry**. If so, try clicking the link again. If it still doesn't work, then there may be a typo in the link's address, or the page to which the link refers may no longer exist. This kind of error could also mean that your Internet connection has been broken. Dial into your service provider again and retry the link.

Busy Signal?   If a page is popular, a lot of people might be trying to connect to it at the same time. In such a case, you'll probably get one of two error messages: **Connection refused by Host** or **Too many users, try again later**. Try again at a less busy time, such as early in the day or late at night. (However, if you get a **403** error or a similar number, you may be locked out of the site.)

Returning to Previously Viewed Pages

As you move from one Web page to another, Netscape Navigator saves the history of where you've been so you can easily return to any previously viewed page. However, Navigator tracks the history for the current session only; that history is erased when you exit the program.

What If I Find a Page I Like?   If you find a Web page that you plan to visit often, you can save its address permanently. See Lesson 4 for details.

Using the history feature in Netscape Navigator is a lot like reading a book: To return to a previously viewed page, you move backward in the "book." In Navigator, you can move backward as many pages as you like simply by clicking the **Back** button. After you back up, you can return to where you were by moving forward through previously viewed Web pages. Simply click the **Forward** button. If you want to return to your starting point, you can click the **Back** button until you get there, or you can click the **Home** button. Either way, you return to your home page, which by default is the Netscape home page.

To find out where the Back or Forward button will take you, rest the mouse pointer on it. To view a list of pages you have visited recently, point to the **Back** or **Forward** button and hold down the mouse button. This opens a menu that displays the names or addresses of pages you can quickly return to. Click the desired page.

CAUTION

Nothing Happens When I Click the Button   If the Forward (or Backward) button is gray, you have moved to the end (or the beginning) of the history. You can't select the button again because you've moved as far forward or backward in the history as you can.

CAUTION

Working with Frames   When a Web page uses frames, moving to a previously viewed page is a bit trickier than described here. See Lesson 3 for more details.

You can also jump directly to any previously viewed page by selecting it from the Location drop-down list. Just follow these steps:

1. Click the **Location** drop-down arrow. The history list appears, as shown in Figure 1.6.

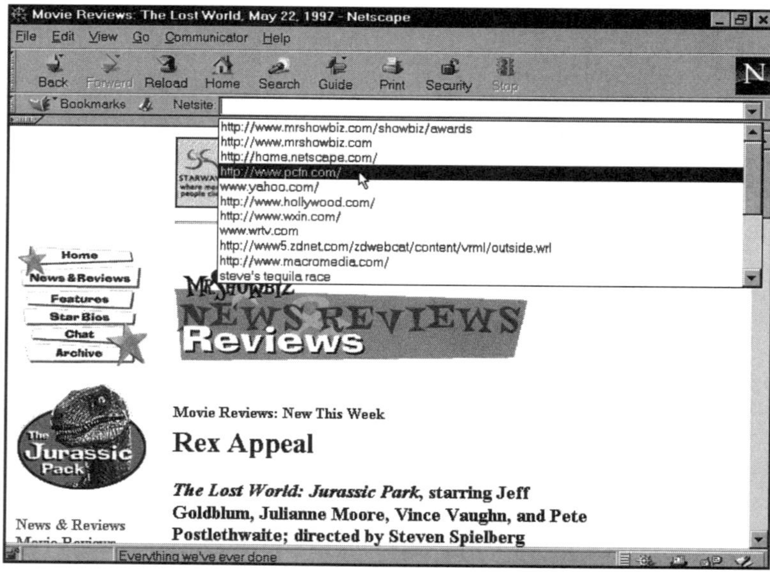

Figure 1.6   A list of pages you've previously visited.

2. Click the address of the page you want to view, and Navigator opens and displays the selected page.

Use the Go Menu You can also find a list of pages you have recently visited at the bottom of the **Go** menu. There, however, the pages are listed by name instead of by address.

If you visited the page a long time ago, you may need to select it from a more comprehensive history list. Open the **Communicator** menu and select **History**. The History window appears, showing a list of all the pages you visited in the current session. Click the name or address of the desired page.

Keyboard Navigation

The mouse makes it easy to work the Web: You just point and click. However, in case you don't like taking your hands off the keyboard, Navigator does offer some keyboard alternatives:

- **Tab** from one link to another on a page and press **Enter** to select one.
- Press **Alt+←** to move back to the previous page; press **Alt+→** to move ahead to the next page.
- Use the up and down arrow keys to move up or down a page.
- Press **Page Up** or **Page Down** to scroll.
- Press **Ctrl+Home** to go to the top of a page or **Ctrl+End** to drop to the bottom.

Also, don't forget that you can use shortcut key combinations, such as Ctrl+O to open a page or Esc to stop loading.

Exiting Navigator

When you're ready to exit Navigator, use whichever of the following methods is appropriate for your system:

- **Windows 95** Open the **File** menu and select **Exit**, or click the **Close** button. To disconnect from the Internet, return to the Connect To dialog box and click **Disconnect**.

- **Windows 3.1**   Open the **File** menu and select **Exit**, or double-click the **Control-menu box**. Disconnect from the Internet by returning to Trumpet Winsock, opening the **Dialler** menu, and selecting **Bye**.

In this lesson, you learned how to start Navigator, how to navigate through the Web using links and Navigator's history list, and how to exit Navigator. In the next lesson, you'll learn how to enter an address so that you can jump directly to a particular Web page.

Using Addresses (URLs)

In this lesson, you learn how to use addresses (URLs) to move directly to a Web page.

Understanding Addresses (URLs)

As mentioned in the previous lesson, each Web page has its own address, or URL (Uniform Resource Locator). A typical URL looks something like this:

http://www.ticketmaster.com/events/ev_home.html

If you know the address for a particular page you want to see, you can type it in the **Location/Go to** box in Navigator. Press **Enter**, and you jump directly to the Web page whose address you entered.

TIP

Where Do I Get the Address for a Page? If you don't know the address for a particular page or even which pages you might want to view, you can search for applicable pages using a Web search tool such as InfoSeek, Yahoo!, or Lycos. See Part 1 Lesson 7 for more information on those tools. You can also get addresses for hot Web sites from any of several Internet magazines such as *The Net*, *Websight*, *Net Guide*, and *Internet World*. In addition, many companies now include their Web page addresses in their advertising, commonly incorporating Web page addresses into TV commercials and magazine ads.

A Web address identifies an official Internet resource. Every URL has two parts: the *content identifier* and the *location*. Take another look at our sample address, and then we'll break it down.

http://www.ticketmaster.com/events/ev_home.html

The first part, the **http://** part in our sample, is the content identifier (or content-id for short). The content-id tells Navigator which protocol or language was used to create the current page. The http:// identifier tells Navigator that this page was written using HyperText Transport Protocol (http for short). Navigator supports other protocols as well, such as ftp:// (for transferring files), gopher://, telnet://, and news:. This flexibility allows you to connect to other resources through the Web. For instance, you can link to a site's FTP directory or a UseNet newsgroup just as easily as you can link to another Web page—just by clicking the link.

Which Protocol Do I Use?!   Don't worry too much about the different protocols. Navigator has what it takes to handle FTP and Gopher. If you enter the URL for a newsgroup, Navigator automatically runs Netscape Collabra, which is designed for newsgroups. And, if you click a link for an e-mail address, Navigator runs Netscape Messenger, allowing you to compose an e-mail message.

How Can I Tell Which Resource a Link Will Connect Me To?   If you want to see what type of resource you're jumping to before you click its link, point to the link but don't click. The address of the link appears in the status bar. The content-id at the beginning of the address tells you whether the link connects to a Web page (http://) or some other type of resource.

The second part of the sample address identifies the location of the particular Web page or resource. To understand the location better, you need to divide it into two smaller parts:

- The first part (**www.ticketmaster.com**) is the *domain name* or *host name*. Each computer connected to the Internet has a unique name that makes it easy to identify it from the thousands of other computers connected directly to the Web. Your PC doesn't have a domain name, but your service provider's does because it's connected to the Web. (You connect to the Web through your service provider's domain.) So the address www.ticketmaster.com refers to the Web-managing portion (www) of a computer called ticketmaster.com.

Domain Type   The **.com** part, by the way, tells you that this computer is basically used for commercial (business) purposes. Other popular extensions include .gov for government, .edu for education, .pub for public, and .net for Internet service provider.

- The second part of the location (**/events/ev_home.html**) is the name of a particular Web resource. This name looks very much like a directory path because that's exactly what it is. You see, every Web page is actually just a document file that exists on some computer connected to the Web. These directory paths follow the UNIX format, which means that they use forward slashes (/) in place of the backslashes (\) you're used to seeing in DOS and Windows. So the address in the sample will connect you to a document called *ev_home.html,* located in the *events* directory of the *ticketmaster* computer.

No Document Name?   Some addresses don't provide an actual document name. For example, you might be given the address http://www.weather.com, which connects you to the Weather Channel's computer. When you connect, that system automatically displays the Weather Channel's home page (a document file located on that computer). You'll encounter a lot of systems set up this way, so don't worry when you encounter an address that doesn't end in a document name.

Using Addresses to Jump to a Page

Once you have the address of a Web resource you'd like to visit, it's easy to jump to that page. Just follow these steps:

1. Click in the **Location** box. The address of the current page becomes selected so that you can replace it with something else. If the current address is not highlighted, double-click inside the **Location** text box.

2. Type the address you want to go to, as shown in Figure 2.1. (You'll probably notice that the text box's name changes to "Go to" as you type.) Make sure that you use forward slashes (/) to separate the parts of the address, and that you use the proper case.

Case Is Important Note that the address www.Weather.com (for example) is different from www.weather.com. The use of upper- and lowercase letters is very important, especially when you are typing the path to a directory. Make sure you write down addresses correctly and enter them accurately.

CAUTION

3. Press **Enter**, and you're taken to the Web resource at the address you entered.

Enter an URL here.

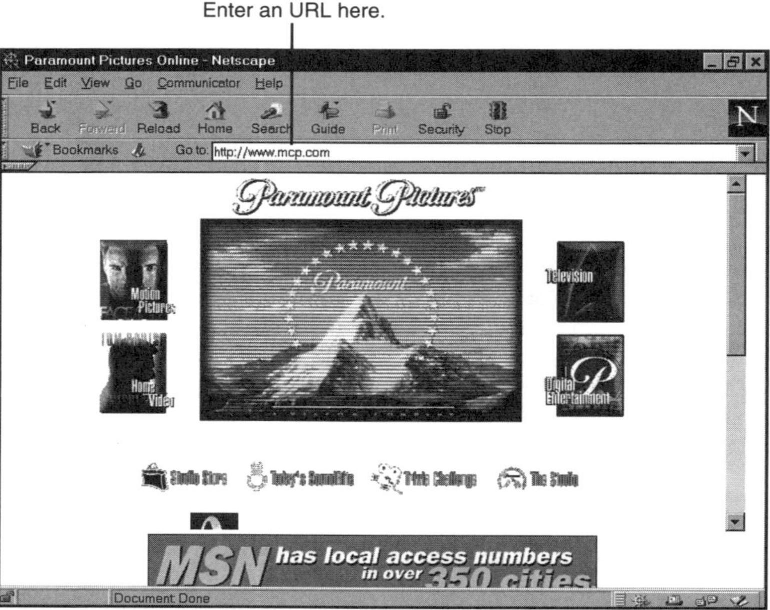

Figure 2.1 Enter an URL in the Location/Go to text box.

If the Location text box contains an URL that's similar to the page you want to go to, you can edit the URL instead of completely replacing it. Click in the URL text box two times, so the insertion point appears inside it. Then use the Delete or Backspace key to remove text, and you can type your desired changes.

You can also open the **File** menu and select **Open Page** to enter an address if you want. Simply type the address in the Open Page dialog box, make sure **Open Location or File in Navigator** is selected, and click **Open** to jump to that Web page.

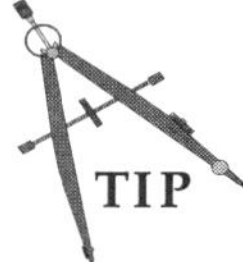

Save Yourself Some Keystrokes   If you're entering the URL of a Web page, you can usually omit the http:// at the beginning of the URL. For example, you might enter **www.yahoo.com** in the Location text box. Better yet, if the URL starts with www and ends with com, just type the in-between part—entering **yahoo** will take you to Yahoo!'s home page. Try it!

Navigator also features Auto Complete. As you start typing the URL of a page you've visited previously, AutoComplete fills in the rest of the address for you. If the address is correct, press **Enter**. If it is incorrect, keep typing.

Opening a Web Page in a Separate Window

Once in a while, you will want to go to one Web page, but you won't want to leave the one where you are. No problem. You can leave the current window open and open a new, separate window for the page you want to load. Take the following steps to do so:

1. Open the **File** menu, point to **New**, and click **Navigator Window** (or press **Ctrl+N**). Navigator opens a new window and loads the Netscape home page.

2. Click in the **Location** text box, type the address of the desired page, and press **Enter**.

3. You can switch between your two Navigator windows the same way you switch between any open program windows. For example, in Windows 95, you can use the Windows taskbar. You can also select a window from the bottom of the Communicator menu.

Another way to open a new window is to right-click a link in the current window and select **Open in New Window**. Whenever you right-click a link, Navigator displays a context menu like the one shown in Figure 2.2, which lists the options available for the link.

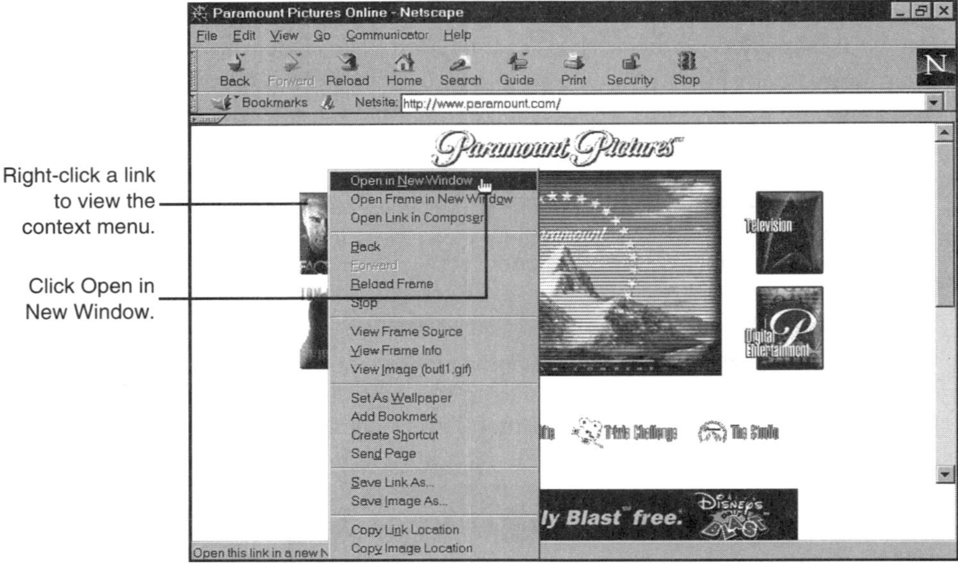

Figure 2.2   You can use your right mouse button to save some keystrokes.

Fun Time   Many well-known companies have Web sites. Try finding their sites by typing in company names. For example, type **mcdonalds** to visit the Golden Arches at www.mcdonalds.com. Enter **microsoft** in the **Location** text box. Or, try a magazine name, such as **time** or **newsweek**. After that, try more general terms, such as **hollywood** or **hair**.

In this lesson, you learned how to enter addresses (URLs) into Navigator to move around the Web. In the next lesson, you'll learn how to work with Web pages that contain frames.

Working with Frames

In this lesson, you learn how to navigate a Web page that has frames.

What Is a Frame?

A *frame* is a section of the Navigator window. Just as panes divide a real window into smaller sections, frames divide the single Navigator window. Frames are typically used to organize a lot of material in a small space so that you can easily jump directly to whatever you're looking for. For example, the frame on the left might display the outline of a Web document, while the frame on the right displays the contents of the currently selected topic in the outline (see Figure 3.1).

Not all Web sites use frames. Among those that do use them, the number of frames varies. Some Web sites use only two frames, while others divide the window into several frames. The person who creates the Web page controls the initial size of the frames, but you can drag the bar that separates frames to change their relative dimensions. In addition, if a frame contains more content than it can display, you can use the frame's scroll bar to bring additional information into view.

The contents of each frame is actually a separate Web document (Web page) with its own URL. Therefore, a window with frames can actually display several Web pages at once—each in its own frame. Many Web sites are designed so that when you click a link within a frame, the Web page to which it is linked appears in a corresponding frame (see Figure 3.2). With both pages still visible, you can view new information while referring to information on a previous page.

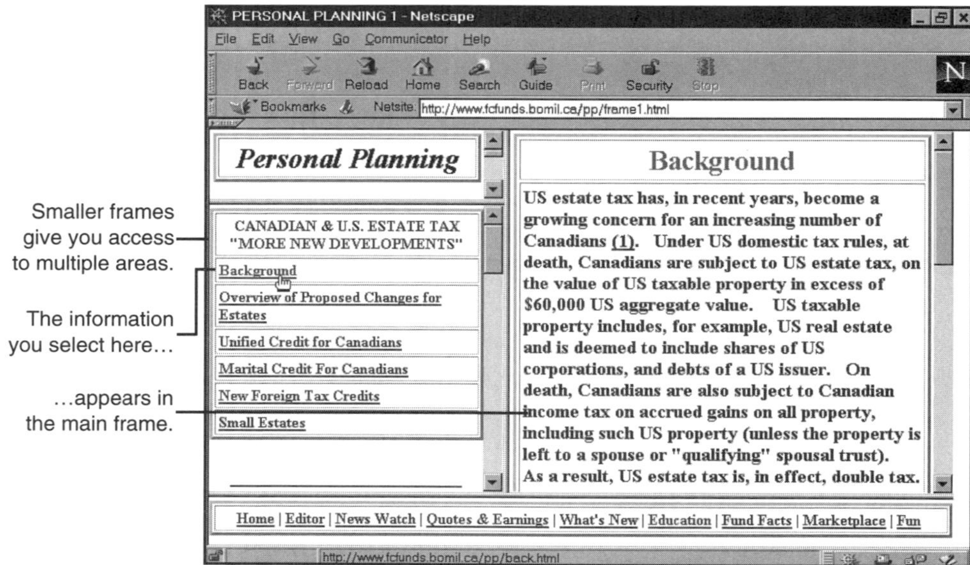

Figure 3.1   Web sites commonly use frames to help people navigate.

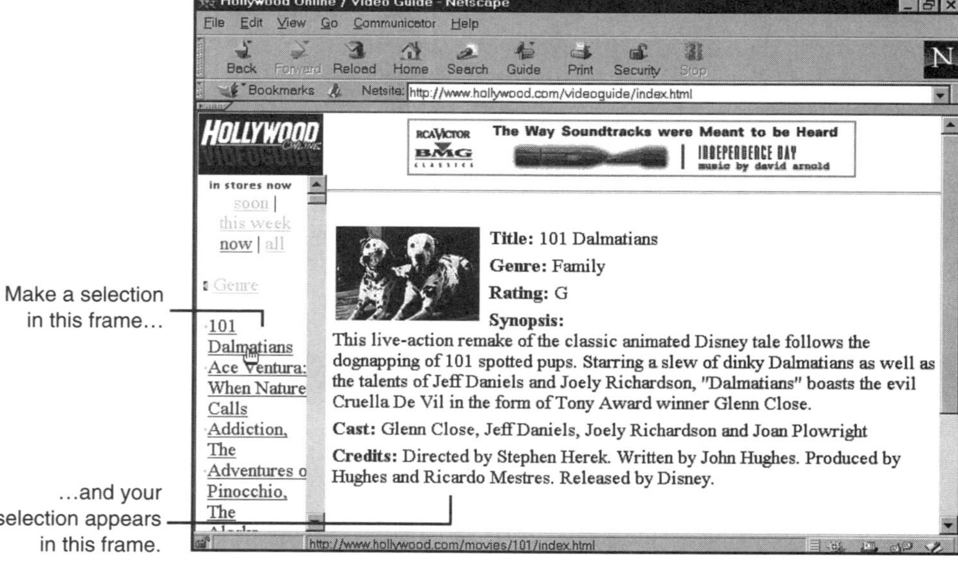

Figure 3.2   You can keep two Web pages visible in frames and easily switch back and forth.

In some cases, the contents of a frame may not change. For example, a special message or a map of the Web site may be fixed in a frame within the Navigator window to provide a constant reference point for the user as he moves through the site.

The frame on the left side of the window shown in Figure 3.3 allows the user to quickly jump from section to section in the Web site by clicking the appropriate link (such as Overview, What's New?, or Concert Reviews). And because the left frame doesn't change, the user can just as easily jump from any of those locations back to the Clouds in My Coffee page.

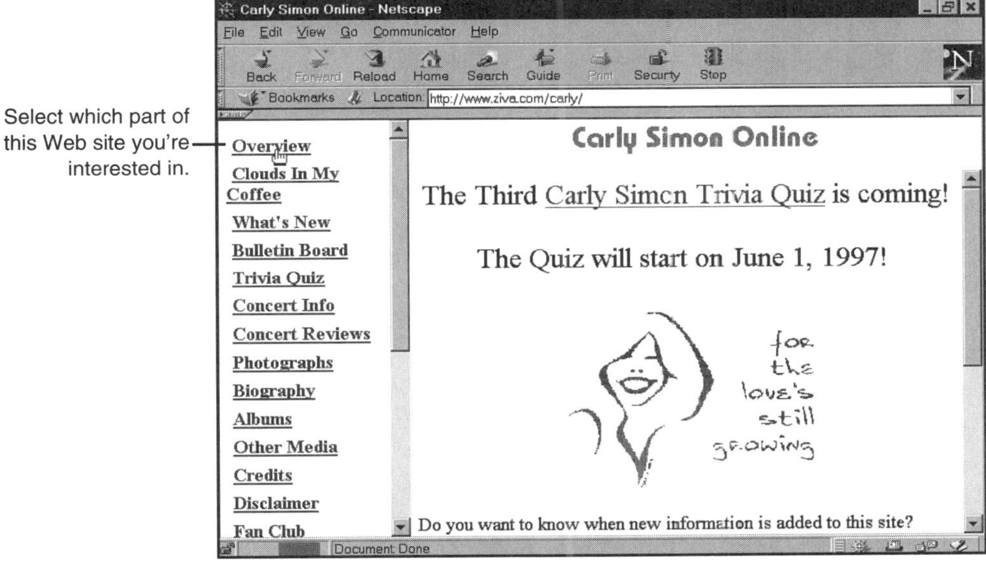

Figure 3.3 One frame might remain constant as a reference point.

Working on a Framed Web Page

It's easy to navigate your way around a framed Web site. For example, let's weave our way through a list of movies at *Hollywood Online*:

1. Connect to the Internet and start Navigator.

2. In the **Location/Go to** text box, type **hollywood** and press **Enter**. Navigator takes you to Hollywood Online, where you are greeted by a four-framed window like the one in Figure 3.4. (You can't resize these frames.)

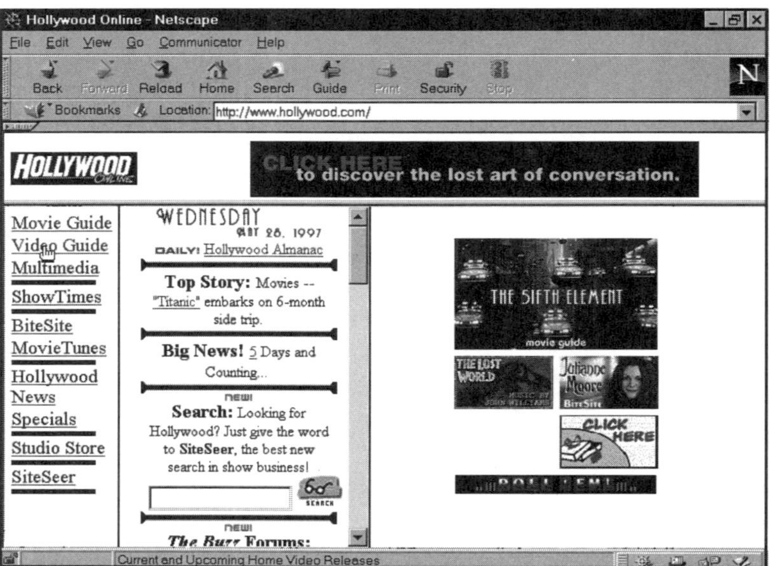

Figure 3.4 At Hollywood Online, you can see frames in action.

3. You use links on a framed Web page as you would the links on any other page: Click a link to go to the corresponding Web page. For example, click **Video Guide** in the frame on the left. Whoa! As you can see in Figure 3.5, the linked page displays an entirely new layout, complete with a different frame outline on the left.

4. Now, let's use a frame that works as a frame should work. In the list of videos on the left, click the title of a video. The left frame doesn't change, but the right frame changes to display information on the video you selected. A lot of Web sites use this technique in order to give you an *anchor*, or stable reference point.

5. Notice that each frame has its own scroll bar. To view more information about the currently selected video, use the scroll bar on the right. To view the names of additional videos in the list, use the scroll bar on the left.

6. Dig deeper into the *Hollywood Online* Web site by clicking the **Reviews** link directly below the video synopsis. The view in the second frame changes again, as shown in Figure 3.6.

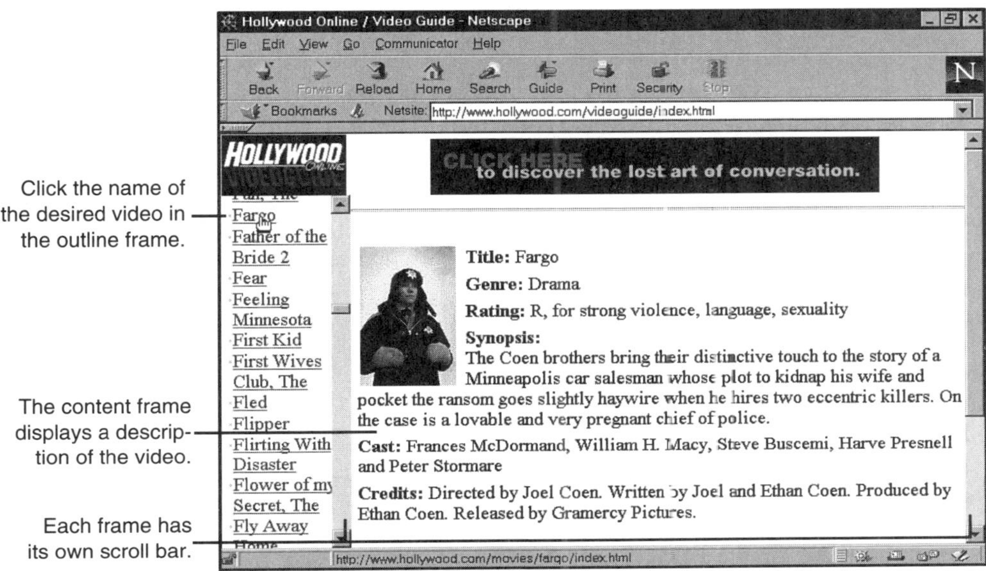

Click the name of the desired video in the outline frame.

The content frame displays a description of the video.

Each frame has its own scroll bar.

Figure 3.5 What's new at the video store?

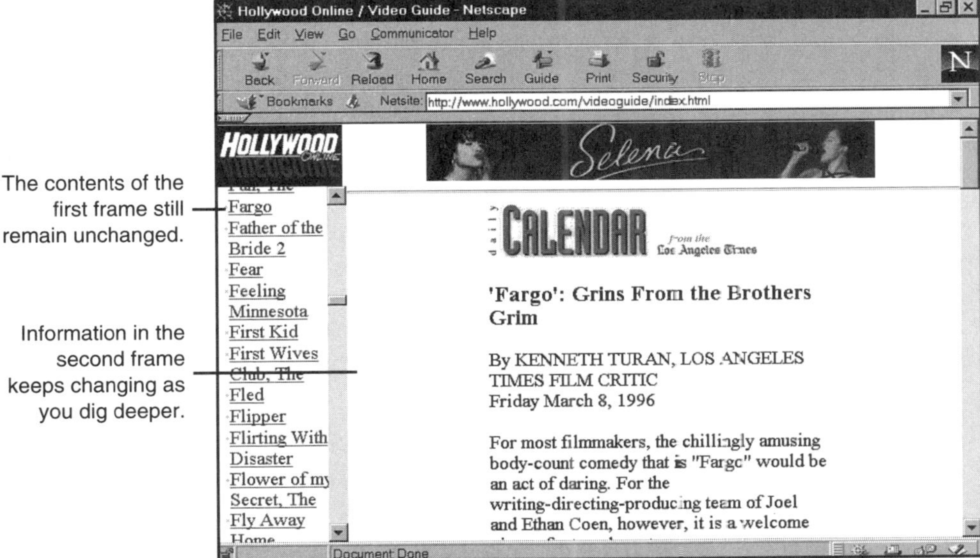

The contents of the first frame still remain unchanged.

Information in the second frame keeps changing as you dig deeper.

Figure 3.6 Typically, the left frame remains unchanged while you move in the right frame.

7. Using the Back button to return to previous pages is tricky with frames. Each click of the Back button takes you back one frame, not back to the previous Web site or page. Try it. Click the **Back** button several times until you return to the previous Web site.

Is Using the Back Button a Hassle?   The problem with a framed system is that it's difficult to get back to the last whole Web page you visited. If you're in a hurry, open the **Go** menu and select the page you want to return to.

8. When you finish practicing with frames, close Navigator and log off the Internet.

I Hate Frames   When used in moderation, frames can help users navigate a Web site. But when frames first became available, many Web page creators went a little too far, dividing windows into six or seven tiny frames, which angered Web surfers. For some humorous criticism of frames, check out the I Hate Frames page at http://wwwvoice.com/hatefrm.html.

In this lesson, you learned how to navigate framed Web pages. In the next lesson, you'll learn how to save the locations of your favorite Web pages so that you can return to them quickly.

Revisiting Your Favorite Sites

In this lesson, you learn various ways to mark your favorite Web pages so that you can return to them at any time.

Going Back to Where You've Been

Navigator offers a couple of options to help you get where you're going. You can type an URL in the Location text box, or you can click a link. However, because there are so many Web pages and because URLs are so difficult to remember, Navigator offers many more options to help you return to sites you have already visited.

In Part 1 Lesson 1, you learned how to use a few of these tools. You can open the Go menu and select the name of a page you visited; you can open the Location drop-down list and select an URL; you can display the history list (Communicator, History); and you can use the Back and Forward buttons. In this lesson, you will learn how to use more sophisticated tools to mark the pages you might want to revisit in the future:

- **Bookmarks** allow you to create a menu of pages and place groups of page names on submenus. For example, you could create bookmark submenus for Sports, Health, Investments, Research, Weather, and so on. To go to a page, you select it from the menu.

- **Personal toolbar** lets you create buttons for the pages you visit most often. You can then click a button to quickly load the associated page.

- **Shortcuts** allow you to create icons for pages or links and place those icons on the Windows desktop or in a folder. To load a page, you double-click its link.

Bookmarking a Page

You'll probably find that browsing the Web is like browsing through the pages of a large book. When you find a particular passage in a book that you want to be able to find again quickly, you insert a bookmark. You can do the same thing with your Web browser: When you find a particular Web page you like and plan to return to often, you add a bookmark.

When you create a bookmark in Navigator, Navigator saves the address for the displayed Web page. Because the addresses are often long and complex, creating bookmarks for your favorite Web pages saves you the time and trouble of trying to remember and enter them correctly.

Navigator offers several options for creating bookmarks, some of which are easier to use than others. Try any of the following techniques:

- Press **Ctrl+D** to bookmark the current page.

- Open the page you want to mark, and then drag the **Location** icon over the Bookmarks icon, as shown in Figure 4.1. When the mouse pointer reaches the Bookmarks icon, a submenu appears. Drag over **Add Bookmark** and release the mouse button.

- To create a bookmark for a link, drag the link from the current page over the Bookmarks icon. When the mouse pointer reaches the Bookmarks icon, a submenu appears. Without dragging over any of the options on the submenu, release the mouse button.

- To create a bookmark for the current Web page, right-click a blank area of the page and select **Add Bookmark**.

- To create a bookmark for a link, right-click the link and select **Add Bookmark**.

- Bookmark options also appear on the **Communicator, Bookmarks** submenu, but who really wants to go through all that trouble?

Bookmarking frames (discussed in Lesson 3) is a little tricky. If you see a link for the frame, you can right-click it and select **Add Bookmark**, or you can drag the link up to the Bookmarks icon. However, if the frame's contents are already displayed, you have to make sure you mark the specific frame and not the entire page. You can do this by right-clicking a blank area inside the frame and selecting **Add Bookmark**. When you click a bookmark for the frame, the frame's contents appear inside a window, not inside a frame.

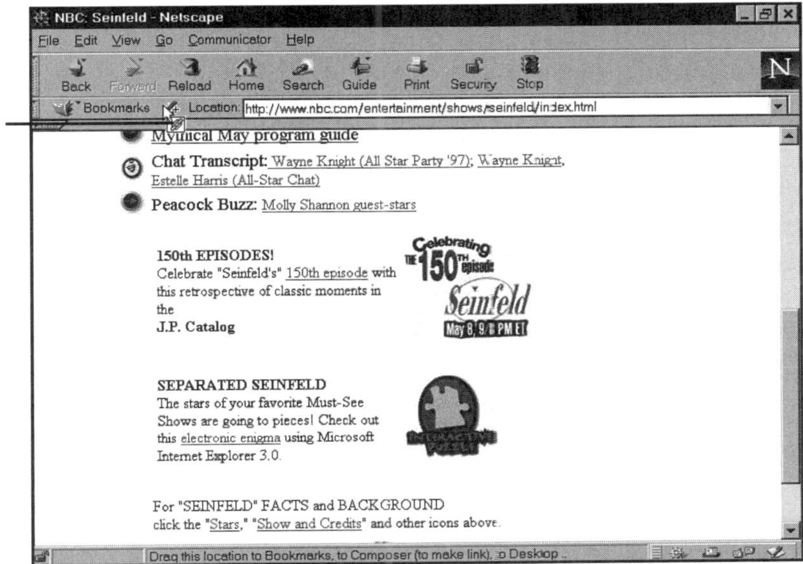

Figure 4.1   The most intuitive way to create bookmarks is to use the drag-and-drop technique.

After you create a bookmark for a page, you can return to that Web page at any time using one of the following methods:

- Open the **Bookmarks** menu and select the page from the list or submenu as shown in Figure 4.2. (Your newest bookmark appears at the bottom of the list.)

- Press **Ctrl+B** to display the Bookmarks window, and then double-click the bookmark for the page you want to go to.

Trade Places   You can trade bookmark files with your coworkers if you want. First, have your friend copy his bookmark file to a disk. (The file is called bookmark.htm, and it's in the Netscape directory.) Insert his disk in your computer, open the **Bookmarks** menu, and select **Edit Bookmarks**. Then open the **File** menu and select **Import**. Select the file on the disk and click **Open**. Voilà! His bookmarks are added to the bottom of your bookmark list.

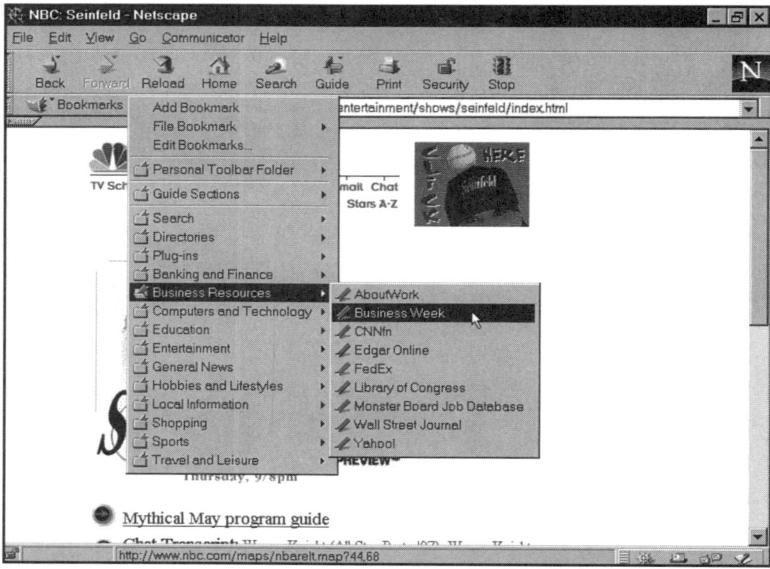

Figure 4.2   To return to a bookmarked page, select it from the Bookmarks menu or one of its submenus.

Organizing Bookmarks

Navigator enables you to sort your bookmarks, organize them in folders (to create submenus), and add comments. If you save very many bookmarks, you'll soon appreciate that you can organize them into a usable list.

You might create a folder so you can store similar bookmarks together. To create a bookmark folder, follow these steps:

1. Open the **Bookmarks** menu and select **Edit Bookmarks** (or just press **Ctrl+B**). The Bookmarks window appears.

2. In the bookmarks list, click where you want the folder to appear. The new folder appears directly below the item you select.

3. Open the **File** menu and select **New Folder**. The Bookmark Properties dialog box appears.

4. Type a name for the folder (submenu) in the **Name** text box. You can type a description in the **Description** text box, but that's optional; the description appears only if you use the Bookmark list as a Web page. When you finish, click **OK**.

5. To add an existing bookmark item to the folder, drag it to the folder as shown in Figure 4.3.

6. Click the **Close** (X) button to close the Bookmarks window.

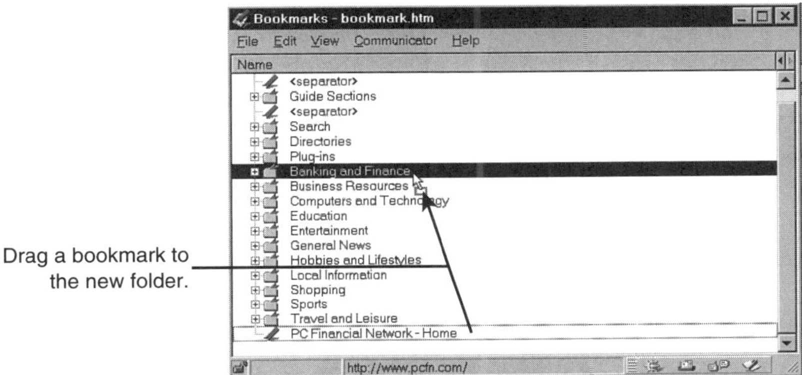

Drag a bookmark to the new folder.

Figure 4.3 You can organize your bookmarks into folders.

Adding Bookmarks to Your New Folder (Submenu)

In previous versions of Navigator, adding bookmarks directly to a submenu was nearly impossible. You had to open the Edit Bookmarks window and then drag the bookmarks around as if you were working in Windows Explorer. Although you can still arrange bookmarks using that technique, Navigator 4.0 now offers an easier way that allows you to add bookmarks on-the-fly. First, display the page you want to add to the Bookmarks menu. Then open the **Bookmarks** menu, point to **File Bookmark**, and click the name of the folder to which you want to add this page. (An easier way to add a bookmark to a submenu is to drag a link or the Location icon over Bookmarks, over the submenu name, and then onto that submenu.)

Another way to add bookmarks to a submenu is to enter a setting that makes a specific submenu the default receptacle for any bookmarks you create. To do this, take the following steps:

1. Open the **Bookmarks** menu and click **Edit Bookmarks**.

2. Right-click the name of the folder you want to use as the default folder and click **Set As New Bookmarks Folder**.

Now, whenever you add a bookmark by selecting Add Bookmark from the Bookmarks menu or from a context menu, the bookmark will be added to the specified submenu instead of to the main Bookmarks menu. To make the main Bookmarks menu the default, right-click the folder at the top of the list in the Edit Bookmarks window and select **Set As Bookmark Menu**.

You can also use one of your submenus as the main Bookmarks menu. Right-click the submenu you want to transform into the Bookmarks menu and select **Use for Bookmarks Menu**. Then, when you open the Bookmarks menu, you will see only the bookmarks that are included in the folder you selected.

Let's Separate!   One way to group bookmarks without using submenus is to use separators. To place a separator between two bookmarks, open the Edit Bookmarks window (**Bookmarks, Edit Bookmarks**). Click the bookmark below which you want to insert the separator line, open the **File** menu, and select **New Separator**. The next time you open the Bookmarks window, a separator line appears below the bookmark or folder you selected.

You can delete bookmarks just as easily as you can delete files on a disk; simply click the bookmark and press the **Delete** key. You can delete a bookmark folder by selecting it and pressing **Delete**. Of course, when you delete a folder, you delete all the bookmarks in it. So be careful!

When working in the Bookmarks window, you can hide the items in a folder by clicking the minus sign in front of the folder icon. To display the items in a closed folder, click the plus sign in front of the folder icon.

Adding Bookmark Descriptions

Sometimes, adding a description can help you identify an obscure bookmark later. (Although you can add a description for a bookmark, you see that description only when you open the Properties window or you open your bookmarks file as a Web page.) Follow these steps to add a description to an existing bookmark:

1. Open the **Bookmarks** menu and select **Edit Bookmarks**.
2. To change the description for a particular item, right-click it and select **Bookmark Properties**. The Bookmark Properties dialog box appears (see Figure 4.4).

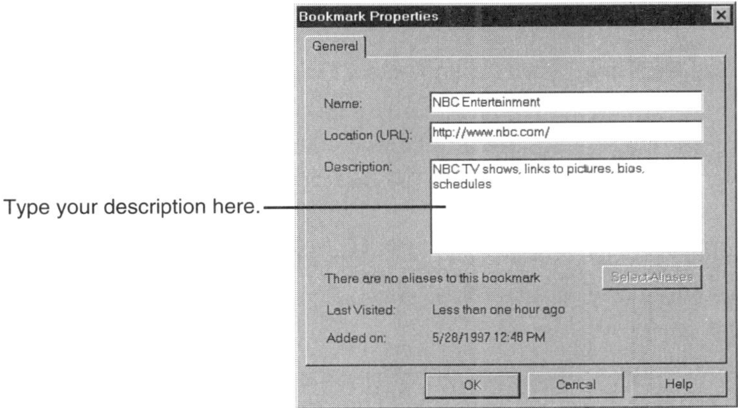

Figure 4.4   Add a description to your bookmark so you can identify it.

3. (Optional) In the **Name** text box, change the name of the item if necessary.

4. In the **Description** area, type a description for the selected bookmark. Then click **OK**.

The Page Moved!   If the Web page associated with one of your bookmarks has moved and you know its new location you can follow these steps to change its address. Type the new address in the **Location/Go to** text box. However, Navigator can automatically update your bookmarks for you, as explained next in "Updating Your Bookmarks."

Updating Your Bookmarks

The Internet changes constantly, and sometimes it's a struggle to keep up. What's the best way to find out what's new?

One way is to have Navigator check your bookmarked pages and notify you of which ones contain new information. Then you only have to visit the changed pages to get a quick update on your favorite topics. It couldn't be simpler—and you don't waste any time visiting Web pages whose information hasn't changed since your last visit.

Follow these steps to set Navigator to check your bookmarked pages:

1. Open the **Bookmarks** menu and select **Edit Bookmarks**.
2. (Optional) If you want to check only a few bookmarks, select them by clicking the first bookmark and **Ctrl**+clicking any additional bookmarks you want to check. (If you want Navigator to check all your bookmarks, skip this step.)
3. Open the **View** menu and select **Update Bookmarks**.
4. Choose whether you want Navigator to check all bookmarks or only the selected ones.
5. Click **Start Checking**. Navigator verifies each bookmark by attempting to connect to its associated Web site. (The amount of time it takes to check out your bookmarked pages will vary, depending on the number of Web sites you selected, how busy they are, and the speed of your connection.)
6. When Navigator finishes checking your bookmarks, it displays a message saying so. Click **OK**.

If you return to the Bookmarks window, you might see that some bookmark icons have changed (see Figure 4.5):

- Bookmarks that point to pages whose information has changed are marked with a highlighted icon.
- Bookmarks that could not be checked are marked with a question mark icon.

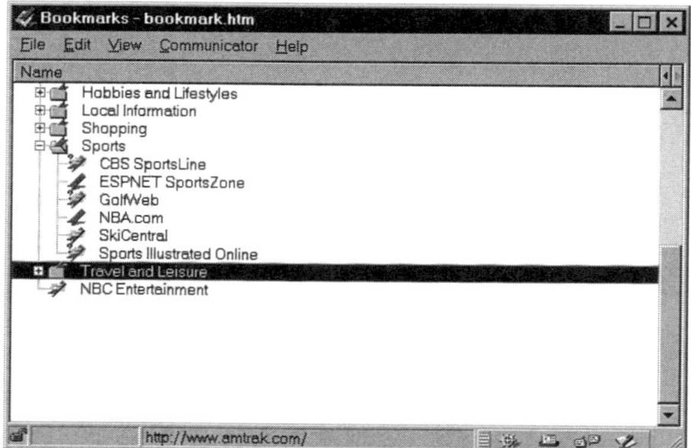

Figure 4.5   Navigator updates your bookmarks and shows you which ones have changed.

Creating a Shortcut for a Web Page

If you often visit a certain Web page at the beginning of your Navigator session, you might want to set up that page as your home page. You'll learn how to change the home page in Part 1 Lesson 5.On the other hand, if you don't want to make the page your permanent home page, you can simply create a shortcut for it. When you create a shortcut, an icon for the Web page appears on the desktop. Then all you have to do is double-click the icon, and Navigator starts up and automatically jumps to that Web page. (It's kind of like creating a temporary starting point that you can use whenever you want.)

Windows 95 Only   Sorry, but only Windows 95 users can create and use shortcuts.

CAUTION

Navigator offers several options for creating shortcuts. Try the following techniques to find out which one you like best:

- Right-click a link and select **Create Shortcut**. The Create Internet Shortcut dialog box prompts you to change the name of the shortcut. If desired, type a new name. Click **OK**.
- To create a shortcut for the current page, right-click a blank area of the page and select **Create Shortcut**. Click **OK** in the Create Internet Shortcut dialog box.
- Drag the **Location** icon to a blank area of the Windows desktop.
- Drag a link to the desired page over a blank area of the Windows desktop.

To use a shortcut, double-click it. If you didn't start Navigator yet, Navigator automatically runs and attempts to open the page. Shortcuts act like any Windows 95 shortcut. You can delete, copy, or move them, and you can create a separate folder for your shortcuts. Here's another trick you might try with shortcuts: Drag a shortcut into the page viewing area of the Navigator window and see what happens.

Adding Buttons to the Personal Toolbar

In addition to placing links on the Bookmarks menu and on the Windows desktop, you can place them as buttons on the Personal toolbar. To display this toolbar, click its tab. (If you hid the toolbar earlier, open the **View** menu and select **Show Personal Toolbar**.) You can then do any of the following to add links:

- Drag a link up to the toolbar, as shown in Figure 4.6.
- Drag the **Location** icon over the toolbar to create a button that points to the current page.
- Display the page you want to add to the Personal toolbar. Then open the **Bookmarks** menu, point to **File Bookmark**, and select **Personal Toolbar Folder**.
- In the Edit Bookmarks window, click the bookmark you want to add to the Personal toolbar. Then open the **File** menu and select **Add Selection to Toolbar**.

You can also have Navigator automatically add any bookmarks you create to the Personal toolbar. First, open the Edit Bookmarks window (**Bookmarks, Edit Bookmarks**). Then right-click **Personal Toolbar Folder**, and select **Set As New Bookmarks Folder**. Now, whenever you select the Add Bookmark command, the bookmark is placed on the Personal toolbar.

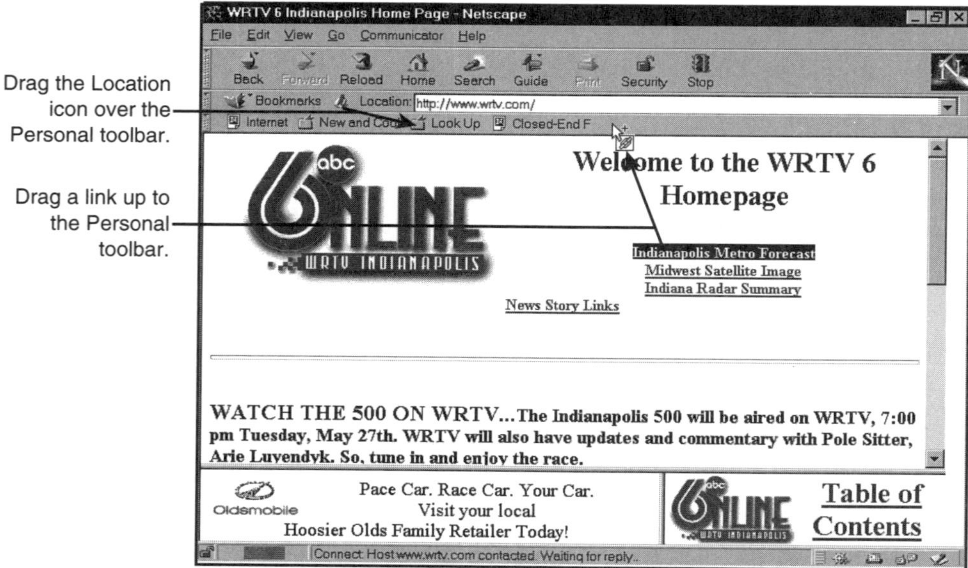

Figure 4.6   You can create buttons for your favorite pages on the Personal toolbar.

In this lesson, you learned how to create and organize bookmarks. In the next lesson, you'll learn about other Navigator features you might want to try.

Other Navigator Features

In this lesson, you learn about other things you can do with Navigator, such as picking the starting Web page for Navigator.

Designating a Different Home Page

Normally, when you start Navigator, you're connected to the Netscape home page. From the home page, you can explore the World Wide Web however you like. But if you often visit the same Web page, why not make it your starting point?

Make Your Own You can also create your own Web page—filled with links to all your favorite spots on the Web—and designate it as your home page. You'll learn how to create Web pages in Part 6.

Once you decide which page you want to use, follow these steps to change your designated home page:

1. Open the **Edit** menu and select **Preferences.** The Preferences dialog box appears.
2. Under Category, click **Navigator.** The **Navigator** preferences appear, as shown in Figure 5.1.

3. Under Browser Starts With, select **Home Page** so you can specify a page to load on startup. (You can select **Blank Page** to run Navigator without opening a Web page, or you can select **Last Page Visited** to make the last page you visited before exiting Navigator become the starting page the next time you run Navigator.)

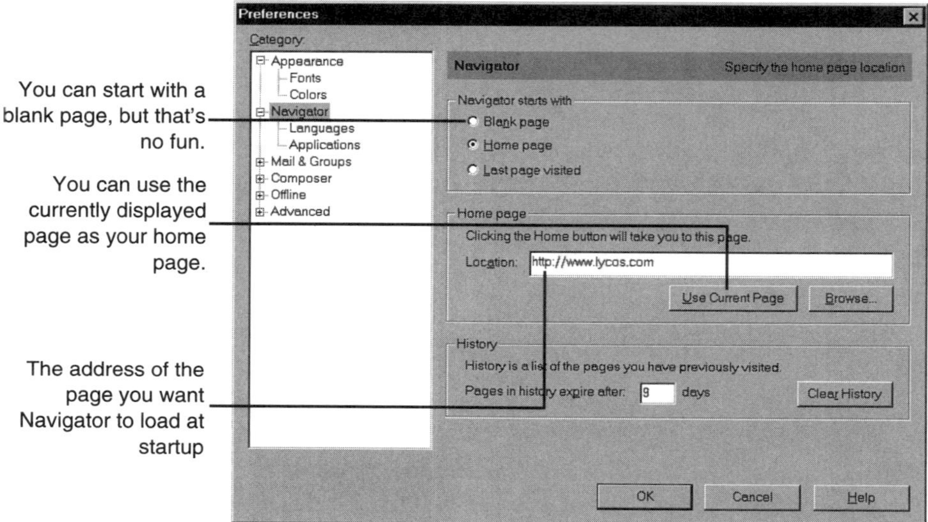

Figure 5.1 Choose any Web page to be your home page.

4. If you selected Home Page in step 3, drag over any text in the **Home Page Location** text box, and then enter the address of the Web page you want to use as your home page. (You can click the Use Current Page button to use the currently displayed Web page as your home page.)

5. Click **OK**.

Now, whenever you start Navigator or click the Home button, Navigator will open the specified Web page.

Instead of using a Web page as your starting page, you can use a page that contains all the bookmarks you created in the previous lesson. Take the following steps:

1. Open the **Bookmarks** menu and select **Edit Bookmarks**. The Edit Bookmarks window appears, displaying your bookmarks.

2. Open the **File** menu and select **Save As**. The Save As dialog box prompts you to name the file and pick a folder in which to store it.

3. You can simply click the **Save** button to accept the default location (C:\Program Files\Netscape\Users*Yourname* and use the file name bookmark.htm). Or, you can give the file a new name and/or save it to a different folder.

4. You can use the bookmarks file as your starting Web page by performing the previous set of steps. Under the Home Page Location text box, click the **Browse** button and use the Browse for Home Page dialog box to select the file named **Bookmarks.htm** (it should be in the C:\Program Files\Netscape\Users*Yourname* folder).

Saving and Printing Web Pages

You'll often find things on the Web that you want to hang onto. Of course, if you just want to be able to visit the page again, you can create a bookmark for it as described in Lesson 4. However, if you want to save the information on the page, a bookmark might not work because the next time you visit that Web page, it might contain different information. Or, if the page contains a lot of information, you might want to save it so you don't waste online time reading it all. Luckily, Navigator enables you to print a Web page or to save it so you can view it later.

To save a Web page, follow these steps:

1. Open the **File** menu and select **Save As**. The Save As dialog box appears. (If the page has two or more frames, first click a blank area inside the frame you want to save, and then select **File**, **Save Frame As**.)

2. Change to the directory in which you want to save the Web page.

3. Enter a name for the document in the **File Name** text box and click **Save**.

To view the document later, open the **File** menu and select **Open Page**. Click the **Choose File** button, use the Open dialog box to select the page, and click **Open**. The document appears in the Navigator window. You do *not* have to be online to view a saved document.

CAUTION

Where Are the Graphics?   If the Web page you save contains fancy graphics, they won't be in your saved copy. If you really want the graphics, you must save each one separately. To save a graphic, right-click it and select **Save Image As** from the shortcut menu. Then enter a name for the graphic and click **Save**. (For best results, save the graphic in the same directory as your document.) If you save the graphics to the same directory as the Web page, they will appear when you open the document later—at least most of the time. If a graphic doesn't load after you open your saved document, right-click its placeholder and select **Show Image** from the shortcut menu.

If you don't want to save the Web page to your hard disk, you can just as easily save its contents by printing it. To print a Web page, click the **Print** button. Or open the **File** menu and select **Print**. Then, in the Print Range area of the Print dialog box, select **All**. Click **OK**. (If the page has two or more frames, first click on a blank area inside the frame whose contents you want to print. Then select **File**, **Print Frame**.)

Speeding Up Navigator

Most Web pages have a lot of pretty graphics. The trouble is, it can take a long time for Navigator to load and display all those graphics on your system. Meanwhile, you sit—waiting very impatiently, I'm sure.

To speed up Navigator, you can set it so that it doesn't display the graphics. Instead, Navigator displays a small placeholder like the one shown in Figure 5.2. If you switch to a page whose graphics you want to load and display, you can do it with a single click.

To set up Navigator so that it doesn't display graphics automatically, open the **Edit** menu and select **Preferences**. Under Category, click **Advanced** and deselect **Automatically Load Images** (remove the check mark from in front of the option to turn it off). From now on, when you switch to a new Web page, its text appears, and placeholders appear where the graphics normally would. You'll also see a new button in the toolbar labeled **Images**. If you decide you want to view the images, click the **Images** button.

You can turn Automatically Load Images back on at any time. Simply display the Preferences dialog box, click **Advanced** (below Category), and select **Automatically Load Images**.

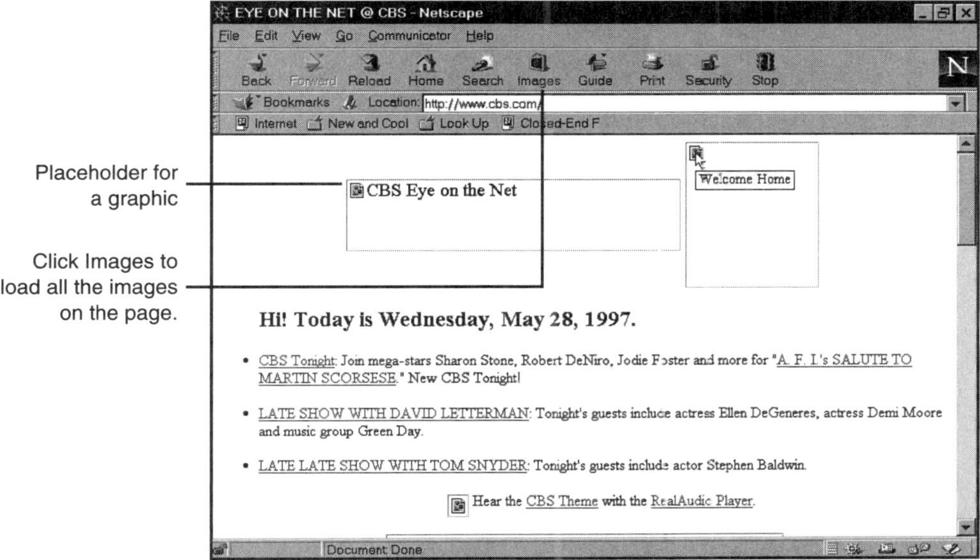

Placeholder for a graphic

Click Images to load all the images on the page.

Figure 5.2   You can speed up Navigator by not displaying graphics.

Setting Up Communicator for Two or More Users

If you share your computer with other people, you might want to create a separate user profile for each person. With a separate user profile, each person can create his or her own bookmarks and customize the various Communicator components separately. Even if you don't share your computer with other people, you might consider creating profiles to work with two or more variations of Communicator. For example, you might customize Communicator one way for business use and another way for personal use.

If you create separate profiles, whenever you start Communicator, it prompts you to select a profile. After you select a profile, Communicator runs using the preferences specified for that profile.

To create a separate user profile, take the following steps:

1. Exit any Communicator components that are currently running.

2. In Windows 95, open the Start menu, point to **Programs**, select **Netscape Communicator**, point to **Utilities**, and then click **User Profile Manager**. The Profile Manager window appears, displaying a list of existing profiles.

3. Click the **New** button. The Profile Setup Wizard appears, explaining the profile option.

4. Click the **Next** button, and then type your name and e-mail address in the text boxes as directed. Click the **Next** button. The next dialog box prompts you to enter a name for the profile and specify the directory in which you want your preferences saved.

5. Make any changes to the profile name entry and directory, as desired. Click the **Next** button. The last dialog box appears, asking if you want to move your settings to the new directory.

6. Continue entering requested details to specify your e-mail server, news server, and other options. In the last dialog box, click the **Finish** button. This returns you to the Profile Manager dialog box.

7. Click the profile you want to use for Communicator, and then click the **Start Communicator** button. This starts Navigator with the settings for the selected profile. The Netscape License Agreement dialog box may appear.

8. If the Netscape License Agreement dialog box appears, read the license agreement and click **Accept**. If you click **Do Not Accept**, Communicator will not run.

Working Offline

As you enter addresses and click links to pages, Netscape Communicator saves the Web pages and all related files and graphics in a temporary storage area on your hard drive, called the disk cache. This enables Navigator to open the pages more quickly if you choose to revisit them. It also allows you to disconnect from the Internet and load the pages from your hard drive instead of from the Web.

To view pages you have visited without going online, open the **File** menu and choose **Go Offline**. The Download dialog box appears, asking if you want to send and receive e-mail and download messages from discussion groups before disconnecting. Enter your preferences and click **Go Offline**. Communicator sends and retrieves any waiting messages, and then goes offline without disconnecting your Dial-Up Connection (you may disconnect to save phone or online charges).

You can still open Web pages by entering URLs and clicking links as you normally would. However, if you attempt to open a page that is not in the cache, Navigator displays a dialog box telling you that you must go online to open the page. Choose **File**, **Go Online**.

Offline Preferences You can choose to start Netscape Communicator in Offline mode and have it display a prompt when you need to go online. Open the **Edit** menu, select **Preferences**, and click **Offline**. Select **Online Work Mode**, **Offline Work Mode**, or **Ask Me**.

Getting Help

Navigator provides *online* help for its software. Therefore, to get help, you must connect to the Internet first. When your Internet connection is established, open the **Help** menu and choose one of the following commands:

- **Help Contents**   Choose this command if you need help using Navigator.

- **Release Notes**   This command provides information about dealing with known "bugs" (glitches in the software).

- **Product Information and Support**   This command gives you access to more help.

- **Software Updates**   Takes you to Netscape's Web site, where you can download the latest Communicator upgrades (so you don't have to reinstall the entire program).

- **Register Now**   Lets you register your copy of Netscape Communicator online, giving you a legal copy of the software. Netscape informs registered users of program updates.

- **Member Services**   Takes you to Netscape's Web site, where you can learn more about Netscape products and add-ons.

- **International Users**   Select this option to find out about issues that affect non-English versions of Netscape Communicator.

- **Security**   Select this to find out more about how Navigator can help keep your information secure.

- **Net Etiquette**   Explains how to behave in UseNet newsgroups.

- **About Plug-Ins**   Lists the Netscape plug-ins that are currently installed. This list will come in handy when you start working with helper applications and plug-ins later in Part 1.

- **About Font Displayers**   Displays a list of font tools installed in Navigator. These tools help Navigator display non-standard fonts used in some Web pages.
- **About Communicator**   Displays a list of Communicator components that are installed, along with their version numbers.

Plug-Ins   Similar to helper apps, plug-ins are special programs designed to enhance Navigator. For example, the RealAudio plug-in enables Navigator to play sound files embedded in a Web page in real-time.

Create Your Own Help   If you use Netscape's Help system a lot, your online time adds up quickly. You might want to save Help pages you need and read them later after you log off. Follow the steps in the section "Saving and Printing Web Pages" to do that.

In this lesson, you learned how to change Navigator's starting page, print and save Web pages, speed up Navigator, and get help. In the next lesson, you'll learn how to complete on-screen forms.

Filling Out Forms

In this lesson, you learn how to complete on-screen forms that you may encounter while surfing the Web.

What Is a Form?

At some Web pages you visit, you may be asked to fill out a *form*. A form is simply a "dialog box" placed on a Web page. You're probably already familiar with dialog boxes; they're part of every program you use, including Navigator, your word processor, your spreadsheet program, and Windows. Dialog boxes enable you, the user, to provide additional information that a program might need in order to complete a task. When you save a file for the first time, for example, you use the options in a dialog box to select a directory in which to save the file and to enter a name for it.

On the Web, you don't use dialog boxes. Instead, you fill out forms to provide the information needed to complete a task. For example, when you use one of the Web search tools such as Yahoo!, InfoSeek, or Lycos, you complete an on-screen form to tell the search tool what you want to search for. Similarly, you might complete a form to leave an opinion on someone's Web page, or to provide an e-mail address to which the owner of the Web page may respond. The uses for forms are as vast as the Web itself.

Be Careful Out There!   As you'll learn later in this lesson, the Web is not the most secure place. Someone with the desire and ability can possibly intercept the information you enter. So be careful when you enter information in a form.

As you might expect, an on-screen form looks like a large dialog box, complete with text boxes, list boxes, check boxes, and option buttons. Figure 6.1 shows an example of a form you might fill out on the Web.

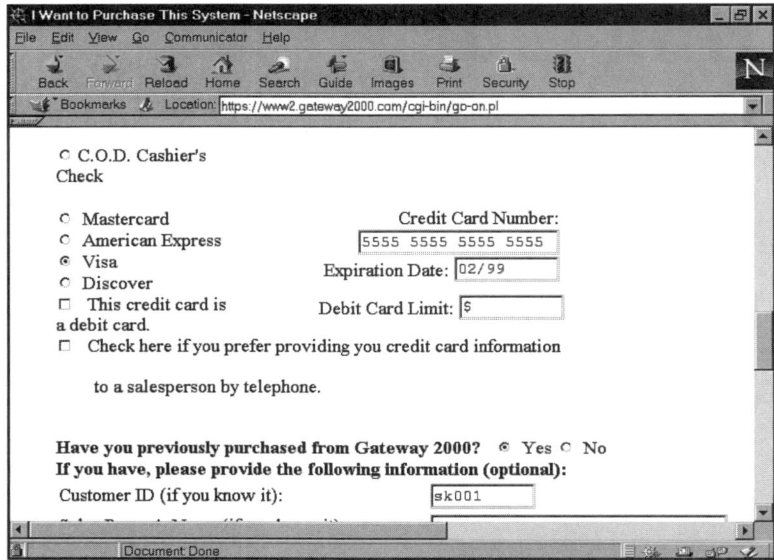

Figure 6.1   A Web form looks like a dialog box.

Completing a Form

When you encounter a form on a Web page, treat it as you would a Windows dialog box. (Keep in mind that you should protect private information on the Web; see the next section for a discussion about security issues.) Follow these guidelines when completing forms:

- To enter text in a Web form, click in the text box and type your information (see Figure 6.2).
- You can move to a text box by clicking in it or by using the **Tab** key.
- If the form uses option buttons or check boxes, click the option you want to select. (Remember that you can select only one option button in a group.)
- To use a list box, click the drop-down arrow to open the list (see Figure 6.3). Then click your selection.
- When you finish filling in the form, click the appropriate command button. (On the form in Figure 6.2, for example, you would click **Search**.)

48

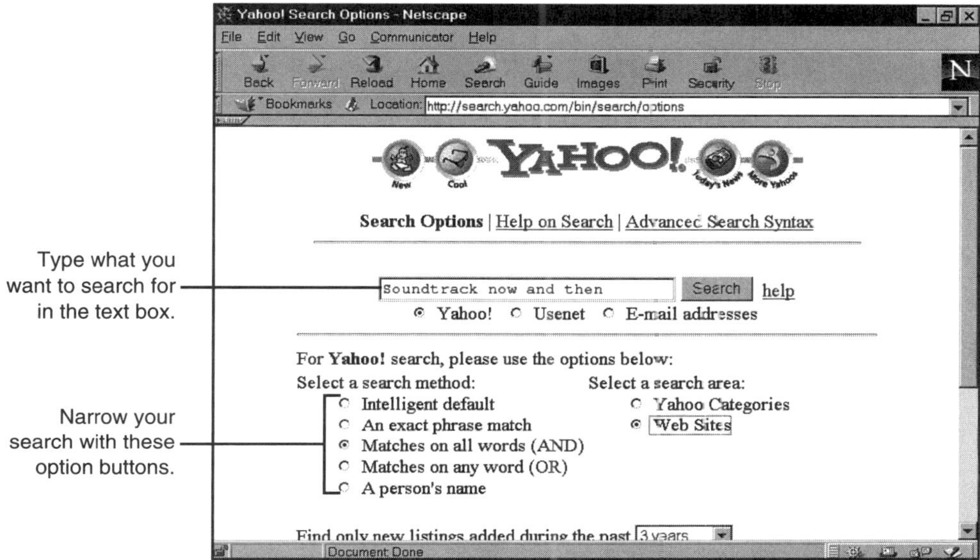

Figure 6.2 Entering information in a form is like completing a dialog box.

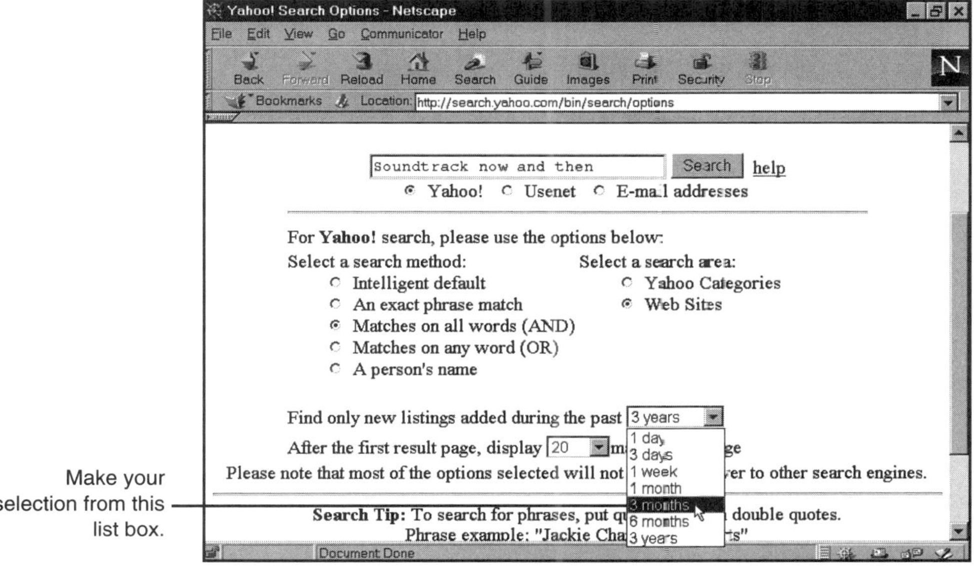

Figure 6.3 Some forms use list boxes.

Security Issues

The problem with sending data on the Internet (by way of forms, e-mail, or other techniques) is that the data bounces around from one computer to another in an attempt to find an open route to its destination. At any one of the points in the data's journey, it can be intercepted, decoded, and read by someone with the proper know-how and desire. How often data is intercepted in transit, nobody really knows. But it *can* happen, and that's the concern.

Should you worry? Usually, no. Most of the data you send isn't very confidential. For example, if you fill out a search form to look for Michael Jordan pages on the Web, you probably don't care if someone intercepts the data and reads it.

As for confidential information (such as a credit card number), you don't have to be on the Internet for someone to steal your number. A person can look over your shoulder at the store, phony companies can ask for your number on the phone, or someone can sift through your trash. The Internet is no more dangerous than the real world.

To protect yourself, however, avoid entering data at any site that looks as though it may not be legitimate. Also, don't give your credit card number, phone number, passwords, PIN numbers, or other confidential information to people who might ask for it (not only on the Web, but also in chat rooms and via e-mail).

To supplement that precaution, Navigator has some built-in security features that can help you transmit your data more safely. These are discussed in the following sections.

Identifying Secure Web Sites

Although no system is completely secure, some systems are more secure than others. The person who creates a Web site can make the site more secure by using the protocol https instead of the usual http. The "s" stands for *Secure Sockets Layer*, a data encryption standard. At a secure site, the data you enter is encoded before you send it, and is then decoded when it reaches its destination. Although any code can theoretically be cracked, SSL makes sending data fairly safe.

Navigator uses various techniques to let you know if you are about to enter data at a secure or insecure site. The following list tells you what to look for:

- If you try to enter data at an insecure site, Navigator displays a warning like the one shown in Figure 6.4. You can choose to ignore the warning or cancel the transmission.

- If **https** appears in the Location text box (instead of **http**), the site is secure.

- Look at the lock icon in the status bar or the Security button on the Navigation toolbar. If the lock is unlocked, the site is not secure. If the lock is locked, the site is secure.

- Click the **Security** button to view additional security information.

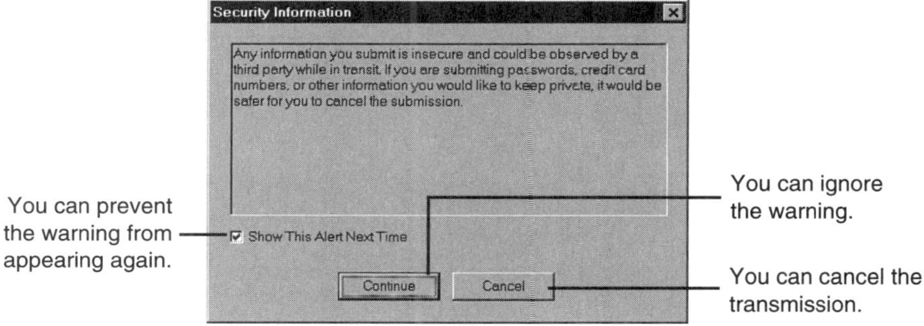

You can prevent the warning from appearing again.

You can ignore the warning.

You can cancel the transmission.

Figure 6.4   Navigator displays a warning if you are sending data at an insecure site.

Although the security warning dialog boxes provide the most obvious indication of whether you are at a secure or insecure site, they can become annoying. Whenever one of these dialog boxes appears, it offers the option of turning off the alert. If you use forms simply to search on the Internet, go ahead and turn off the alerts.

Another way to turn the alerts off (or back on) is to change the security settings. Click the **Security** button to display Netscape's Security dialog box. In the list on the left, click **Navigator**. As you can see in Figure 6.5, there are four **Show A Warning Before** options at the top of the dialog box. Click an option to turn it on or off. (A check mark next to an option indicates that it is on.) Click **OK**.

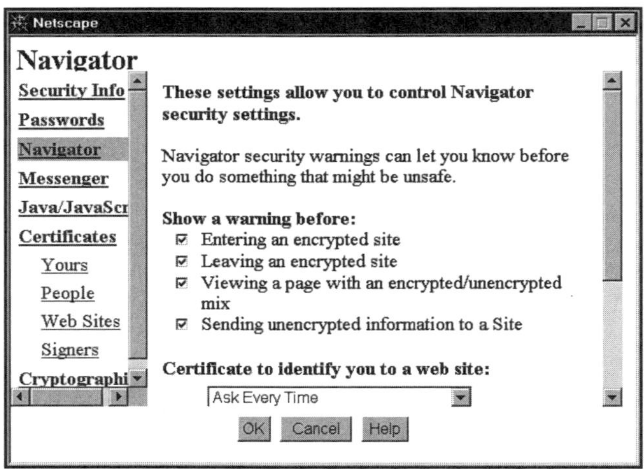

Figure 6.5   You can turn the security warnings on or off.

Security Through Certificates

Another way to improve security is with *certificates*. During the registration process, you may have been asked if you wanted to sign up for a security certificate (digital ID). If you chose to do so, you provided your e-mail address and some other personal information, and in return, you received a certificate file that contained your digital ID. When doing business over the Internet at a secure site, you might be asked for that certificate in order to access the site. The digital ID replaces multiple passwords for accessing the secure site. In other cases, you might be asked for a certificate in order to validate a charge card order. This prevents any potential thief from successfully using your credit card number or your password for a secure site; he won't have the certificate file needed to complete the transaction. See Part 1 Lesson 13 for more information on certificates and Internet security.

In this lesson, you learned how to complete Web forms, and you learned how to enter data securely on the Web. In the next lesson, you'll learn how to search for information on the Web.

Searching for Information on the Web

In this lesson, you learn how to search the Web for information using the most popular Web search tools.

How Search Tools Work

Up to this point, you've probably found the information you were looking for on the Web by jumping from one link to another or by entering the URLs (addresses) for specific Web pages. Although they work, those are not the most efficient methods.

A better way to locate what you need is to use *Web search tools*. With a search tool, you fill out a form describing what you want to search for and click a Search button, and the search tool looks through its list of Web pages to find a match. As it searches, it makes a note of the number of *hits*, or matches, it finds for each Web page.

Hit   A match between your search criteria and something found in the description of a Web page. The more hits the tool finds within its description of a particular Web page, the more likely it is that the Web page contains the information you want.

When it finishes searching, the search tool lists the sites it thinks match your search criteria. This list is basically a set of links pointing to various Web pages, arranged so that the pages with the most hits (matches) are at the top. You browse through this list and click the links for the Web sites you want to visit.

Obviously, for the best results, you should start with the pages at the beginning of the list. If you want, you can save your search results so you can browse through them later. To do so, follow the steps in Lesson 5 for saving a Web page.

Search Tool   A searchable index of Web pages. Popular Web search tools include Yahoo!, Lycos, and Excite!.

Because each search tool maintains its own independent list of Web pages, some search tools are better than others. You'll soon find your favorite. Navigator makes it easy to connect to the most popular search tools, including InfoSeek, Excite!, Yahoo!, Lycos, and Magellan.

Search tools typically fall into two categories based on how you specify the information you want to find. With one type of tool, you simply enter a word or two to search for, and click a button to start the search. The popular search tool called Lycos works this way. To use the other type of tool, you select a major category, a subcategory from that, another subcategory, and so on until you find what you need or until you've narrowed the subject matter for the search. The popular search tool Yahoo! works in this manner (although it also has a search box in which you can type specific words to search for).

Web Only   The search tools you'll learn about in this lesson work mainly for information on the World Wide Web. (Some Web search tools can help you find newsgroups and other resources.) Remember that the Web is only one part of the Internet. If a search tool doesn't find any pages that match your criteria, you can still search other parts of the Internet such as FTP or Gopher sites. You'll learn how to search FTP sites in Lesson 10 and Gopher sites in Lesson 11.

In this lesson, I'll walk you through the specific steps for using Lycos and Yahoo!. Table 7.1 contains a list of other available tools and their URLs.

Table 7.1   Web Search Tools

Search Tool	Address
AltaVista	http://www.altavista.com
Lycos	http://www.lycos.com
Excite!	http://www.excite.com

continues

Table 7.1 Continued

Search Tool	Address
InfoSeek	http://www.infoseek.com
Magellan	http://www.mckinley.com
WebCrawler	http://www.webcrawler.com
Open Text Index	http://index.opentext.net/
Point	http://www.pointcom.com

Quick Seek You can access one of several popular Web search tools by clicking the **Search** button at the top of the Navigator window. Note, however, that Navigator changes the search tool associated with this button from time to time so you don't really know which search tool you'll get when you click it. It might be Excite!, WebCrawler, InfoSeek, Lycos, Yahoo!, or another search tool.

Getting Better Results

As you'll see in a moment, most of the Web search tools function in a similar manner. Basically, you type in what you want to search for, click a button, and off it goes. For example, you could search for the word "fishing," and the search tool would list pages that have "fishing" somewhere in the description.

Forget It The Web search tools ignore certain words, including "a," "an," "the," "it," and common words such as "computer" and "Internet," so don't bother to use those words in your search. One or two well-chosen words are always best ("Windows utilities" or "stock quotes," for example).

Using a simple search term like "fishing" will probably result in a long list of potential Web sites that you'll have to wade through. To make your search more effective, try to narrow it by using more specific search text. For example, you might type "bass fishing" or "fresh water fishing" instead of just "fishing."

The better search tools, such as Yahoo! and InfoSeek, allow you to narrow your search further by setting additional criteria. For example, if you enter "vegetable gardening," most search tools will come up with a list of Web sites that mention either the word "vegetable" or the word "gardening." But the better search tools allow you to specify an exact match, which tells the tool that you want a listing of only the Web sites that contain both "vegetable" and "gardening."

Another common mistake is typing a word that can be found in other words that do not relate to what you want. For example, if you type "stock," you might find matches for stocks, stock brokers, stockyards, soup stock, and stock exchange. If the search tool you're using allows you to specify exact matches only, choose that option in order to avoid this problem.

The Magical Location Text Box   Instead of connecting to a particular search site, you can just type your search phrase in the **Location** text box and press **Enter**. Navigator randomly picks a search engine to use and enters your search phrase for you.

Using Lycos

Lycos is popular because it's one of the best search tools. If you can't find what you're looking for by browsing the Web, chances are you'll find it with Lycos. But if that's not enough, you can also access another helpful tool through Lycos: Point's Top 5% Web Sites. Point provides direct links that *point* you to the more popular pages on the Web and provide reviews of these pages.

Like most Web search tools, Lycos provides a simple text box into which you enter the word or words you want to search for. Lycos also offers options with which you can narrow the search and improve the results. To use Lycos, follow these steps:

1. Type **www.lycos.com** in the **Location/Go to** text box and press **Enter**. You'll find yourself at the main Lycos screen, shown in Figure 7.1.

A Faster Way   You can also access Lycos with Navigator's Search button. At the top of the Net Search page are five buttons for various search tools including Lycos. Click the **Lycos** button.

2. Open the **Search** list and click the desired category: **The Web, Sounds, Pictures, Top 5% Sites,** or **WPS Tracking#**.

3. If you do not want to limit your search, type the word or words you want to search for in the **For** text box. Click **Go Get It**, and you are finished.

   If you want to narrow your search, do not type anything in the For text box. Instead, proceed with step 4.

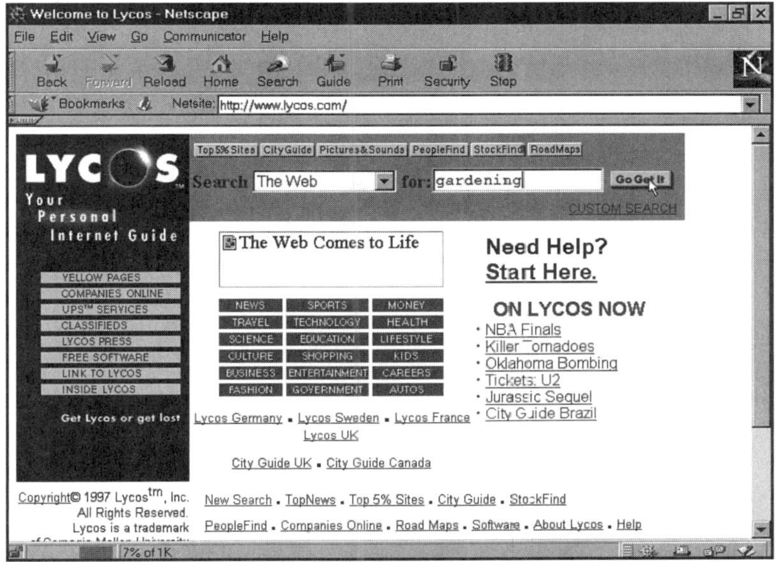

Figure 7.1   You can search the Web with Lycos.

4. Click **CUSTOM**. The Lycos Search Form appears (see Figure 7.2).

5. Type the word or words you want to search for in the **Search For** text box.

6. Normally, Lycos lists Web pages that contain any of the search words. If you want Lycos to list only pages that contain *all* of the search words (providing a more narrow search), open the first **Search Options** drop-down list and click **Match All Terms (AND)**.

7. If you want Lycos to list only the Web pages with a lot of hits, open the second **Search Options** drop-down list (on the right) and select an option that specifies how close you want your matches to be.

8. Lycos normally displays 10 matches at a time. To display more matches per page, open the first **Display Options** drop-down list and select a different number.

9. Lycos also displays a brief description for each match. To control the length of this description, open the second **Display Options** drop-down list (on the right) and choose **summary results** (short), **standard results** (medium), or **detailed results** (long).

10. When you're ready to start the search, click the **Go Get It** button.

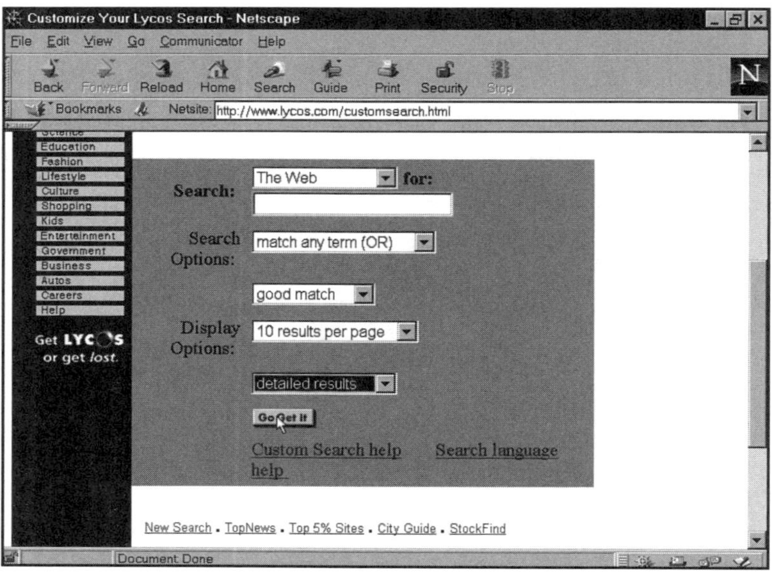

Figure 7.2   Use these options to narrow your search in Lycos.

Lycos performs the search and displays a list of items that match your search criteria. Click any item to jump to the associated Web page. Remember that the pages with the most hits (the ones which come closest to matching your search criteria) appear at the beginning of the list. If the list fills more than one page, scroll down to the bottom of the page and click the link that advances you to the next page of search results. If necessary, you can return to a previous search results page by clicking the **Back** button at the top of the Navigator window.

Save That Search!   You can save your search results on a single page by opening the **File** menu and selecting **Save As**. You can then view the saved Web page later by starting Navigator and opening the file (see Lesson 5). You can also save the results with a bookmark by opening the **Bookmarks** menu and selecting **Add Bookmark**. The only problem (if you want to call it that) is that the bookmark saves the search criteria—not the results. So when you revisit the page, you might find that the results have changed because new Web pages have been added and others have been dropped from the Internet.

Using Yahoo!

Yahoo!, like Lycos, enables you to search its listing of Web pages by entering a few keywords. However, it also provides you with another way of searching. In Yahoo!, you can browse for what you're looking for by selecting a category that interests you from the Yahoo! Web page. From there, you can select another category and another, until you've narrowed your search sufficiently. At the bottom of the screen, you'll see a number of sites that fit the category you selected. So by using Yahoo!'s category method, you can even find a Web page without entering any keywords at all.

In addition, Yahoo! lets you combine the two methods. You can select a few categories first and then enter a keyword to search for. This enables you to limit your search to a smaller portion of the Web.

Another Way You can also access Yahoo! with Navigator's Search button. As you learned earlier, Navigator connects you to one of several search tools when you click this button. Click the **Yahoo** button at the top of the page.

To select a category in Yahoo! that interests you, follow these steps:

1. Type **www.yahoo.com** in the **Location / Go to** text box and press **Enter**. You'll see the Yahoo! opening screen, shown in Figure 7.3.
2. Click a category that interests you. For example, click **Arts**.
3. Yahoo! presents a list of subcategories. Continue clicking links until you find a category you like.
4. Click a link to jump to that Web page.

Alternatively, you can search for a keyword within a category. Simply enter a keyword or two into the text box, and click the **Search** button. Yahoo! searches for the requested topic and displays a list of links that match your entry. Click an entry to change to that Web page.

Narrow That Search You can narrow your Yahoo! search as you did with Lycos: by looking for only exact matches, for example. To do so, click the **Options** link next to the Search text box. Make your selections to limit the search, enter keywords to search for, and click **Search**.

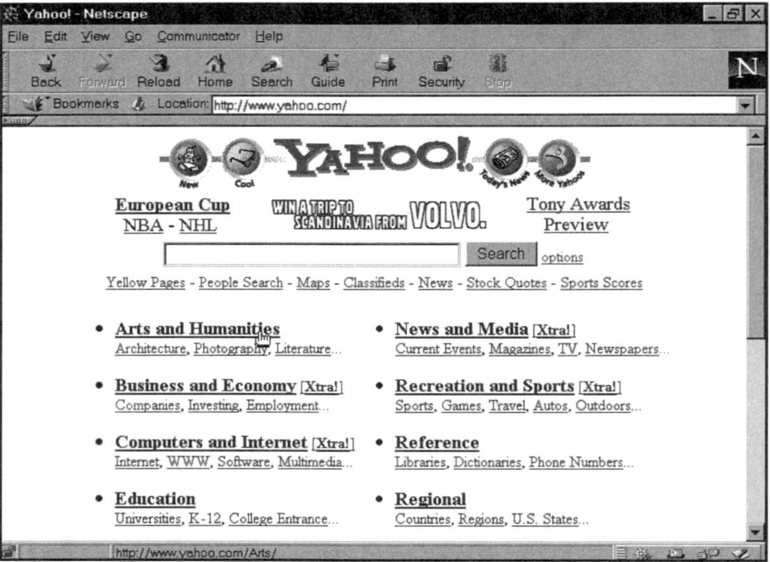

Figure 7.3   With Yahoo!, you can search for a Web page by category.

After jumping to a particular Web page, you can return to the list of items that Yahoo! found by clicking the **Back** button.

Search Twice   If your search results were pretty skimpy, Yahoo! allows you to search the Web again using a different Web search tool. At the end of the list of found items, Yahoo! provides links to other search tools. Click one, and the other search tool automatically performs a search using the same search criteria.

In this lesson, you learned how to use several different Web search tools. In the next lesson, you'll learn how to search for people.

Searching for People on the Internet

In this lesson, you learn how to search for friends and coworkers on the Web.

Finding People Using Web Tools

Several companies (mostly phone companies) have transformed their paper telephone directories into electronic versions and placed them on the Web. You can search for a person by last name if you know the city or state in which they live. This is sort of like dialing the person's area code followed by 555-1212 and asking the operator. The following list provides the URLs for some of these search tools.

http://www.four11.com/

http://www.bigfoot.com

http://www.nova.edu/Inter-Links/phone.html

http://www.switchboard.com/

http://www.yahoo.com/search/people/

http://www.tollfree.att.net/

Follow these steps to see one of these search tools in action.

1. Run Navigator, type **www.four11.com** in the **Location** text box, and press **Enter**. Navigator loads the Four11 White Pages.

2. On the left, click the directory you want to search: E-mail, Telephone, Netphone, Government, or Celebrity (see Figure 8.1).

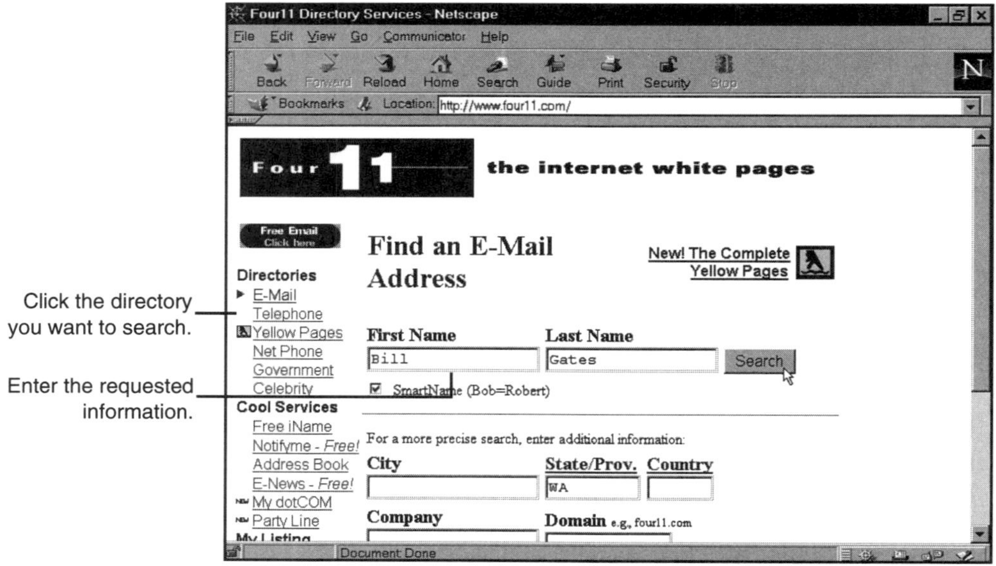

Click the directory you want to search.

Enter the requested information.

Figure 8.1   You can search for people in electronic phone books.

3. Complete the form to specify as much information as possible about the person you're looking for. For example, type the person's last name and the city in which that person lives in the appropriate text boxes.

4. Click the **Search** button. The search tool pulls up a list of all the people that matched your specifications.

Search for E-Mail Address   To search for people using a variety of tools, click the **Guide** button in the Navigation toolbar, and then click **People**. This displays a search form at Netscape that allows you to use any of several people search tools. Click the tool you want to use, complete the form, and click the button to start the search.

Finding Someone Using a Finger Gateway

Although the Web search tools offer the easiest way to search for long lost friends and relatives, there are a few other Internet tools you can try. One such tool is *finger*.

Finger is a tool that you can use to locate a user for whom you have at least a partial e-mail address. Obviously, if you had an e-mail address for the person, you wouldn't be wasting your time looking all over the Internet for him. But it is handy if the address you have is incomplete—and its usefulness doesn't end there. Finger can also tell you whether an e-mail message reached its intended recipient, it can tell you whether a message has been read, and it can sometimes provide a street address and phone number for your friend.

When you want to try using finger, the first thing you have to do is connect to a finger gateway. Here are some addresses you can use:

http://www.nova.edu/Inter-Links/cgi-bin/finger.pl

http://www.cs.indiana.edu/finger/gateway

http://rickman.com/finger.html

http://www.louisville.edu/~jadour01/mothersoft/gf/

http://www.POPULUS.net/cgi-bin/HyperFinger

To use finger, follow these steps:

1. Type the address of a finger gateway in the **Location/Go to** text box and press **Enter**.
2. Enter the e-mail address of the person you're looking for in the search text box.
3. Press **Enter** to start the search. Finger lists its results in a screen similar to the one in Figure 8.2.

Sometimes finger displays a *plan* file for the person you are searching for. If it does, you'll find additional information such as a person's address and phone number in that plan file.

Plan   A text file that contains additional information about a person (such as his name, address, and phone number). Because the contents of a plan file are only displayed when someone fingers you (is searching for you), you might want to create this simple text file, fill it with information you want others to know, and place it in your directory on your service provider's computer.

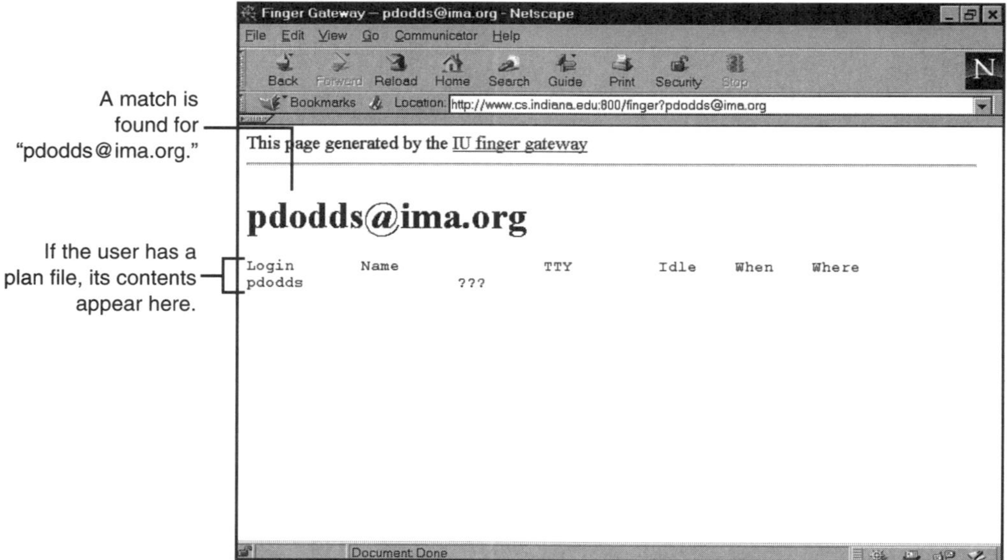

A match is found for "pdodds@ima.org."

If the user has a plan file, its contents appear here.

Figure 8.2   Finger displays its results.

Other Ways to Search for People

Although Web search tools and finger are the best ways to locate people on the Internet, there are other search sites you can try. However, most of them charge you something (most searches are under $100). If you're looking for another way to find someone, though, try one of these electronic detectives (the first of which is shown in Figure 8.3):

Nationwide Investigations	http://www.nwin.com
People Locator Service	http://www.clickit.com/bizwiz/homepage/plsform.htm
Internet Address Finder	http://www.iaf.net

Finally, if you know that the person you're looking for uses a certain online service, such as CompuServe, you (or someone you know who also uses that service) can search the service's member list for your lost pal. You never know what might work.

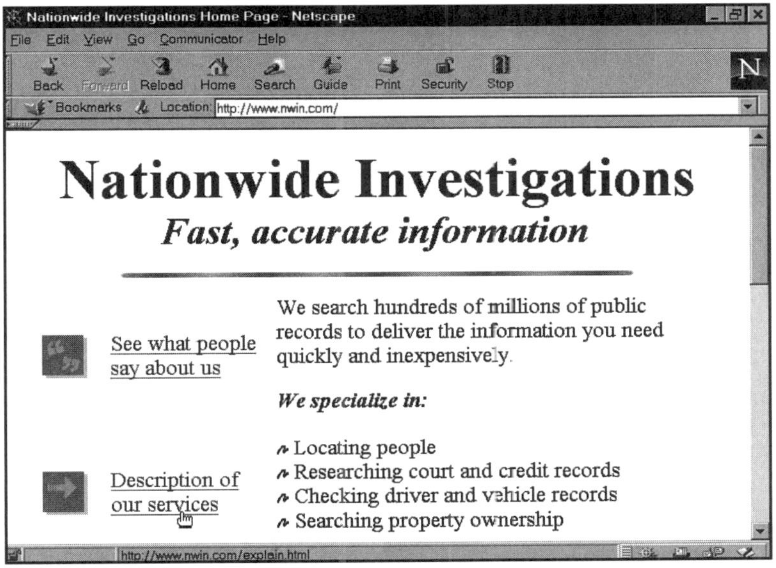

Figure 8.3 If you've tried everything else, hire a detective.

In this lesson, you learned how to search for people on the Web. In the next lesson, you'll learn how to view and save graphics.

Viewing and Saving Graphics

In this lesson, you learn how to view graphic files with Navigator and how to save them to your PC.

A Word About Graphic Viewers

Navigator can display the ordinary graphics, such as jpeg and gif images, that you find on most Web pages. However, to display certain graphic files (bmp, pbm, pgm, and tiff files, for example), Navigator requires some help, which it gets from *in-line plug-ins* and *helper applications*.

Helper apps and in-line plug-ins do just what their names suggest: They help Navigator perform tasks it is not designed to do. The difference between in-line plug-ins and helper applications is a small one that has to do with the method in which they enhance Navigator's capabilities. You'll learn more about helper applications and plug-ins in Part 1 Lesson 18.

In addition to a helper app or in-line plug-in that enables Navigator to display graphic files, you'll probably need helper apps and in-line plug-ins to play sound in real-time, to view incompatible 3-D worlds, or to print PDF documents. You'll learn how to download and install various in-line plug-ins and helper apps later in this part; here, you'll learn how to install an image viewer.

What Happens When Navigator Can't Play a File?

In most cases, Navigator displays graphic images as they appear on Web pages. Sometimes the images are tiny, and you can click the image to view it full-size. Other times, the Web page may display a link that points to a particular graphic. You click the link, and Navigator displays the file.

If you click a link for a graphic or other file type that Navigator cannot play and Navigator "knows" that you need a specific plug-in for that file type, the Plugin Not Loaded dialog box appears (see Figure 9.1). Click **Get the Plugin**.

If Navigator does not know which plug-in you need, Navigator displays the Unknown File Type dialog box asking you what to do. Click the **More Info** button. If Navigator knows of a plug-in you can get to play the file, Navigator displays the Plug-In Finder Page with a link for connecting to the page that features the required plug-in. See Lesson 18, "Using Plug-Ins and Helper Applications," for details.

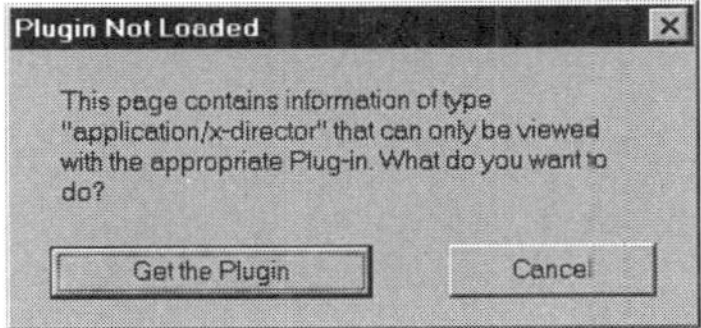

Figure 9.1 If Navigator knows of a plug-in that can play the selected file type, Navigator offers to help you find it.

If Navigator does not know about a plug-in for a selected file type, you have a couple of other options. If you have an application on your system that can play the selected type of file, click **Pick App** (see Figure 9.2), and then select the program to assign it to this file type. If you don't have an application that can play this type of file, you can click **Save File** to save the file to your hard drive so you can play it later.

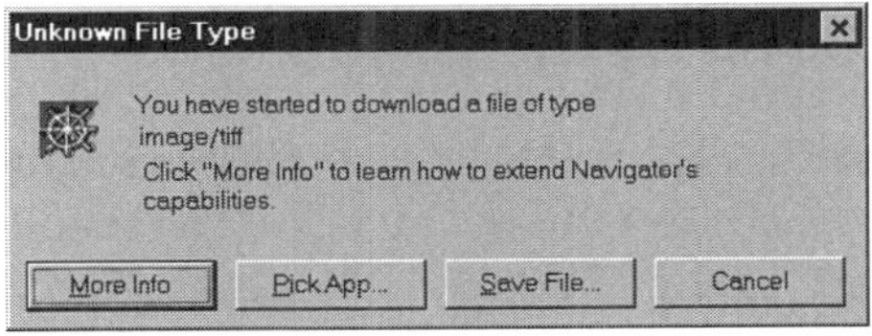

Figure 9.2 If Navigator and its plug-ins cannot play a file, Navigator notifies you.

Downloading and Installing a Graphic Viewer

There are several graphic viewers that you might want to use with Navigator, including LView Pro, VuePrint, ACDSee, or ViewDirector. In addition, you might need to install Fractal Viewer if you think you'll encounter any fractal graphic files (which have the .FIF extension) and FIGleaf Inline or InterCAP Inline if you want to display CGM (Computer Graphics Metafiles). If you need to view CAD (computer aided design) drawings, you'll need a good viewer such as DWG/DXF by SoftSource, WHIP!, or SVF by SoftSource.

You can find Navigator-related files such as graphic viewers in a number of places on the Web. If you don't already have your favorite sources, try one of the ones in Table 9.1.

Table 9.1   Sources for Graphic Helper Apps and In-Line Plug-Ins

Site	*URL*
Stroud's	http://cws.internet.com
Stroud's second main site	http://www.stroud.com
Stroud's main alternate site	http://www.enterprise.net/cwsapps
ZDNet's Software Library	http://www.hotfiles.com
TUCOWS main site	http://www.tucows.com
Shareware.com	http://www.shareware.com
Windows 95.com	http://windows95.com
Thor's WinTools	http://TOOLS.ofthe.NET
Winsite Archive	http://www.winsite.com

Follow these steps to download and install a graphic viewer:

1. Connect to the Internet and start Navigator.
2. Enter the address of a source, such as **http://cws.internet.com**, in the **Location/Go to** text box and press **Enter**.
3. Locate the file you want to download. (At Stroud's, for example, you need to first click the Stroud's logo to get to the main menu. Then you click **Graphic Viewers** to get to a list of available graphic viewers.)
4. Select a viewer and click it to download it.

5. Depending on the type of file you selected, Navigator may display the Unknown File Type dialog box. Click **Save File**. If a warning dialog box appears, click **Save It to Disk** and click **OK**. In either case, the Save As dialog box appears (see Figure 9.3).

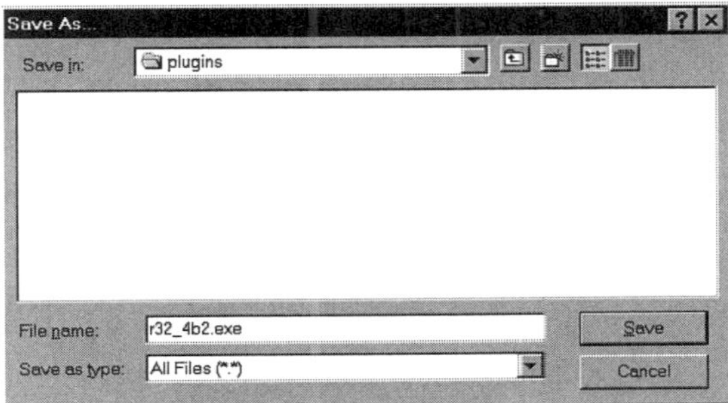

Figure 9.3   The Save As dialog box prompts you to save the file.

6. Select a directory into which you want to save the file, and then click **Save**. When the download is complete, you're returned to the Navigator window.

The process to install your new viewer will vary from viewer to viewer, but here are the basic steps:

1. Open File Manager or Explorer and change to the directory/folder into which you downloaded your file.

2. Double-click the zipped file to start WinZip. If the file you downloaded is self-extracting—if it ends in .EXE—WinZip will not start. Instead, the file will decompress (unzip) itself into the current directory, and you can skip to step 5.

WinZip   WinZip is a handy utility that makes using PKUNZIP and PKZIP a lot easier. PKUNZIP is the DOS utility that you use to unzip (decompress) the files you get off the Web. If you don't have a copy of WinZip, get back on the Internet and download it (you can find WinZip at http://www.shareware.com). Install WinZip on your system, and then come back here to finish installing your new viewer. (WinZip includes a copy of the PKZIP and PKUNZIP utilities.) Note that WinZip is a shareware program, which means that after a short trial period, you're required to register it and pay a small fee. *Be sure you do that.*

3. Click the **Extract** button, select a directory into which you want the decompressed files placed (the same directory as the zipped file is okay), and then click **Extract** again.

4. Close WinZip, and then switch to the directory that contains the decompressed files. You'll probably find something called SETUP.EXE or INSTALL.EXE.

5. Double-click the **SETUP.EXE** or **INSTALL.EXE** file to start the installation process.

I Don't See a Setup File   Some smaller programs don't really have an installation routine. If you don't find a setup file, the program is probably already installed. Double-click a **README.TXT** or similar file and read it. This usually clears up any questions you might have about installation. Then double-click the main file (such as lviewp.exe) to start the program to test it.

CAUTION

If the graphic viewer you selected is an in-line plug-in, when you double-click it, it decompresses and starts its setup routine automatically. Follow the on-screen instructions to link the in-line plug-in to Navigator.

If the graphic viewer you selected is a helper application, you need to start Navigator and tell it where the graphic viewer is located. Follow these steps:

1. Start Navigator. (You don't need to connect to the Internet to complete these steps.)

2. Open the **Edit** menu and select **Preferences**.

3. Click the plus sign next to Navigator and select **Applications** (see Figure 9.4).

4. From the **Description** list, select a file type associated with your viewer. For example, LView Pro supports bmp files, so select **Windows Bitmap**.

5. Click the **Edit** button, and the Edit Type dialog box appears, allowing you to assign an application to this file type.

6. Click **Application**.

7. Click **Browse**, and the Open dialog box appears.

8. Select your application's main program file and click **Open**. (For example, switch to the LView Pro directory and select the lviewp.exe file.)

9. If you don't want Navigator to display a warning before opening files of this type, click the **Ask Me Before Opening Downloaded Files of This Type** check box to remove the check. Then click **OK**.

10. Repeat steps 4 through 9 to associate your graphic viewer with other file types as needed. For example, LView Pro also supports ppm, pgm, pbm, and tiff files, so you should repeat the steps for each of those file extensions.

11. When you're done, click **OK**.

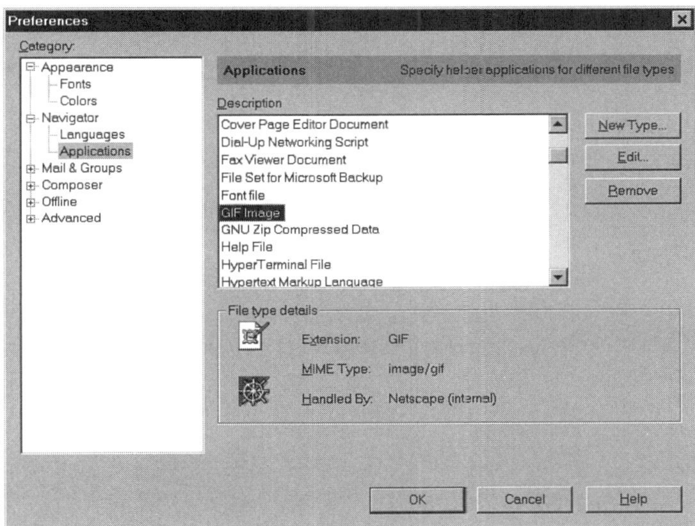

Figure 9.4 Options for installing your graphic viewer.

If you need a graphics file type that is not listed, you can add it. To do so, click the **New Type** button and type a description of the file type. Next, tab to the **File Extension** text box and enter the file type (such as jpeg, bmp, or tiff). If you know the MIME type, tab to the **MIME Type** text box and enter the MIME type (if you're not sure, leave this blank, but be sure to enter a file name extension). Then under **Application to Use**, click the **Browse** button, select the desired application, and click **Open**. Click **OK**.

From now on, whenever Navigator encounters a file type that matches one associated with your graphic viewer, it will automatically launch the appropriate program (such as LView Pro) and display the graphic for you.

Reassociate Files with Navigator   Initially, Navigator is set up to play several types of files, including GIF, JPEG, and AIFF files. If you change that by associating these file types to other plug-ins or helper applications, you can always reassociate them to Navigator. In the Preferences dialog box, under **Navigator**, click **Applications**. Then select the desired file type, click **Edit**, and click the **Navigator** option. Click **OK**.

Saving a Graphic to Your PC's Hard Disk

You can save to your hard disk any graphic you encounter during your Web surfing sessions. If you save a graphic to your hard disk, you can view it later or reuse it for your own purposes (as a desktop background, for example).

Graphic Royalty   If you do reuse a graphic for any commercial reason—such as republishing it on the Web—you should make sure that the graphic is in the public domain (meaning that you do not have to pay a royalty to use it).

To save a graphic to your hard disk, follow these steps:

1. Right-click the graphic.

2. Select **Save Image As**, and the Save As dialog box appears.

3. Select a directory in which to save the graphic, and then click **Save**.

You can set up Navigator to automatically save files of a particular type to your hard drive. Display the Preferences dialog box, and under **Navigator**, click **Applications**. Select the file type that you want to save to disk and click **Edit**. Then click the **Save to Disk** option and click **OK**.

Can't See What You're Getting?   Some graphics aren't visible because you need a graphic viewer to view them. Even so, you can right-click the link itself to save the graphic to your hard disk. If you want to preview the graphic first, click the link and let Navigator load the appropriate graphic viewer. You can then save the file to your hard disk by using the viewer's **File**, **Save As** command.

In this lesson, you learned how to install a graphic viewer for Navigator and how to save a Web graphic to your hard drive. In the next lesson, you'll learn how to copy (download) files from the Internet.

Downloading Files

In this lesson, you learn how to download files from the Web using a variety of methods.

Copying Files from the Internet

The Internet is packed with all sorts of goodies. You'll find Web pages full of images, sounds, and video clips; sites that offer programs you can try for free; and places where you can download collections of clip art and other files.

But how do you get those files from the Internet to your computer? In most cases, the process is fairly easy. You right-click the image or a link that points to the file you want, and then you click a Save command (Save Image As or Save Link As). The Save As dialog box appears—and you know what to do from there.

You can also use Navigator to go to file repositories on the Web called *FTP servers*. An FTP server is sort of like a big hard disk on the Internet. You can use Navigator just as you use Windows Explorer or File Manager to change directories, select files, and copy them to your hard drive.

In this lesson, you learn how to copy (download) files from Web pages, how to find files and programs on the Web, and how to download from FTP sites.

Another Way to Save Files   Later in Part 1, you will learn how to use helper applications and plug-ins to play the media files you encounter on the Web. Many of these programs contain their own Save option, which you can use to save the file after playing it.

CAUTION

Saving Files from Web Pages

As you skip from one Web page to another, you will no doubt encounter items that you want to save for your future enjoyment. For example, you might visit an art museum and pick up a few electronic versions of your favorite master-pieces. The following steps explain how to copy those files from the Web to your computer:

1. Run Navigator and open the Web page that contains the image you want to copy or that contains a link that points to the file you want (a video or audio clip, or any other file type).

2. Right-click the image or link. Navigator displays a context menu (see Figure 10.1) offering a couple of Save options.

3. Click the **Save Image As** option. Navigator displays the Save As dialog box, prompting you to name the file.

4. Pick the drive and folder in which you want to save the file and type a new name for the file if you want. Click **Save**, and Navigator saves the file.

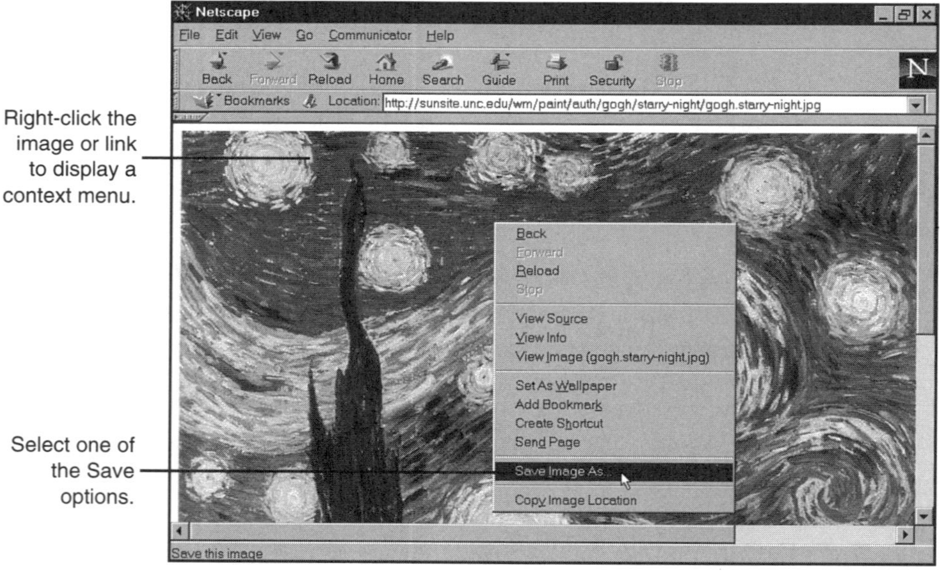

Right-click the image or link to display a context menu.

Select one of the Save options.

Figure 10.1   Right-click to quickly save a file.

Transform an Image into Windows Wallpaper   If you see an image you really like, you might want to use it as the background for your Windows desktop. To do so, right-click the image and select **Set as Wallpaper**.

Locating a File on the Web

There are several good sources for files on the Web. Of those, some sites allow you to search for just about any kind of software, while others specialize in Windows applications, Internet applications, and so on. Search tools such as Lycos, Yahoo!, Excite!, and InfoSeek often supply links to the more popular software sources. However, if you don't feel like searching around, try some of the good general sources listed in Table 10.1.

Table 10.1   General Software Sources

Source	URL
Shareware.com	http://www.shareware.com
Windows95.com	http://windows95.com
ZDNet	http://www.hotfiles.com
BC's Win95 Net Apps	http://bcpub.com/w95netapps.html
Thor's WinTools	http://TOOLS.ofthe.NET
Winsite Archive	http://www.winsite.com
Papa Winsock	http://papa.indstate.edu:8888/ftp/main.html

If you're looking for Internet apps in particular, try some of the sites listed in Table 10.2.

Table 10.2   Internet Software Sources

Source	URL
Stroud's main site	http://www.cwsapps.com
Stroud's second main site	http://www.stroud.com
Stroud's main alternate site	http://www.enterprise.net/cwsapps
TUCOWS main site	http://www.tucows.com
TUCOWS main alternate site	http://tucow.niia.net

When you connect to one of these pages, you'll typically find a search tool that you can use to find your file. In other cases, files are categorized by type so that all you have to do is select a category that interests you, and then select your file from among those listed. After you find your file, downloading it from the Web is an easy process. Figure 10.2 shows you what to expect at Stroud's.

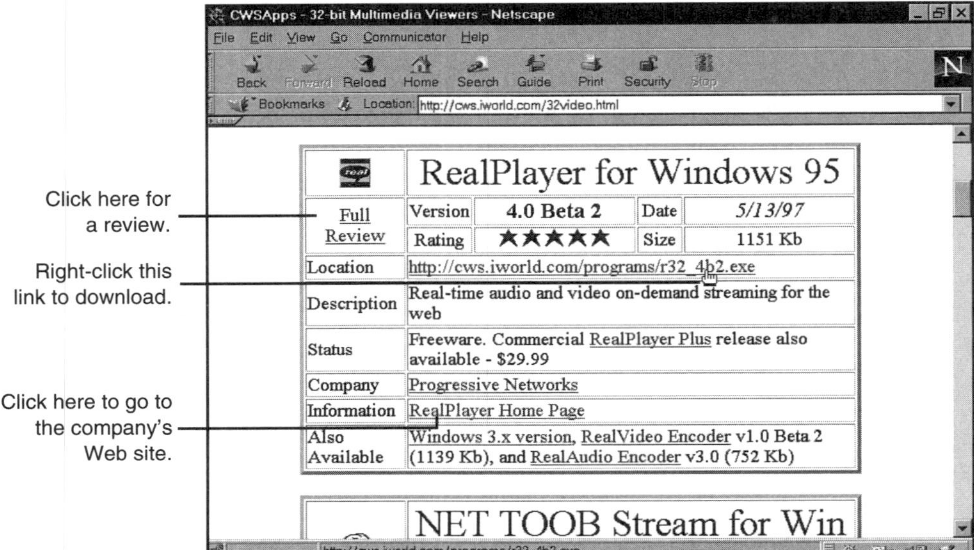

Figure 10.2   Stroud's reviews applications and provides links with which you can download and learn more about the file.

Searching for Files on an FTP Site with Archie

One of the main reasons people connect to the Internet is to download a copy of a *shareware* program such as WinZip (a Windows interface for PKZIP) or Eudora (an Internet e-mail program). The Internet uses *FTP* (File Transfer Protocol) to transfer files over the Internet to your computer. Netscape comes with built-in FTP support, so you don't need a separate FTP program to download files from the Internet. However, you can always use one if you want.

If you have trouble locating the program you're looking for on the Web but you know the file's name, you might want to go directly to the source: an FTP site. To search for a file on an FTP site, you use *Archie*. Archie servers search FTP sites periodically for downloadable files and then make a catalog of the files that you can search through. If Archie's catalog contains the name of the file you're looking for, Archie provides the location (the FTP site and directory) of your file. You can then use Navigator or an FTP program to download the file.

Why Bother with an FTP Program?   Although you can use your Web browser to download files, FTP programs often make the process easier in a couple of ways. First, they contain preset links to the most common FTP sites—something a Web browser lacks. Second, you can download multiple files at once with an FTP program, but not with a Web browser. Also, if you need to manage files in your own directory on an FTP server, the FTP program offers commands for deleting and renaming files, and creating, deleting, and moving directories.

In the old days, you had to use a separate Archie program to search for files. However, now the Web has Archie pages that make searching for a file as easy as filling out a search form. The only trouble is that you need to know the exact name of the file, or at least a unique portion of the file's name. To search for a specific file with Archie, follow these steps:

1. Click in the **Location** text box and type one of the following URLs:

   http://hoohoo.ncsa.uiuc.edu/archie.html

   http://alfred.uib.no/cgi-bin/archie.pl

   http://www.wg.omron.co.jp/AA-eng.html

2. Press **Enter**, and then wait for the Archie Request Form to appear. The form you see varies depending on the URL you entered in step 1. Figure 10.3 shows the form for the first URL listed above.

3. Enter the name or partial name of the file you're looking for. (If you type a partial name, make sure you enter a setting to search for a substring instead of an exact match.)

4. Enter any other information or settings as desired. For example, most Archie search forms ask if you want the search to be case-sensitive.

5. If you're given a choice, click the **By Host** or **By Date** button to select a sorting preference. By Host tells Archie to sort the found files by host name. By Date lists newer files first.

6. If you see a drop-down list labeled **Priority** or **The Impact on Other Users Can Be**, select how pushy you want to be. If you select Not Nice At All, the Archie server will drop everything to search for your file. Select **Nicer** to be at least somewhat nice.

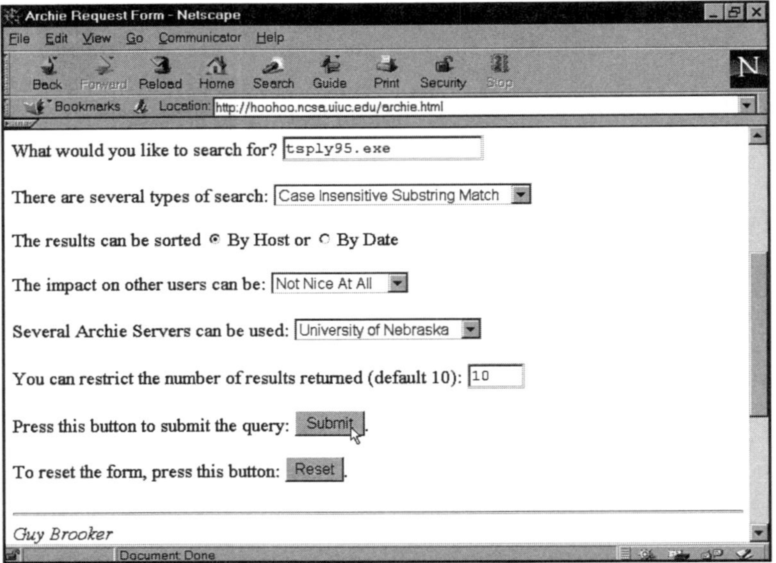

Figure 10.3 An Archie request form.

7. If you're given a choice of Archie servers to use, open the drop-down list and select the Archie server you want to use for this search. A closer server may be faster in off-hours, whereas a distant server (one located in a time zone where it is evening or early morning) might work better during business hours.

8. If you see a text box that allows you to limit the number of copies of the file you want Archie to find, type a number in the text box. Archie searches can take a long time, so I usually type **30** in this text box.

9. Click the **Start Search** button (or its equivalent). Archie searches can take a while, so don't expect a list of files to pop up immediately.

10. If Archie finds the file, it displays a list of links that point to various locations where the file is stored. Right-click a link and select **Save Link As**.

Archie Is Slow   Don't be surprised if an Archie search takes several minutes. Archie sites are typically busy, especially during business hours. If you want a faster search, try searching in the middle of the night.

CAUTION

Downloading a File from an FTP Site

Many people locate the files they want to download on the Web, and many Web pages feature links to FTP sites. However, those sites are often busy. In such cases, you might find it easier to connect directly to an FTP site with Netscape.

You can connect to one of several FTP sites and rummage around for a file, but it's easier if you have the address of the file's exact location on the FTP system. You might get that address in any number of ways. You might, for example, find the address for a file in a book or a magazine that recommends that particular program, or you might locate the address for a file through an Archie search (see "Searching for Files on an FTP Site with Archie" for more information). Table 10.3 lists some popular public FTP sites where you can start.

Table 10.3 Recommended FTP Sites

Site	URL
CICA Windows Archive	ftp.winsite.com
Netscape	ftp1.netscape.com
Mosaic	ftp.ncsa.uuic.edu
Oakland Archives	oak.oakland.edu
Microsoft	ftp.microsoft.com
America Online	ftp.aol.com
Mirrors to Popular Sites	mirrors.aol.com
SimTel Archives	ftp.coast.net
ESNET	ftp.esnet.com
GARBO Archives	garbo.uwusa.fi

Connecting to Public and Private FTP Servers

All the FTP sites listed in Table 10.3 provide public access. In most cases, Navigator handles the login procedure for you, entering the proper generic information to get you connected. If you have trouble connecting to a particular site, the site may be busy, or it may require that you enter your e-mail address as a password.

To set up Navigator to send your e-mail address, follow these steps:

1. Open the **Edit** menu and select **Preferences**. The Preferences dialog box appears.

2. Click the plus sign next to **Mail & Groups**, click **Identity**, and then type your e-mail address in the **Email Address** text box. Click **OK**.

3. Click **Advanced**.

4. Make sure there is a check mark in the box labeled **Send Email Address As Anonymous FTP Password** (see Figure 10.4), and then click **OK**.

If you still have trouble connecting, the site may just be too busy.

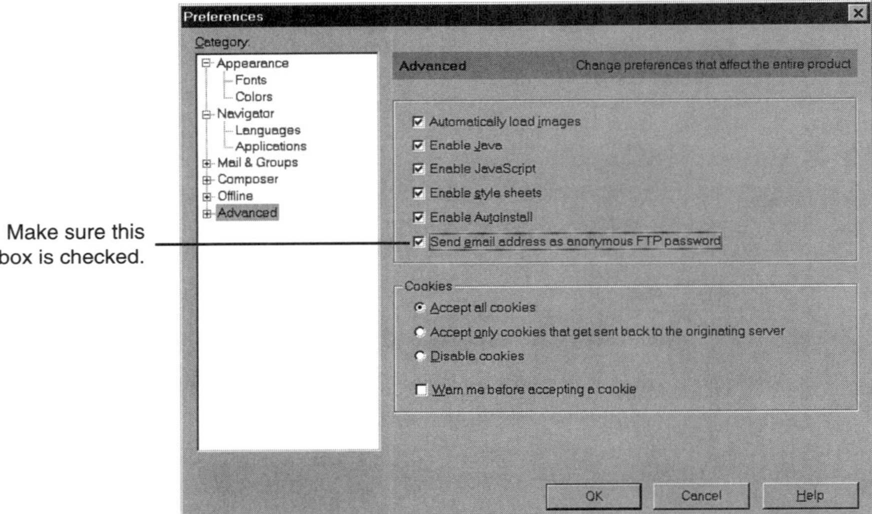

Figure 10.4 Navigator can send your e-mail address as the password.

Some FTP sites are private. For example, your service provider probably has a private FTP server that you use (unknowingly) for e-mail and other data. The service provider doesn't want non-members to be messing with members' files, so it protects the server by requiring members to enter their username and password in order to access the server.

If you need to access files on a private server, you must obtain a username and password from the server's administrator. Once you have a username and password, you must enter it correctly into Navigator. To connect to a password-protected FTP server, enter your name and password into the **Location** text box in the following form:

ftp://*username:password*@ftp.*sitename.domain*

For example, you might enter:

ftp://bfink:x23qrtvg@ftp.internet.com

Navigating an FTP Server

When you log onto an FTP site, you see its folders (those files and folders to which you've been given some level of access). You can move about these folders in much the same way that you move from folder to folder within File Manager or the Explorer:

- To open a folder, click it (see Figure 10.5).
- To move up the directory tree, click the double dots (..), or click **Up to Higher Level Directory** at the top of the tree, or click Navigator's **Back** button.
- When you find a file you want, right-click its link and click one of the Save commands. See the next section, "Downloading a File," for further instructions.

Downloading a File

When you've located a file you want, you're ready to download it to your PC. Netscape makes downloading files as simple as point-and-click. When you see a link that points to the file you want, take one of the following steps to download it.

- Right-click the link and select **Save Link As**. The Save As dialog box appears, prompting you to name the file and select a drive and folder in which to store it.
- If you want to download a file that Navigator or one of its helper applications can play, **Shift+**click the link. This tells Navigator that instead of viewing the file, you want to save it. The Save As dialog appears.
- If you are downloading a program file—or any other file that Navigator or one of its helper applications cannot play—simply click the link for the file. Navigator prompts you to save it.

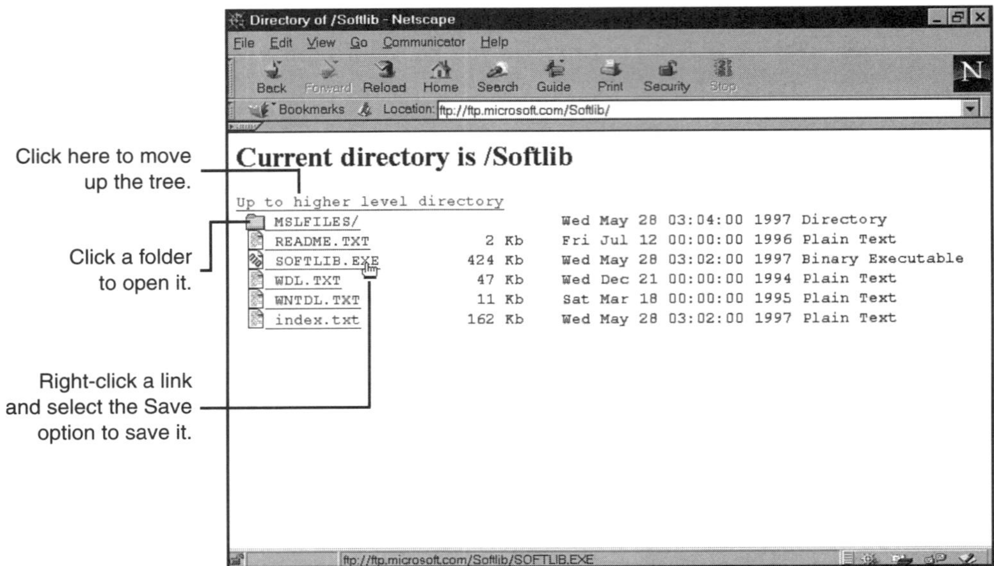

Click here to move up the tree.

Click a folder to open it.

Right-click a link and select the Save option to save it.

Figure 10.5   Navigating at an FTP site is like navigating in Windows Explorer.

Most program files available for download from the Internet have been *compressed*. Compressing a file makes it smaller so that it can be downloaded more quickly. After you download a file from the Internet, you'll probably have to decompress it using a utility called PKUNZIP. You can identify zipped (compressed) files by the file extension .ZIP.

Some compressed files are *self-extracting*, which means that you won't need PKUNZIP (or a similar utility) to decompress them. When you double-click a self-extracting file, it decompresses automatically, placing its newly restored file(s) in the current directory. Self-extracting zip files have the file extension .EXE. (As a side note, keep in mind that not all files that end in .EXE are zipped files.)

The easiest way to unzip files is to use WinZip (which contains a licensed copy of the PKZIP Utilities). So before you start downloading files from the Internet, download a copy of WinZip and install it. You can download WinZip from http://www.winzip.com/. Or look for it at Stroud's or TUCOWS.

Beware of Viruses The most common way you can introduce a virus into your computer is to download and run an infected program file. Before running the file, check it for viruses with an antivirus program. For additional tips on virus prevention, see Lesson 13, "Digital Passport, Cookies, and Other Security Topics."

Uploading Files

Although you will usually want to take files from an FTP server, you might find occasion to place files on an FTP server (for example, to publish a Web page). The easiest way to do this is to connect to the FTP server, change to the directory in which you want the files placed, and then drag the file from Windows Explorer or File Manager into the Navigator window.

Another way to upload files is to change to the FTP directory in which you want the file(s) placed, and then open Navigator's **File** menu and select **Upload File**. This displays the File Upload dialog box, which you can use to select the file(s) you want to upload. After selecting the files, click the **Open** button.

Access Denied Very few FTP servers let just anybody upload files. This could introduce viruses into their system or overload their storage capacities. In order to upload files, you typically must receive permission from the administrator at that site, who will then give you a username and password for a higher level of access.

In this lesson, you learned how to download files from the Internet. In the next lesson, you'll learn how to navigate a Gopher site with Navigator.

Visiting a Gopher Site

In this lesson, you learn how to connect to a Gopher site and search for items of interest within Gopherspace.

What Is Gopherspace?

The Gopher system originated at the University of Minnesota, whose Internet engineers promptly named it after the University of Minnesota mascot, the Golden Gopher. Gopherspace was designed to create an interconnected index of files and documents located on various Gopher servers throughout the Internet. You navigate Gopherspace using a menu system.

How Do I Get to Gopherspace? Gopherspace (like the Web) is a subset of the Internet. You can connect to Gopherspace using a Gopher program, but it's easier to use Navigator and connect to Gopherspace through the Web.

When you connect to a Gopher server, you see a menu of subjects or sites, as shown in Figure 11.1. Select a subject off the main menu (directory), and you'll see another menu (subdirectory) with which you narrow your choice. This continues until you get to something useful, such as a text document or a graphic file that you can view, download, or print.

For example, suppose you start by selecting Publications from the main menu. Then you select something like Consumer News from the next menu. Eventually, you find a document you want to look at, such as "How to Get Cheap Airline Tickets." In other words, you browse Gopherspace just as you might browse the Web, but instead of clicking links, you select subjects from Gopher menus. There's even a way to search for information in Gopherspace, as you'll see later in this lesson.

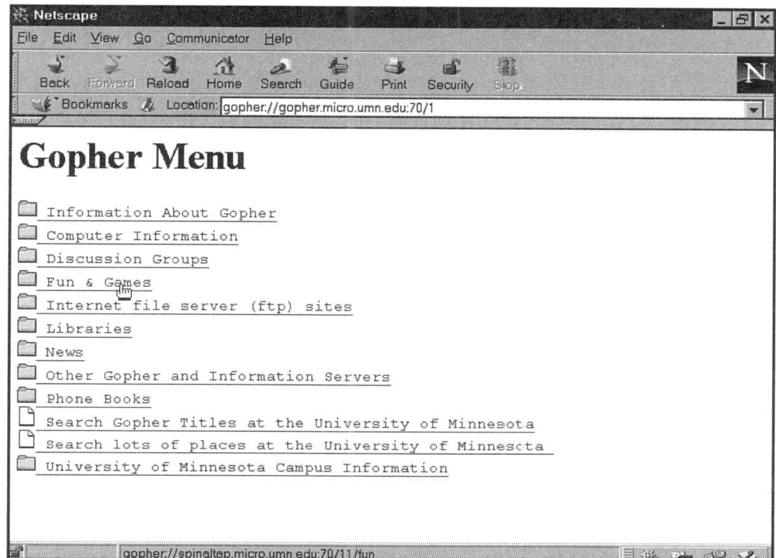

Figure 11.1 Gopher displays a full-page menu that looks a lot like an FTP server's directories.

Not everything on a Gopher menu actually resides on that particular Gopher server. But don't worry; as you move from menu to menu, you're automatically connected to whichever server contains the proper information.

Ask Forms While browsing Gopherspace, you might also encounter *ask forms*, which are like dialog boxes. These forms help you search special Gopher+ sites for information.

Gopher+ Sites Gopher+ sites are enhanced versions of regular Gopher sites; they are called "enhanced" because they provide ask forms for quick searching, and they usually provide more than one version of a file for downloading.

Connecting to a Gopher Site

When you connect to a Gopher server, what you see looks something like Explorer or File Manager: a menu with icons for folders (directories), text files, program files, and so on. To change from one menu (directory) to another or to select a file, you click the appropriate icon.

The information you typically find in Gopherspace differs considerably from what you find on the Web. Most Gopher servers are associated with universities, so the information in Gopherspace tends to be fairly academic. If you need to do research, though, you might find information in Gopherspace that has not yet made its way to the Web.

You can travel Gopherspace with a specialized Gopher program or with Navigator. To connect to a Gopher site with Navigator, you enter its address in Navigator's **Location** text box. A Gopher address looks like this:

gopher://gopher.tc.umn.edu

The first part of the address tells Navigator to use the gopher protocol to read the information on the site. The second part is the actual address of the Gopher site.

When you're ready to try out Gopher, check out the Gopher server named above or one of these others:

gopher://gopher.berkeley.edu

gopher://gopher.indiana.edu

gopher://infoeagle.bc.edu

gopher://gopher.uiuc.edu

To connect to a Gopher site with Navigator, follow these steps:

1. Connect to the Internet as usual and start Navigator.

2. To connect to a Gopher site, type its address in the **Location**/**Go to** text box and press **Enter**. Navigator displays the opening Gopher menu (see Figure 11.2).

3. Click a link or a folder to open the associated menu. Continue to change from menu to menu until you find a file you want to view, print, or download.

Moving Up One Level   To return to the previous menu, click Navigator's **Back** button.

4. To view a file, click it. You can then print it by clicking the **Print** button. To download a file, press and hold the **Shift** key and click the file name.

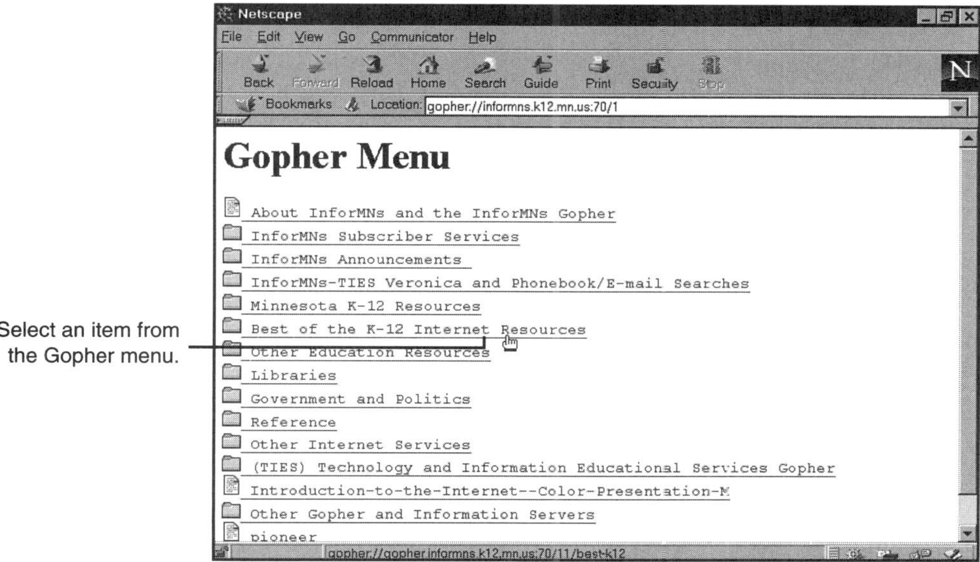

Select an item from the Gopher menu.

Figure 11.2   You surf Gopherspace using menus.

Search Forms   If you encounter a search form during your travels in Gopherspace, see the next section, "Searching for Items with Veronica and Jughead," for help.

CAUTION

Searching for Items with Veronica and Jughead

Gopher provides two search tools you can use to locate items in Gopherspace: *Veronica* and *Jughead*. Veronica searches for your item all over Gopherspace, while Jughead searches only the current Gopher server. You can identify Veronica and Jughead searches on Gopher menus by their distinctive magnifying glass icon.

Veronica An Internet search tool that you can use to find resources at a Gopher site. Veronica searches all Gopher sites to find something that matches your criteria.

Jughead A Gopher search tool that's similar to Veronica. Unlike Veronica, however, Jughead searches only the current Gopher site to find the specified resources.

Faster Searches Because it takes a long time to search Gopherspace, Veronica allows you to choose between searching all of Gopherspace and searching directory names only.

When you select Veronica or Jughead from a Gopher menu, you're taken to an ask form (similar to a dialog box). Enter the information for which you want to search. Veronica or Jughead locates an item for you, which you can view by clicking it.

Search Tips

In the ask form, if you type a search string such as "English poetry," Veronica or Jughead searches for any item with both the words "English" AND "poetry" in it. Keeping your search very specific like this means that you'll have fewer results to wade through.

You can use NOT in a search string to narrow a search even more if you want. For example, you could type "poetry NOT French" to display all kinds of poetry except French poetry. You can also use the asterisk wild-card character (*) to aid your search. The asterisk represents any character or characters in a search string. For example, if you were to type "drug*," you'd get "drug," "drugs," and "drugstore" among your results. Note, however, that you can't use an asterisk in the middle of a search string (as in dr*g). All you'll get for your cleverness is an error message.

You can also use OR in your search string—but it's not very useful. If you type the string "English OR poetry," Veronica or Jughead will display all files that contain either the word "English" or the word "poetry." This actually expands your search area, when your primary goal is probably to narrow the search. Therefore, you should avoid using OR in your search string if possible.

What's OR For?   Okay, there is one way to use OR to aid in a search. If you are looking for information on English or Irish poetry, you can use the search string "poetry (English OR Irish)," which includes parentheses to group the two related items. This will find items related to either English poetry or Irish poetry.

Normally, Veronica limits its results to the first 200 items it finds that match your search string. You can also narrow a search by limiting the number of items listed, and/or by limiting the type of file Veronica searches. (Jughead doesn't allow you to limit your searches in this manner.)

- To limit the number of files listed in the result, add **-mnumber** to the end of your Veronica search string, like this:

english literature -m10

- To have Veronica list everything it finds, add **-m** but don't type a number, like this:

english literature -m

- To limit the type of file Veronica searches for, add **-ttype** to the end of your search string, where **type** is a number from Table 11.1. Your search string might look like this:

utilities -t1

This example requests a search for only file type #1, which finds directories.

Table 11.1   Valid File Types

Number	Type
0	Text file
1	Directory
2	CSO name server (phone book)
4	Mac HQX file (BINHEX)
5	PC binary file (program file)
6	Uuencoded file
7	Gopher menu

continues

Table 11.1 Continued

Number	Type
8	Telnet session
9	Binary file
s	Sound
e	Event
I	Image (other than GIF file)
M	MIME e-mail message
T	TN3270 session
c	Calendar
g	GIF image
h	HTML document

Searching Gopherspace

To search Gopherspace with Navigator, follow these steps:

1. To start your search, click a magnifying glass or similar icon (such as a Phone icon). You're connected to a Veronica or Jughead search site.

I Can't Find a Veronica or Jughead Site!   Some Gopher sites don't actually list Jughead as an option. Look for a Search option instead, such as "Search Gopher titles at the University of Minnesota." To locate a Veronica site, try typing one of these addresses: gopher://liberty.uc.wlu.edu:70/11/gophers/ veronica or gopher://veronica.scs.unr.edu:70/11/veronica. Both of these list Veronica sites.

2. Enter the keyword(s) you want to search for and click **Search** or press **Enter**. If you enter "Oklahoma weather" as in Figure 11.3, for example, you'll get any item that contains both the word "Oklahoma" and the word "weather."

3. The results of your search appear on-screen. To view a file, click it. If a folder appears, you can click it to display its contents.

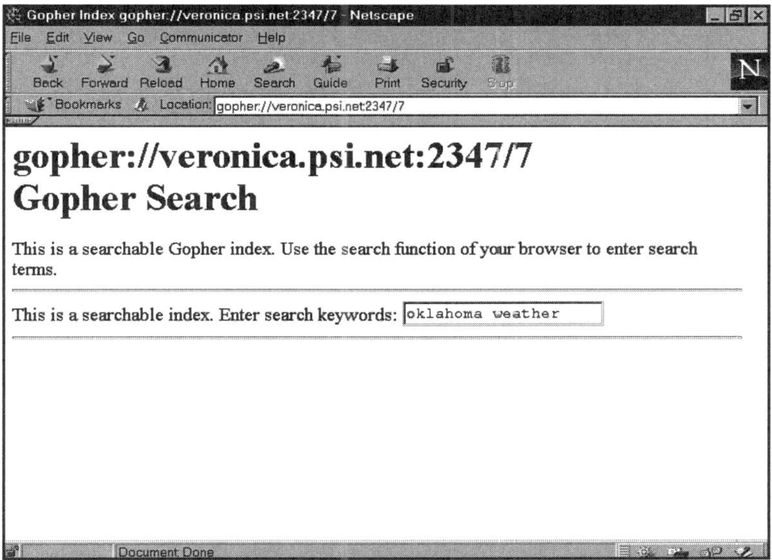

Figure 11.3   You can search Gopherspace with Veronica or Jughead.

In this lesson, you learned how to search Gopherspace with Navigator. In the next lesson, you'll learn how to customize Navigator.

Customizing Navigator to Make It Your Own

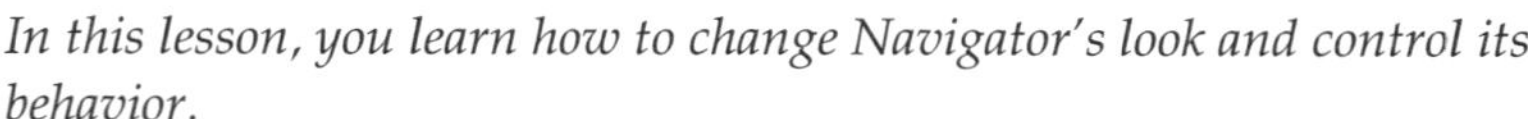

In this lesson, you learn how to change Navigator's look and control its behavior.

Customization Basics

Although Navigator is set up to run immediately with settings that anyone can use, Navigator allows you to customize it to make it look and act the way you want it to. You can enlarge the viewing area by turning toolbars off, create your own toolbar buttons (as you did in Part 1 Lesson 4), change the screen colors, load pages without loading graphics, and much more.

In this lesson, you will learn to take control of Navigator's toolbars and to change some of the settings that control Navigator's look and behavior. You can change most settings by opening the Edit menu, selecting Preferences, and then choosing the set of options you want to change: Appearance, Navigator, Mail & Groups, Composer, Offline, or Advanced. This lesson deals mostly with the Appearance, Navigator, Offline, and Advanced Preferences. For instructions on entering the other settings, see the following lessons:

- **Mail & Groups Preferences:** See Part 3 Lesson 1, "Setting Up Netscape Messenger."

- **Composer Preferences:** See Part 6 Lesson 1, "What Can Composer Do for Me?"

- **Security Preferences:** See Part 1 Lesson 13, "Digital Passport, Cookies, and Other Security Topics."

Controlling Navigator's Toolbars

There are a few things you can do to Navigator's interface without hunting through the menu system for customization options. For one, you can create more screen space by hiding any of the toolbars. To hide a toolbar, click its tab (see Figure 12.1). You can also drag a tab to move the toolbar up or down.

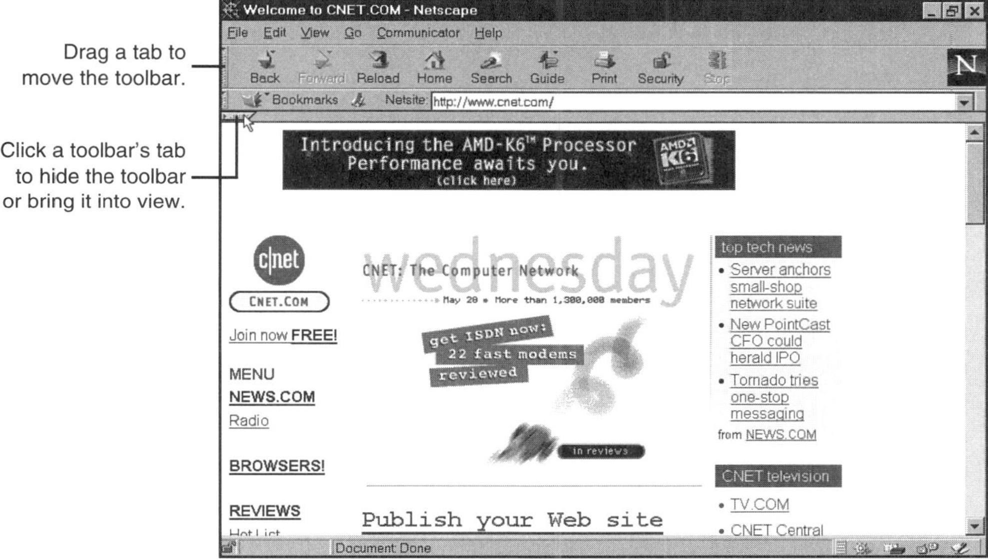

Figure 12.1   You can use the toolbar tabs to hide or display each toolbar.

To turn a toolbar completely off so that not even the tab is showing, open the **View** menu and click the **Hide** command for the toolbar you want to hide. To redisplay a toolbar, open the **View** menu and select the **Show** command for the desired toolbar.

Entering General Preferences

The Appearance Preferences panel contains most of the options you might want to adjust. Here, you can change the background and text color for Web pages, the appearance of Navigator's toolbars, and the way in which Navigator displays images. To enter any preferences, take the following steps:

1. Open the **Edit** menu and select **Preferences**. The Preferences dialog box appears, as shown in Figure 12.2, offering categories of settings.

2. Click the category that looks as though it might contain the settings you want to change, and then enter your changes. (When you click a category, the panel on the right changes to show the available options.) The following sections explain the options for five panels that deal with Navigator.

3. When you finish entering changes, click **OK**.

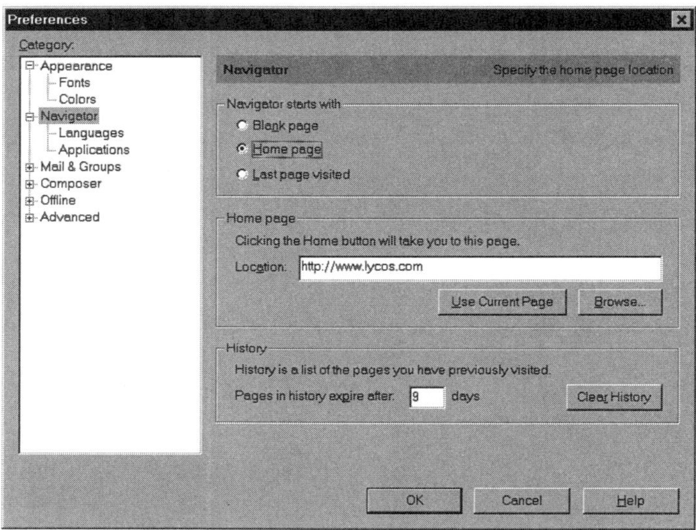

Figure 12.2   The Preferences dialog box.

Setting Your Appearance Preferences

When you open the Preferences dialog box, the Appearance category should be selected. If the category is not selected, click it. You can then change the following options:

On Startup Launch   This setting gives you the option of starting Navigator, Messenger Mailbox (for incoming e-mail), Collabra Discussions (for accessing newsgroups), Page Composer (for creating Web pages), or Netcaster automatically when you double-click the Netscape Communicator icon that's on the Windows desktop.

Show Toolbar As   This option allows you to control the appearance of the buttons in the toolbar. You can choose **Pictures and Text** (for large buttons that show the button names), or **Pictures Only** (for small buttons without names), or **Text Only** (for small buttons without pictures). If you choose Pictures Only, you can still see the name of a button by resting the mouse pointer on it.

Setting Font Preferences

Web pages consist of text and of codes that provide instructions to the Web browser on how to display text, insert and position images, and display the page in the correct layout. The codes typically provide general instructions that the Web browser must interpret. That's why no page looks the same displayed in two different Web browsers.

Because Navigator is in charge of assigning fonts, you can pick the fonts you want to use to style the text. With the Preferences dialog box displayed, click the **Fonts** category (directly below Appearance). If Fonts is not displayed, click the plus sign next to Appearance. The Fonts panel allows you to enter the following font settings:

- **Variable Width Font**   A *variable width font* gives each character only the amount of space it needs. A skinny "i" gets less space than a wide "w." Variable width fonts are used for most of the text on a Web page.

- Fixed Width Font   A fixed width font gives each character the same amount of room. A slender "i" gets the same space as a wide-body "w." Fixed width fonts are usually used to display file names at FTP sites, and to display other types of "computer" text.

- **Use My Default Fonts, Overriding Document-Specified Fonts**   This option tells Navigator to always use the fonts you selected instead of using the fonts specified on the Web page.

- **Use Document-Specified Fonts, but Disable Dynamic Fonts**   Select this option to use the fonts that are built into the Web page. If additional (dynamic) fonts will increase the download time for the page, Navigator won't use the dynamic fonts.

- **Use Document-Specified Fonts, Including Dynamic Fonts**   Choose this option if you want Navigator to always use the fonts built into the Web page, even if they increase the download time for the page.

To change a font, open the drop-down list for the font you want to change, and then click the desired font. To change the size of the text, select the size from the drop-down list next to the font's name.

CAUTION

Encoding Font   Leave the **For the Encoding** setting alone. Most sites in the United States and in other countries that use the Roman alphabet use codes based on Latin letters. If you try to visit sites in China or Turkey and the pages do not display properly, you can change this setting.

Changing Navigator's Colors

Unless a Web page specifies which colors to use for the page background, links, and other items on the page, Navigator uses its default color settings. To change these settings, display the Preferences dialog box and click the **Colors** category (below Appearance). You can then change the following color settings:

Text   This option lets you specify the color to use to display most of the text on the page (not including links). You should probably leave this set to black; but if you're going to pick a dark background, select a lighter color for your text.

Background   Lets you pick a background color for any Web page that does not have a background color. The Default setting gives pages a gray background, which makes dark text easy to read. To pick a different color, click the **Background** button to display a dialog box that lets you change the background color.

Use Windows Colors   This option tells Navigator to use the same color settings that Windows uses.

Unvisited Links   Controls the colors of the links you haven't yet tried. If you like blue links, don't change this setting. If you would prefer some other color, click the color button next to this option. In the Color dialog box, click the desired color and click **OK**.

Visited Links   Sets the color for links that you've already tried. To change this color setting, perform the same steps you performed for the Unvisited Links setting.

Underline links   Typically, Navigator displays links in a different color and underlined. You can turn the underlining on or off.

Always Use My Colors, Overriding Document   Tells Navigator to use your colors and background setting even if the Web page you load is set to display a different color or background.

Clashing Colors Be careful when setting the background and text colors. If you pick a light background color and then load a page that has yellow or white text, you may not be able to see that text.

Entering Navigator Preferences

Next in the list of preference categories are the Navigator preferences. You may have already worked with most of these options in Lesson 5. The following list provides a brief review of these options:

Navigator Starts With   This option lets you specify which page you want Navigator to load when you start it. You can select **Blank Page** (if you don't want Navigator to load a page), **Home Page** (to specify a starting page), or **Last Page Visited** (Navigator starts with the page that was open when you last exited Navigator). See Lesson 5, "Other Navigator Features," for instructions.

Home Page   This option lets you specify the URL of the Web page you want to use as a starting page (assuming you selected Home Page under Browser Starts With). You can select **Use Current Page** to use the currently displayed Web page as your starting page.

History   This option lets you specify the number of days you want Navigator to keep track of pages you have visited. You can click the **Clear History** button to delete the history from your hard disk and reclaim some disk space.

Setting the Offline Preferences

Navigator lets you work offline to view pages you have already opened. This allows you to download pages during the evening and morning hours when the Internet is less busy, and then view the pages at your convenience. To set the Offline preferences, open the Preferences dialog box and click **Offline**. You can then choose **Online Work Mode** (to always open pages when you are online), **Offline Work Mode** (to always open pages from your hard disk), or **Ask Me** (to have Navigator display a dialog box when you first start it, asking if you want to work online or offline).

The Download option (directly below Offline) allows you to set options for reading discussion groups (newsgroup messages) offline.

Increasing Performance with the Cache Settings

You can improve the speed at which Navigator loads pages by tinkering with the cache preferences. These preferences allow you to change the size of the cache (a temporary storage area) so that Navigator can use more disk space for storing pages you have already visited. Follow these steps to change the cache size:

1. Open the **Edit** menu and select **Preferences**. The Preferences dialog box appears.

2. Under Category, click the plus sign (+) next to Advanced, and then click **Cache** (see Figure 12.3).

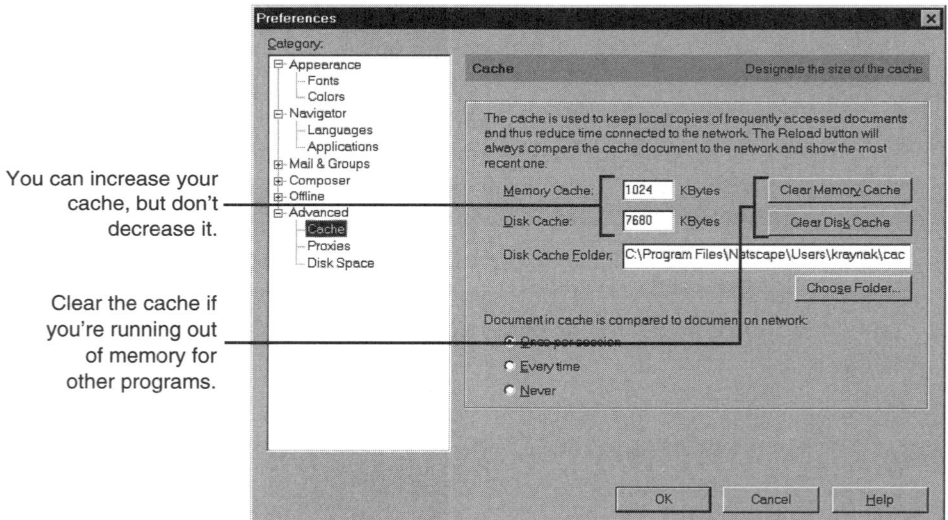

Figure 12.3   You are in control of the disk and memory caches.

Cache   A *cache* (pronounced "cash") is memory or disk space that Navigator (or any other program) uses to temporarily store data. In Navigator's case, the cache is used to store Web pages you've already loaded, so if you go back or forward to a page, Navigator doesn't have to reload the page from the Web site.

3. The minimum numbers for the disk and memory cache are already entered for you; don't go any lower. If you have scads of disk space or memory, click in the **Memory Cache** or **Disk Cache** text box and type the desired amount in kilobytes. (1,000 kilobytes is approximately 1 megabyte.)

4. The buttons next to the disk and memory cache settings (**Clear Memory Cache** and **Clear Disk Cache**) are useful if you have trouble running your other Windows programs because your system is low on memory. These buttons clear the cache, freeing that storage space for other use.

5. Under Document in Cache Is Compared to Document on Network, you can specify how often you want Navigator to check a Web document you've loaded against the original (**Once per Session, Every Time**, or **Never**). The less often Navigator has to verify documents, the faster Navigator will run.

6. Click **OK** to save your settings.

In this lesson, you learned how to change the appearance of Navigator and the pages it displays. You also learned some strategies for improving its performance. In the next lesson, you will learn how to use Navigator's security settings to protect yourself on the Internet.

Digital Passport, Cookies, and Other Security Topics

In this lesson, you learn about Internet security issues and how to do your part to keep your private information secure.

Understanding Internet Security

"Internet security" is a broad term encompassing many aspects of the Internet. The following list introduces some of the more important security issues:

- **Secure transactions:** Because the Internet is one of the best ways to exchange data on the Web, it's important to be able to send and receive data without it being intercepted and read by unauthorized parties.

- **Viruses:** When you open your computer to the world via a network connection or modem, and you start to copy program files and run them, you run the risk of infecting your computer with a virus.

- **Offensive material:** The Internet is an electronic world that offers everything the real world offers—both good and bad. If you have kids, you probably worry that they might stumble across sites that promote pornography, violence, and bigotry.

In this lesson, you will learn more about these issues and what you can do to protect your data, your computer, and yourself. You will also learn how to make the most of Navigator's built-in security features.

Transmitting Data Securely

As you learned in Lesson 6, "Filling Out Forms," whenever you transmit data across the Internet, it is possible that someone with the proper know-how can intercept the data and read it. Fortunately, Navigator supports the SSL security standards, which make transmitting data across the Internet fairly secure. Navigator can warn you whenever you are about to send data at an insecure site. See Lesson 6 to learn how to turn these warnings on or off.

Transmitting data via forms is only one aspect of performing transactions on the Internet. The following sections introduce additional issues concerning secure data transfers.

Sending Private E-Mail

Although you hear a lot about security issues on the Web, you rarely hear about security issues in newsgroups or e-mail. This gives us a false sense of security about posting messages in newsgroups or sending e-mail messages across the Internet.

To help you send e-mail messages securely, Netscape Messenger encrypts outgoing messages. When the message arrives at its destination, the recipient's e-mail program can then decrypt it. You can check Messenger's security settings whenever you compose a message. (See Part 3 Lesson 1 for more details on Netscape Messenger.)

What About Newsgroups?

In most newsgroups, you don't worry about security issues. Newsgroups are typically public forums where people openly express their ideas and opinions, share their knowledge, and ask for help.

So why bother with the security protocol? You may want a degree of privacy— even anonymity—when posting newsgroup messages. If you subscribe to a role-playing game group, for instance, and you use a pseudonym like "Zoltar the Omnipotent," you don't want an enterprising enemy magic-wielder to intercept one of your messages, trace it to its source, eliminate it, and post his own message in its place using your pseudonym.

SSL security standards (the same standards used to secure the Web) can help ensure that people reading your newsgroup messages see only what you want them to see. In Navigator, you can determine if you are at a secure news server by checking out the server's URL. If the URL begins with snews:// instead of just news://, you are at a secure server. (See Part 4 for more information on Collabra.)

A Word About EDI

If you frequently do business over the Internet with only a handful of select clients, you may want to ask your Internet service provider if it supports *Electronic Data Interchange* (EDI). Using special software in conjunction with your e-mail, EDI sets up a special mailbox on your service provider's computer to be used exclusively for messages sent between you and your designated trading partners. Messages between you and your partners are automatically sent to this mailbox, where the service provider encrypts them. Only the messages' final recipients have the tools necessary to decrypt them. There is some cost involved with EDI, but you might find that using EDI is much safer and much less expensive than using express delivery services to ensure privacy.

Banking and Buying Stuff on the Internet

When it comes to the issue of Internet security, one area of concern is the process of paying for purchases. Most users fear the idea of a hacker getting hold of their charge card numbers and running up thousands of dollars' worth of charges on their accounts. Sure there are limits to which you're supposed to be liable, but this kind of thing can really mess up your credit rating (or at the very least, it will be a huge inconvenience).

However, suppose you see something on the Net that you can't resist—some great new piece of shareware or a hard-to-find antique, for example. Is it possible to buy something over the Internet without risking your credit rating?

Buyer Beware!   Even if you feel safe spending your hard-earned e-cash online, you still should know something about the merchant with whom you are dealing. Once a purchase is made, if the merchant fails to ship your merchandise, or if it arrives broken or damaged, you won't be able to picket the guy's storefront (or take someone to court who does business halfway around the world).

The answer to that question may soon be a resounding, "Yes." Several companies are gearing up to offer various forms of e-cash (electronic cash) for use in transactions over the Net. One company, DigiCash, offers a system that allows a user to set up an account with a bank by mailing it a check and an application. After the account is set up, the bank sends you electronic "cash," in the form of an encrypted e-mail message containing a unique combination of 64-bit numbers. You send your e-cash to whomever you want, and they forward it back to the bank for verification. If the number matches the cash in your account, the cash is transferred to the recipient's account. Every number is issued only once, so you can't "copy" your e-cash. The unique numbering system also makes fraud an improbability.

Another company, CyberCash (www.cybercash.com), offers a software-based solution. When you find something you want to buy online, you ask the merchant to send you an electronic invoice. You use CyberCash software to add your encrypted credit card number to the invoice, which you then send back to the merchant. The merchant adds a confirmation number and sends the whole thing to a CyberCash server on the Internet. That server decrypts it and sends it through its banking system as a normal credit card transaction.

Protecting Your System Against Viruses

A computer virus is any computer code that performs some undesirable act, such as deleting files, formatting your hard drive, or just making funny or obnoxious messages pop up on your screen when you least expect it. Because most viruses hang out in program files and macros (shortcut command sequences that users can create in applications), you usually won't introduce a virus to your computer by downloading media files, including graphics, video clips, and sound clips.

When you start downloading programs, however, you should be a little careful and take the following precautions:

- Download and install programs only from reputable companies.
- Download programs from the original site or one of its certified mirror sites. Most of these places check their files for viruses. If you pick up a copy of a copy of a copy, the program may have picked up a virus somewhere along the line.
- If someone sends you a program file (via e-mail), don't run it. Ask the person where he or she obtained the file, and then download it from the original site.

- Purchase and install an antivirus program. One of the best is McAfee AntiVirus, which you can download at www.mcafee.com. Scan program files *before* you run them. You rarely introduce a virus to your system by downloading files; you have to open the document that contains infected macros or run the infected program to unleash the virus.

When you download program files and run them, you're in control. However, Navigator commonly downloads and runs programs (such as Java applets) automatically. Java applets have a built-in security system that prevents programming vandals from building viruses into the applets. Although these built-in safeguards are not foolproof, they provide fairly good protection; you rarely hear reports of Java viruses. However, if you want to be completely safe, you can prevent Navigator from automatically downloading and playing Java applets.

Java   Java is a programming language that allows people with the proper know-how to develop programs for the Internet that can run on any platform: Windows 95, Windows 3.1, Mac OS, OS/2, UNIX, etc. With Java, the browser downloads the code behind the program and then interprets that code, creating the executable program.

To set up Navigator so it doesn't automatically download and play Java applets, follow these steps:

1. Open Navigator's **Edit** menu and select **Preferences**. The Preferences dialog box appears.

2. Under Category, click **Advanced**. The Java options appear, as shown in Figure 13.1. By default, Navigator is set up to automatically play Java applets and JavaScript programs.

3. Click **Enable Java** and **Enable JavaScript** to turn both options off (remove the checks from the boxes).

4. You can also click the **Enable Auto Install** option to prevent programs from automatically installing themselves on your computer.

5. While the Advanced preferences are on-screen, click **Warn Me Before Accepting a Cookie**.

6. Click **OK** to close the Preferences dialog box and save your changes.

For more details about running Java applets, see Lesson 14, "Finding and Playing Java Applets."

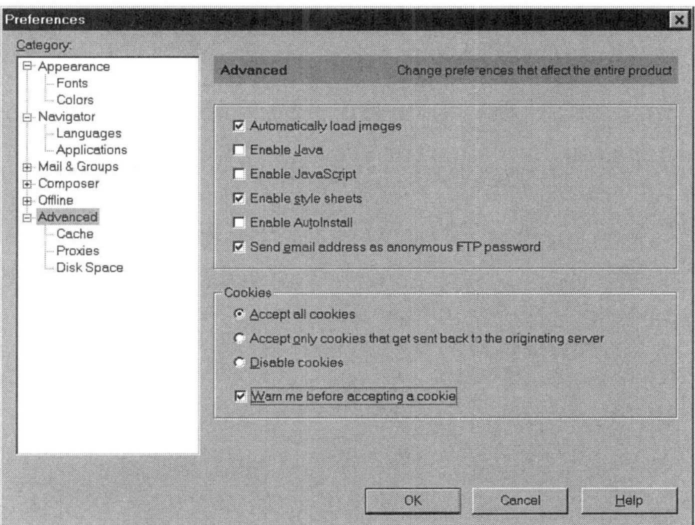

Figure 13.1 You can prevent Navigator from playing Java applets.

Cookies Cookies are like tokens that a Web page hands you when you connect to the page or enter information. These cookies stay with Navigator, so that the next time you visit the site or visit another area at the site, the Web server can identify you. Cookies are commonly used to log such statistics as who visits a particular site and where each person goes at that site. Cookies are also used at shopping pages on the Web. As you add items to your "cart," the page gives you a cookie for each item. When you go to check out, the page knows (from the cookies) which items you have in your cart. Although cookies do not pose a strong security risk, you might like to know when a site is sending you something.

Enhancing Security with Certificates

Although security and encryption technology can provide a fair level of security and privacy on the Internet, it cannot ensure that the companies and the people you are dealing with are who they say they are. To help, some companies have devised electronic IDs called *digital certificates* or *digital passports* that companies and individuals can use to prove their identity.

You can use two types of certificates in Navigator: personal and site certificates. A personal certificate is one that you use to prove your identity (and verify that you can pay your bills). A site certificate is one that a company uses to verify its authenticity to you. The following sections provide instructions on how to use certificates.

Personal Certificates

To obtain a personal certificate, you must connect to a company that issues certificates and fill out the appropriate "paperwork" (via a Web form). This process varies from company to company and is forever changing, so I can't give you specific instructions. However, here are basic instructions for obtaining a certificate from VeriSign:

1. Run Navigator and click the **Security** button.

2. Under **Certificates**, click **Yours**. This displays a list of any certificates you may have obtained.

3. Scroll down and click the **Get a Certificate** button. Navigator connects you to a Netscape page that lists companies that provide digital certificates. (As of the time of writing of this book, only VeriSign was on the list.)

4. Click the **VeriSign** link. This takes you to VeriSign's home page.

5. Follow the trail of links to obtain an individual certificate. You eventually reach a form you must fill out. Specify the application for which you want a digital certificate (Navigator) and enter personal and billing information (see Figure 13.2).

6. VeriSign then sends you a temporary digital certificate. (You will receive your permanent digital certificate via e-mail.) A dialog box appears, telling you that it is about to generate a private key; click **OK**. Navigator then displays a window asking if you want to password-protect your certificate.

7. If you are on a network or you share your computer with others, you should click **Next** and then enter a unique password. (You have to type the same password into two text boxes.) If you're using a computer that no one else has access to, you can choose not to use a password.

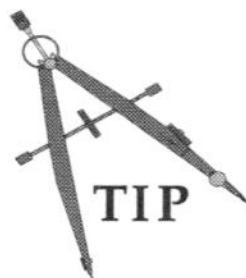

Passwords   If you choose not to password-protect your certificates right now, you can do so at any time later. Simply click the **Security** button and select **Passwords**. Then follow the on-screen instructions to add or change your password.

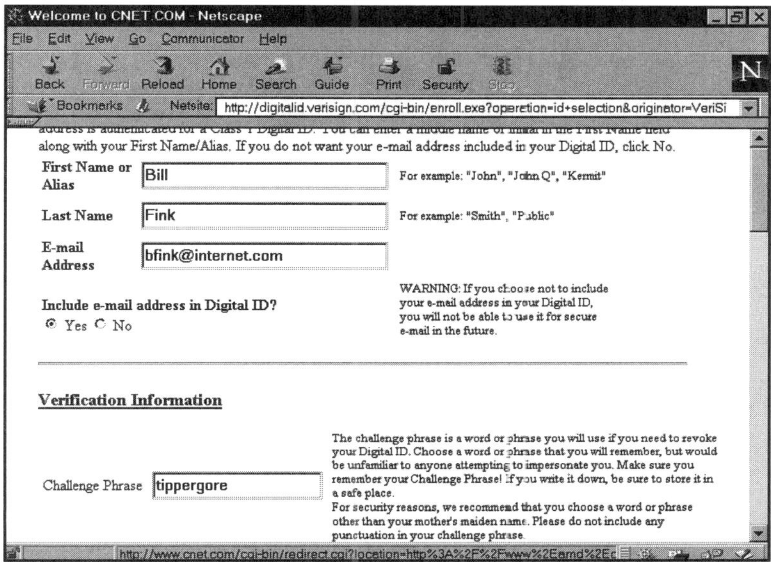

Figure 13.2 VeriSign asks for information to validate your ID.

8. The next dialog box asks how often you want to be prompted for the password. Select the desired frequency, and then click the **Finished** button.

9. VeriSign e-mails a PIN number to you. Check your e-mail, get the PIN number, switch back to Navigator, and enter the PIN number in the specified text box. VeriSign then sends you your certificate.

10. When you're done, check to see if your certificate has been set up in Navigator. Click the **Security** button, and then select **Your** under **Certificates**. You should see the nickname you entered for the new certificate.

Site Certificates

Each secure Web site is certified by a licensed authority. If you open the Security Preferences dialog box (by clicking the Security button) and select **Signers** under **Certificates**, you can view a list of these authorities, as shown in Figure 13.3.

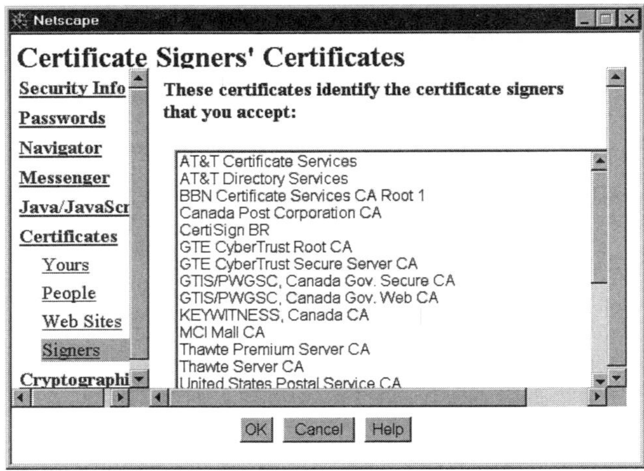

Figure 13.3   Many companies verify the identity of companies on the Web.

In most cases, you can ignore this list. However, if you hear that the sites certified by a particular authority have had security problems, you can prevent access to sites that this particular authority certified. To delete a site certificate entirely (so any sites certified by that authority will appear as insecure), follow these steps:

1. Click the **Security** button.
2. Under **Certificates**, click **Signers**.
3. Click the name of the authority you want to remove, and then click **Delete**.

If you do not want to completely delete a company from the list, you can edit the certificate. To display a warning whenever you attempt to send data to a site that has been certified by an authority, click the name of the authority and click the **Edit** button. You can then block access to the site or have a warning displayed.

Censoring the Internet

If you are a parent or teacher and you want to introduce your kids to the Internet, you need some way to prevent them from accessing sites that broadcast sex, violence, strong language, and other objectionable material. And there are plenty of these sites on the Internet.

Netscape Communicator does not have any built-in features that you can use to censor the Internet. However, there are several specialized programs that can work along with Communicator to block access to objectionable Web pages and Internet newsgroups. The following list names some of the better censoring programs and provides addresses for the Web pages where you can find out more about these programs and download shareware versions of the products.

- *Cyber Patrol* (at http://www.cyberpatrol.com) is the most popular censoring program. It allows you to set security levels, prevent Internet access during certain hours, and prevent access to specific sites. Passwords allow you to set access levels for different users (see Figure 13.4).

- *CYBERsitter* (at http://www.solidoak.com) is another fine censoring program. Although a little less strict than Cyber Patrol, CYBERsitter is easier to use and configure. CYBERsitter has a unique filtering system that judges words in context, so that it won't block access to inoffensive sites (such as the John Sexton home page).

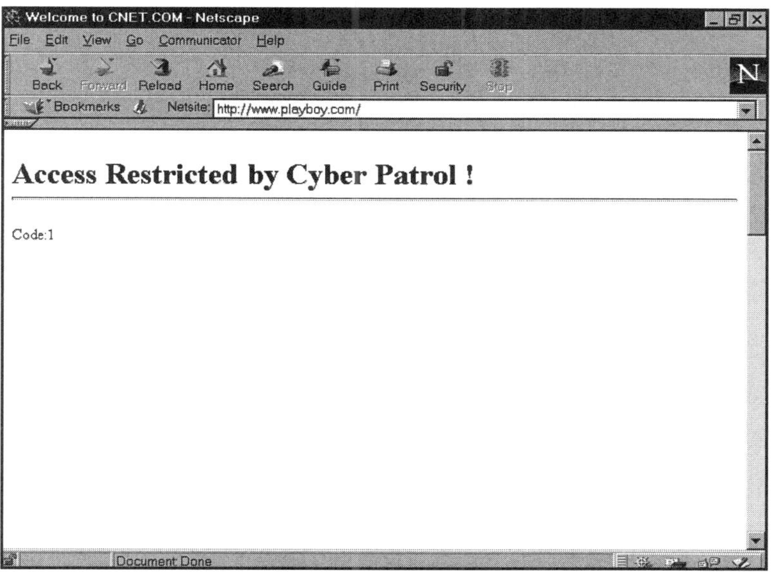

Figure 13.4   Cyber Patrol blocks access to a potentially offensive site.

- *Net Nanny* (at http://www.netnanny.com/netnanny) is unique in that it can punish the user for typing URLs of offensive sites or for typing any word on the no-no list. If a user types a prohibited word or URL, Net Nanny can shut down the application and record the offense. Net Nanny's configuration options are a little tricky.
- *Surf Watch* (at http://www.surfwatch.com) is one of the easiest censoring programs to install and use. Surf Watch comes with a list of prohibited sites deemed offensive by its panel of parents and teachers. It also blocks access to pages that contain offensive language.

Network Security

If you don't work on a network, you don't have to worry much about network security. If you do work on a network, you have a network administrator whose job it is to secure the network. In many cases, the network administrator secures the network by setting up a computer that acts as a middleman between the network and the Internet. This computer is called a *proxy*.

If your network uses proxies to access certain Internet features, such as the Web or FTP, you may need to obtain the proxy's URL from your network administrator and then enter it into Navigator. Once you obtain the proxy server's URL, open Navigator's **Edit** menu, select **Preferences**, and click **Proxies** (below the Advanced category). Then enter the required information.

In this lesson, you learned about many of the security issues you need to be aware of and how to protect your computer and your data. In the next lesson, you'll learn where to find Java applets and how to play them.

Finding and Playing Java Applets

In this lesson, you learn how to find and play Java applets, as well as the basics of putting JavaScript applets into a Web page.

Understanding Java

Java is a hot topic on the Internet right now—but what exactly is it? Java is a programming language you can use to create mini-programs (called *applets*) that you can embed in Web pages. Java applets can be played on any type of computer—Windows, Mac, or UNIX—which makes them perfect for inclusion on Web pages.

Applet   A small single-purpose application such as a loan calculator or a tic-tac-toe game. Java applets cannot run by themselves; you must use a compatible Web browser (such as Netscape) in order for them to work.

Java applets take many forms, including painting programs, games, and animations. Java is a quickly growing programming language. Because Java is still in developmental stages, most of the examples of Java applets you'll find out on the Internet are small, dynamic user interfaces like stock tickers or scrolling lines of text. However, Java is fast becoming a standard, and as such, it will be used more and more as an integral part of a functional Web page.

Examples of Java Applets

You'll often encounter a Java applet without even knowing it. If you run into some part of a Web page that seems to function almost automatically, you've probably run into a Java applet (see Figure 14.1). For example, some financial Web pages include a "live" stock ticker; that automation is a Java applet.

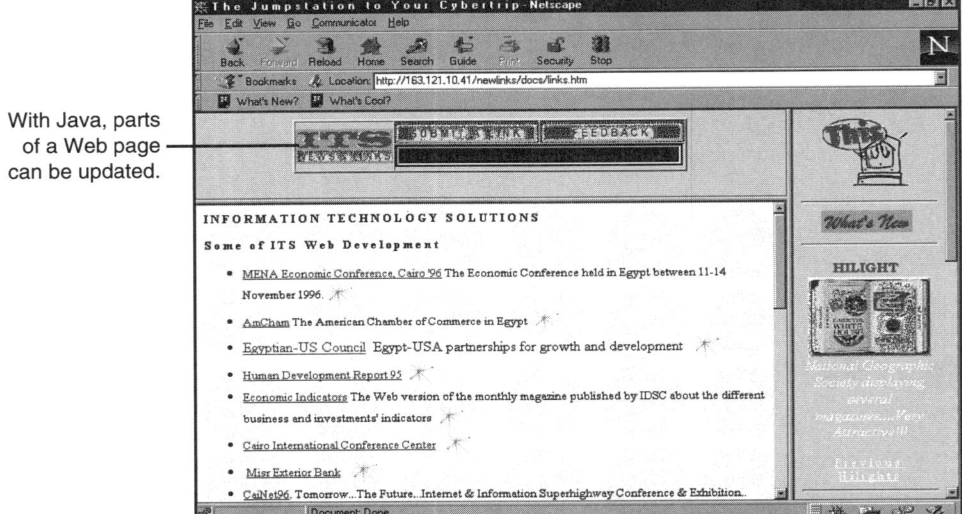

Figure 14.1   A Java applet can automatically update portions of the Web page with current information.

The benefit of including Java applets in a Web page is live interaction with the user. For example, a Java applet might perform a calculation for you—*live*—based on information you just entered into a form. In addition, a graph embedded in the Web page might change to reflect your variable input (see Figure 14.2).

Some Java applets, such as blinking or scrolling text, draw the reader's attention to particular parts of the Web page. Other Java applets, such as a cute animation, a video that is replayed automatically, or a game (see Figure 14.3) are just for fun.

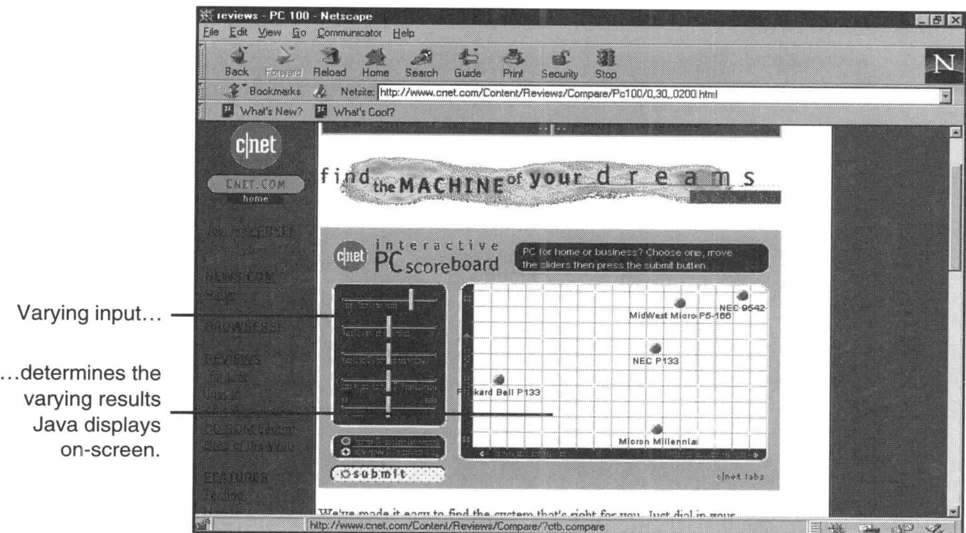

Varying input… …determines the varying results Java displays on-screen.

Figure 14.2 A Java applet can change the display according to varying user input.

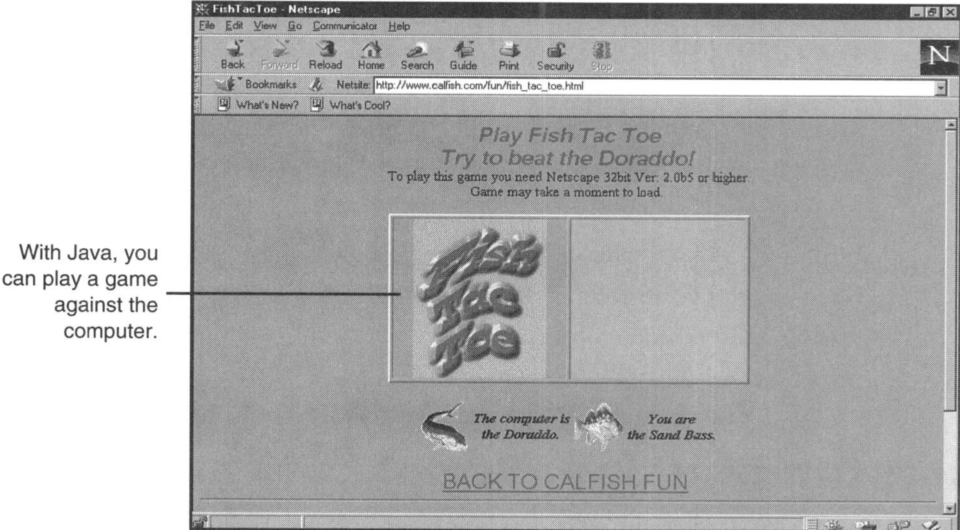

With Java, you can play a game against the computer.

Figure 14.3 Some Java applets are just for fun.

You could run into a Java applet just about anywhere on the Web, but because Java is still kind of new, you might want to go to the source (Sun Microsystems) first to see some demonstrations. Their Web site is at http://java.sun.com. To visit the Sun site and play one of the demos, follow these steps:

1. Connect to the Internet and start Netscape.
2. Type the address **http://www.java.sun.com/applets** into the **Location/Go to** text box and press **Enter**.
3. In the list of links, click **applets**.
4. Scroll down to **Games and Other Diversions**.
5. Select a demo from the list. For example, click **Hangman**. The game you select appears on-screen (it may take a while to download the applet). To play Hangman, select a letter that you think belongs in the missing phrase. Continue to select letters until you uncover the phrase or you're hanged.
6. When you finish playing the demo, you can click the **Back** button to return to the list of applets and select another demo if you want.

The following list names some other sites where you can find Java applets.

http://www.gamelan.com

http://www.npac.syr.edu/projects/vishuman/VisibleHuman.html

http://www.npac.syr.edu/projects/java/magic/Magic.html

http://www-md.fsl.noaa.gov/eft/internal/GFVUsersMan.html

http://www.jars.com

http://www.java.co.uk

http://www.vector.co.za/vst/java/vstj-01.htm

http://www.teamjava.com/links

http://www.rssi.com/info/java-info.html

Understanding JavaScript

JavaScript is a set of commands that you place within a Web page to make it more interactive. For example, you can insert a JavaScript command to create an animated control button such as a spinning wheel. With JavaScript, you can ask the user some questions on a form, and then you can respond in varying ways based on his answers. JavaScript also contains the commands needed to embed a Java applet (a program you create with the Java programming language) into a Web page.

If you don't plan to create your own Web pages, you don't need to worry about JavaScript. However, if you want to create a Web page with some pizzazz, you can include some simple JavaScript commands within the HTML code for your page. For example, this script by Tomer and Yehuda Shiran (which you can copy, if you'd like) allows you to add a nice clock to your Web page:

```html
<html>
<head>
    <title>The JavaScript Date and Time</title>
    <meta name="GENERATOR" content="Mozilla/2.01Gold (Win32)">
<script>
<!--
/* This script and all others are copyright (c) 1996 by Tomer Shiran
and Yehuda Shiran. They will all be posted in our upcoming book on
JavaScript, along with many others. The book will give you the
ability to write scripts and not just copy them. Feel free to steal
the code. Drop me a line if you choose to do so. Thanks. */
var Temp;
var CurHour; var CurMinute; var CurMonth; var CurDate; var CurYear;
var DayNight;

getData()
function getData() {
        var location = getPath();
        var ImageOpen = '<IMG SRC="'+location+'dg'
        var ImageClose = '.gif" HEIGHT=21 WIDTH=16>'
        var Copyr='This script and all the others are copyright &#169
        1996 by <BR>
        <BLINK><STRONG>Tomer Shiran</STRONG>'+'</BLINK> and
        <BLINK><STRONG>Yehuda Shiran</STRONG></BLINK>.
        Please feel free to '+'copy <BR>this script and add it to
        your homepage.'
        Temp = ""
        var now = new Date();
        CurHour = now.getHours();
        CurMinute = now.getMinutes();
        CurMonth = now.getMonth();
        CurDate = now.getDate();
        CurYear = now.getYear();now = null;
        CheckData();
        Temp += "<CENTER><TABLE BORDER=3 CELLPADDING=4><TR><TD>"
        Temp += "The current time is: "
        for (Count = 0; Count < CurHour.length; Count++) {
                Temp += ImageOpen + CurHour.substring (Count,
                Count+1) + ImageClose
        }
        Temp += ImageOpen + "c" + '.gif" HEIGHT=21 WIDTH=9>'
        for (Count = 0; Count < CurMinute.length; Count++) {
                Temp += ImageOpen + CurMinute.substring (Count,
                Count+1) + ImageClose
```

```
        }
        Temp += "<p>The current date is: "
        for (Count = 0; Count < CurMonth.length; Count++) {
                Temp += ImageOpen + CurMonth.substring (Count,
                Count+1) + ImageClose
        }
        Temp += ImageOpen + "p" + '.gif" HEIGHT=21 WIDTH=9>'
        for (Count = 0; Count < CurDate.length; Count++) {
                Temp += ImageOpen + CurDate.substring (Count,
                Count+1) + ImageClose
        }
        Temp += ImageOpen + "p" + '.gif" HEIGHT=21 WIDTH=9>'
        for (Count = 0; Count < CurYear.length; Count++) {
                Temp += ImageOpen + CurYear.substring (Count,
                Count+1) + ImageClose
        }
        Temp += "</TD><TD>"+Copyr+"</TD></TR></TABLE></CENTER>"
        return(Temp)
}

function getPath() {
        PathEnd=location.href.lastIndexOf('/', location.href.length- 1);

        FinalPath=location.href.substring(0, PathEnd+1);
        return(FinalPath);
}

function CheckData() {
        if (CurMinute < 10) {CurMinute = "0" + CurMinute} else
        {CurMinute = "" + CurMinute}
        CurHour = "" + CurHour;
        CurMonth = ++ CurMonth;
        CurMonth = "" + CurMonth;
        CurDate = "" + CurDate;
        CurYear = "" + CurYear;
}

document.write(Temp);

// -->
</script>
</head>
<body>

<h1 align=center>The JavaScript Date and Time
<br>24 Hour Clock</h1>

<p><b>This is an example of presenting the date and time graphically
using JavaScript only. This example is from the book we are currently
writing on JavaScript.</b></p>
```

```
<p> A set of images is available for
<a href="http://www.geocities.com/Hollywood/4250/
digits.zip">downloading</a>.
You may use any set of digit images which match the following names:
</p>

<ul>
<li>The digit image files (<i>dg0.gif</i> through <i>dg9.gif</i>)
</li>

<li>The colon and point separators (<i>dgc.gif</i> and <i>dgp.gif
</i>)
</li>
</ul>

<p>If you would like to use this clock in the middle of the page,
just copy the SCRIPT section to the desired place. The table can
be removed by deleting the specified lines in the source. </p>

<p>Help me make the JavaScript book suitable for your needs.
<a href="http://www.geocities.com/Hollywood/4250/suggest.htm">
Send me comments and suggestions</a> so I know what coverage you
would like to see. </p>

<p><a href="http://www.geocities.com/Hollywood/4250/index.html">
<img src="headsm.gif" border=0 height=38 width=250 align=center></p>

</body>
</html>
```

The JavaScript commands appear between the `<SCRIPT>` and `</SCRIPT>` tags. The rest of the codes you see here are HTML commands.

Want to Learn More?   If you'd like to learn more about JavaScript so that you can create your own scripts, pick up a copy of *The Complete Idiot's Guide to JavaScript, Second Edition*, also from Que.

Because JavaScript is interactive, you can program many such examples, where your Web page gets information from the user and then acts on it.

In this lesson, you learned about the purpose of Java applets and how to recognize them. You also learned how JavaScript code is incorporated into a Web page. In the next lesson, you'll learn about virtual reality on the Internet.

117

Playing in a VRML Virtual World with Cosmo Player

In this lesson, you learn about VRML virtual reality files and how to view them using Cosmo Player.

Understanding VRML

In Lesson 14, you learned about a programming language called Java, with which you can make your Web page interactive. VRML, *Virtual Reality Modeling Language*, is similar to Java. With the VRML programming language, you can create animations on your Web pages, run video files, and respond to user input.

Sounds Cool! Let's Go!   Before you decide to add VRML animations to your Web page, let me warn you: Coding VRML instructions is a lot more difficult than using HTML. However, as with HTML, several editors out there (such as Virtual House Space Builder) make the process of working with the VRML language less of a pain.

The main difference between VRML and Java is that you can use VRML to create a *virtual world*—a world that seems to have three dimensions, complete with texture, light, and shadow. Why is 3-D so important? A person can navigate a three-dimensional Web site very intuitively by seemingly "walking through" the site (see Figure 15.1). With 3-D, even simple animations can make a Web site come alive. In addition, VRML creates the potential for 3-D Web-based games such as flight simulators, DOOM clones, and the like.

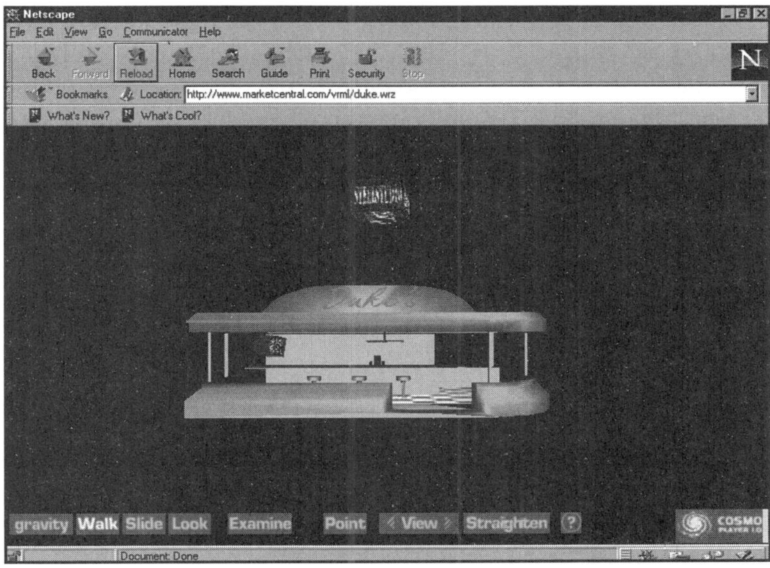

Figure 15.1 A VRML applet can simulate a 3-D world.

What Is Cosmo Player?

Cosmo Player is Netscape's newest entry into the VRML plug-in field. Netscape teamed with Silicon Graphics to use Cosmo Player, which replaces Live3D as Netscape's default VRML browser.

I Can't Find Cosmo Player! If you're using the 16-bit version of Communicator (for Windows 3.1), you will not have Cosmo Player. Instead, Live3D will be your default VRML browser.

CAUTION

A VRML (*Virtual Reality Modeling Language*) browser is used to navigate three-dimensional scenes called *worlds*. These worlds are described in files using the VRML language. Like many other VRML browsers, Cosmo Player supports the new VRML 2.0 specification. VRML 2.0 includes many new features such as animation, scripting, and interaction. The most important change, however, allows for objects in the world to move; in VRML 1.0, everything in the world stood still.

In addition, Cosmo Player supports streaming audio and video mixed in with the world. It also allows the world to be integrated with Java programs, allowing it to be used for virtual reality games, conferences, and more. These are benefits that give Cosmo Player an edge over other VRML browsers, but it remains to be seen whether people will actually develop worlds that take advantage of this. Because experimenting with these browsers is free, you should try several and see which works best for you.

Finding and Playing VRML Applets

Numerous Web sites on the Internet include VRML applets, one of which you'll visit in a moment. To visit a VRML Web site, you need a compatible VR plug-in or helper app. Because Netscape comes with Cosmo Player built right in, you've probably already got what you need. But if you somehow encounter a VRML site that doesn't work with Cosmo Player, you can add other VR viewers as needed.

The Fast Way   Cosmo Player is designed to support files that end with .wrl (a *world* file) or .wrl.gz (a *world* file *geometrically zipped* or compressed). If you're offered the option of viewing the same world as a .wrl or a .wrl.gz file, pick the latter because it will download faster.

Closing Time   VRML is powerful, but it takes a toll on your PC. To keep up, your PC will need a fast CPU (a Pentium or better) and a lot of memory to run most VRML apps. If you notice that your PC is a lot slower when running a VRML applet, close as many other applications as you can.

Follow these steps to visit the Cosmo Player test site:

1. Connect to the Internet and start Netscape.

2. Type the address **http://vrml.sgi.com/worlds** in the **Location/Go to** text box and press **Enter**.

3. Scroll down the page and click the **VRML Apartment** link. After a few minutes, an image of the inside of an apartment appears, as shown in Figure 15.2. To view the apartment from different angles, move the mouse pointer. For example, to "walk" closer, drag the mouse pointer (within the VRML window) toward the middle of the room.

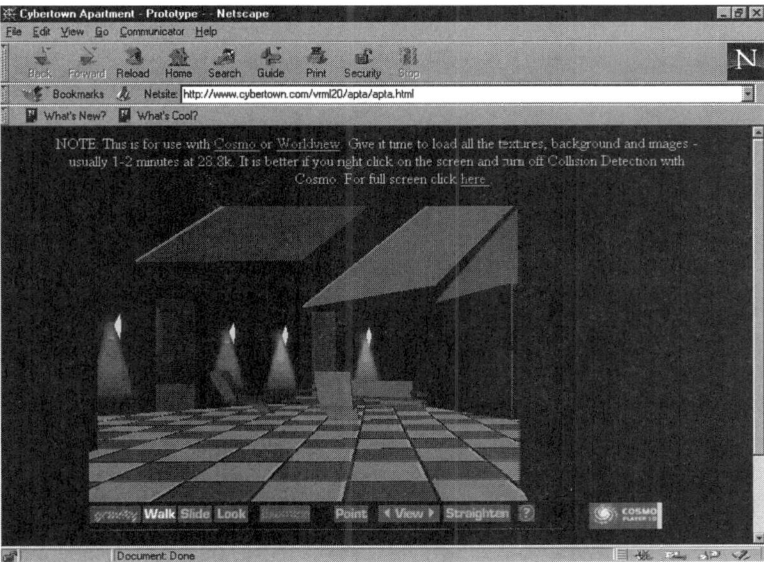

Figure 15.2 Change your view by dragging the mouse pointer.

4. (Optional) You can use the Dashboard to help you explore this virtual world. The Dashboard appears at the bottom of the VRML window. Here's a brief description of each control:

> **Gravity** With Gravity on, you can walk through the world. If you turn it off, you can fly.

> **Walk** In Walk mode, you move in a lateral plane, as along a surface. To move, drag the mouse in the direction in which you want to "walk." For example, drag the mouse forward to move toward an object; drag backward to move away.

> **Slide** In Slide mode, you move quickly in a single direction without spinning. To slide, drag the mouse pointer in the direction in which you want to go.

> **Look** In Look mode, you are stationary, but the view changes as you look left, right, up, or down. To look left, drag the mouse pointer left; to look down, drag the mouse pointer downward; and so on.

> **Examine** In Examine mode, the object in the center of the screen rotates. Drag the mouse pointer left or right to get a better view of the object you are examining. Examine mode works best when there are objects floating in space.

Point   In Point mode, you move toward an object by pointing at it. When you click the object in Point mode, you move toward it.

View   Takes you back to the starting point or to one of several other viewpoints. Select the viewpoints you want with the left and right arrows.

Straighten   Takes your rotated world and returns it to a straight position.

?   Opens the Help page.

6. To leave the VRML world, click the **Back** button.

You might also want to check out these other popular sites that contain VRML applets.

http://www.virtus.com/vrmlsite.html

http://www.virtuocity.com

http://vrml.sgi.com/worlds

http://www.construct.net/projects/planetitaly/Spazio/
    VRML/siena.wrl

http://www.tcp.ca/gsb/VRML/

http://cedar.cic.net/~rtilmann/mm/vrmllink.htm#SITES

http://www.sdsc.edu/vrml

http://www.netscape.com/comprod/products/navigator/live3d/
    cool_worlds.html

http://www.marketcentral.com/vrml

http://www.virtualtoys.comhttp://www.graphcomp.com/vrml

http://www.intel.com/procs/ppro/intro/vrml/nav.wrl

http://www.pointcom.com

http://www.photomodeler.com/vrml.html

http://www.clark.net/theme/worlds/ab2.wrl.gz

http://www.zdnet.com/~zdi/vrml/content/vrmlsite/outside.wrl

http://www.ncsa.uiuc.edu

In this lesson, you learned about virtual reality on the Internet. In the next lesson, you'll learn about listening to sound files.

Listening to Sound Files with LiveAudio

In this lesson, you learn how to play sound files embedded in Web pages.

What Is LiveAudio?

LiveAudio is Netscape's built-in sound file player. Whereas in the past you had to install a sound file helper application or in-line plug-in to play a sound file, now Netscape will automatically play any WAV, MIDI, AU, or AIFF sound file you select.

How does LiveAudio work? Whenever you select a sound file on the Web, Netscape displays the LiveAudio player console shown in Figure 16.1. As you'll learn later in this lesson, the player console contains simple controls with which you pause, stop, or replay a sound file. In addition, the console enables you to adjust the volume easily.

CAUTION

What About RealAudio?   If you have heard of RealAudio (the in-line plug-in for Netscape), you may be wondering how RealAudio is different from LiveAudio. While LiveAudio does a great job of playing simple audio files, RealAudio allows you to listen to near-to-live audio transmissions over the Internet. Think of it as radio for the Internet. You'll learn more about the RealAudio plug-in in Lesson 23.

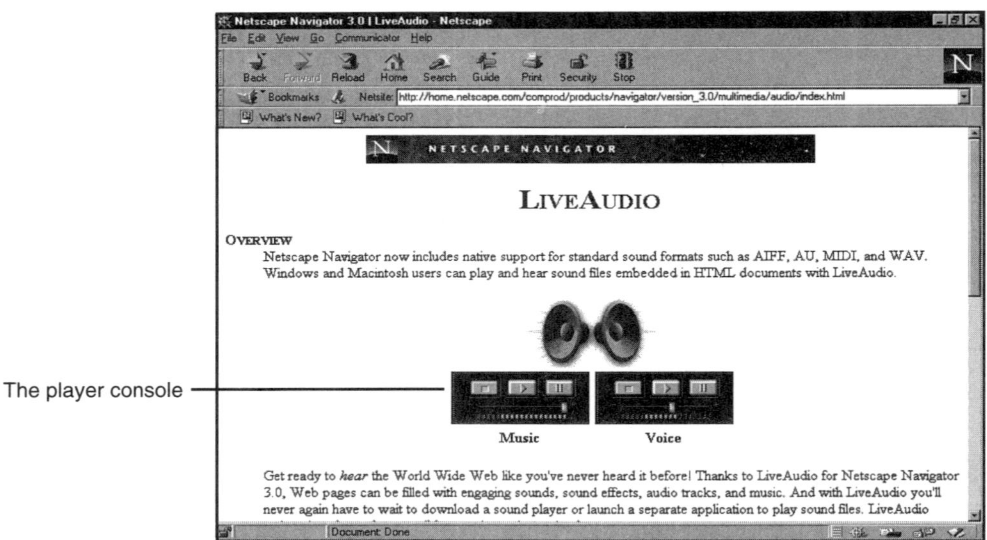

The player console

Figure 16.1   Netscape can now play sound files automatically.

Playing a Sound File

On the Web, you might encounter a sound file just about anywhere. When you do, LiveAudio takes over automatically—there's no setup involved.

Sound Card Required   Of course, for LiveAudio to work, your PC must be equipped with a sound card.

CAUTION

If you're anxious to test LiveAudio, follow these steps to visit a Web site that has some good examples of LiveAudio files.

1. Connect to the Internet and start Netscape.

2. In the **Location/Go to** text box, type **http://www.wsservice.com/media/sound/index.htm** and press **Enter**.

3. After the page loads, music will begin playing, and you will see the screen shown in Figure 16.2.

4. Click **Minuet** from the image map.

Figure 16.2 Select your type of music.

5. A new window opens, and a picture of a minuet appears. The audio file downloads and begins to play. At the same time, the player console appears (see Figure 16.3).

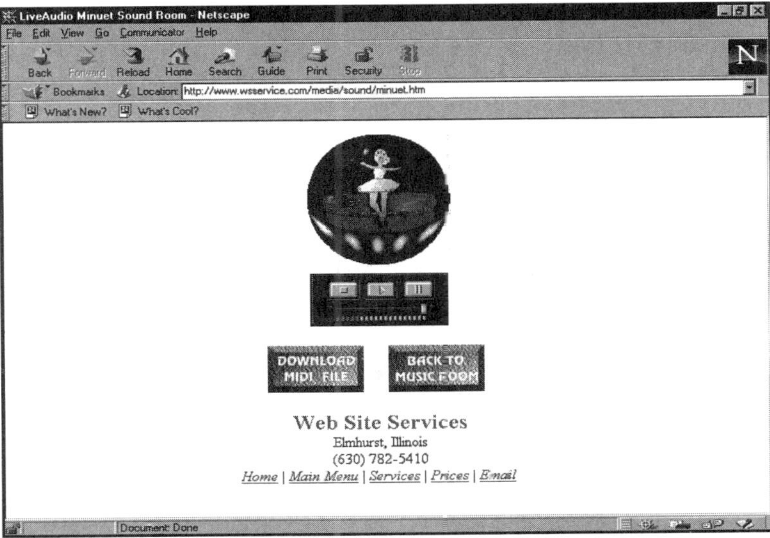

Figure 16.3 The RealAudio console opens to play the song.

6. To return to the menu, click the **Back to Music Room** button.

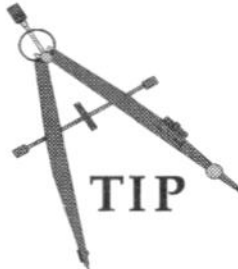

Not Fast Enough?   You might notice that it takes a while for Netscape to play the audio file. That's because the entire file must be downloaded before Netscape can begin playing it. If you get impatient with this, you might want to try another audio plug-in (such as TrueSpeech or Crescendo Plus) that uses a faster method called *streaming*. Streaming allows audio files to be played as they are being downloaded. See Lesson 21 for information on TrueSpeech or Lesson 22 for more on Crescendo Plus.

Using the LiveAudio Console

When an audio file is playing, you might want to adjust its volume. Or perhaps you'll want to pause it for a moment, or to replay the entire audio file. All of these tasks are easy to do with the player console. The following steps take you to a Web site that features a musical audio file. Work through them to learn about using the player console.

1. Connect to the Internet and start Netscape.

2. In the **Location/Go to** text box, type **http://www.thevervepipe.com/ music.html** and press **Enter**. The Verve Pipe Web page appears (see Figure 16.4).

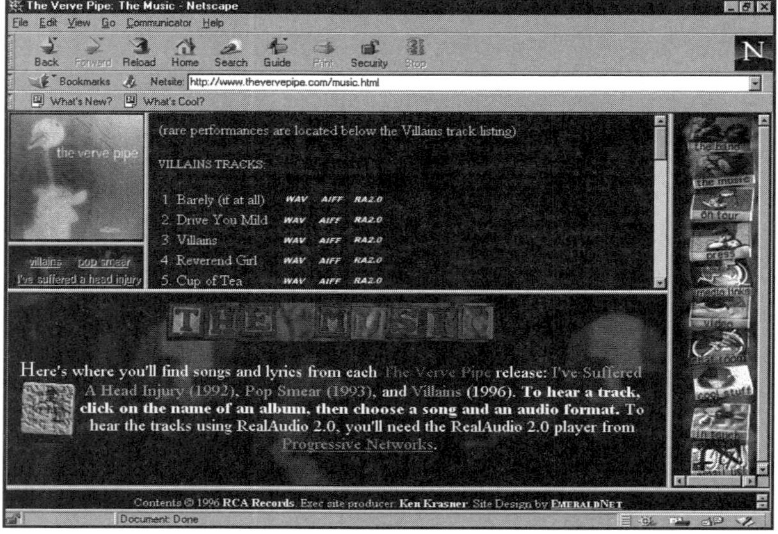

Figure 16.4   Welcome to The Verve Pipe.

3. The main frame displays a list of songs. Click in the WAV column or the AIFF column next to one of the songs to select it. The file is downloaded, and then the player console appears (see Figure 16.5).

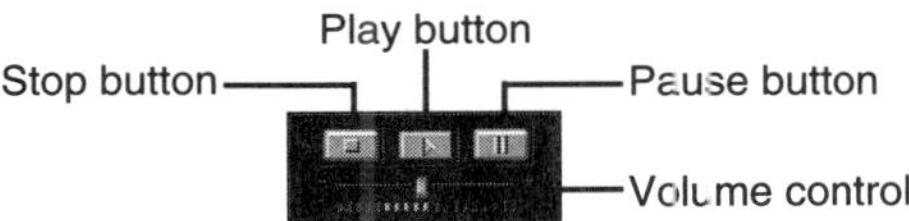

Figure 16.5   You can control the audio file with the player console.

4. Use the player console's buttons as described here to control the audio file:

Click the **Stop** button to stop the audio file from playing.

Click the **Play** button to replay the audio file.

Click the **Pause** button to pause the recording temporarily. Then click **Pause** again to restart the recording where it left off.

Drag the volume control indicator to the left to decrease the volume, or to the right to increase it.

In this lesson, you learned how to play audio files with LiveAudio. In the next lesson, you'll learn how to play video files.

Playing Video Files with LiveVideo

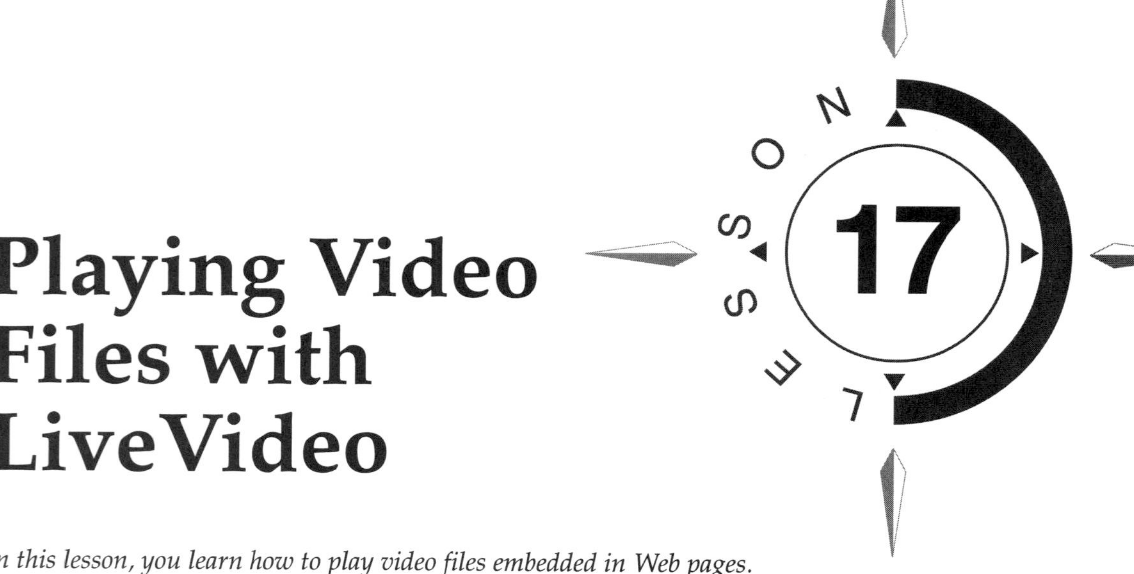

In this lesson, you learn how to play video files embedded in Web pages.

What Is LiveVideo?

LiveVideo is Netscape's built-in video file player. LiveVideo supports the AVI file format. Anytime you click a link to an AVI video file, LiveVideo automatically plays it.

CAUTION

One Might Not Be Enough   AVI is not the only video format used on the Internet. You might also run into such video formats as QuickTime or MPEG. To play one of them in Netscape, you have to download and install a compatible video player. See Lesson 24 for details.

Playing a Video File

Because LiveVideo is built into Netscape, you don't have to do much to play an embedded video file. The following steps take you to a Web site that includes a video file you can play to experiment with LiveVideo.

1. Connect to the Internet and start Netscape.

2. In the **Location/Go to** text box, type the address **http://www.ducks.ca/ iwwr/tracker/aviclips.htm** and press **Enter**.

3. An index appears, showing several images and AVI movies available. Scroll down to the AVI files and click **Mallard Tracker In Action**.

4. If you're asked, choose whether you want to **Open It** or **Save It to Disk**. Netscape opens a blank page with a picture in the center of the window (see Figure 17.1). Click the picture to start the movie.

5. (Optional) When the video ends, click the **Back** button and select another video to view.

Click here to play the video. ——

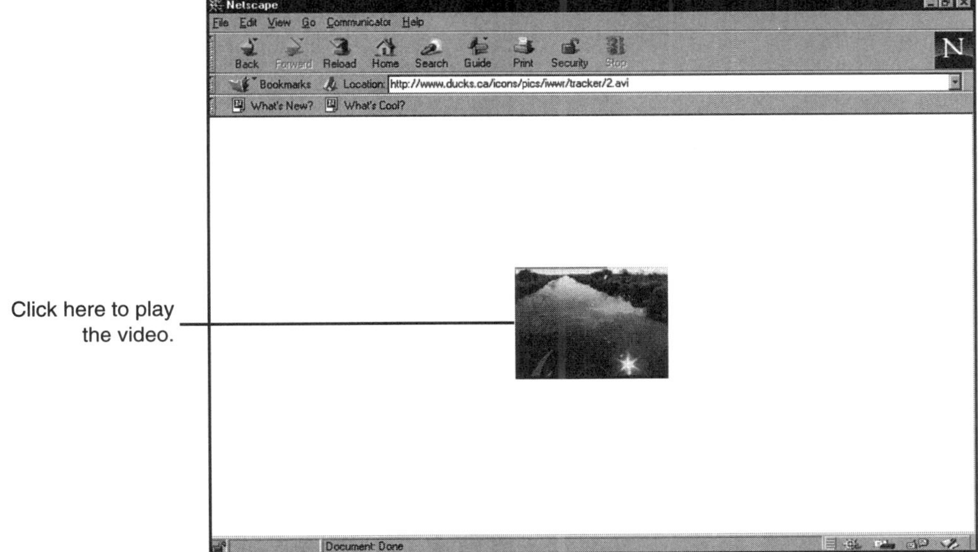

Figure 17.1   Tracking a mallard.

CAUTION

Not So Fast!   Although it's good at playing video files, LiveVideo is not terribly fast. The reason is that LiveVideo must download the entire video file before it can begin playing the file. If you have a need for speed, you might try to find a *streaming* video player such as VDOL ve, StreamWorks, or InterVU MPEG Player. Streaming video players are capable of playing video files as the files are being downloaded. See Lesson 20 for information about VDOLive or Lesson 24 for information about InterVU MPEG Player.

Using the Video Controls

LiveVideo makes it easy for you to replay a video file. You can also pause the video or forward it to the end if you want. And if you're a real videophile, you can advance or reverse the video frame by frame. To use the video controls, follow these steps:

1. After the video is downloaded and begins playing, right-click the video window. A shortcut menu appears, as shown in Figure 17.2.

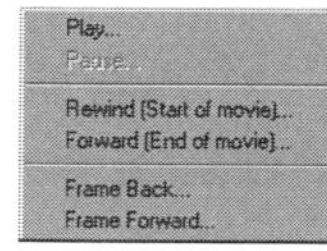

Figure 17.2   You can control the video with the commands on this shortcut menu.

2. Select the appropriate command:

> **Play** restarts the video after it's been paused.
>
> **Pause** temporarily halts the video.
>
> **Rewind** returns the video to the beginning.
>
> **Forward** advances the video to the end.
>
> **Frame Back** reverses the video one frame at a time.
>
> **Frame Forward** advances the video one frame at a time.

In this lesson, you learned how to play AVI video files. In the next lesson, you'll learn about plug-ins and helper applications.

Using Plug-Ins and Helper Applications

In this lesson, you learn the difference between in-line plug-ins and helper applications.

What Is a Plug-In?

A *plug-in* is a special program that extends the capabilities of Netscape Navigator. You can add plug-ins that enable you to visit virtual reality Web sites to listen to live radio broadcasts over the Net or to carry on a near-to-live "conversation." There are many plug-ins for Netscape that you can download from various sites throughout the Internet; you'll learn how to download the most popular plug-ins in upcoming lessons. Once you download a plug-in and install it, Netscape uses the plug-in's capabilities as if it were built in. Figure 18.1 shows a document Netscape can display with the help of a plug-in called Adobe Acrobat Reader.

Plug-ins can work in one of three ways: embedded in a Web page frame, expanded to fill the whole Netscape window, or hidden from view (running in the background). A lot of plug-ins work either in hidden or in full window mode, as you'll see in upcoming lessons. However, regardless of which mode a plug-in uses, its functions appear fully integrated to you, the user. In other words, you don't have to learn any special commands to use the plug-in; after you install it, the plug-in's capabilities become a part of Netscape.

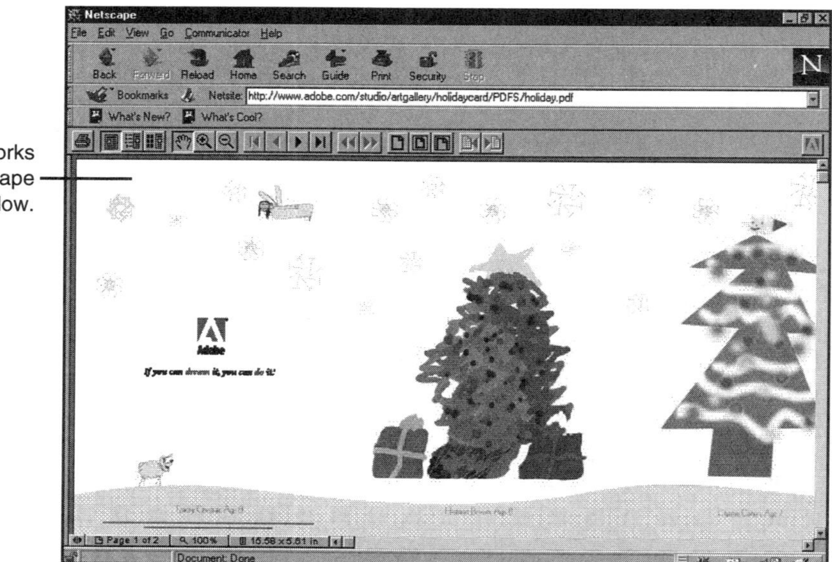

This plug-in works within the Netscape window.

Figure 18.1   A plug-in like Adobe Acrobat Reader extends the capabilities of Netscape.

Installing Plug-Ins

Plug-ins are designed to work seamlessly with Netscape Navigator. Because of that, installing plug-ins is as simple as installing Navigator. You'll find the details for downloading and installing specific plug-ins in upcoming lessons.

Twins?   Many programs are available in both a plug-in and a helper app format. When selecting which format to use, keep this in mind: A plug-in works invisibly (within the Netscape window) so it might be easier to use and understand. However, helper apps are more versatile because you can use them with any compatible file (outside of Netscape).

Also keep in mind that if you have a plug-in (such as Cosmo Player) and a helper app (such as WebSpace) both which handle the same file type (such as .vrml), Netscape will use the plug-in before it will use the helper app. To tell Netscape to use the helper app instead, you have to uninstall the plug-in.

For now, here are the basic steps that you'll need to follow to install a plug-in:

1. Open File Manager or Explorer and double-click the plug-in file. The installation program starts.

2. Follow the on-screen instructions.

3. At some point during installation, you'll be asked to select the directory in which Netscape is stored (see Figure 18.2). You might want to create a new directory within the \Netscape\Program\Plugins directory in order to keep all your plug-ins in one place. In any case, select the directory you want to use and click **OK** to return to the main dialog box. Setup copies the plug-in's files into its directory.

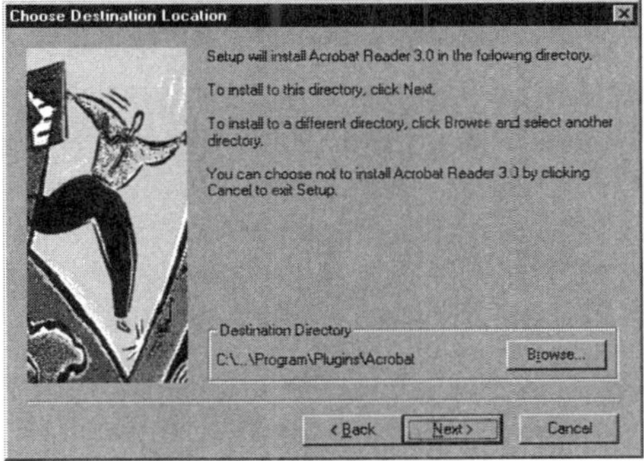

Figure 18.2   You can change the directory into which the plug-in is installed.

4. When you see a message telling you that installation is complete, click **OK**.

As you can see from these steps, you do not have to do anything to tell Netscape that the plug-in exists. The installation process takes care of any configuring that's necessary. So once the plug-in is installed, it's ready to use. Anytime you point Netscape to a file type that the plug-in supports, Netscape automatically calls on the plug-in's capabilities to display the file's contents.

Popular Plug-Ins to Try

As you'll see in upcoming lessons, there are many popular plug-ins for Netscape Navigator. This section tells you about some of the more popular plug-ins you might want to try.

Which Windows?   Some of these plug-ins are available only for Windows 95, and not for Windows 3.1.

Where Do I Get the Plug-Ins?   Although most of these plug-ins are covered in upcoming lessons (along with instructions on how to download and install them), some are not covered because of their limited applicability. The location of these programs is noted in the description so you can download them if you like. You can also find most of them on the Netscape home page. Open the **Get the Latest Netscape Software** pull-down menu and select **Navigator Plug-ins**.

Acrobat Reader by Adobe
http://www.adobe.com/prodindex/acrobat/readstep.html

This version of the popular Acrobat Reader lets you view, navigate, and print Portable Document Format (PDF) files within the Navigator window. PDF is a format used over the Internet to produce printer-independent, formatted documents that can be reprinted at the user's end *exactly* as they were created.

ASAP WebShow by Software Publishing Corporation
http://www.spco.com/ DOWNLOAD/DOWNMAIN.HTM

With WebShow, you can view and print graphically rich reports and presentations created with ASAP WordPower.

Astound Web Player
http://www.golddisk.com/awp/download.html

This plug-in plays multimedia documents created using Astound or Studio M, which can include sound, animation, graphics, and video. Some documents are even interactive! And Astound Web Player is fast because it downloads each slide in the background while you're viewing the one before it.

Carbon Copy/Net by Microcom
http://www.microcom.com/cc/ccdnload.htm

With Carbon Copy/Net, you can control a remote PC through the Internet, running applications, copying and deleting files, and even editing documents—just as if you were using your own PC. (The remote PC must also have Carbon Copy/Net installed and must be ready to receive your call.) With Carbon

Copy/Net, you can provide remote support for your product, perform demos in remote locations, and access remote resources such as programs and data. Carbon Copy/Net is not available for Windows 3.1.

Chemscape Chime by MDL Information Systems
http://www.mdli.com/chemscape/chime/download.html

Whether you're a scientist or just interested in science, you can use Chemscape Chime to view 2-D and 3-D chemical structures within an HTML page or table.

ClearFusion by Iterated Systems
http://www.iterated.com/coolfusn/download/cf-loadp.htm

With ClearFusion, you can view standard video (AVI) files almost live, using a process called *streaming*, in which the video file appears as it's being received (without a time gap). ClearFusion is not available for Windows 3.1.

CMX Viewer by Corel
http://www.corel.com/corelcmx/

You can use CMX Viewer to view vector graphics. CMX Viewer is not available for Windows 3.1.

Crescendo PLUS by LiveUpdate
http://www.liveupdate.com/midi.html

This plug-in enables you to listen to MIDI files without a time-delay, using a process called *streaming*.

DWG/DXF Plug-In by SoftSource
http://www.softsource.com/ plugins/dwg-plugin.html

With DWG/DXF Plug-In, you can view AutoCAD (DWG) and DXF drawings *dynamically*. This means that you can manipulate them by panning or zooming the drawing, and hiding or displaying layers—right on the Web page! DWG/DXF Plug-In is not available for Windows 3.1.

EarthTime by Starfish Software
http://www.starfishsoftware.com/getearth.html

EarthTime displays the local time and date for eight geographic locations—all within the Netscape window. With its animated map, you can also see which countries around the world are in daylight and which are in darkness at the current point in time. This can be helpful if you're doing Internet business with people all over the world. EarthTime is not available for Windows 3.1.

Envoy by Tumbleweed Software
http://www.twcorp.com/plugin.htm

You can view documents created with Envoy software exactly as they were designed—complete with multiple fonts, graphics, and complex layouts.

Formula One/NET by Visual Components
http://www.visualcomp.com/f1net/download.htm

With Formula One/NET, you can create Excel-compatible spreadsheets with live charts, buttons and controls, and links to URLs.

Fractal Viewer by Iterated Systems
http://www.iterated.com/fracview/download/fv-loadp.htm

This plug-in enables you to view fractal images (such as digitized photographs) that have been compressed using Iterated's Fractal Image Format. You can zoom, stretch, flip, and rotate images, and specify the amount of image detail you prefer.

InterCAP Inline by InterCAP Graphics Systems
http://www.intercap.com/about/DownloadNow.html

You can use InterCAP Inline to view, zoom, pan, magnify, and animate Computer Graphics Metafiles (CGM) vector graphics. InterCAP Inline is not available for Windows 3.1.

KEYview For Windows by FTP Software
http://www.ftp.com/mkt_info/evals/choice.html

With this plug-in, you can view, print, convert, and manage nearly 200 different file formats (including Microsoft Word, WordPerfect, Microsoft Excel, EPS, PCX, and even compressed files) from inside Netscape Navigator. KEYview For Windows is not available for Windows 3.1.

Lightning Strike by Infinet Op
http://www.infinop.com/html/extvwr_pick.html

You can use Lightning Strike to compress your Web pages.

Look@Me by Farallon
http://collaborate.farallon.com/www/look/download.html

With this plug-in, you can view a remote Look@Me user's screen through the Net in *real time*. (You can't, however, control the other PC remotely.) This is great for reviewing presentations or providing training and support. Look@Me is not available for Windows 3.1.

MovieStar by Intelligence At Large
http://www.beingthere.com

This plug-in enables you to view QuickTime movies in Netscape. MovieStar is not available for Windows 3.1.

OLE Control by NCompass
http:// www.ncompasslabs.com/

With OLE Control Plug-In, you can embed OLE controls in your Web pages as applets. OLE Control Plug-In is not available for Windows 3.1.

InterVu Player by InterVU
http://www.intervu.com/player/download.html

With InterVu Player, you can watch MPEG videos in almost-live mode, using a process called *streaming*. (Streaming enables you to view a video file even while it's still being downloaded.) InterVu Player is not available for Windows 3.1.

QuickSilver by Micrografx
http://www.micrografx.com/quicksilver/download.htm

With QuickSilver, you can view and edit object-oriented graphics created with Micrografx products. QuickSilver is not available for Windows 3.1.

QuickTime
http://quicktime.apple.com.

This plug-in makes it possible for you to experience multimedia video and sound in a near-live format.

RealAudio by Progressive Networks
http://www.realaudio.com

With RealAudio, you can listen to live or on-demand audio files in real-time.

Shockwave for Director by Macromedia
http://www.macromedia.com

Shockwave for Director enables you to view multimedia presentations created with Director.

Sizzler by Totally Hip
http://www.totallyhip.com/Support/SizzlerSupport.html

You can view Sizzler animations before they are completely downloaded, using a process called *streaming*.

SVF Plug-In by SoftSource
http://www.softsource.com/softsource/plugins/plugins.html

With this plug-in, you can view SVF images such as CAD drawings and other complex graphics. You can pan and zoom an SVF image, and you can hide and display layers. SVF Plug-In is not available for Windows 3.1.

ToolVox by Voxware
http://www.voxware.com/download.htm

ToolVox enables you to add high-quality real-time audio to your Web pages.

VDOLive by VDONet
http://www.vdolive.com/download/

This plug-in lets you view VDO compressed video images *fast*.

VR Scout by Chaco Communications
http://www.chaco.com/vrscout

This plug-in enables you to play VR (Virtual Reality) worlds. VR Scout is not available for Windows 3.1.

VRealm Browser by Integrated Data Systems
http://www.ids-net.com/ids/downldpi.html

This is another VR (Virtual Reality) viewer.

Wavelet Image Viewer by Summus
http://www.summus.com/download.htm

With Wavelet Image Viewer, you can quickly view Wavelet graphic images, and you can control the amount of detail Netscape shows.

WIRL by VREAM
http://www.vream.com/3dl1.html

This plug-in is a VR (Virtual Reality) viewer. WIRL is not available for
Windows 3.1.

Word Viewer Plug-In by Inso Corporation
http://www.inso.com/ frames/consumer/qvp/plug.htm

You can use Word Viewer Plug-In to view, copy, or print any Microsoft Word
6.0 or Microsoft Word 7.0 document on the Web. Word Viewer Plug-In is not
available for Windows 3.1.

What Is a Helper Application?

A helper application is like a plug-in in that it also extends the capabilities of
Netscape. However, a helper application goes about it in a different way.

Unlike a plug-in, whose functionality interacts seamlessly with Netscape
(so much so that the plug-in almost seems to be built into Netscape), a helper
application works independently of Netscape. A helper application specializes
in handling specific file types, such as ZIP or WAV files, for example. When
Netscape encounters one of these file types, it launches the appropriate helper
app and lets it display what's in the file. The helper app then deciphers and
displays the contents of the file inside its own window—*not* within the Netscape
window (see Figure 18.3). You might think of this process in terms of football:
When the quarterback (Netscape) runs into trouble, he passes the ball to the
wide receiver (the helper app), who then carries it into the end zone.

Because a helper application runs in its own window, it can be used separately
from Netscape. This flexibility allows you to use the helper application in other
scenarios. For example, you can install WinZip as a helper app so that Netscape
automatically launches it whenever it encounters a zipped (compressed) file.
You can then view the contents of the zipped file before you download it. But
because WinZip is not integrated into Netscape, you can also use it independently to zip and unzip your own files.

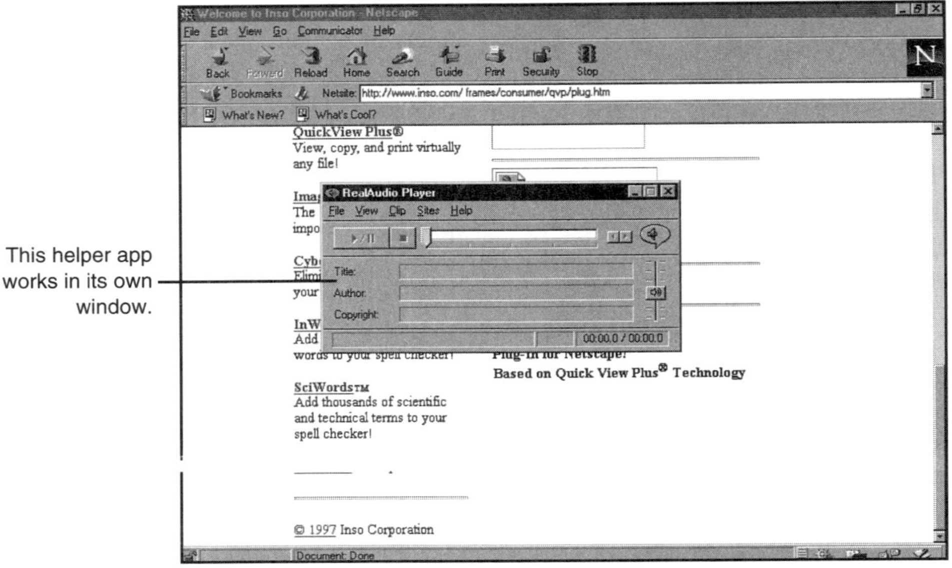

Figure 18.3 A helper app displays the contents of the file in its own window.

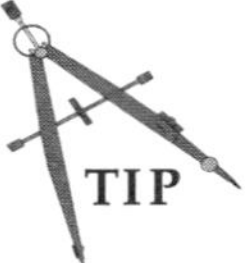

Which to Choose? Some plug-ins discussed in the upcoming lessons are also available as helper applications. Remember that a helper app can be used independently of Netscape, and it might contain some additional features that can prove useful. Some helper apps are faster than the plug-ins because Navigator does not have to load in order to run them. Taking this into consideration, choose the type of program (in-line plug-in or helper app) that best suits your needs.

You can even use a helper app in place of Netscape's viewer. For example, Netscape is perfectly capable of displaying simple graphic images such as JPEG, GIF, and XBM files. If you want to be able to manipulate those images, though, you might prefer to use a helper app such as LView instead.

Installing Helper Apps

Netscape can understand many file types, including HTML (the format used on most Web pages) and the graphic file types JPEG, GIF, and XBM. To display the contents of other file types, Netscape requires the expertise of a helper app.

On the Internet, each file is identified by its MIME type. MIME (Multipurpose Internet Mail Extensions) is a system that organizes various file types into groups, listing similar file types together as the same MIME type. Netscape keeps a list of MIME types in its Preferences dialog box.

When Netscape attempts to display a file, it first looks at the file's MIME type. If the MIME type is one that Netscape itself can handle, the process continues as usual. If Netscape determines that the MIME type is associated with a particular helper app, Netscape automatically launches that helper application and turns the file over to it for display.

What If I Don't Install a Helper App?   If Netscape encounters a file type that it can't handle, and for which you have not assigned a helper app, it displays an error message asking you what you want to do. You can choose to install the helper app at that time, to not display the file, or to save the file to your hard disk for viewing at a later time.

CAUTION

How does Netscape know when you've installed a helper app for a particular file type? Netscape keeps track of MIME types in its Preferences dialog box. There you'll see a list of the various helper applications that are associated with them (see Figure 18.4). To let Netscape know that you want it to launch a certain helper app when it encounters a particular file type, you need to add the name of your helper app in the appropriate place on this list.

Sometimes, the helper app's installation program takes care of the process of adding its name to this list. Other times, you have to do that manually.

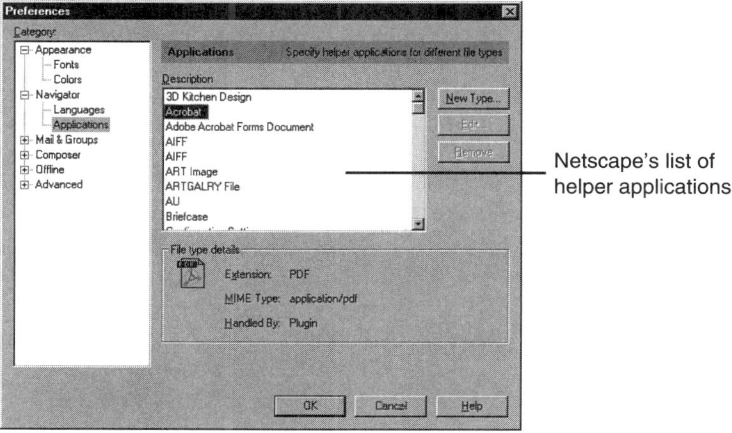

Netscape's list of helper applications

Figure 18.4   Netscape keeps track of helper applications in its Preferences dialog box.

The specifics for installing many popular helper apps are covered in upcoming lessons. But this gives you an idea of the general steps you must follow to install a helper app to the MIME list manually.

1. Use the helper app's install program to copy its file onto your PC's hard disk.

2. Start Netscape (you do not need to connect to the Internet).

3. Open the **Edit** menu and select **Preferences**.

4. In the **Category** box, choose the **Navigator** category and click **Applications**.

5. In the **Description** list, select the file type you want to associate with the helper app, and then click the **Edit** button (see Figure 18.4).

Missing Type   If you don't see the file type you need, you can add it by clicking the **New Type** button, entering the **MIME Type** (such as video, audio, image, or application), entering the **Application to Use** (such as RealAudio or QuickTime), and clicking **OK**.

6. Click in the **Application** text box.

7. Click **Browse**, select the program's starter (executable or .EXE) file, and click **Open**.

8. Click **OK**. The next time Navigator encounters a file with the extension(s) you specified, it will pass that file to the associated helper app for viewing.

Popular Helper Apps to Try

You'll learn about several helper apps in upcoming chapters, but for now, here are a few of the more popular ones.

Where Do I Find These Helper Apps?   A lot of these helper apps are covered in upcoming lessons (along with instructions on how to download and install them). However, some are not covered because of their limited applicability. The location of these programs is noted in the description so you can download them if you like.

Acrobat Reader
http://www.adobe.com

This version of the Acrobat Reader by Adobe enables you to view and print Portable Document Format (PDF) files in a separate window.

AVI Pro
ftp://gatekeeper.dec.com/pub/micro/msdos/win3/desktop/avipro2.exe

This helper app plays MPEG video clips with AVI Pro.

GhostScript
http://www.cs.wisc.edu/~ghost/

You can print PostScript documents on a non-PostScript printer.

LView Pro
http://www.lview.com

With this helper app, you can view many types of graphic files, including JPEG, BMP, TRG, PCX, PGM, PPM, PBM, TIFF, and GIF files.

Smart Bookmarks
http://www.firstfloor.com

This helper application enables you to organize and update your bookmarks with automatic updates.

MPEGPlay
ftp://gatekeeper.dec.com/pub/micro/msdos/win3/desktop/mpegw32g.zip

MPEGPlay enables you to view MPEG video files with MPEGPlay.

PolyView for Win95
http://www.kagi.com/authors/polybytes/

You can view a variety of graphic files, including BMP, GIF, JPEG, PNG, and TIFF files with PolyView for Win95.

QuickTime
http://quicktime.apple.com

With QuickTime, you can experience incredible multimedia video and sound in a near-live format.

RealAudio
http://www.realaudio.com

This helper app enables you to listen to live or on-demand audio files presented in real-time on the Net.

TrueSpeech
http://www.dspg.com

With TrueSpeech, you can listen to near-live audio transmissions over the Internet.

VMPEG Lite
www.stroud.com/svideo.html

You can view MPEG video files with VMPEG Lite.

WebSpace
http://www.sd.tgs.com/~template/WebSpace

WebSpace enables you to visit 3-D worlds with this VR (virtual reality) viewer.

WHAM
ftp://gatekeeper.dec.com/pub/micro/msdos/win3/sounds/wham133.zip

Use WHAM to play and edit audio files, such as AU, AIFF, IFF, VOC, and WAV files.

WinCode
http:// http://www.stroud.com/inx.html.

WinCode handles all your e-mail encoding needs, including MIME, uuencoding, and BinHex.

WinZip
http://www.winzip.com/

WinZip compresses and decompresses zipped (PKZIP) and LHArc files.

WPlany
http://www.stroud.com/inx.html

WPlany is a simple sound player that plays AU, IFF, SND, VOC, and WAV sound files.

In this lesson, you learned the difference between in-line plug-ins and helper applications. You also learned the names of many popular plug-ins and helper apps you might want to try. In the next lesson, you'll learn how to install and use Shockwave.

Shockwave by Macromedia

In this lesson, you learn how to get Shockwave and how to use it to view multimedia presentations over the Web.

What Is Shockwave?

Shockwave is a plug-in created by Macromedia, whose Director program is the leading tool for putting together multimedia presentations. With Director, you can combine still pictures, animations, and sounds, and include point-and-click interaction. If you play CD-ROM-based adventure games or use a CD-ROM reference program, odds are good that you've been using a Director presentation. Macromedia Flash is a program that puts together small and fast Shockwave multimedia. Many Web sites contain presentations created with Flash.

Shockwave lets you view Director and Flash presentations over the Web. (You *don't* need a copy of Director or Flash, unless you want to design your own presentations.) A Web site designed for use with Shockwave can present video and sound without your having to request each animation and sound file. It also allows you to use more complex interactivity than simple HTML links allow.

Downloading Shockwave

You can download Shockwave from Macromedia's Web site by following these steps:

1. Type **http://www.macromedia.com/shockwave/download/** in Netscape's **Location**/**Go to** text box and press **Enter**. This takes you to the Macromedia Shockwave Web site.

2. Scroll down to the text boxes that ask for your name and e-mail address and enter that information.

3. The Web page automatically selects which operating system you are using. Click the **Download Now** button to download the software.

4. From the Save As dialog box shown in Figure 19.1, choose a temporary directory in which to store the downloaded file (you probably have one named C:\TEMP or C:\TMP). Then click the **Save** button, and the download begins.

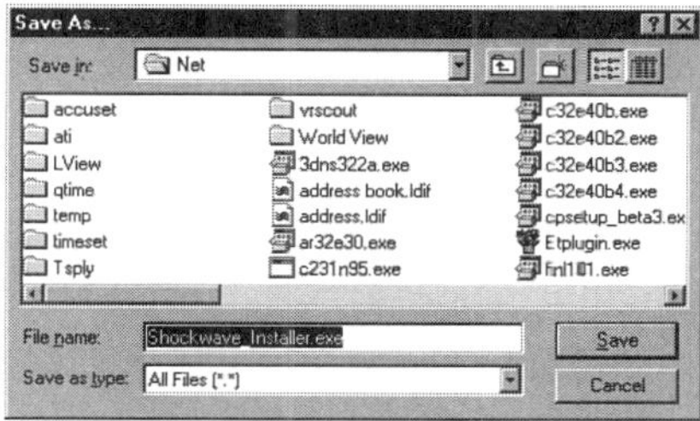

Figure 19.1 Choose a destination for the downloaded file.

5. When the download is complete, you're ready to install the program. Close Netscape and disconnect from the Internet.

Installing Shockwave

When you finish downloading Shockwave, you will need to install it. The entire install program is contained in the single file you downloaded.

Crowded Disk? When you need to clear some disk space, you should always look in your TEMP directories for files that have been there for some time and that you no longer need.

Follow these steps to run the Setup program for Shockwave:

1. In Windows 95, click the **Start** button and select the **Run** command. In earlier versions of Windows, pull down File Manager's **File** menu and select the **Run** command.

2. Click the **Browse** button, and then locate the temporary directory to which you downloaded the Shockwave file. Select the **Shockwave_Installer.exe** file.

3. Click the **Open** button to close the Browse dialog box. Then click **OK** in the Run dialog box to run the setup program. The installation program starts.

4. First you'll see a small dialog box asking if you want to install Shockwave. Click **Next**.

5. Next you'll see a dialog box full of boring legal stuff. Read this (you don't want to agree to something without knowing what you're agreeing to!) and click **Yes** to continue the installation.

6. The installation program will ask you where you want to install Shockwave. The default location should be fine, so just click **Next**.

7. The setup program starts putting the files in place, and a meter appears, displaying the progress of the installation.

8. When the installation is complete, a dialog box appears, asking if you want to go to the Macromedia site. Leave the check box checked and click **Finish** (make sure Netscape is not open before you click the Finish button). Netscape opens and takes you to the Shockwave welcome page. After a few minutes, a movie appears, indicating that Shockwave was installed correctly.

Save on Connect Charges   While some Shockwave presentations link to other presentations, most are self-contained. After the presentation is downloaded to your hard disk, you can disconnect from the Web and continue viewing the presentation without running up your Internet bill!

Shockwave Sites

You can find a number of good Shockwave presentations by starting from the Macromedia Gallery page, or you can look them up in the gallery located at http://www.macromedia.com/shockzone/. In addition, you might want to try some of the pages listed in Table 19.1.

Table 19.1 Pages with Shockwave Content

Site	*URL*
Mudball Wall Game	http://www.broderbund.com/studio/activemind/mudball.html
Daily Tortoise game	http://www.sirius.com/~jtaylor/shockwave/shockwave.html
Demolition Graphics	http://www.halcyon.com/flaherty/
Art Exhibit Educational Demos	http://www-leland.stanford.edu/~dmiller/
Etch-A-Sketch toy simulator	http://members.aol.com/dkimura/etch.html
FaceMaker	http://users.aol.com/jrbuell2/ShockFace.html
Fortune Cookie	http://www.slip.net/~maniaman/fortune.html
CleverMedia Arcade	http://clevermedia.com/arcade/
Hollywood Online	http://hollywood.com/movies/shocked.html
Michael's Haunted House	http://yip5.chem.wfu.edu/yip/haunted_house/mhhmain.html
Nando.net games	http://www2.nando.net/nandox/shock.html
Pop Rocket games	http://www.poprocket.com/shockwave/
Tulane University guide	http://www.bentmedia.com/bentmedia/dtulane/Shockwave.html
Velma Apparelizer	http://www.headbone.com/home.html
Virtual Drums	http://www.cybertown.com/virtdrum.html

In this lesson, you learned how to download, install, and view a presentation with Shockwave. In the next lesson, you'll learn about the VDOLive plug-in.

VDOLive by VDOnet

In this lesson, you'll learn how to get the VDOLive plug-in and use it to view video displays over the Web.

What Is VDOLive?

VDOLive is a plug-in created by VDOnet. Its goal is to allow you to view movies that you might find on some Web sites. VDOnet lets you see these movies in real-time so you don't have to wait for them to download before you can start watching them. This not only makes for faster viewing, it also limits the amount of open disk space you need for a long movie.

VDOnet claims that their product can receive 10 to 15 frames per second on a standard 28,800 bps modem—an impressive rate. For a Web site to provide a VDOLive movie, it must have VDOnet's server software, which the owner has to pay for. However, the viewing software is free and is available over the Web (as are most plug-ins).

Downloading VDOLive

You can download VDOLive from VDOnet's Web site, using the following steps:

1. Connect to the Internet and start Netscape.
2. Type **http://www.vdolive.com/download** in the **Location/Go to** text box and press **Enter**.
3. Click the **VDOLive Player** link, as shown in Figure 20.1.

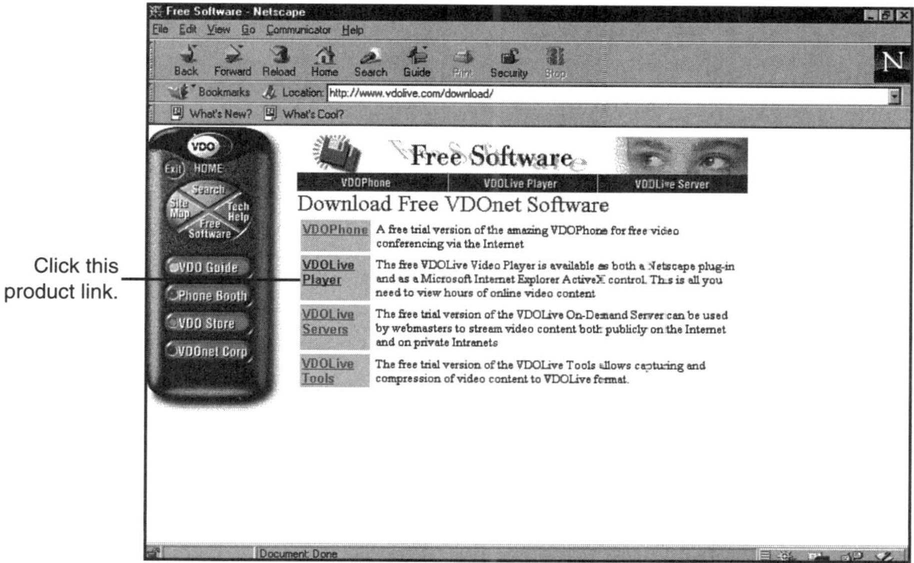

Figure 20.1   The VDOLive page has several products you can download, including VDOLive Video Player.

4. The next Web page shows you that you will be downloading the VDOLive Player for Windows 95 or Windows NT. Click the **Download** link to begin downloading the file.

5. The next page asks you to enter your name and e-mail address. Type them, and then click the **Go to Download and Instructions Page** button.

6. The next page will contain the link to download the file. Click the link.

7. In the Save As dialog box, choose a temporary folder or directory to store the downloaded file in (such as a TEMP directory). Click **OK**, and the download begins. (Be sure to note the name of the file you're downloading and the directory or folder you're saving it to. You'll need both names later to install VDOLive.)

8. When the download is complete, close Netscape Navigator and disconnect from the Internet.

You're now ready to install the plug-in. It's always a good idea to log off the Internet while you install programs so you don't waste valuable online time.

Installing VDOLive

You can run the VDOLive program directly to install the software. Follow these steps to install VDOLive:

1. In Windows 95, click the **Start** button and select the **Run** command. In older versions of Windows, pull down File Manager's **File** menu and select the **Run** command.

2. Click the **Browse** button and locate the folder with the downloaded file in it. Then click the name of the file.

3. Click the **Open** button to return to the Run dialog box.

4. Click **OK** to start the program, and the opening screen appears.

5. Click **OK** in the Welcome! dialog box to start the installation.

6. When the license agreement appears, read it over. (Yes, it's boring, but using this software indicates that you agree to the terms of this document—and it's good to know what you're agreeing to.) Click **OK** to continue.

7. Another dialog box appears, asking where you want to put your VDOLive files (see Figure 20.2). This will default to some standard program file directory, but you probably don't want it there. It's a good idea to organize all your plug-ins in a subfolder of the folder that contains Communicator. If you already have a plug-ins folder, select it, and a new folder called "vdoplay" is created in that folder. If you don't have a plug-ins folder, edit the **Destination Directory** field to include it (the end of your folder path should read **Communicator\plugins\vdoplay**). A plug-ins folder is created for you. Click **OK**.

8. VDOLive displays a dialog box, asking for confirmation of your name and e-mail address (which it got from the Netscape registration file). Click **OK** to continue.

9. As files are copied to their appropriate directories, a meter shows you the progress. When it finishes, the program asks which Program Manager (Start Menu) group you want the icons in. If you want them in a new group, click **OK**. If you want to add them to an existing group, click the group name and click **OK**.

10. A final dialog box tells you that installation is complete. Click **Yes** to view the Readme file. The Readme file contains any additional information you need about this revision of the software. When you are finished reading, click the **Close** button in Notepad.

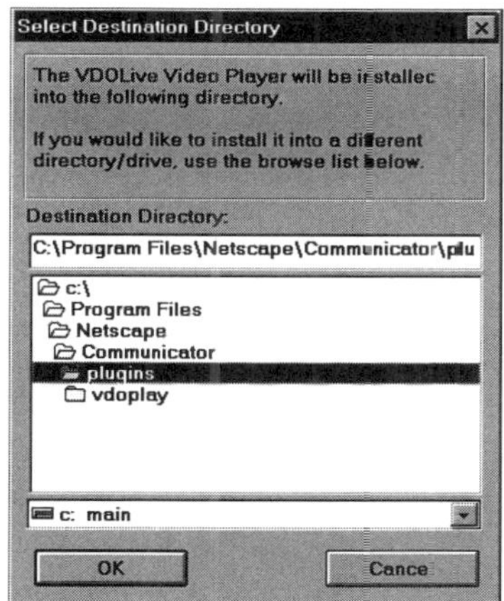

Figure 20.2   The VDOLive installer asks you to designate a location for the program files.

Check out the program group where you indicated the icons should go, and you will find that you now have not only an icon for the player, but also an icon for uninstalling the program if you no longer need it, some sample HTML files, a Help file, and a Readme file.

VDOLive Basics

Once you have VDOLive installed, it's time to start watching some videos! To test your new VDOLive Video Player, load up the demo page by selecting its icon or by opening the **Start** menu, pointing to **Programs**, pointing to **VDOLive Video Player,** and clicking **VDOLive Plugin Demo Page**. When the page loads, you'll see two little areas on-screen with test pattern images in them (see Figure 20.3).

Click the picture on the right side of the page under **Netscape Navigator Plug-In**. After a few seconds, the image opens in its own window, and a line appears under the image saying **Connecting....** This indicates that the VDOLive player software on your system is connecting with the special VDOLive server software on the Web server. When the connection is established, this status line changes to **Requesting** and then **Loading** as it preloads some information (it is **not** loading the whole video). A percentage counter tells you how much of that information is loaded.

When the counter hits 100%, the video begins. The status line splits into two parts: The left part displays how much time has passed in the video (in minutes and seconds), and the right side shows a reception level both as a percentage and as a colored meter. The more green on the meter or the higher the percentage, the more of the video you are getting. At lower percentages, the image is slightly jumpy. At very low percentages, you'll hear significant skips in the sound.

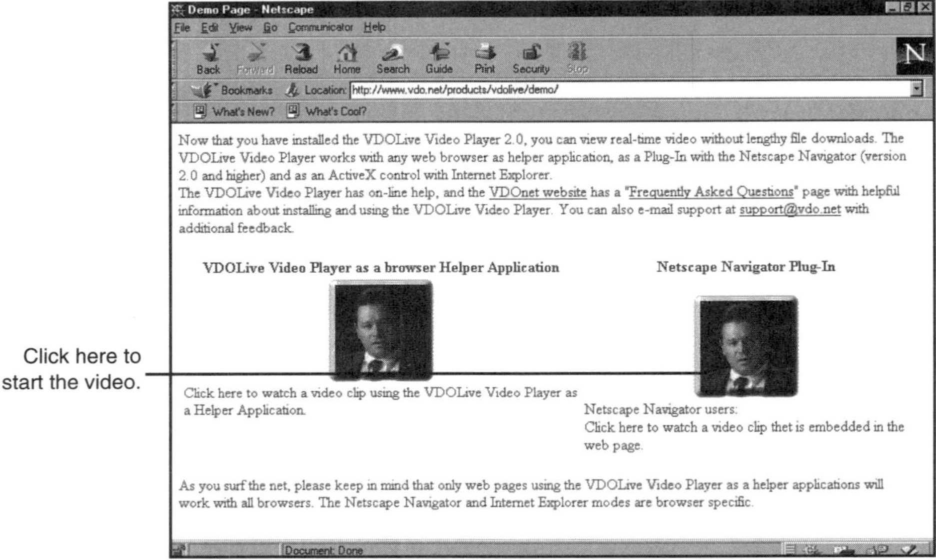

Figure 20.3   The VDOLive demo page.

The limiting factor in watching the video is the communications speed. Theoretically, you should be able to get 100% reception from a 28,800 modem. If you're seeing significantly lower figures and you want to watch and listen to a certain video more cleanly, you might try viewing it at a time when the Internet and the server are likely to be less busy.

Some Videos Need a Nudge   Not all VDOLive videos start automatically. For some, you have to click the video display area to start them.

Setting Options

A site can contain two types of videos. One is *embedded*, which means that the video is included on an HTML page. The other is *stand-alone*, which means the page contains a link that points directly to the video. When viewing stand-alone videos, you can choose whether to view them using a separate VDOLive window or using a Netscape viewer. The VDOLive window is better because it gives you more control.

When you view an embedded video, you have easy access to a menu that lets you control the video and set the options for the VDOLive window. To set options for the VDOLive window, follow these steps:

1. Right-click in the video display area, and a menu appears.

2. This menu contains the commands Play (which starts a stopped video), Stop (which stops playing a video), Go VDO! (which takes you to the VDOLive Web page), Setup (which lets you set options), and About (which opens a window of information about your system). Select **Setup**, and the Setup dialog box shown in Figure 20.4 appears.

3. Click the **Show Session Statistics** box to put a check in it. When turned on, this replaces the reception display in the VDOLive window with more detailed information about how much video and audio is being lost. (This option works only when you're running VDOLive in its own window.)

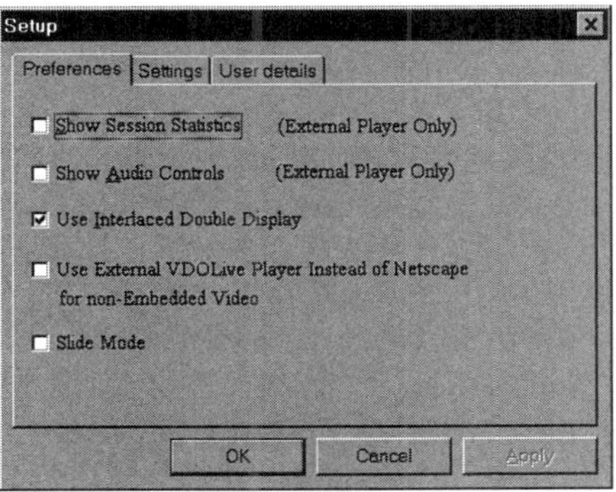

Figure 20.4 VDOLive's optional settings.

4. If you're using Windows 95, check the **Show Audio Controls** check box. Otherwise, leave it empty. When you check this box, volume controls appear in the VDOLive window—but the controls only work with Windows 95. (This option only works when you're running VDOLive in its own window.)

What Do I Do About the Third One?   The third option lets you control how the display is drawn when you ask to see the video double-sized. This is an option you can experiment with, but for the most part, you'll leave it as it is.

5. Put a check in the **Use External VDOLive Player Instead of Netscape for Non-Embedded Video** check box to tell the system that you do want to use the VDOLive window for non-embedded videos.

6. The last check box allows you to display the video in a slide show instead of motion video. This is useful if you have a slow Internet connection, but leave it unchecked for now.

7. Click **OK** to save these options and close the Setup dialog box.

Using the VDOLive Window

The VDOLive window is a complete console with a full set of easily accessible controls. This makes it a better choice to use for viewing movies that aren't embedded. Viewing it in a Netscape window may make the product seem more a part of Netscape, but it really doesn't gain you anything.

To view a sample video, follow these steps:

1. Enter **http://www.chron.com/content/interactive/space/vdo/** in Netscape's **Location/Go to** text box and press **Enter**. Click one of the Shuttle mission links, and a list of available videos is shown. Click one of the video links.

2. When the connection is made, the video starts playing (see Figure 20.5). Right-click the transfer status to see a list of status information items you can display. Choose **Frames/Sec** to see just how often the image is being updated.

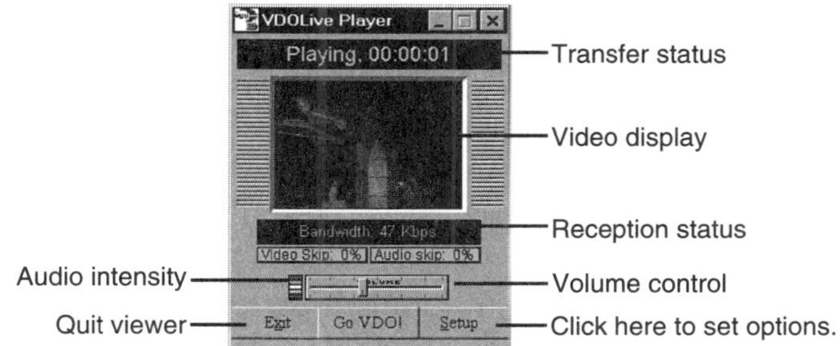

Figure 20.5   The VDOLive Player window.

3. Double-click in the video screen. The window resizes itself, doubling the size of the image (see Figure 20.6). Notice that the image doesn't actually become more detailed when it gets larger, so the quality of the image degrades.

4. When you're done with the video window, click **Exit**.

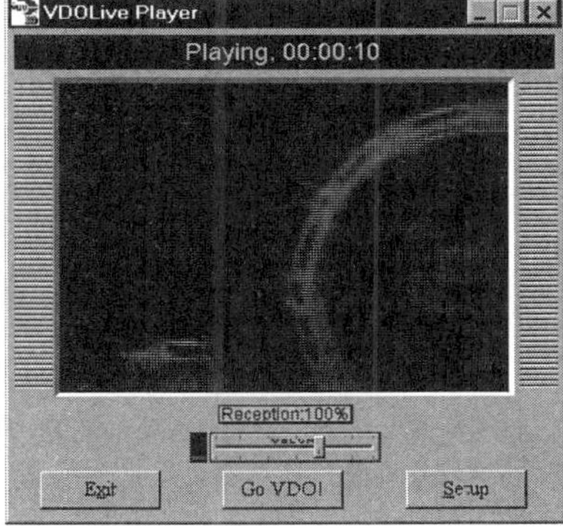

Figure 20.6   An enlarged image looks more grainy than a smaller one.

Figure 20.5 shows the video with the Session Statistics option on. Notice that you can see the actual data bandwidth (the higher the better, topping out at the speed of your modem), as well as the percentage of the video and audio being lost (the lower the better). Figure 20.6 shows the video with the Session Statistics option off. There you see just the reception percentage summary, like you saw on the embedded video.

Other VDOLive Sites

The number of VDOLive sites is growing rapidly. VDOLive seems to be popular with news and information organizations. However, other sites have more artistically oriented movies, and new sites are popping up all the time with other uses.

Still, VDOLive movies are not yet so common that you're likely to run into them while casually surfing the Web. Table 5.1 lists a handful of movies you might want to check out.

Table 5.1 VDOLive Sites

Site	*URL*
Brainworks	http://www.brainworks.net
CBS Up To The Minute	http://uttm.com
Grolier's Club Internet	http://www.clubinternet.com/vdolive/index.html
Hollywood Network	http://www.hollywoodnetwork.com/vdolive
Houston Chronicle	http://www.chron.com
InterneXperts	http://www.InterneXperts.com
KPIX TV channel 5	http://www.kpix.com/video/cnet.vdo (San Francisco)
netvideo	http://www.netvideo.com/netvideo/netstream.html
NowTV	http://NowTV.com
phuture.com	http://www.phuture.com/vdo.html
Preview Vacations	http://www.vacations.com/Multimedia/VDOLive
Sawyer Brown	http://www.sawyer-brown.com/video.html
Talk 101	http://www.talk-101.com
WCVB NewsCenter 5	http://www.wcvb.com/wcvb/webmate/wcvb/page/wcvb/5ol_vdo
Yard Productions Inc.	http://www.yrd.com/yrd/vdos/

In this lesson, you learned to download and install VDOLive and use it to view video clips. In the next lesson, you learn about TrueSpeech.

TrueSpeech Audio Player by DSPG

In this lesson, you learn how to get TrueSpeech and how to use it to listen to audio recordings over the Web.

What Is TrueSpeech?

TrueSpeech is a program that enables you to listen to recorded audio over the Web. Although Netscape has a built-in audio player, it requires you to download the whole sound file before you can listen to it. With TrueSpeech, however, you listen to the audio as it arrives, which is much better for long recorded pieces. Because it uses compressed audio files, the files can usually be transferred as quickly as they are read and there's less of a chance of the Net falling behind, causing a gap in the sound.

Catch the Wave   Another advantage of using TrueSpeech is that it plays files in .wav format. Wav files are common to all windows machines, making it a very popular sound format. Wav files are also readily available on the Internet.

The TrueSpeech player program is currently available on an indefinite trial basis. The version currently available combines both a helper and a plug-in. Some sites will require the plug-in, which shows its controls as part of the Web page. Most sites, however, will *only* work with the helper, which opens a separate window for the audio controls. It's good that most sites are set up to work with the helper, which gives you a better set of controls than the plug-in.

To use TrueSpeech, your computer will need a Windows-compatible sound card and speakers (or headphones).

Downloading TrueSpeech

You can download TrueSpeech from DSPG's Web site, using the following steps:

1. View the Web page at **http://www.dspg.com/allplyr.htm** using Netscape. On this page, you will find links for downloading versions of TrueSpeech for different operating systems.

2. Click any of those links. Navigator displays the Save As dialog box, and a file name something like TSPLY95.EXE appears in the File Name text box.

3. Choose a temporary directory to store the downloaded file in (you probably have one named C:\TEMP or C:\TMP), and click the **Save** button. The download begins. A meter appears, showing you the progress of the download. When the download is complete, the meter disappears.

What's in a Name?   In the file name TSPLY95.EXE, TS stands for TrueSpeech, PLY stands for player, and what follows that is an indication of the Windows version you're using (such as 95 for Windows 95).

This file is about one megabyte. Under ideal conditions, it will download in approximately 10 minutes using a 14,400bps modem. Under normal conditions, expect it to take 15–20 minutes. It will, of course, take less time with a faster modem, and more time with a slower one.

Installing TrueSpeech

The program is delivered as a self-extracting archive file that contains the setup program. Your computer needs the setup program only when you install the program. Because you stored such files in a temporary directory, they are set aside for you to delete them later.

The first thing you need to do is to extract the setup files from the archive. To do so, follow these steps:

1. If you're using Windows 95 or Windows NT 4, click the **Start** button and select the **Run** command.

If you're using Windows 3.1 or Windows NT 3.51, pull down Program Manager's **File** menu and select the **Run** command.

2. In the Run dialog box, click the **Browse** button.

3. In the dialog box that appears, select the directory with the downloaded file in it, and click the name of the file. Click the **Open** button to return to the Run dialog box.

4. Click **OK**, and the WinZip Self Extractor window opens (see Figure 21.1).

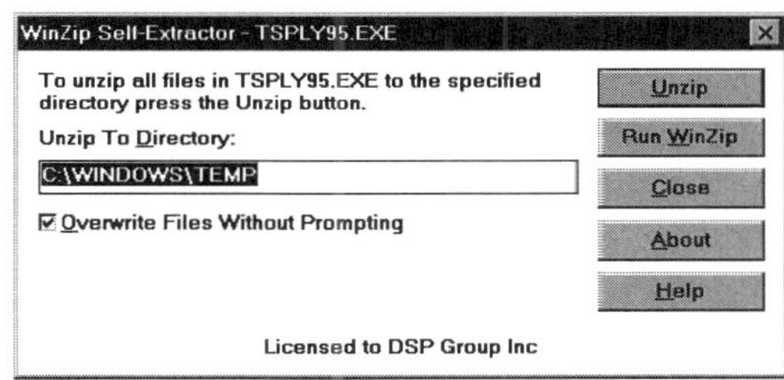

Figure 21.1 The WinZip self-extractor.

5. In the **Unzip to Directory** text box, type the folder where you want the files stored (the default is the Windows\temp folder which is a good choice). Then click **Unzip**. Each file is listed at the bottom as it is extracted.

6. When the program finishes extracting files, the line at the bottom tells you how many files were unzipped successfully. Click the **Close** button to close the WinZip dialog box.

After you extract the setup files, it's time to run the setup program. Follow these steps:

1. Close Communicator and any programs that you have open that you don't need.

2. If you're using Windows 95 or Windows NT 4, click the **Start** button and select the **Run** command.

If you're using Windows 3.1 or Windows NT 3.51, pull down Program Manager's **File** menu and select the **Run** command.

3. Click the **Browse** button, and then select the **SETUP.EXE** file from the Browse dialog box. (You should still be in your temporary directory, assuming you haven't used the Run command since the previous procedure.)

4. Click the **Open** button to close the Browse dialog box; then click **OK** in the Run dialog box to run the setup program.

5. A TrueSpeech title screen appears, and then a meter appears showing the progress of the setup program. Once that is complete, a setup background fills the screen, and a Welcome dialog box appears. Click the **Next** button to continue.

6. When you are asked to choose the directory to install the program files in, click the **Browse** button.

7. In the Choose Directory dialog box (see Figure 21.2), navigate to your plugins folder in your Communicator program folder and add **tsplay** to the end of the path name. This tells it to create a new folder in the plugins folder to store the TrueSpeech player program. Click **OK**.

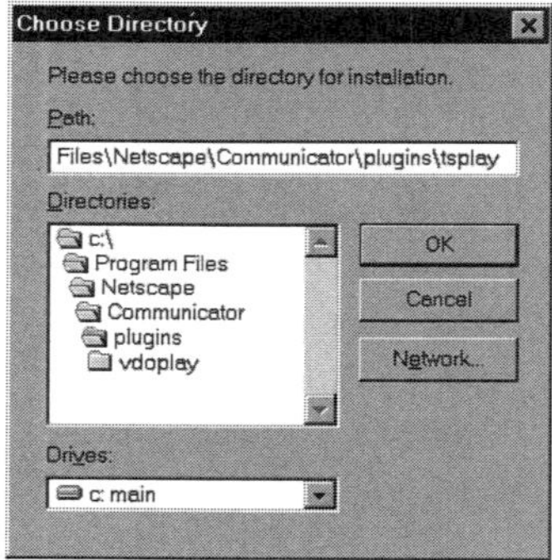

Figure 21.2   Create a new folder called tsplay in which to store TrueSpeech.

8. Another dialog box appears to ask if you want to create a new directory. Click the **Yes** button.

9. You are returned to the Choose Destination Location dialog box, where you clicked the Browse button. Click the **Next** button to continue.

10. Select a program folder for the TrueSpeech icons. By default, setup creates a new folder for them. If you want them in any other folder (such as the folder where you keep Communicator), click that folder name. Click **Next**.

11. Next you're asked which browser you are using TrueSpeech with. Click the **Netscape Navigator** check box to select it and click **Next**. The installation begins, and a meter shows the progress of the installation.

12. When you are asked to enter the Netscape Navigator path, click the **Browse** button.

13. Again, a Choose Directory dialog box appears. Navigate to your main Netscape directory (probably C:\Program Files\Netscape\ Communicator\Program). Click **OK**.

14. You are returned to the Choose the Netscape Navigator Path dialog box, where you clicked the Browse button. Click the **Next** button to continue.

15. When the installation is complete, a dialog box appears asking if you want to read the README file now. Click **Yes**.

16. An editor or word processor opens and displays the README file. Read through it; it may contain information on new features. When you finish, close the editor.

17. A dialog box appears telling you that the setup is complete. Click **OK**. The TrueSpeech player program opens a window like the one in Figure 21.3, and a recorded message plays through your speakers.

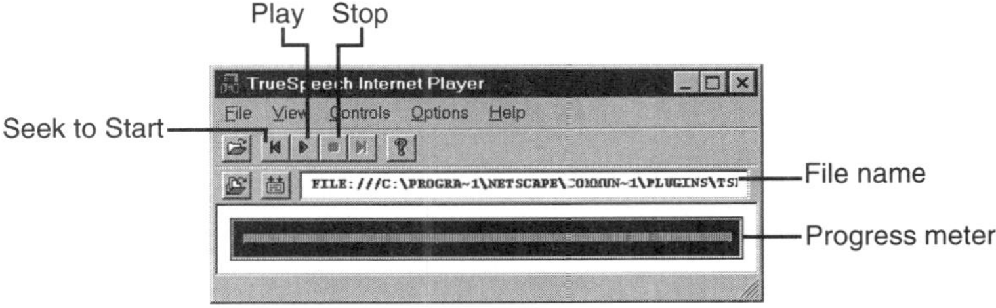

Figure 21.3 TrueSpeech starts and plays a greeting.

TrueSpeech Basics

The TrueSpeech player has the capability to play both TrueSpeech compressed files (file names that end with .tsp) and uncompressed wave-format files (.wav). Both .tsp and .wav Web links transfer files that end in .wav; when Netscape sees a link that ends in .tsp, it knows to request the .wav file and then play it as compressed audio. Originally, the player only sets itself up for the compressed files; see the section "Playing Noncompressed Files" to learn about setting up TrueSpeech to play .wav files.

To see TrueSpeech at work, get online and follow these steps:

1. Close the TrueSpeech player if it is still open from the installation process.

2. In Netscape Navigator, go to the sample sounds page located at **http://www.dspg.com/tsampl85.htm**. This page includes a list of links for recordings.

3. Click any link. A file transfer meter appears, followed by the TrueSpeech Player helper window. The two numbers at the bottom of the player indicate (respectively) how many bytes of the recording have been downloaded and how many bytes the recording has total. After a few seconds, the recording should start playing.

While the recording is playing, notice the lines on the progress meter (see Figure 21.4). The width of the progress meter represents the length of the recording. The single green line indicates how much of the recording has been downloaded and decompressed so far, and the bluish-green lines that build from the left indicate how much of the recording has played so far.

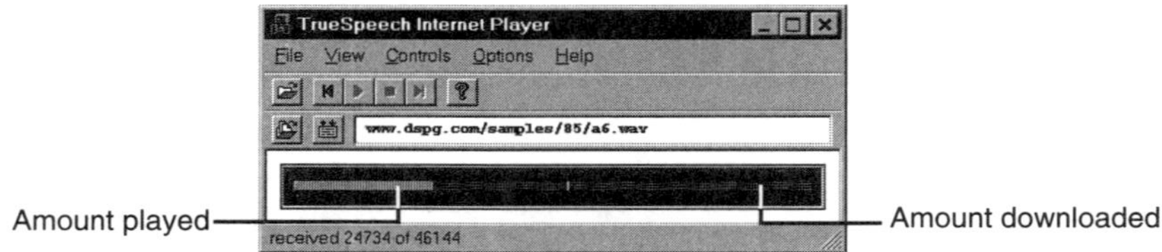

Figure 21.4   The meter tells you how much of the recording has been downloaded and how much has been played.

If the bluish-green lines catch up to the green line before the green line gets all the way to the end, it means that you've heard all the sound that has downloaded so far. Unfortunately, this can happen when the Internet is slow. If it does, the player pauses until it gets more data, and then it plays until it runs out of data again.

Use the **Stop** button to stop the sound from playing, the **Play** button to resume the sound, and the **Seek To Start** button to stop playing and reset the bluish green lines to the beginning, so that next time you hit the **Play** button it plays over from the start. These functions are also available as commands on the Controls menu.

Playing Noncompressed Files

To set up the player to also play noncompressed .wav files, follow these steps:

1. Open Navigator's **Edit** menu and select **Preferences**. A Preferences dialog box appears.

2. In the **Category** box, choose **Navigator** and click **Applications** to see the options shown in Figure 21.5.

3. Scroll through the **Description** list and select the **WAV** entry. Then click the **New Type** button.

You Don't Need This If a path name appears in the **Handled By** field, you already have a .wav player selected. To leave that one configured, click the **Cancel** button.

CAUTION

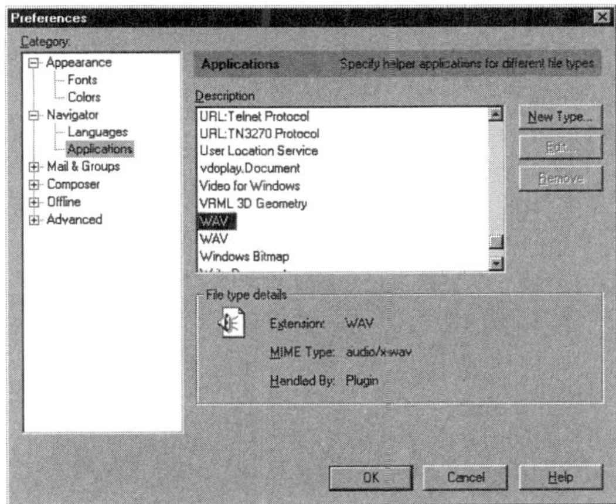

Figure 21.5 The Applications folder in the Preferences dialog box.

4. Enter **TrueSpeech** in the **Description of Type** text box.

5. In the **File Extension** text box, type **wav.**

6. In the **MIME Type** text box, type **x-wav.**

7. Click the **Browse** button, and a folder dialog box appears.

8. Locate the tsplay folder that you created when installing TrueSpeech and select the **tsplay16.exe** or **tsplay32.exe** file (whichever you have).

9. Click the **Open** button and click **OK** to return to the Preferences dialog box.

10. The file name you selected is now listed at the bottom of the dialog box. Click **OK**.

When you use the TrueSpeech player to play uncompressed .wav files, it waits until the entire file has been downloaded before it starts to play.

Where Can I Find More?   To find other Web sites with TrueSpeech files, check out **http://www.dspg.com/cool.htm**, which is where DSPG keeps its guide to sites.

In this lesson, you learned about TrueSpeech. In the next lesson, you'll learn how to get the Crescendo program to listen to MIDI files.

Listening to MIDI Files with Crescendo by LiveUpdate

In this lesson, you learn how to get the Crescendo plug-in and how to use it to listen to music stored on Web pages in MIDI format.

Understanding MIDI

Crescendo is a plug-in that lets you listen to music stored as MIDI files on Web pages. *MIDI* (Musical Instrument Digital Interface) stores music in a way that's very different from that of the digitized sound recordings that other audio plug-ins play.

The MIDI file doesn't contain a recording of a performance of the music. Instead, it is the computer equivalent of sheet music: a list of which notes are played, by which instruments, and in what order. Your sound card knows how to re-create the sounds of many different instruments. When Crescendo feeds this MIDI information to your sound card, the sound card performs the music.

MIDI has advantages and disadvantages when compared to digitized audio. You don't get any vocals with MIDI. Standard PC speech synthesis is certainly not developed enough to synthesize a good singer! You also don't get the nuances of a fine artist's performance from a MIDI file; you merely get the notes in the right order. What you hear may be very different from what the person who created the file heard, because the final sound depends heavily on how your sound card generates the music. (Cards that have *wave tables* tend to sound much better than the cheaper sound cards that merely synthesize the instruments. Also, the original composer may have been using professional-quality MIDI-controlled electronic instruments, which sound better yet.)

Wave Table   The digitized sounds of various instruments stored on a sound card. When a card with a wave table plays the sound of the instruments, it's producing an actual recording of the instruments instead of a mathematically designed computer simulation.

The capability to vary the sound is actually one of MIDI's strengths, however. Because you have the sheet music, you can change how it is interpreted. You'll need separate MIDI editing software to do so (Crescendo is just a player, not an editor), but once the file is on your disk, you can change which instruments play which parts, you can change the tempo, or you can rearrange the notes.

Compose Yourself   If you want to create your own MIDI music or edit other people's music, you will need a MIDI editor program, which is often called a *sequencer*. Popular sequencers include Powertracks and Dr. T's.

The biggest advantage of MIDI for Web use, however, is file size. The typical tune, for example, has 16 instruments playing for almost a full minute. Yet the file is less than 13 kilobytes. It can be downloaded in one-twentieth of the time it would take to download a typical low-quality digitized sound that you might find on the Web; it can be downloaded in less than one-five-hundredth of the time that it would take to download pure CD-quality audio.

Crescendo is available for Windows 3.1, Windows 95, and Windows NT, as well as for the Macintosh. You need to have a sound card to use Crescendo.

There is an enhanced version available called Crescendo Plus, which doesn't have to wait until the file is finished downloading before it starts playing. That version costs more, though, so I'll show you how to get the shareware version. If you want Crescendo Plus, you can look into upgrading later. Registering the shareware version costs $9.95; buying the Plus version costs $19.95.

The Crescendo file is 800K. Under ideal conditions using a 14.4 modem, it will take about 10 minutes to download. If the Web is busy, don't be surprised if it takes 20–30 minutes.

Downloading Crescendo

Crescendo is available for download from LiveUpdate's Web site. To get your copy, follow these steps:

1. Go to **http://www.liveupdate.com/dl.html** using Netscape.

2. In the form that appears, fill in your name and e-mail address and click the **Submit** button.

3. Scroll down to the bottom of the page until you see the OS logos shown in Figure 22.1. Click the logo for your operating system.

4. At the bottom of the new page is a list of download sites. Click one of them, and Netscape displays the Save As dialog box, which points to your Program directory.

5. If you don't already have a plugins folder, click the **New Folder** button and type **plugins** as the folder name.

6. Double-click the **plugins** folder icon to indicate that you want the file stored there.

7. Click the **Save** button, and the download begins. The file you receive will be called something like C231N95.EXE.

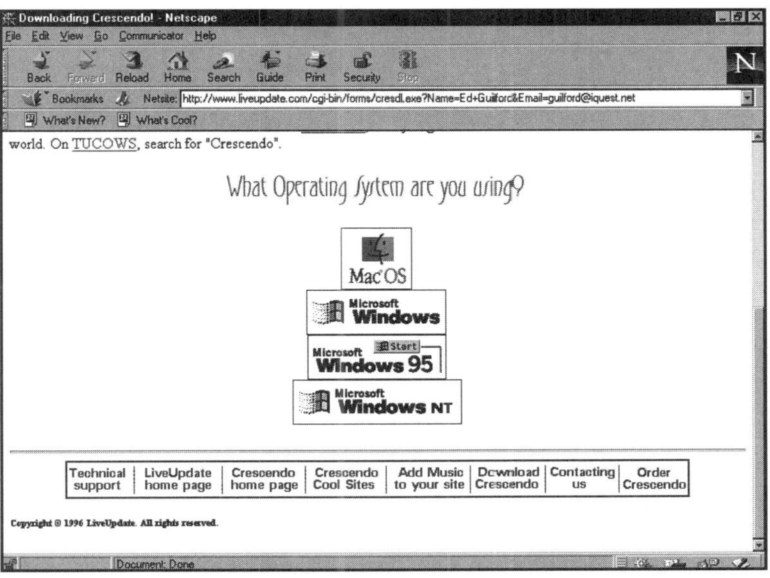

Figure 22.1 Choose the version that works with your operating system.

A meter is displayed while the file downloads. When the meter disappears, the download is complete. You can disconnect from the Internet now, but installation is so quick that you might not want to bother doing so because you'll have to get back on the Net to try it out.

Installing Crescendo

Because it's a rather simple product, Crescendo installs quickly and easily. Use the Run command to run the program you downloaded. You can accept the defaults in the installation program; just keep clicking **Next**. When the installation program is finished, you will be asked if you want to view the release notes. Click **Yes** to read through the file. When you finish, close the WordPad window.

Crescendo Basics

Basics are really all there is to Crescendo. It's a useful and fun utility, but it is not at all complicated. To test Crescendo, follow these steps:

1. Head to **http://www.liveupdate.com/exper.html** using Navigator.
2. Click the **Hear Crescendo StreamSites NOW!** link, and the Crescendo control panel appears in the upper-right corner of the page (see Figure 22.2). Drag the slider above the buttons to increase or decrease the volume.
3. Click the **Stop** button to stop playing the MIDI file at any time.
4. Click the **Pause** button to pause or resume play.
5. You can move forward and back in the song with the **Forward 10 Seconds** and **Back 10 Seconds** buttons.
6. To hear the song again, click the **Back to Beginning** button.

Embedded Tunes   Some embedded tunes play automatically: As soon as the page loads, the tune starts playing. To start other tunes, however, you have to click the Play button.

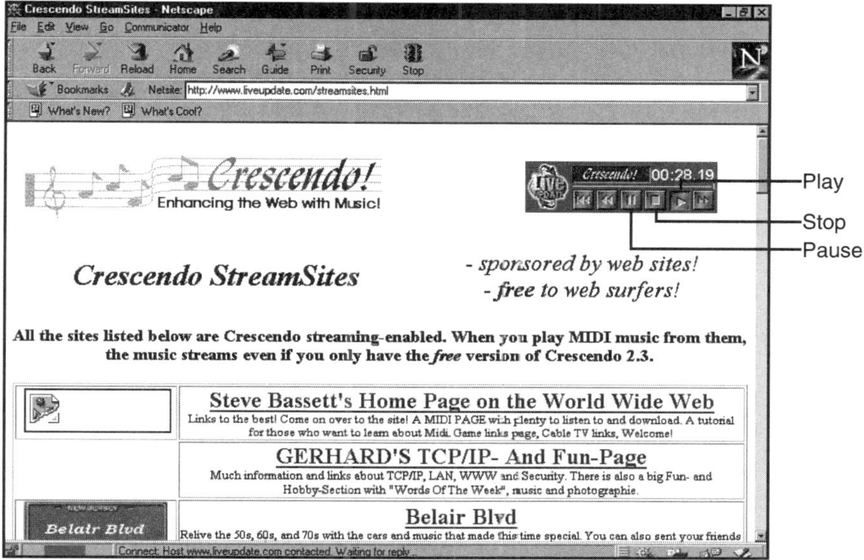

Figure 22.2   The control panel lets you play MIDI files

More MIDI

There are tens of thousands of MIDI scores available on the Web. Some are great, some are horrible, and some will sound good only if you have a good sound card. (As a rule, music that's designed for play on the computer will sound okay on a cheap sound card, but transcriptions of music intended for performance will really sound good only on a high-quality sound card that uses wave table synthesis.)

You cannot play all MIDI files off of the Web. There are two main reasons for this:

- The MIDI files have been compressed—as you can tell by the .ZIP file extension. Compressing makes sense for a file that someone will download and listen to later because it reduces the download time. However, Crescendo (and other MIDI players) can't understand such a file until it has been run through a decompression program such as WinZip. As MIDI capability becomes a more common Web browser feature, fewer MIDI files will be zipped. But those that are out there for a long time to come will be zipped.

- The file is in the proper form and has an extension of .mid or .midi, but the server on which it is stored does not know what those extensions stand for. If you click a MIDI file and end up with a Navigator window with a small amount of garbled text, this is the problem. The server has to be able to tell Navigator that this is a MIDI file in order for Crescendo to be able to pick it up.

Despite these problems, there are plenty of good sites with Crescendo-friendly MIDI files. Here are just a few (many of which have links that will lead you to others):

- **http://digiscape.com/jukebox/jukefram.htm** has the MIDI Jukebox, a selection of popular songs available at the click of a button.

- **http://www.prs.net/midi.html** is the site of The Classical MIDI Archives, a gargantuan collection of long-hair music that contains more than 1,800 MIDI files.

- **ftp://ftp.cs.ruu.nl/pub/MIDI/SONGS/** is a constantly growing archive with hundreds of tunes in various categories.

- **http://www.eeb.ele.tue.nl/midi/** doesn't have much in the way of actual tunes. What it does have, however, are some good articles about MIDI. If listening to some of these files makes you curious about what these files are and how you can make them, this is a good source for information.

- **http://www.dzp.se/midi/** is the home of The MIDI Music Pages, a good source for rock and pop music.

- **http://math.idbsu.edu/gas/midi** is the Gilbert and Sullivan Archive. In addition to files for the music of this classic musical theater team, this site also offers text files with the words to the songs. If you've ever tried to figure out the lyrics to "The Major General's Song," you'll enjoy this.

In this lesson, you learned how to use Crescendo to play MIDI music files over the Web. In the next lesson, you'll learn how to get RealAudio Player and use it to receive near-live radio transmissions over the Web.

Hearing Real-Time Broadcasts with RealAudio Player

In this lesson, you learn how to use RealAudio Player.

What Is RealAudio Player?

RealAudio Player is a program through which near-to-live audio transmissions are sent over the Internet. Think of it as radio on the Internet.

But don't confuse it with radio transmissions, because unlike live radio, RealAudio Player produces only near-to-live transmission. This means that when you listen to a RealAudio transmission, there's a small delay between the time that the sound signal is sent and the time that you actually hear it—about two seconds or so. In other words, it's almost "live."

To hear a RealAudio broadcast, you'll need a copy of RealAudio Player. In this lesson, you'll learn how to install the RealAudio Player and how to use it. By the way, there are other programs that can perform near-to-live transmission of sound over the Internet, but RealAudio Player is, by far, the most popular.

How does near-to-live sound transmission differ from regular sound transmission over the Net? Well, normally, when you encounter a sound file, such as an .AU or .VOX file, on a Web page, Netscape has to receive the entire sound file and save it to disk before launching a sound player application, which reads the sound file in its entirety and, finally, starts playing it. Since many sound files are large (256K or so), this means you'll spend a lot of time online before you can hear the sound.

RealAudio Player cuts a lot of time out of this audio transmission process. When you encounter a Web page with a RealAudio Player sound file, RealAudio Player begins decompressing it after it receives just the first few thousand bytes. It then starts playing the decompressed portion; meanwhile, the rest of the sound file is still being transmitted. Also, you can save a RealAudio Player transmission as a file if you want, but you don't have to in order to hear it just once.

How Do I Create a RealAudio Sound File?   If you create your own Web pages and you'd like to include a RealAudio Sound file, you can easily convert a conventional .AU or .WAV file using the RealAudio Encoder program you can download from the RealAudio Web site.

Downloading RealAudio Player

In order to install RealAudio Player, your PC must have at least a 486/33 MHz CPU, with 8M of RAM, 2M of free hard disk space, a sound card, and at least a 14.4 Kbps Internet connection. (If you use a 28.8 Kbps connection, you'll need at least a 486/66 MHz CPU.)

RealAudio Player comes in two versions: as a helper application (which runs outside the Netscape window as a separate program) and as a plug-in (which runs invisibly, within Netscape). The choice is yours.

Which One Should I Choose?   Unless you have a big need for a helper application that you can use without Netscape to play sound files, choose the plug-in version of RealAudio Player. It works automatically once installed, and it takes up less space on your hard disk.

You download RealAudio from the RealAudio site at http://realaudio.com. During the download process for RealAudio Player, you'll complete a form with your name, address, and computer information. This form gives the RealAudio developers information about their users so they can fine-tune their product. In addition, you'll need to apply for a password that RealAudio will send you via e-mail, which you'll need in order to visit the RealAudio site and play a test sound file. Once you download RealAudio Player, you'll install it, which is described in the next section.

RealAudio comes in a standard edition, as well as RealAudio Plus. RealAudio Plus gives you better sound quality and more controls for RealAudio. The standard edition can be downloaded for free. You can try out the standard edition first and upgraded to RealAudio Plus later if you like it.

To download RealAudio Player (the plug-in version), follow these steps:

1. Connect to the Internet and start Netscape.

2. In the **Location/Go to** text box, type **http://www.realaudio.com** and press **Enter**.

3. Click **RealPlayer** (see Figure 23.1).

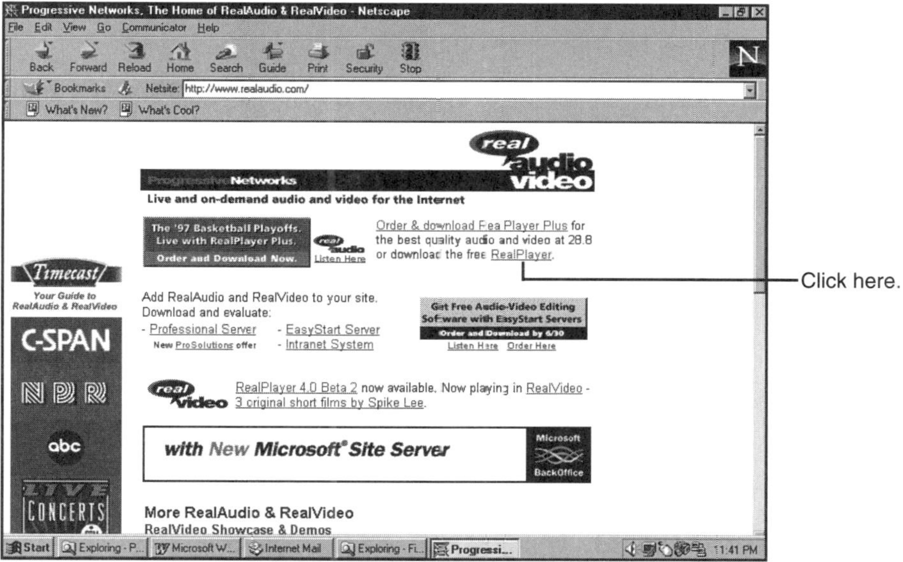

Figure 23.1   The RealAudio Web site.

4. In the RealPlayer column, click **Download Now**.

5. Select your operating system, processor, and Internet connection speed from the drop-down list boxes provided.

6. Complete the form for downloading RealPlayer by entering your name and e-mail address.

7. When you're ready, click **Download Now** to download RealPlayer.

8. Click a download site.

9. Select a folder in which to save the file, and then click **Save**. You may want to save the file in a TEMP directory so that you can check it for possible viruses before you install it.

10. After the file is downloaded to your PC, disconnect from the Internet so that you can install RealAudio Player without racking up connect-time charges.

Installing RealAudio Player

RealAudio Player comes in two forms: a helper application which works outside of Netscape as an independent program, and as an in-line plug-in, which works within Netscape, enabling it to recognize and play RealAudio transmissions whenever you encounter them.

During the process of installing the RealAudio Player, it automatically ties itself into your Web browser. This allows your Web browser to activate the RealAudio player whenever it encounters a RealAudio page on the Web.

The file you downloaded will install the RealAudio Helper application and the plug-in all at once. To run the installation use the Run command and browse for the file you just downloaded. The install program is pretty self-explanatory; just follow the instructions. (Refer to Lesson 19 for an example of the full installation procedure.)

After you install the program, the RealAudio Player will open automatically and play an example.

RealAudio Player Basics

RealAudio Player is easy to use. When you connect to a Web site with a sound file, your Web browser automatically launches RealAudio Player to play it.

There are several Web sites that use RealAudio Player, and more appear every day. The best place to start is to simply visit the RealAudio Web site, located at http://www.realaudio.com. The site contains links to other Web sites that feature RealAudio sound files (files that end in .RA or .RAM), such as the National Public Radio Web site and the ABC Internet Hourly News site.

To visit the RealAudio site and play a test file, follow these steps:

1. Connect to the Internet and start Netscape.

2. In the **Location/Go to** text box, enter the address
   http://www.realaudio.com and press **Enter**.

3. On the left side of the page, you will see many RealAudio Web
   sites, as shown in Figure 23.2.

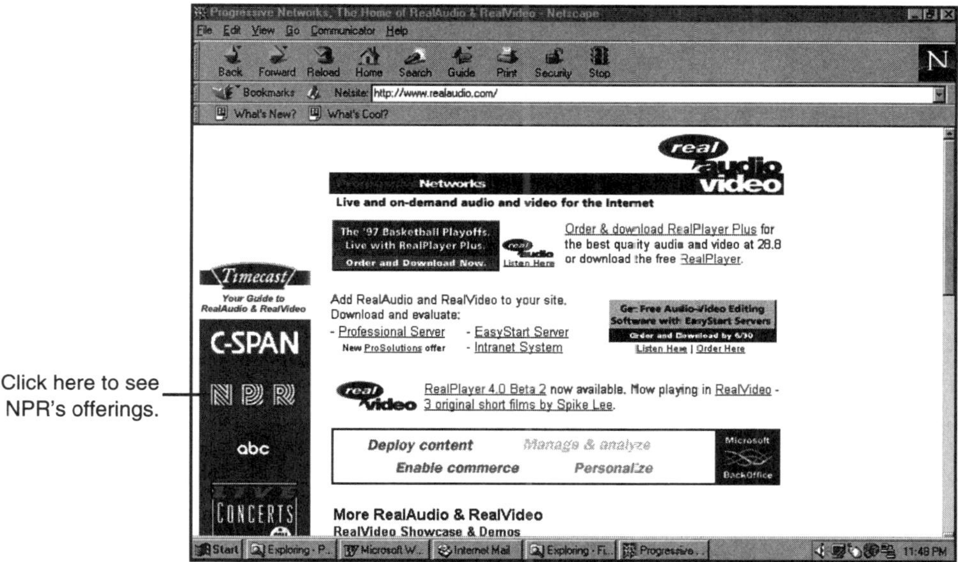

Figure 23.2   The RealAudio Web page contains links to many RealAudio test sites.

4. Click the **NPR** logo, and you're taken to a page that lists many NPR
   RealAudio sites.

5. Click the **Morning Edition** link. When the Morning Edition page opens,
   click the **Morning Edition** link.

6. (Optional) To pause the transmission at any time, click the **Pause** button
   shown in Figure 23.3. To resume the transmission, click the **Play** button.

7. (Optional) Use the **Volume** slider to increase or decrease the volume,
   or click the **Stop** button to stop the transmission at any time.

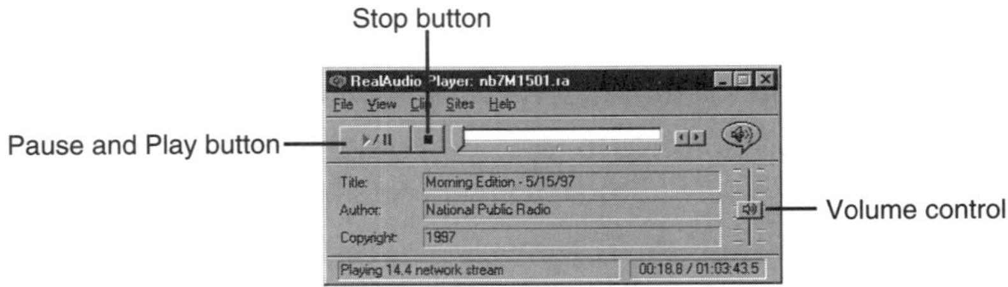

Figure 23.3   You can pause the transmission if you want.

You can continue to use your Web browser to visit other non-RealAudio sites. The RealAudio transmission continues as you work. When the transmission ends, the RealAudio player automatically closes.

I Want to Stop!   You don't have to play the entire audio transmission if you don't want to. Simply click the **Close** button anytime to close RealAudio Player instantly.

In this lesson, you learned how to install and use RealAudio Player. In the next lesson, you'll learn about InterVU MPEG Player, an MPEG video player.

Watching MPEG Movies with InterVU MPEG Player

In this lesson, you learn how to play MPEG videos using the InterVU MPEG Player plug-in for Navigator.

What Is InterVU MPEG Player?

MPEG video is a format for storing a full-motion color video "movie" with a soundtrack together in a single file. That's the good part. The bad part is that MPEG video files are typically very large.

Most MPEG viewers work like this: When you click a link that points to an MPEG file, the entire file is downloaded to your hard disk, and then the viewer begins to play it. MPEG files, even for the shortest videos, are quite large and you can end up waiting a long time for them to download before you start to view them.

Using a process called *streaming*, InterVU MPEG Player lets you see the contents of the MPEG video *as you're downloading it*, albeit at the speed of the download (which is generally slower than the playback speed). This gives you the opportunity to cancel the download if the video contains nothing you particularly want or need. After the file is downloaded, of course, the playback continues at normal speed. In addition, InterVU MPEG Player provides controls for starting and stopping the video as needed.

Because InterVU MPEG Player is an in-line plug-in, you view the video within the Netscape Navigator window, so that the movie remains an integral part of the Web page. With other MPEG viewers, you typically view the MPEG video within a separate window, outside of the Web page. This makes the whole experience a bit disconnected.

What If I Have a Video File Saved on My Hard Disk?   Because InterVU MPEG Player is an in-line plug-in, it can't act as a stand-alone program. In other words, you can't launch InterVU MPEG Player without Navigator. But if you want to view an MPEG video file from your hard drive, simply start Navigator, and then drag and drop the video file into the Navigator workspace. The video will then play at normal speed (because it's not being downloaded).

What About MPEG-2 Video?   MPEG-2 is a more highly compressed video format than regular MPEG, complete with stereo soundtracks. Because MPEG-2 is so very different from regular MPEG format, it is not supported by the current version of InterVU MPEG Player.

Downloading InterVU MPEG Player

The current version of InterVU MPEG Player runs only on Windows 95 or Windows NT and can be installed on any system that can run Netscape Navigator. In reality, on some systems, its performance may be limited. For optimal performance, your PC should have at least a 486 66 MHz CPU. Also, for at least moderately smooth viewing during the downloading of a video file, your modem should be no slower than 14.4Kbps. With this latest version of InterVU MPEG Player, if your PC is equipped with a sound card, you will be able to hear what you see (that is, if the video has sound).

In the next section, you'll learn how to install InterVU MPEG Player following the download. To download InterVU MPEG Player, follow these steps:

1. Connect to the Internet and start Netscape.

2. In the **Location/Go to** text box, type **http://www.intervu.com/player/player.html** and press **Enter**. You'll be taken to the download page (not the home page) of InterVU MPEG Player's Web site.

3. System requirements for InterVU MPEG Player may change without notice. To double-check whether your system can accommodate InterVU MPEG Player, click the **Help** link and click **About the InterVU Player** (see Figure 24.1).

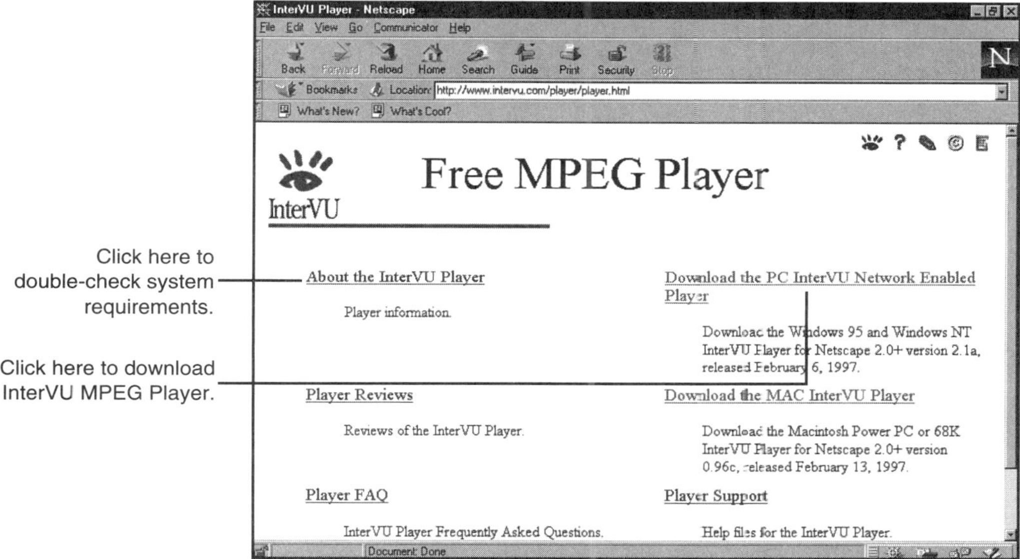

Figure 24.1   InterVU's main download page.

4. Current system requirements will be listed here. If your PC meets these standards, click Navigator's **Back** (left-arrow) button to continue the download. If your PC is lacking the requirements, you can still download InterVU MPEG Player, although it may not function properly (if at all).

5. Click **Download the PC InterVU Network Enabled Player** (see Figure 24.1), and then download instructions appear. Click **Download**.

6. Read the license agreement, and then click **I Agree** at the bottom of the page. A form appears, asking for your name and e-mail address.

7. Complete the form and click **Download MPEG Player**. If you have Netscape security options set, a confirmation dialog box appears; click **Continue**.

8. Click the **Download** link. A dialog box appears, prompting you to select the folder in which you want to place the downloaded file.

9. Select a folder in which to save the file, and then click **Save**. You may want to download the file into a TEMP directory, in order to check it for possible viruses before actually installing it.

10. After the file is downloaded to your PC, disconnect from the Internet so you can save on connect charges while you install InterVU MPEG Player.

Installing InterVU MPEG Player

Like most other in-line plug-ins, InterVU MPEG Player automatically ties itself into Netscape during the installation process. This allows Netscape to activate InterVU MPEG Player whenever it encounters an MPEG video on the Web.

Another interesting side note is that, unlike most other installation programs, InterVU MPEG Player's setup does not allow you to select the directory where InterVU MPEG Player will be installed. Instead, it is installed into its default directory, where Netscape Navigator will know to find it.

CAUTION

What If I Have More than One Netscape Navigator on My System? As silly as that might sound, you can possibly be evaluating and comparing two versions of Navigator on the same system. As a Navigator plug-in, InterVU MPEG Player can be installed for only one copy of Navigator—or rather, on one copy at a time. If you want InterVU MPEG Player to work for both copies, you'll need to install it twice.

Here's what you do: Run the copy of Navigator for which you want to install InterVU MPEG Player first; then exit the program and run the InterVU MPEG Player installation program. When you're done, run the *other* copy of Navigator and exit. Having an entry in a file located in the Windows directory tells the InterVU MPEG Player installer that, for all intents and purposes, that second copy is the "active" copy. Run the installation program a second time, follow the same instructions, and InterVU MPEG Player will work for both copies.

Once you've downloaded the InterVU MPEG Player installation program, follow these steps to install it on your system:

1. Start File Manager or Explorer and change to the directory where you downloaded the InterVU MPEG Player file.

2. Double-click the **InterVU MPEG Player** file (its file name should be something like IVSMSetup2_1.exe). The InterVU MPEG Player Installation program starts.

3. Click **OK** to begin the setup process, and the standard license agreement appears.

4. Read the license agreement and click **OK**. A meter appears showing the progress of the installation.

5. A dialog box will appear asking you for information about your Internet connection. Fill in the information and click **OK**.

6. Click **Finish** to complete the information and start a demo of the program. Navigator opens and takes you to the InterVU test page (see Figure 24.2). The video starts automatically.

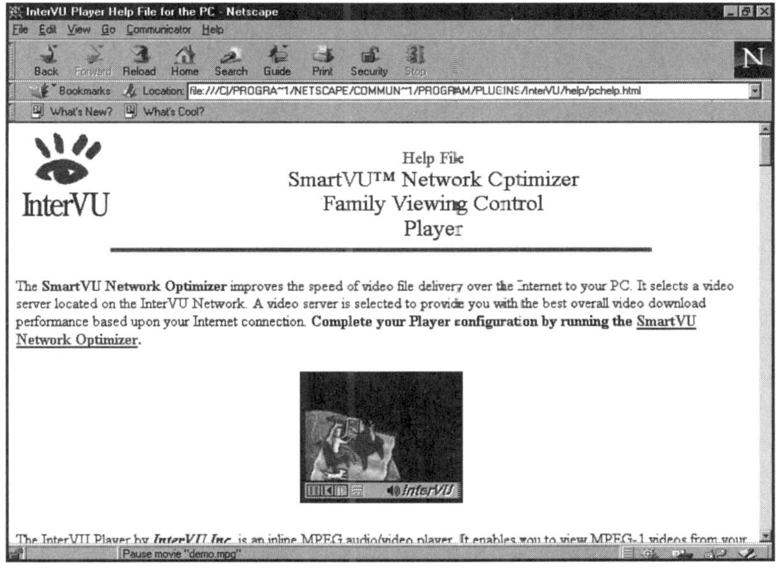

Figure 24.2   The InterVU test video.

7. This MPEG video is already on your disk, so you won't be downloading it, just testing to see if it plays. The video will stop automatically.

8. You're finished installing InterVU MPEG Player. Close the Netscape window.

InterVU MPEG Player Basics

Like most in-line plug-ins, there's not much to running them. Click a link to an MPEG file, and Netscape automatically launches InterVU MPEG Player.

If you were using some other MPEG video viewer and you clicked a link, you'd have to wait until Netscape Navigator downloaded the entire video, after which the MPEG video player would finally begin playing it. Between clicking the link and starting to play the video, there can be an interval of anywhere up to a half-hour of thumb twiddling.

However, with InterVU MPEG Player installed, you can view the video almost as soon as your system begins to receive it. Of course, this early preview is not perfect. It runs in a slower-than-real mode, so the video seems a bit jerky at times. In addition, during the preview, sound is omitted. Once the file is completely downloaded, you can play it, complete with sound, at real speed.

So, if you're anxious to try out your new toy, follow these steps to connect to the demo page on the InterVU MPEG Player Web site:

1. Connect to the Internet and start Netscape.
2. In the **Location** text box, type **http://www.intervu.com/partners/menu.html** and press **Enter**. InterVU's video guide page appears.
3. Scroll down to see a list of demos. Then click any link to see a list of videos available at that site.
4. Click a link to see the video. Begin downloading by clicking the green right-arrow **Play** button.
5. InterVU MPEG Player begins playing the portion of the video it has downloaded thus far in regular time (but without sound). When InterVU MPEG Player gets to the part it hasn't downloaded yet, it pauses. InterVU MPEG Player then plays the next frames of the video as they become available. To cancel the downloading of the video at any time during playback, click the red square **Stop** button.
6. When the video finishes downloading, the Disk button will appear just to the right of the Stop button on the InterVU MPEG Player control panel, as shown in Figure 24.3. If you want to save the video on your hard disk, click this button. Select a directory in which to save the file; then click **OK**.

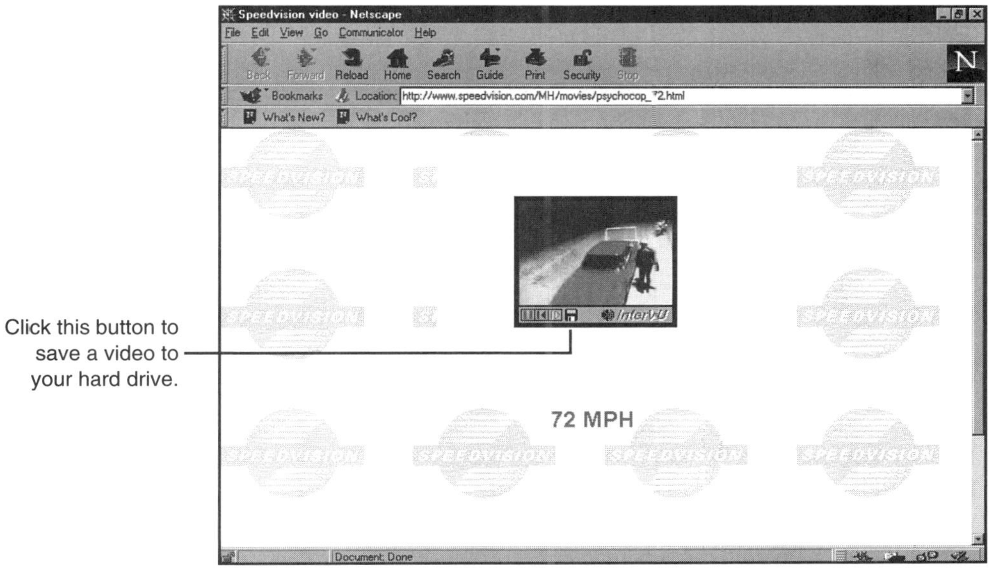

Click this button to save a video to your hard drive.

Figure 24.3 Click the Disk button to save the video permanently.

Playing Saved MPEG Video Files

Although InterVU MPEG Player is not a stand-alone program, it can play MPEG files you've saved to your hard drive. Follow these steps to get InterVU MPEG Player to play a saved MPEG video:

1. Open Explorer or File Manager, and change to the directory that contains the MPEG video file you want to play.

2. Start Netscape Navigator. (You do not need to connect to the Internet.)

3. Resize the Netscape window, if necessary, so that you can see File Manager or Explorer.

4. Drag the MPEG file into the Netscape Navigator window (where the Web pages are generally displayed) and drop it (release the mouse button). InterVU MPEG Player plays the video, as shown in Figure 24.4.

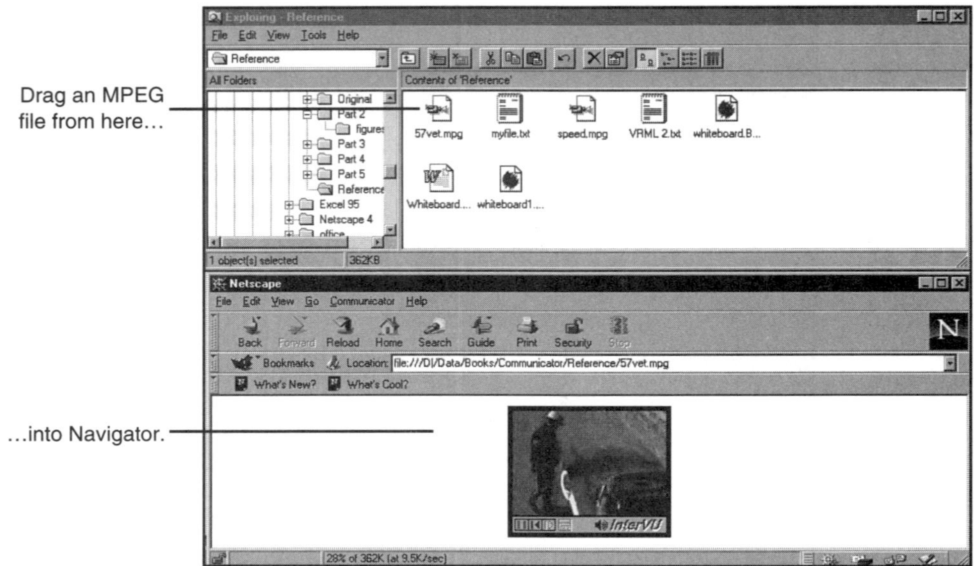

Figure 24.4   Use drag-and-drop to play a saved MPEG video file.

I Want More Control   InterVU MPEG Player provides only basic controls for your video. Playback is at standard MPEG speed, and you cannot resize the playback frame. If you need more control over the video playback, consider using Apple's QuickTime viewer, which plays back both QuickTime and MPEG videos and offers many more controls.

In this lesson, you learned how to install and use the InterVU MPEG Player plug-in to play MPEG video files.

Netscape Netcaster

The Basics of Netscape Netcaster

In this lesson, you learn the basics of using Netscape Netcaster.

What Is Netscape Netcaster?

Netscape Netcaster is the newest component of Communicator. Netcaster
does something you probably haven't seen before. It enables you to receive
information from the Internet automatically. Netcaster enables *push* delivery
of information right to your desktop.

Push   Push technology is a new form of information transfer over the Internet.
With push technology, information is *pushed* to you automatically instead of you
pulling it off the Web with your browser.

When information is pushed to Netcaster, Netcaster automatically downloads
the information to your hard drive, so you will be able to view the information
even when you are not connected to the Internet. You can then set up Netcaster
to update the information at regular intervals

Not Quite the Same?   Netcaster was not included in the first public
release of Communicator, upon which this book is based. Therefore, the
information in the Netcaster section is based on preliminary beta-test information. The final release version of Netcaster may differ from this beta version in
subtle or even significant ways.

The main focus of Netcaster is to receive *channels*. Content providers push their information through these channels to your computer (see Figure 1.1). Netcaster includes a channel finder you can use to locate the latest and greatest channels. Netcaster also provides built-in support for Castanet by Marimba. (Marimba developed Castanet for channel providers to bring you the best in push content. What this means is that you will be able to receive a wide variety of channels.)

The Page I Want Is Not a Channel   One great thing about Netcaster is that it works with any Web page. If you want Netcaster to update a specific Web page automatically, Netcaster can do it, even if the Web page wasn't designed as a channel.

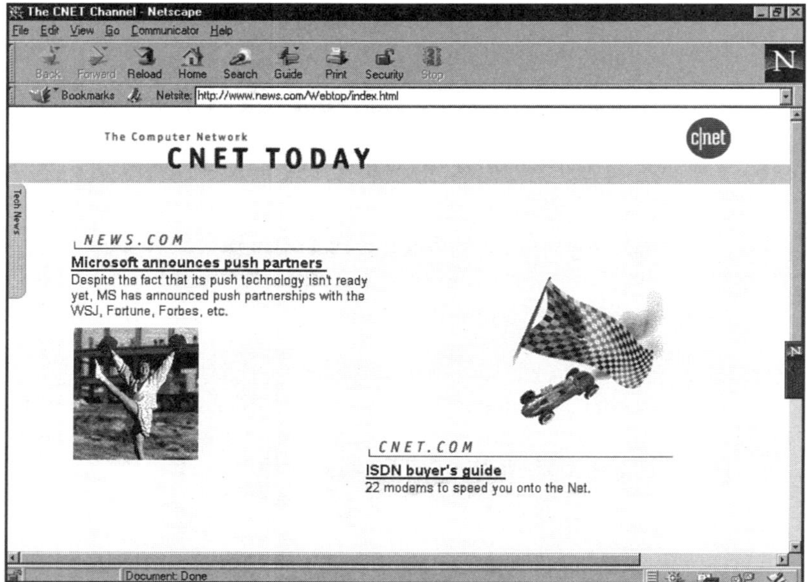

Figure 1.1   The CNET Channel.

Another interesting feature of Netcaster is its capability to display channels as a *Webtop*. A Webtop is a Netcaster page that anchors itself to a certain area on your desktop. Once it's there, it will remain behind the applications you are working on until you decide to use it. You can also set the Webtop to fill your entire desktop. This maximizes the amount of content you will be able to see on your screen (see Figure 1.2).

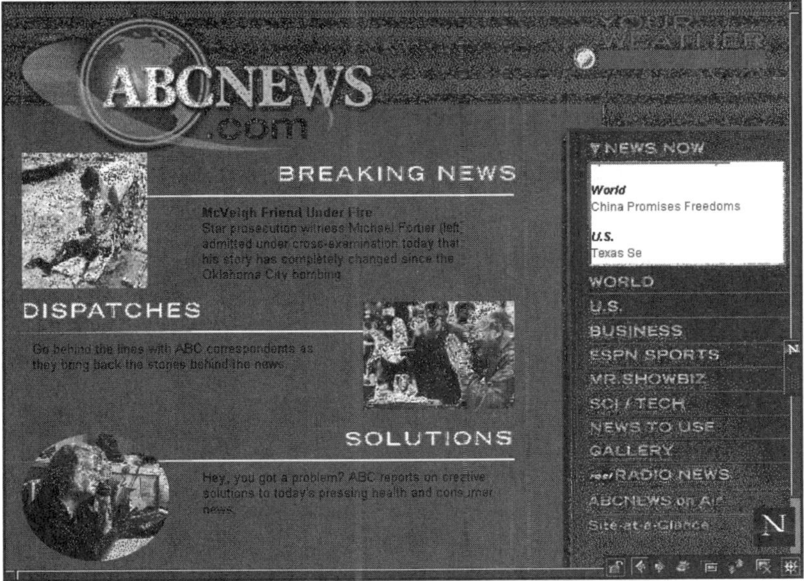

Figure 1.2   The ABCNEWS Channel as a Webtop.

Using Netcaster

Now that you know a little about Netcaster, let's take a look at it. To start Netcaster, do one of the following:

- From any Communicator program, open the **Communicator** menu and choose **Netcaster**.

- Or open the **Start** menu, point to **Programs**, point to **Netscape Communicator**, and select **Netscape Netcaster**.

The Netcaster window opens on the right side of your screen (as shown in Figure 1.3), and the Channel Finder opens by default. Click **My Channels** to open the menu of available channels. At first, the Netscape Channel will be the only channel available (you'll learn how to add more channels in Lesson 2). Click **Netscape Channel**, and the Netscape Channel opens (see Figure 1.4).

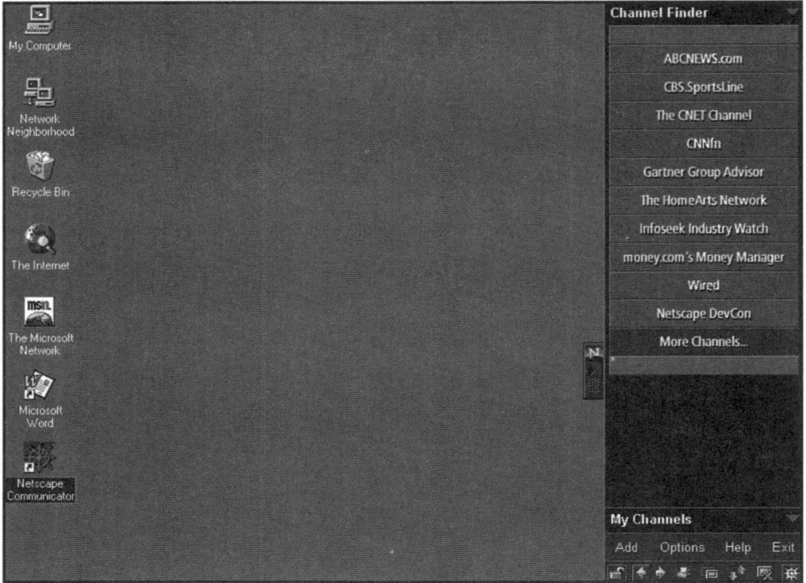

Figure 1.3 The Netcaster window.

Figure 1.4 The Netscape channel.

The Netscape Channel has various links that you can click just as you would on a normal Web page. If you click a link, Navigator opens and takes you to the Web page the link refers to. When the channel first loaded, it downloaded all the links to your hard drive. This is an advantage when you are clicking through the links because they will load much more quickly. The disadvantage is that it will take a while to load the Netcaster channel because it downloads all the links at once. When you have the channel loaded, you can continue to work at your computer as you normally would. If you get bored, just switch over to the Netcaster Channel window and click a link.

By default, the Netcaster window hides when a Netcaster channel is open. To reopen Netcaster, click the **Netcaster** tab at the right of your screen (see Figure 1.5).

Figure 1.5   The Netcaster tab.

When you are finished with the Netscape Channel, click the **Close** (X) button.

In this lesson, you learned the basics of Netscape Netcaster. In the next lesson, you'll learn how to subscribe to channels.

Subscribing to Channels

In this lesson, you learn how to subscribe to channels to get the content you want from Netcaster.

What's a Channel?

A *channel* is nothing more than a Web site that has been specially set up to deliver information to your desktop automatically. Channels are created the same way as Web sites using HTML codes. They can also support Java programs and other specialized Web authoring features.

Channels are usually set up to deliver specific content. For example, the ABCNEWS channel provides the latest news stories; CBS.SportsLine gives you sports information; and CNNfn has financial updates. When Netcaster was first released, dozens of information providers were committed to producing channels that can be used by Netcaster. By the time you read this, channel providers will probably number in the hundreds.

Netcaster contains two lists of channels. One is called Channel Finder and contains some of the channels available on the Internet. The other is called My Channels and contains a list of your favorite channels.

Using the Channel Finder

Now that you know there are so many interesting channels out there, you probably want to learn how to find them. Netcaster has included a very useful utility called Channel Finder. The Channel Finder is a list of channels you may be interested in exploring. With Channel Finder, you can preview the channels before you add them to your personal list. This enables you to see what you might be getting without taking the time to download the entire channel. If you decide you like a channel, you can add it to your personal list of channels called My Channels. (These are the channels that Netcaster downloads at regular intervals to keep them up to date.) The Channel Finder is updated regularly by connecting to Netscape's Web site, so check it often to see what is available.

When you first open Netcaster, the Channel Finder opens automatically. Follow these steps to use it:

1. Open Netcaster by clicking the **Start** button, pointing to **Programs**, pointing to **Netscape Communicator**, and selecting **Netscape Netcaster**.

2. If the Channel Finder is not open, click the **Channel Finder** bar to open it. A list of channels appears under the Channel Finder bar as shown in Figure 2.1.

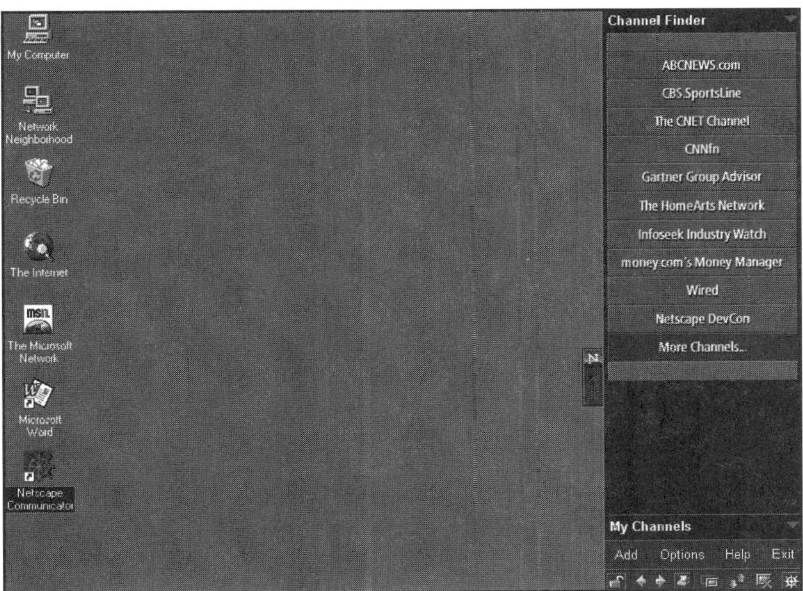

Figure 2.1   The Channel Finder window.

3. Click one of the channel bars to see a description of the channel (see Figure 2.2). To preview the channel, click the **+ ADD CHANNEL** button.

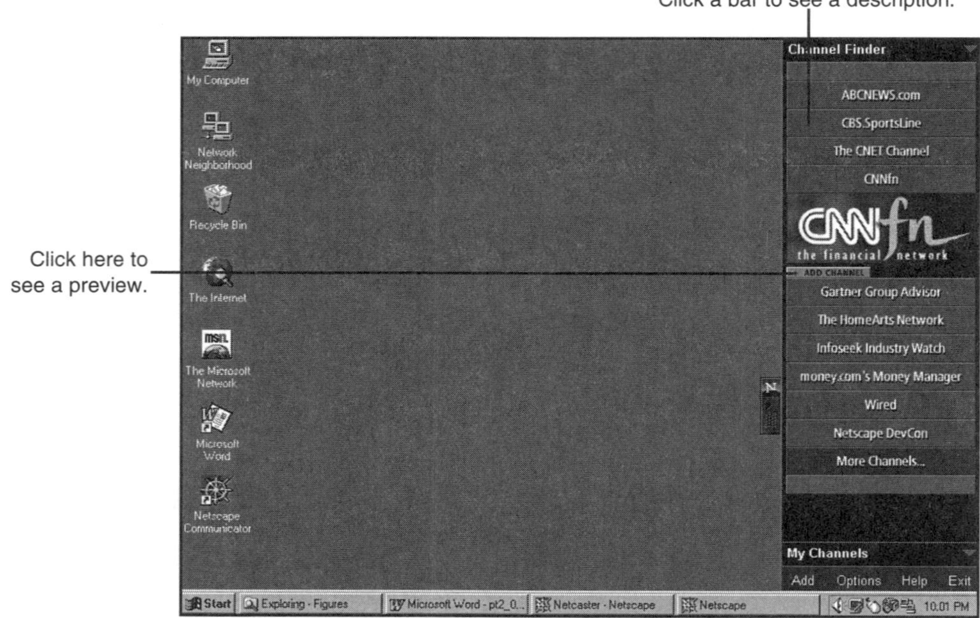

Figure 2.2   You can view a description or a preview of the channel.

4. If you like what you see, click the **Add Channel** button in the preview window (see Figure 2.3). If you don't want to add the channel to your My Channels list, click the **Cancel** button to close the preview window.

5. If you clicked the Add Channel button, the Channel Properties dialog box appears. For now, just click **OK** to accept the defaults (if you want to learn more about channel properties, see Lesson 5).

6. (Optional) Repeat steps 3–5 to add more channels to your list.

7. (Optional) Click the **More Channels...** bar to connect to Netscape's site to see a list of other channels you might want to try (see Figure 2.4). If you would like to add one of those to My Channels, go back to steps 3–5.

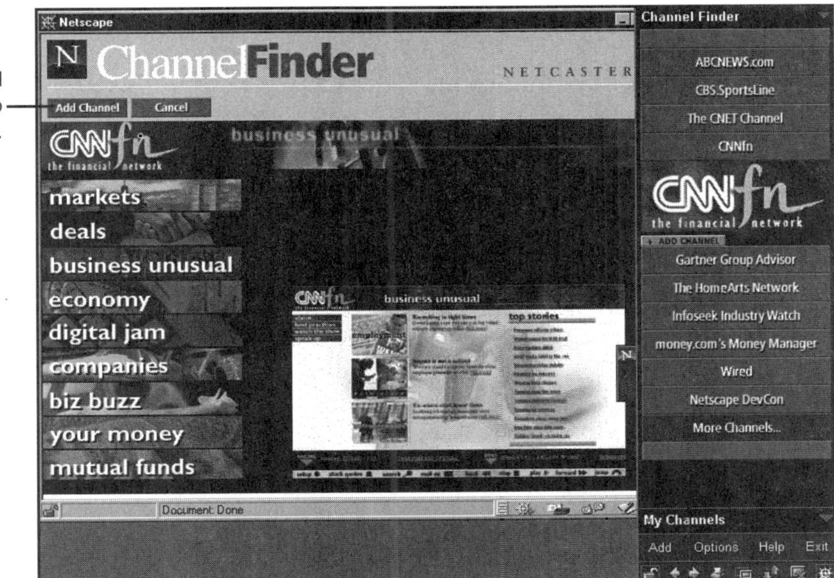

Figure 2.3   You might want to add the preview page for the CNN Financial Network.

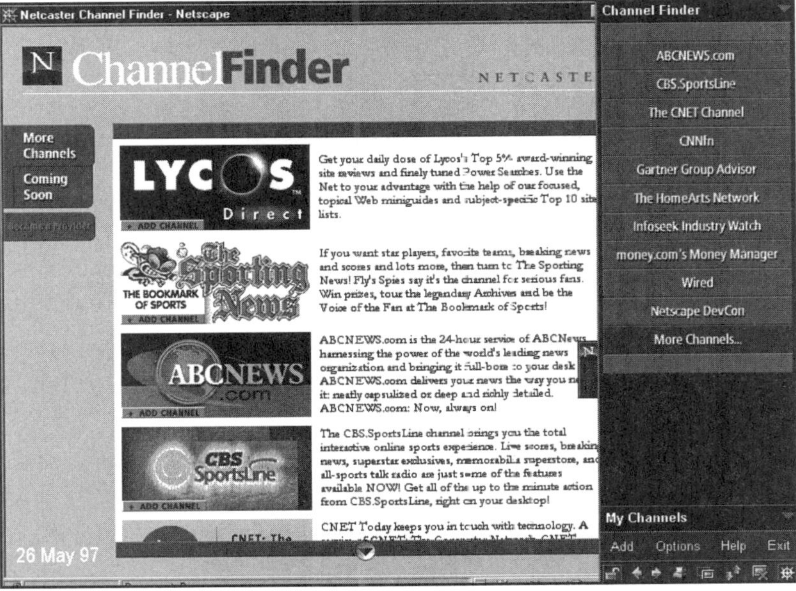

Figure 2.4   Netscape's Channel site.

I Want More!   You can find more channels at Marimba's Web site at http://
www.marimba.com. To add a channel from this site, click the **Channels** link to
go to the list of channels. When you see a channel you like, click the **Add
Channel** button. A dialog box opens, showing you the address of the channel.
Click **OK** to add it to My Channels.

Adding a Channel Manually

You can add any Web page to your list of channels. Although Web pages are not
optimized for Netcaster, Netcaster can still update them at specified intervals as
it does channels.

Follow these steps to add a channel or a Web page manually:

1. At the bottom of the Netcaster window, click the **Add** button. The Channel
Properties dialog box opens (see Figure 2.5).

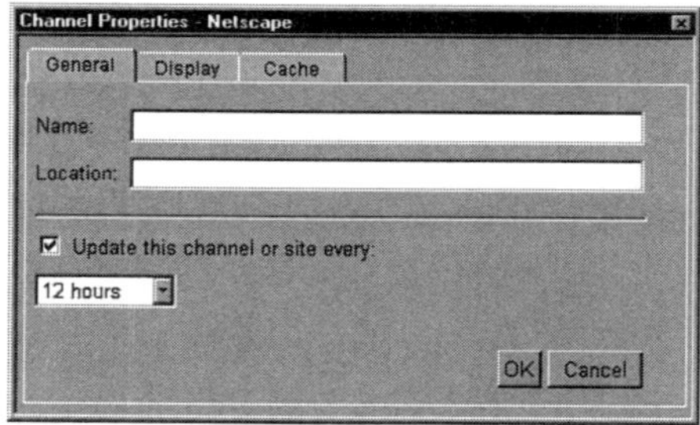

Figure 2.5   The Channel Properties dialog box.

2. In the **Name** text box, type a name for the channel or Web page you are
adding (this is the name that will appear in My Channels).

3. Type the site's URL in the **Location** text box.

4. From the drop-down list at the bottom of the dialog box, select how often
you would like the site to be updated.

5. Click the **Display** tab. Then indicate whether you want the site to be
displayed as a window or a Webtop.

6. Click the **Cache** tab. In the **Download** text box, type the number of levels
deep you would like to download at a site.

What's a Level?   A level is a page at a Web site. When you're at one site and you click a link, you go to the next level. If you use the default value of 2 in step 6, two levels of a site will be downloaded with your channel. That means all the links for those two levels will be downloaded to your hard drive.

7. Type a number in the **Don't Store More Than** text box to specify the maximum amount of disk space a downloaded channel can occupy. The default is 5 megabytes. If you are low on hard drive space, you may want to decrease that number.

8. Click **OK** to close the Channel Properties dialog box.

It's So Slow!   Netcaster uses a lot of memory. If you have less than 32M of RAM, Netcaster will have to use virtual memory to run. Virtual memory uses your computer's hard drive to swap information out of memory. Because access time on your hard drive is much slower than RAM, this process slows up your computer. Closing all unnecessary programs could help, but the only way to significantly increase performance is to add more memory.

Displaying and Updating Channels

After you add channels to your My Channels list, either manually or with Channel Finder, you are ready to display your channel. Follow these steps:

1. Click the **My Channels** bar to display your list of channels.

2. Click the channel you would like to display. Depending on the options you chose, it will be displayed in a window or as a Webtop.

When you added channels to My Channels, you set the options on how often you wanted the channel to be updated. Sometimes it might be more convenient to update the channel at another time. Maybe you want the score of the big game or you want to see the updated stock quotes. Whatever the reason, Netscape gives you a way to update your channel whenever you want. Just follow these steps:

1. From the Netcaster window, click **Options**. The Options dialog box shown in Figure 2.6 appears.

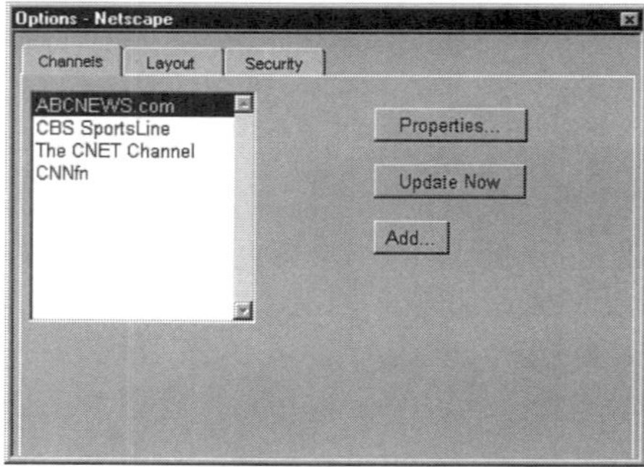

Figure 2.6   The Options dialog box.

2. Highlight the channel you would like to update and click the **Update Now** button.

3. (Optional) Highlight another channel and click **Update Now** to update it. Continue to update other channels as necessary.

4. Click **OK** to close the Options dialog box.

Deleting a Channel

After you have tried a channel, you might decide that you don't like it. To remove a channel from the My Channels list, follow these steps:

1. From the Netcaster window, click the **Options** button.

2. Highlight the channel you want to delete, and then click the **Delete** button.

3. A dialog box opens, asking if you're sure you want to delete this item. Click **OK** to delete.

4. (Optional) Repeat steps 1-3 as necessary to remove unwanted channels.

5. Click **OK** to close the Options dialog box.

In this lesson, you learned how to work with channels. In the next lesson, you'll learn how to use Webtops.

Using Webtops to Display Information

In this lesson, you will learn how to create and use Webtops.

What's a Webtop?

A *Webtop* is simply a channel that anchors itself to your screen. A Webtop is full screen, so it maximizes the amount of information that can be displayed. In this mode, your Webtop acts as a sort of interactive wallpaper for your Windows desktop. It remains in the background until you decide to use it. Figure 3.1 shows the ABCNEWS site displayed as a Webtop. When you click a link on a Webtop, Navigator opens to display the information you requested.

When you first saved your channel to My Channels, you told Netcaster whether you wanted the channel to be displayed in a window or as a Webtop (see Lesson 2). If you can't remember how you configured your channels, just look at the title in My Channels. The channels that are configured as Webtops have a video monitor icon to the right of the title (see Figure 3.2).

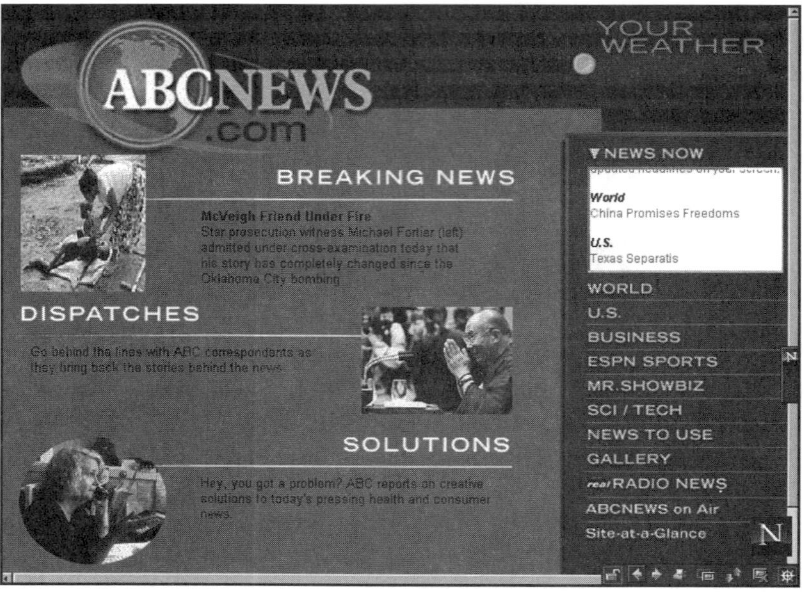

Figure 3.1 The ABCNEWS channel as a Webtop.

These channels are configured as Webtops.

Figure 3.2 My Channels lists the channels available to display.

Click one of the Webtop channels to display the Webtop. After the Webtop opens, you will notice that it fills your entire screen. In the lower-right corner of the screen, a small toolbar is displayed (see Figure 3.3). This toolbar controls the Webtop.

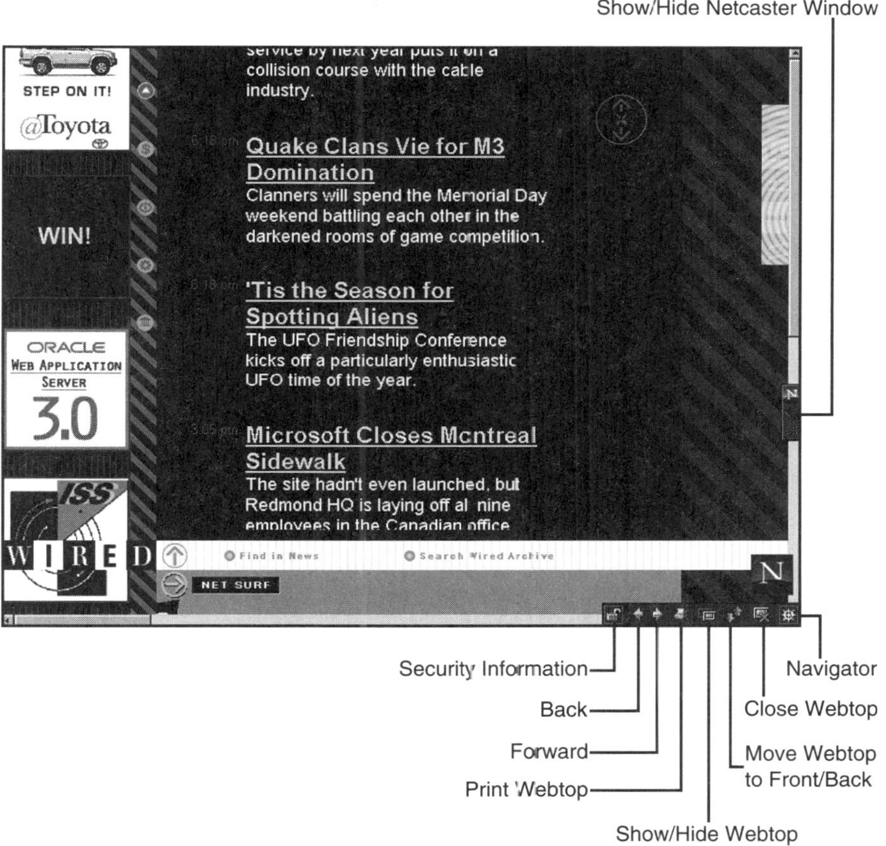

Figure 3.3   The Webtop toolbar lets you control the display.

Toolbar Controls

The Webtop toolbar contains a variety of controls, as outlined in the following list:

> **Security Information**   Shows information about the security of a site.
>
> **Back**   Returns you to the previous Webtop page.

Forward Goes to the next Webtop page.

Print Prints the Webtop.

Show/Hide Webtop Hides the Webtop if it is open, or shows the Webtop if it is hidden. When you hide a Webtop, the toolbar remains visible.

Move Webtop to Front/Back Moves the Webtop to the front (or back) of your desktop. If the Webtop is in the back, your application windows will be visible. If it is in the front, you will see only the Webtop.

Close Webtop Closes the Webtop.

Navigator Opens a Navigator window.

Changing or Updating a Webtop

If you're getting tired of the current Webtop and you'd like to see something different, follow these steps:

1. Click the tab on the right side of your screen to open Netcaster.
2. Click the **My Channels** bar to open My Channels.
3. Click the title of the Webtop you would like to change to. The new Webtop opens, and the old Webtop closes automatically.

Sometimes you may need to update the information on your Webtop at times other than the automatic updates. Maybe you know the big game has started and you want to see the score, or maybe you want to see an update on the weather. To update the Webtop, follow these steps:

1. Click the tab on the right side of your screen to open Netcaster.
2. Click the **Options** button to open the Options dialog box.
3. Select the Webtop you would like to update.
4. Click the **Update Now** button.
5. Click **OK** to close the Options dialog box.

Isn't There an Easier Way? A quick way to update a Webtop is to right-click any link on the Webtop and select **Update** from the shortcut menu that appears.

Deleting a Webtop

After you have tried a Webtop for a while, you might decide that you don't like it. To remove a Webtop from the My Channels list, follow these steps:

1. From the Netcaster window, click the **Options** button.

2. Highlight the Webtop you want to delete, and click the **Delete** button.

3. A dialog box opens, asking if you're sure you want to delete the Webtop. Click **OK** to delete.

4. Click **OK** to close the Options dialog box.

Changing a Channel to Display It As a Webtop

When you first started adding channels, you probably added some as Webtops and others that would open in a window. If you want to change one of the channels that appears in a window so it will be displayed as a Webtop, follow these steps:

1. Click the tab at the right of the screen to open the Netcaster window.

2. Click the **Options** button to open the Options dialog box.

3. Select the channel you would like to change and click **Properties** (you can also right-click the channel in My Channels and select **Properties** from the menu).

4. Click the **Display** tab to see the options shown in Figure 3.4.

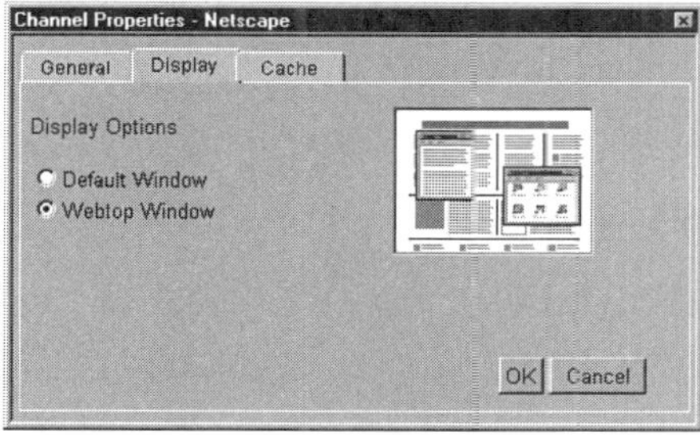

Figure 3.4 The Channel Properties dialog box.

5. Click the **Webtop Window** option button.

6. Click **OK** to close the Channel Properties dialog box.

7. Click **OK** to close the Options dialog box. The next time you open this channel, it will be displayed as a Webtop.

I Don't Like the Webtop   If you want to change a Webtop back to a channel that is displayed as a window, follow the previous steps except choose **Default Window** in step 5.

In this lesson, you learned how to use Webtops. In the next lesson, you'll learn about working offline.

Viewing Channels Offline

In this lesson, you learn how to view channels offline.

About Viewing Offline

If you use Netcaster at work and are connected to a high speed T1 line, you may never have a reason to view channels offline. Web content comes to you for free (free to you anyway), at speeds almost as fast as if you had the data on your hard drive. Most of us do not have that luxury, however.

There are several advantages to viewing a channel offline. If you have only one phone line, you can minimize the time your phone is tied up on the Internet. Offline viewing can be faster than viewing online because information is downloaded to your hard drive when you first load the channel. When you view the information, it comes to you as fast as the hard drive allows (which is much faster than a dial-up Internet connection). One major advantage to offline viewing is that you can view information even when you're not near a phone. If you take your notebook computer when traveling, you can download the information before you leave and read it at your leisure. And of course, if you're charged for connect time, you can save yourself a lot of money by offline viewing.

How Does It Work?

Offline viewing works automatically in the background. You may not even notice that offline viewing is taking place except that there will be a lot of disk activity when the channel first loads and when it updates. When you open a channel in Netcaster, the information from the site is downloaded to your computer to a *cache*. A cache is simply a place on your hard drive where Netcaster stores files for later viewing.

When you use the channel shortly after you open it, you are assured that the information is up-to-date. After the channel has been displayed a while, it will no longer be current. That's why Netcaster automatically updates your channels at regular intervals. By default, Netcaster updates its channels at noon and midnight. When you first set up a channel, you can set the intervals for updates, and you can change the update interval using the Options dialog box. Netcaster will automatically update your site at the intervals you specify even if you're not connected to the Internet. However, if you are using another Communicator application and select **Go Offline** from the **File** menu, Netcaster will not update the channel. Netcaster also will not update channels if it is not running when the scheduled update is supposed to take place.

Netcaster also gives you several different ways to update the channel information manually. You'll learn about those later in this lesson.

Turning Off Automatic Updates

There may be times when you do not want Netcaster to update channels automatically (for example, if you are using a notebook computer and are not near a phone, or if you are using your phone line for voice communications). Follow these steps to turn off automatic updates:

1. If the Netcaster window is not open, click the tab at the right side of the screen to open it.
2. Click the **Options** button to open the Options dialog box (see Figure 4.1).
3. Select the channel that you want to disable from the channel list and click the **Properties** button. The Channel Properties dialog box appears (see Figure 4.2).

Quick Properties   To quickly get to the Channel Properties dialog box, open **My Channels** and right-click the channel you want to change. Then select **Properties** from the shortcut menu that appears.

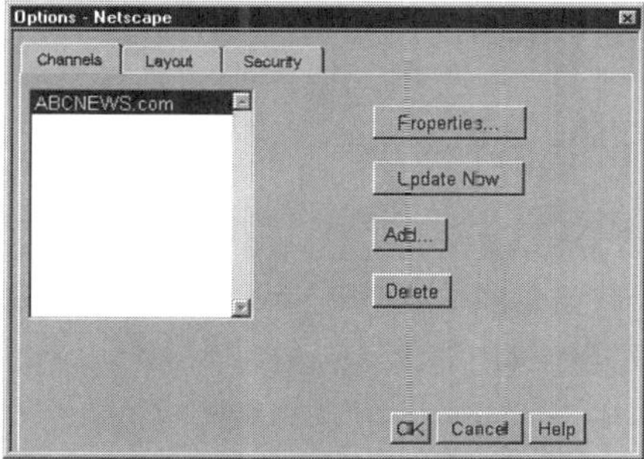

Figure 4.1   The Options dialog box.

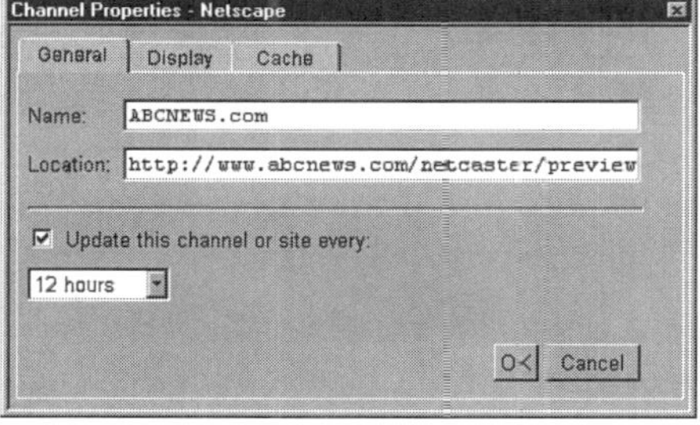

Figure 4.2   The Channel Properties dialog box.

4. Click the **Update This Channel or Site Every:** check box to remove the check mark.

5. Click **OK** to close the Properties dialog box.

6. (Optional) Select other channels as necessary and repeat steps 3–5.

7. Click **OK** to close the Options dialog box.

Adjusting the Update Frequency

You may decide that you want the channel to update more or less frequently than the default of every twelve hours. Follow these steps to change the update frequency:

1. Click the **Options** button from the Netcaster window.
2. In the channel list, select the channel you want to change. Then click the **Properties** button.
3. Choose an update frequency from the drop-down list under **Update This Channel or Site Every:**. You can choose from as little as every thirty minutes to as long as once a week.
4. Click **OK** to close the Properties dialog box.
5. Click **OK** to close the Options dialog box.

Manually Updating a Channel

There may be times when you don't want to wait for a scheduled update to refresh your information. There are several ways to update a channel manually:

- Right-click any link on the channel and select **Reload** from the shortcut menu.
- From the Netcaster window, click the **Options** button. Then select the channel you want to update and click the **Update Now** button.
- If the channel is a Webtop, click the **Update Webtop** button on the Webtop toolbar.

Changing How Much Is Downloaded for Offline Viewing

By default, Netcaster downloads all the information two levels deep at a site. In other words, it will download all the links from the first page, as well as all the links that are associated with each of the links on the first page. This could result in a lot of information. For example, if a channel had 20 links on the opening page and each of those links had 20 links on their page, Netcaster would download the information from 400 links. As you can see, you probably wouldn't want to download much more than two levels.

You can also change the size of the cache to create more or less storage room for the downloaded sites. The cache is the temporary storage area on your hard drive where the downloaded information is stored. The cache size overrides the number of levels downloaded. Therefore, if your cache fills up before the specified number of levels is downloaded, Netcaster will stop retrieving information from the channel.

Follow these steps to change how many levels are downloaded from a channel and/or the cache size:

1. If the Netcaster window is not open, click the tab at the right side of the screen to open it.

2. Open **My Channels** and right-click the channel that you would like to change. Select **Properties** from the shortcut menu. The Properties dialog box opens.

3. Click the **Cache** tab to see the options shown in Figure 4.3.

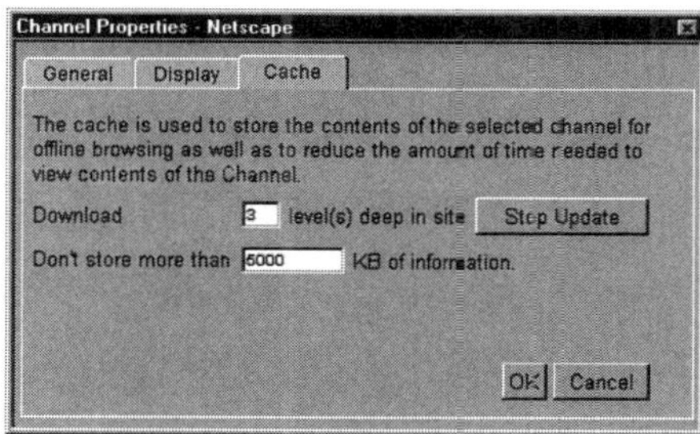

Figure 4.3   You can adjust the number of download levels and the cache size.

4. Indicate the number of levels you want to download in the text box next to **Download**.

5. Change the maximum cache size in the box next to **Don't Store More Than**. (This number is in kilobytes, so 5000 means 5 megabytes.)

6. Click **OK** to close the Properties dialog box.

Stopping an Update in Progress

One of the disadvantages of offline viewing is that updates can be fairly time-consuming, especially if you have a slow Internet connection. These updates can be very resource intensive, so they may slow up your computer considerably. If you really don't have the time to wait for an update, you can stop it manually. To do so, follow these steps:

1. Open the Netcaster window by clicking the tab at the right edge of the screen.

2. Open **My Channels** and right-click the channel that is being updated. Then select **Properties** from the shortcut menu.

3. Click the **Cache** tab and click the **Stop Update** button.

4. Click **OK** to close the Properties dialog box.

In this lesson, you learned how to control offline viewing. In the next lesson, you'll learn how to change the Netcaster options.

Customizing Netcaster

In this lesson, you learn how to customize Netcaster.

Changing the Layout of the Netcaster Window

By default, the Netcaster window opens on the right side of your screen. You have the option of changing which side cf the screen Netcaster opens on. You change the layout options using the Options dialog box. In this dialog box, you also have the opportunity to set a default channel. The default channel will open automatically whenever you open Netcaster. Follow these steps to change the window layout:

1. From the Netcaster window, click the **Options** button.

2. Click the **Layout** tab. The position controls appear, as shown in Figure 5.1.

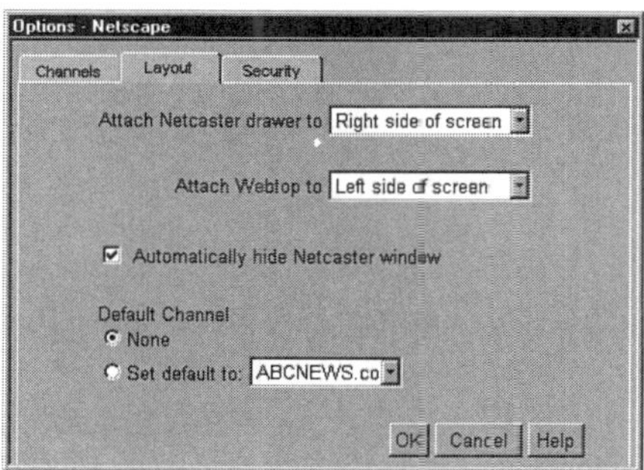

Figure 5.1   Changing the position of the Netcaster window.

3. To change the position of the Netcaster window, open the drop-down list next to **Attach Netcaster Drawer To**. You will be given the option to open the Netcaster window on the left side of the screen or the right side.

4. You can also change the position of Webtops by opening the drop-down list next to **Attach Webtop To**.

5. The Automatically Hide Netcaster Window check box is selected by default so that the Netcaster window closes when you launch a channel. If you would rather leave the Netcaster window open, click to remove the check mark from the box.

6. The next section allows you to select a default channel. The default channel will open automatically when you start Netcaster. If you want to set a default channel, click the **Set Default To** option button and choose a channel from the drop-down list.

7. Click **OK** to close the Options dialog box.

Setting Security Options

In addition to the standard security options available in Netscape Communicator, Netcaster has a few security options of its own. The Netcaster security options deal with Castanet and how much control of your PC you are willing to give it. As you learned in Lesson 1, Castanet is a program by Marimba that information providers use to create channels. The security tab in the Options dialog box (see Figure 5.2) enables you to control the security of these Castanet channels.

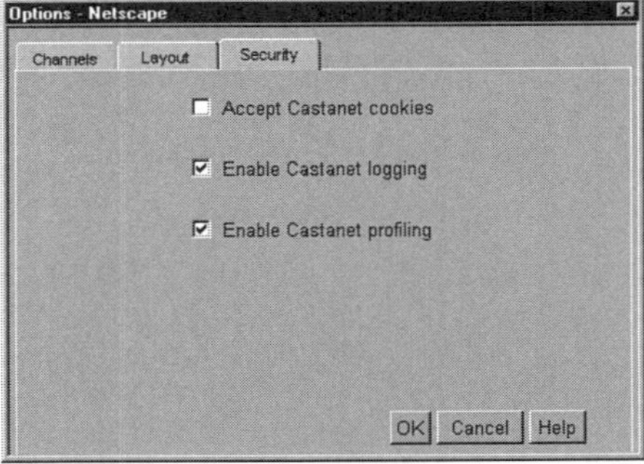

Figure 5.2   Netcaster's security options.

You can select the following options on the Security tab:

Accept Castanet Cookies   A Castanet cookie is similar to any other cookie, but it is specific to Castanet channels. Remember, cookies offer a standard way for Internet sites to interact with you and to store user-specific information. By default, this option is turned off.

Enable Castanet Logging   When Castanet logging is turned on, Netcaster records your mouse clicks and image displays on a specific channel. This enables the channel you are viewing to customize itself to your needs. For example, if you frequently click links related to a certain topic, the channel can offer more links related to your interests. This option is turned on by default.

Enable Castanet Profiling   Profiling is similar to logging, but it stores more permanent information (such as your e-mail address, what language you use, and so on). When Netcaster creates a Castanet Profile, the information is available to all Castanet channels. This option is on by default.

Changing Channel Options

Anytime you need to change a property for a specific channel or how the channels interact, you can use the Channels tab in the Options dialog box. Follow these steps to change channel options:

1. Click the **Options** button in the Netcaster window.

2. Click the **Channels** tab, and the dialog box shown in Figure 5.3 opens.

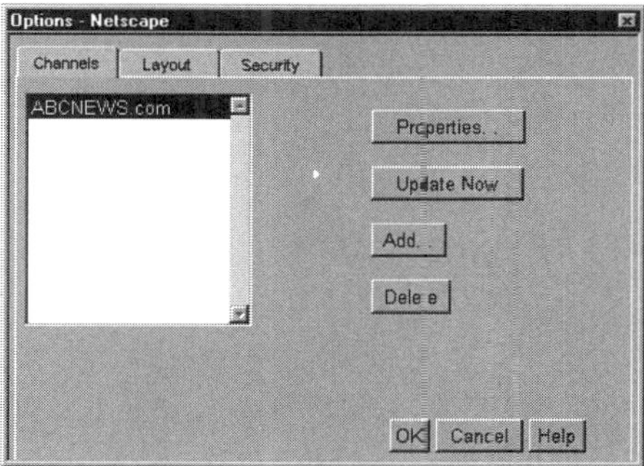

Figure 5.3   You can change the channel options from here.

3. If you need to change a channel's properties, highlight the channel and click the **Properties** button (Lessons 2 and 4 go into detail on channel properties).

4. If you want to update a channel, highlight it and click the **Update Now** button.

5. To add a new channel, click the **Add** button. (See Lesson 2 for more details on adding channels to your My Channels list.)

6. If you no longer want a channel to be part of your list, highlight it and click the **Delete** button.

7. When you finish changing the channel options, click **OK** to close the dialog box.

In this lesson, you learned how to customize Netcaster.

Netscape Messenger

Setting Up Netscape Messenger

In this lesson, you learn how to configure Netscape's e-mail program, Netscape Messenger.

What Is E-Mail?

E-mail (short for *electronic mail*) is the process by which messages are sent electronically from one PC to another. E-mail can be transmitted over network cables from one person to another on the same company network, or it can be sent over the Internet to a person located further away by use of a *modem*.

Before the advent of electronic mail, businesses used either the snail-like postal service to send their correspondence or some high-priced delivery service. But with e-mail, you can send information across the U.S. or across the world in a relatively short time—from a few minutes to a few hours, depending on Internet traffic.

Modem   Short for *modulator-demodulator*, a modem is a device that translates computer information into sound and then transmits those sounds over conventional telephone lines. The modem at the receiving end translates the sounds back into computer data.

Netscape Communicator includes its own e-mail program called Netscape Messenger. With Netscape Messenger, you can send e-mail to anyone else on the Internet and to people who use any of the popular online services such as CompuServe, The Microsoft Network, and America Online. You'll learn how to send and retrieve e-mail messages using Netscape Messenger in upcoming lessons.

Configuring Netscape Messenger

Before you can use Netscape Messenger, you'll need to get some information from your Internet service provider. You need to know the following things:

- The address of your Internet provider's POP (Post Office Protocol) server
- The address of your Internet provider's SMTP (Simple Mail Transfer Protocol) server
- Your specific e-mail address
- Your password for receiving mail (which is probably the same as your Internet logon password)

To configure Netscape Messenger, you'll complete five dialog box screens. Luckily, you don't have to make many changes to the information on those screens.

Completing the Appearance Screen

Follow these steps to begin configuring Netscape Messenger:

1. The first thing you need to do is open Netscape Messenger. If you are already in Navigator, you can just click the **Mailbox** icon in the Communicator taskbar. If you are not running Navigator, open the **Start** menu, point to **Programs**, point to **Netscape Communicator,** and click **Netscape Messenger**.

2. Open the **Edit** menu and select **Preferences**.

3. Double-click the **Mail & Groups** category to see the options shown in Figure 1.1.

4. (Optional) Change the settings of any of the following options as necessary.

   Plain Quoted Text Beginning with ">" Is Displayed With   When you receive a reply to a message, the text from the original message will begin with >. To make the original message text stand out more, you can change the style, the size, and the color. For example, if you want the original text to be italic, select **Italic** from the **Style**

drop-down list. To change the size of the font, use the **Size** box, and to change the color of the original text, click in the **Color** text box.

Display Messages and Articles With   You can use a variable width font if you like. A fixed width font displays each character using the same amount of space, which might be important if you're reading a message whose characters seem to be "misaligned." Otherwise, you may find a variable width font easier to see, especially if your monitor is not very big.

Reuse Message List (Thread) Window   If this option is checked, when a new thread is read, it uses the same window as the previous thread. If you deselect this option, each new thread opens in a new window. (Your screen could get cluttered rather quickly if you choose not to reuse the thread window.)

Reuse Message Window   Keep this option checked to have Messenger use the same window for new messages. (This option is similar to the Reuse thread window option.)

Enable Sound Alert When Messages Arrive   Check this option to have Messenger sound a chime when new messages arrive.

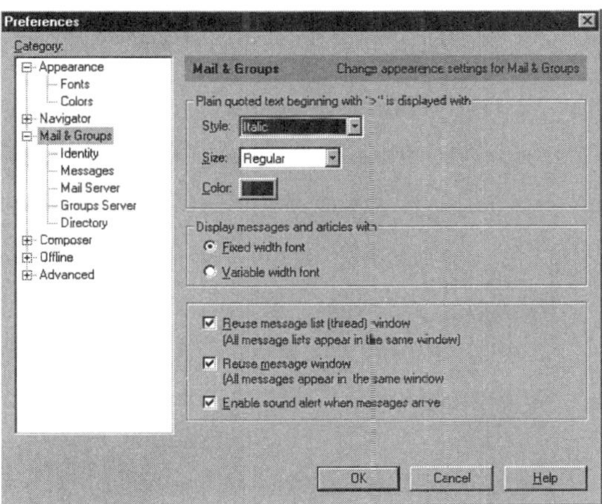

Figure 1.1   Configuring the Mail & Groups screen.

Don't close the Preferences dialog box; you still have several screens to complete.

Completing the Identity Screen

With the Preferences dialog box still open, follow these steps to complete the
Identity screen:

1. Click the **Identity** category to see the options shown in Figure 1.2.

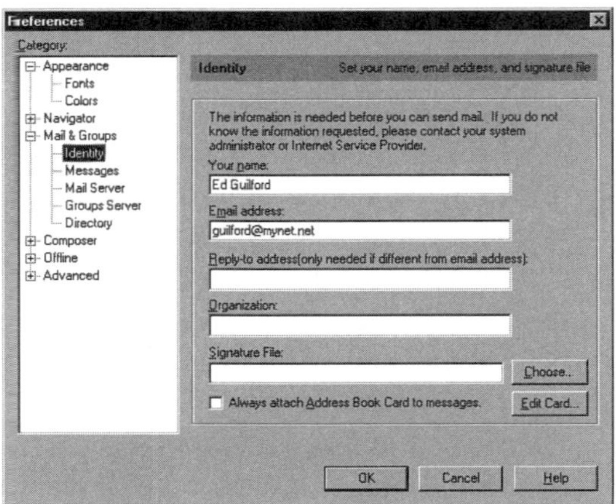

Figure 1.2   Configuring the Identity screen.

2. Fill in the **Your Name** text box.

3. Enter your full e-mail address in the **Email Address** text box.

4. (Optional) Fill in any of the following information that you want to
provide:

> **Reply-to Address**   If you want replies to go to an e-mail address
> other than the one above, fill in this box.
>
> **Organization**   Fill in this text box if you want users to see where you
> work.
>
> **Signature File**   If you want to attach a signature file with your
> e-mail messages, type the path to that file in this text box. (Or click
> **Choose**, select your signature file, and click **Open**.)
>
> **Always Attach Address Book Card to Messages**   Check this option
> to attach an address book entry to messages you send. (This is like
> enclosing your business card with each e-mail.)

Signature File   A text file that usually includes your name and some kind of logo or picture (or maybe a quotation or some other feature that uniquely identifies you to the reader). A signature usually consists of spaces and other characters such as x, l, and - that form a particular pattern, like this:

J Byrd   8-)

To create a signature file, open Notepad or WordPad, type your name, and then create a simple picture. Save the file as SIGN.TXT. Then return to the Identity tab of the Preferences dialog box and select the file. The signature file will always be appended to the end of your outgoing messages.

If you're going to attach a personal address book card to every outgoing message, you might want to edit the card to meet your own needs. To edit the address book card follow these steps:

1. Click the **Edit Card** button at the bottom of the Identity screen. The Card dialog box opens (see Figure 1.3)

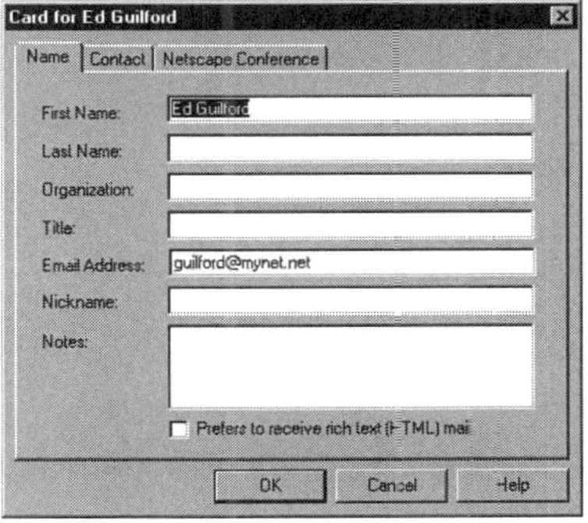

Figure 1.3   Your personal information can be entered in this card.

2. Enter your personal information in the Name screen.

3. Click the **Contact** tab, and then enter your address, phone, and fax numbers.

4. When your Personal Address Book Card is complete, click **OK**.

Leave the Preferences dialog box open and go on to the next section.

Completing the Messages Screen

With the Preferences dialog box open, follow these steps to continue configuring
Netscape Messenger:

1. Click the **Messages** category, and you'll see the options shown in
Figure 1.4.

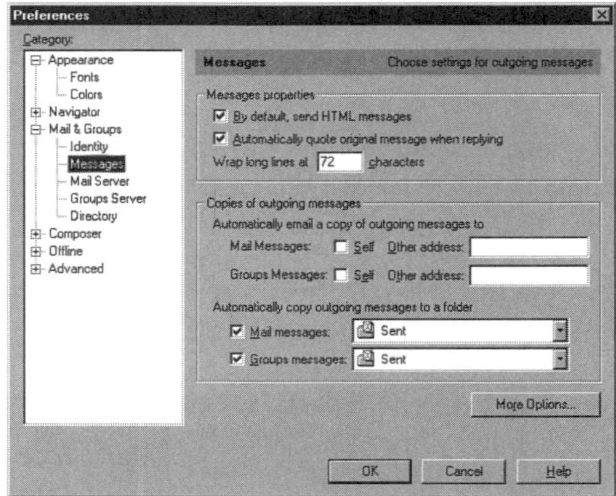

Figure 1.4   Configuring the Messages screen.

2. (Optional) Change the settings of any of the following options as necessary
to suit your needs:

By Default, Send HTML Messages   You can check this box to send
messages in HTML format.

Watch That HTML   Be careful about sending messages in HTML format.
Whoever is going to read the message must have an HTML-compliant e-mail
program (such as Messenger) to make any sense of the message.

CAUTION

Automatically Quote Original Message When Replying   This is
turned on by default. Turn it off if you don't want to follow the
convention of including a copy of the original message in your reply.

I Don't Want to Include All of the Message   If you don't want to
include all of the original message in your reply, or if you don't want to include

TIP

any of it in a particular reply, you should leave this option checked and just delete all or part of the copied text.

> **Wrap Long Lines At**   Change this number if you want long lines of text to wrap to the next line. When you read your messages, if the text at the end of the lines is not visible, you may want to use a smaller number here.

> **Automatically Email a Copy of Outgoing Messages To**   If you want to send a copy of all your e-mail messages to some other e-mail address, enter that address here. (This might be useful if you wanted to always send a copy of your messages to your boss, for example.) If you want to send a copy of every message to yourself, click the **Self** check box.

What About the Groups?   Don't worry about the Groups options right now. You'll learn about those in Part 4.

CAUTION

> **Automatically Copy Outgoing Messages to a Folder**   Netscape Messenger automatically saves copies of your e-mail messages in a file called "Sent." If you want the messages saved in another location, specify a folder path here.

Don't click OK just yet; it's time to complete the information on the Mail Server screen.

Completing the Mail Server Screen

In the Preferences dialog box, complete the Mail Server screen by following these steps:

1. Click the **Mail Server** category to see the options shown in Figure 1.5.

2. In the **Mail Server User Name** text box, enter your e-mail name (the part of your e-mail address that comes before the @ sign).

3. Enter the addresses of your service provider's outgoing and incoming mail servers in the appropriate text boxes.

I Don't Have an Outgoing Server   If your service provider didn't give you the name of the outgoing server, it is probably the same as the incoming server.

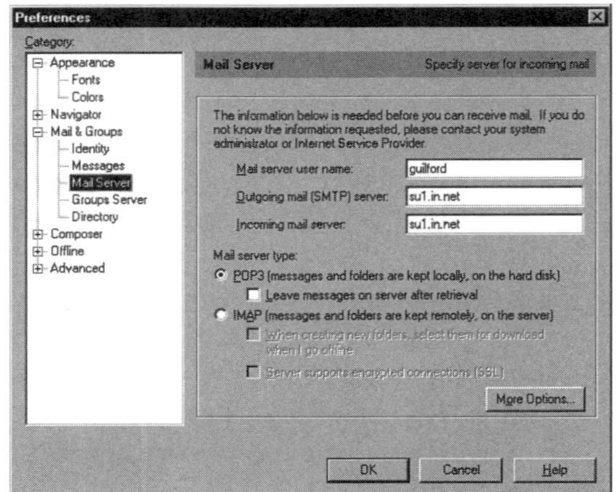

Figure 1.5 Configuring the Mail Server screen.

4. (Optional) Change any of the following options to suit your needs:

> **Mail Server Type**   Most mail servers use POP3. If there is any question, contact your service provider.

> **Leave Messages on Server After Retrieval**   When this box is checked, a copy of your messages remains on the server after you download them. After you get used to using Netscape Messenger, you should deselect this option, which deletes messages from your Internet provider's hard disk after you receive them. (Your Internet provider likes this option best because it saves disk space on his server.)

5. To view the rest of the options, click the **More Options** button at the bottom of the screen.

> **Local Mail Directory**   Enter a new path in this text box (or click the **Choose** button) if you want to change the directory in which Netscape Messenger saves your incoming messages.

> **IMAP Mail Directory**   If you are using an IMAP mail server, type in a local directory to save a copy of your folders.

> **Check for Mail Every**   Type an interval (such as 10) in the text box if you want Netscape to automatically check for your e-mail whenever it's running.

Remember My Mail Password   Check this box so Messenger will not prompt you for a password every time you check your mail. If you have people use your computer that you don't want to see your messages, leave this option unchecked.

Use Netscape Messenger from MAPI-Based Applications   Check this box if you want Messenger to be your default e-mail program in your applications. (For example, if you use the **File, Send** command in Microsoft Word, Messenger will open to send the message.)

Click **OK** to close the More information dialog box, but don't close the Preferences dialog box quite yet. You still have one more screen to complete.

Completing the Directory Screen

Follow these steps to complete the final screen for configuring Netscape Messenger.

1. Click the **Directory** category to see the options shown in Figure 1.6.

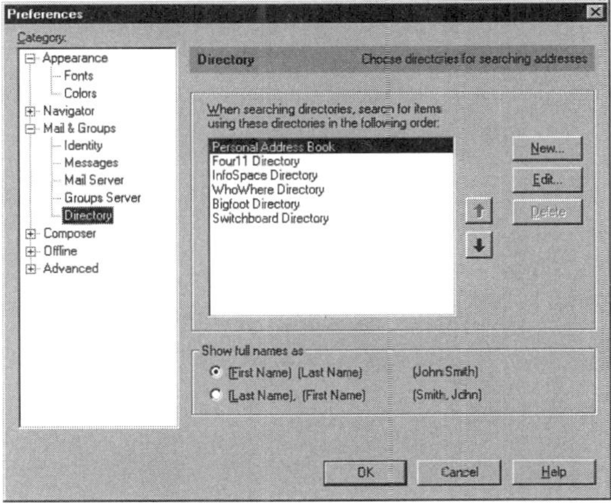

Figure 1.6   Configuring the Directory screen.

2. For the most part, you can leave this screen as it is. If you want, you can change the order in which a directory will appear when you use it. For example, if you use your personal address book the most, leave it at the top. If you want to move one, click the directory to highlight it, and then click the arrows to move it.

What's Bigfoot?   Bigfoot and Four11 are e-mail search pages that allow you to search for e-mail and street addresses, as well as phone numbers.

3. (Optional) If you want Netscape Messenger to show names with the last name first, select the **(Last Name), (First Name)** option.

4. Congratulations, you're done configuring Netscape Messenger! Click **OK**.

If you weren't sure which options to choose as you were making your selections throughout this lesson, just keep in mind that you can return to the Preferences dialog box at any time.

In this lesson, you learned how to configure Netscape Messenger. In the next lesson, you'll learn how to send e-mail messages.

Sending E-Mail Messages

In this lesson, you learn how to send e-mail messages with Netscape Messenger.

Understanding E-Mail Addresses

After you've configured Netscape Messenger, you're ready to send or receive messages. You'll learn about receiving e-mail in the next lesson. But before you learn how to send an e-mail message, you need to learn about e-mail addresses and how they work.

You can send e-mail to anyone who's connected to the Internet directly or anyone who's connected indirectly through an Internet service provider or an online service such as CompuServe, The Microsoft Network, or America Online. To send an e-mail message to someone, you have to know his e-mail address. An Internet e-mail address looks something like this:

jnoname@que.mcp.com

The part of the address before the @ sign is the person's user name (the name by which he is known to his home system). Most user names consist of the person's first initial and last name run together, as in *jnoname*. The at symbol (@) separates the user name from the second part of the address, which is a location. The example address above is that of Que Corporation (the publisher of this book), which is part of Macmillan Computer Publishing. Therefore, part of the location is *que.mcp*. The last part of the location (*.com*) tells you that que.mcp is a commercial (business) venture. Other endings you will see include .edu (educational), .net (an Internet server), .org (nonprofit organization), .gov (government), and .mil (military).

All together, the example address tells the Internet system to send messages with this address to jnoname, located at que.mcp.com, which is some type of business or commercial enterprise.

CAUTION

Watch That Case!   When entering an e-mail address, be careful to use upper- and lowercase letters *exactly* as they are given to you. If someone tells you that his address is SAMBeldon@imagineTHAT.com, you must type the address exactly that way. He will not receive his mail if you send it to sambeldon@imaginethat.com because that is a completely different (or nonexistent) address.

E-mail addresses are a little different for persons connected to the Internet indirectly, such as through CompuServe or The Microsoft Network or users connecting via Internet service providers. In such cases, the person's e-mail location is his online service. The following list shows you the e-mail address format for each of the most popular online services.

Online Service	*Sample Address*
CompuServe	71354.1234@compuserve.com
America Online	joeblow@aol.com
Prodigy	joeblow@prodigy.com
The Microsoft Network	joeblow@msn.com

Creating and Sending E-Mail Messages

As soon as you have an e-mail address, you can start sending out e-mail messages. If you have several e-mail messages to send, you should create them offline (that is, while you're not connected to the Internet). This saves you from paying online charges while you're creating your missives. When you finish creating a message, you save it in your Outbox. Then, when you're ready to send all of your messages, you connect to the Internet and send everything in the Outbox at once.

Only Text Please   A basic e-mail message contains only text. If you want to include a file (such as a spreadsheet, chart, graphic, or word processing document) with your e-mail message, see Lesson 6 for help.

CAUTION

To create an e-mail message, follow these steps:

1. If you are running Netscape Navigator, click the **Mailbox** icon in the Communicator taskbar. (You do not need to connect to the Internet in order to create e-mail messages.)

If you're not running Navigator, open the **Start** menu, point to **Programs,** point to **Netscape Communicator,** and click **Netscape Messenger.**

2. Open the **File** menu, point to **New,** and select **Message.**

Quick Message   Instead of using the File menu, you can click the **New Msg** button on the Netscape Messenger toolbar to quickly create a message.

TIP

3. Click in the **To:** text box and enter the recipient's address. To enter a second address, separate it from the first address with a comma, as in **jfake@mcp.com,jblow@iu.edu.**

4. (Optional) To send a copy of your message to a third party, click the button to the left of the Address field and select **Cc:.** Enter that address in the **Cc:** text box. You can also choose from these other types of addresses by clicking the same button:

> **Reply-To**   Includes your e-mail address
>
> **Bcc**   Sends a blind carbon copy
>
> **Group**   Posts a message to a newsgroup
>
> **Followup-To**   Includes a different e-mail address for follow-ups to your message

Fast Addressing   Netscape Navigator lets you save and reuse the addresses of people to whom you send e-mail often. See Lesson 5 for details.

TIP

5. Enter a subject in the **Subject**: text box.

6. Click in the message area and type your message (see Figure 2.1).

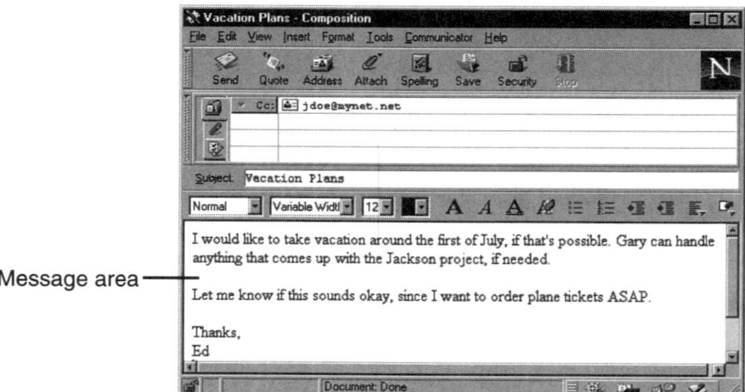

Figure 2.1 Type your e-mail message in the message area.

Getting Attached You can attach a file to send with your message if you want. See Lesson 6 for instructions.

7. To send your message now, first, connect to the Internet. Then click the **Send** button. (Alternatively, you can defer delivery until you've created all the messages you want to send. Don't click Send; instead, see the next section for help.)

8. Repeat steps 2 through 7 to create additional e-mail messages.

Messages sent over the Internet often take a rather circuitous route to their destination. So your e-mail message may take anywhere from a few minutes to a few hours to reach its intended party. Even so, e-mail is a lot faster than regular mail.

When your messages have been sent, they are moved from the Outbox to the Sent folder. (The first time you send messages, the Sent folder is automatically created.) To view a message you've sent, click the folder list drop-down arrow and select **Sent**; then click the message you want to view. It appears in the bottom pane, as shown in Figure 2.2. (If the bottom pane is not visible, click the blue arrow at the left end of the status bar.)

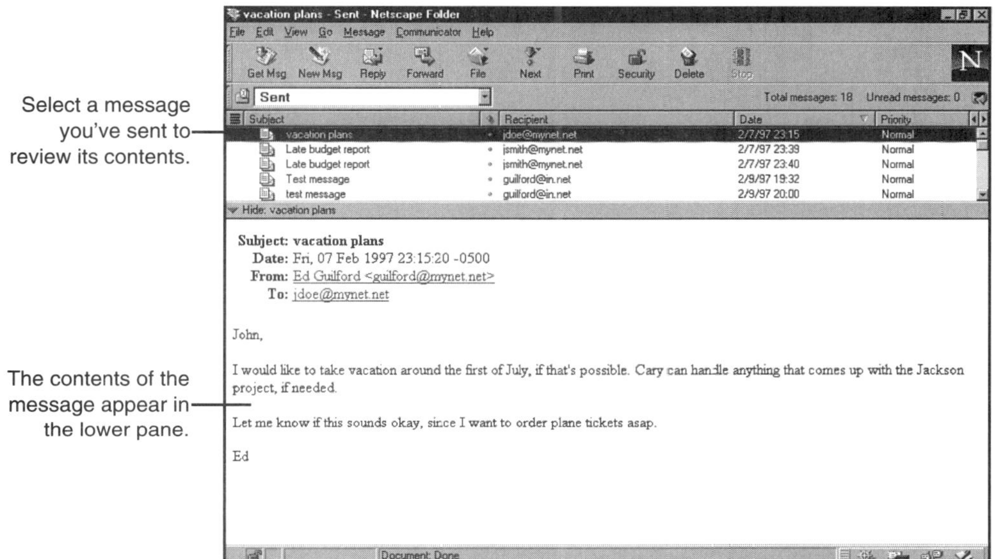

Select a message you've sent to review its contents.

The contents of the message appear in the lower pane.

Figure 2.2   You can review any message you've sent

Not Really Sent   If a message cannot be delivered because the address is invalid, you'll receive a message from your service provider's mail program letting you know (although you may not receive the message for hours or even days). So after you send messages, you should check your Inbox (as explained in Lesson 3) to see if you've been notified that any of your messages didn't reach their destination.

CAUTION

Many Web pages include a button you can use to send messages to the Web page's owner (usually known as the Webmaster). When you click such a button, Netscape automatically displays the Netscape Messenger New Message window so you can type your message. (The address of the Webmaster is automatically inserted for you.) When you finish creating the message, follow the previous steps to send your comments to the Webmaster.

Sending E-Mail Messages at a Later Time

You can create messages and save them for sending at a later time. This allows you to work offline, creating several messages and sending them later, after you connect to the Internet.

To delay sending your messages, follow these steps:

1. Create your message as usual.

2. Before you click the **Send** button to send your message, open the **Edit** menu, select **Preferences**, click the **Offline** category, and select **Offline Work Mode**.

CAUTION

Offline Work Mode   When you turn on the Offline Work Mode option, all of your messages from that point forward will be stored in the Outbox whenever you click Send. They will not be delivered until you tell Netscape Messenger to deliver what's in the Outbox. To change this setting so that Netscape Messenger delivers your mail immediately when you click the Send button, open the **Edit** menu, select **Preferences**, and select **Online Work Mode**. Of ccurse, if you're not connected to the Internet when you click Send, you'll get an error when Netscape Messenger tries to deliver your mail.

3. Click the **Send** button, and Netscape Messenger places your message in the Outbox for delivery at a later time.

4. Create and save additional messages as needed.

5. When you're ready to send your messages, connect to the Internet in the usual manner.

6. Start Netscape if needed.

7. Open the **File** menu and select **Send Unsent Messages**.

Copying Text from Other Messages

You can copy text from another message or any document file (such as a word processing document) using the Edit, Copy and the Edit, Paste commands. The following steps teach you how to copy and paste data into your messages.

1. Open the message or document that contains the text you want to copy to your message, and select the text.

2. Open the **Edit** menu and select either **Copy** (to copy the text) or **Cut** (to move it).

3. Start **Netscape Messenger** and open a new message window by clicking the **New Msg** button.

4. Click in the message area where you want the copied text to appear.

5. Open the **Edit** menu and select **Paste**. If you want the recipient to know that the copied text came from another document, select **Paste As Quotation** instead of Paste. The text appears with > marks in front of it, which indicates that it came from another source (see Figure 2.3).

Fast Copy   Because Netscape supports drag and drop, you can use a shortcut to the preceding steps. To do so, open a new message window. Then open an old message, select the text you want to copy, and drag it into the new message window.

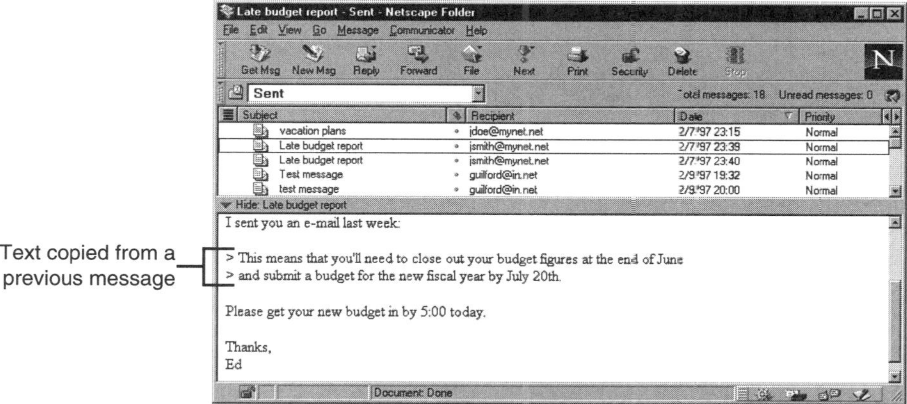

Text copied from a previous message

Figure 2.3   You can make copied text appear as a quotation.

In this lesson, you learned how to send e-mail messages. In the next lesson, you'll learn how to retrieve and read messages sent to you.

Retrieving Your E-Mail Messages

In this lesson, you learn how to retrieve messages sent to you over the Internet.

Retrieving an e-mail message is like going to your mailbox and checking for mail. When you find mail in your mailbox, you take it out, open it, and read it. Netscape Messenger does basically the same thing: It goes to your electronic mailbox (located on your Internet provider's computer), checks for mail, and brings back anything it finds.

By default, Netscape Messenger checks for new mail only when you tell it to. You can have it check for mail whenever you want with a click of your mouse. However, if you prefer to do things simply, you can configure Netscape Messenger to check for mail automatically at regular intervals.

Password-Protected   You'll need your e-mail password to retrieve your mail. This is usually the same password that you use to log on to the Internet. If you're not sure what your password is, or if your logon password doesn't work, contact your service provider for help.

CAUTION

After Netscape Messenger retrieves your mail, you open each message to read it. You can print an open message if you want, or you can save its contents in a text file. You can also reply to the message by sending an e-mail message back to the originator.

Retrieving Your E-Mail

To retrieve your e-mail, follow these steps:

1. Connect to the Internet and open Netscape Messenger. If you are already in Navigator, you can just click the **Mailbox** icon in the Communicator taskbar. If you are not running Navigator, open the **Start** menu, point to **Programs**, point to **Netscape Communicator,** and click **Netscape Messenger.**

2. Click the **Get Msg** icon on the toolbar (or open the **File** menu, point to **Get Messages**, and click **New**). The Password Entry Dialog dialog box appears (see Figure 3.1).

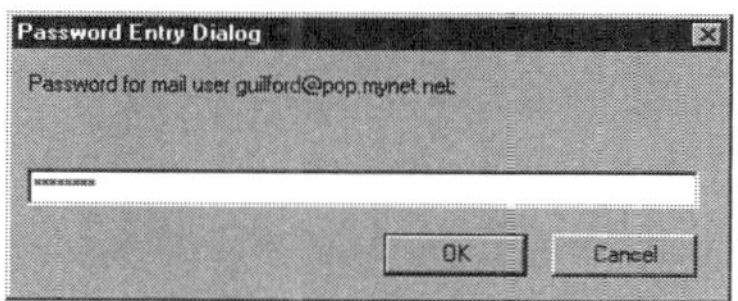

Figure 3.1   Enter your e-mail password.

3. Enter your password and click **OK.** (Asterisks are displayed in the password box when you type to keep observers from seeing your password.) Netscape Messenger checks for mail. If you have new messages, Mail copies them to your system and places them in the Inbox. If you don't have any messages, you'll see a dialog box telling you so.

Repeat steps 2 and 3 whenever you want to check for new mail. To view your new messages, see the section "Opening an E-Mail Message," later in this lesson.

Save Money   After you retrieve your e-mail, when you're ready to read through it, disconnect from the Internet so you won't pay connect charges while you view your messages.

Configuring Messenger to Remember Your Password

You can configure Netscape to allow you to check your mail without having to enter your password each time. (You will still have to enter the password the very first time you use Netscape Messenger, though.) Follow these steps:

1. From Netscape Messenger, open the **Edit** menu and select **Preferences**.

2. Click the **Mail Server** category (under **Mail & Groups**) and click the **More Options** button near the bottom of the dialog box (see Figure 3.2)

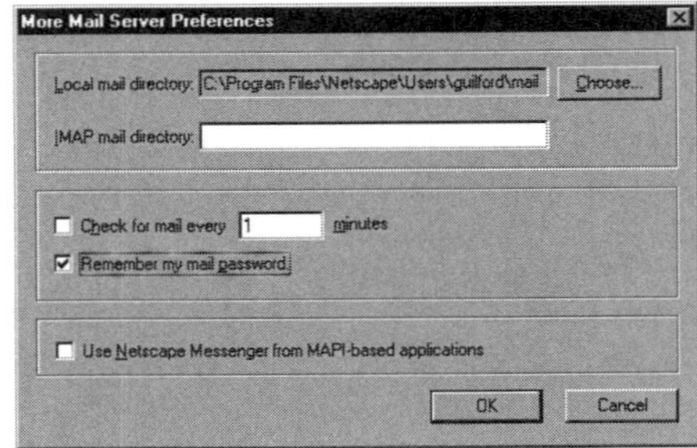

Figure 3.2   Configuring Messenger to remember your password.

3. Check the **Remember My Mail Password** check box.

4. Click **OK,** and then click **OK** again to close the Preferences dialog box.

The next time you check for mail, Messenger will ask you to type in your password. Every time you check your mail after that, you will not be asked for your password.

I Want Messenger to Ask for the Password   If you later change your mind and want Messenger to ask for your password every time you check your mail, just repeat the steps above and uncheck the check box in step 3.

Checking Your Mail Automatically

You can easily configure Netscape Messenger to check for mail at regular intervals when Messenger is running. When it finds new mail, Netscape Messenger notifies you by changing the envelope icon on the status bar to a folder icon with a green diamond next to it. You can then decide whether to retrieve it or not.

What About Navigator?   You don't have to have Messenger running in order to receive notification when you get mail. The envelope icon in the Communicator taskbar changes when you get a new message.

Follow these steps to set up Netscape Messenger to check for e-mail automatically:

1. Open the **Edit** menu and select **Preferences**.

2. Under **Mail & Groups**, click the **Mail Servers** category and click the **More Options** button near the bottom of the dialog box.

3. Enter a time interval in the **Check for Mail Every __ Minutes** text box, and then make sure the check box is checked.

4. Click **OK**.

Error! If Netscape Messenger doesn't know your password (because you aren't using the Remember Mail Password option), or if you haven't yet opened the Netscape Messenger window (so you can enter the password), Messenger will try to check periodically for mail, but it will fail. When this happens, a question mark appears next to the envelope icon at the right end of the Messenger status bar.

CAUTION

Using Netscape Mail Notification

Communicator comes with a program that can monitor your e-mail without even opening Messenger. It's called Netscape Mail Notification. This program checks your e-mail and lets you know when you get a new message. When you do, you can just double-click the Mail Notification icon to open Messenger. Netscape Mail Notification works best when you have a dedicated Internet line to your computer. Otherwise, you will have to constantly dial in to the Internet.

To turn on Netscape Mail Notification, follow these steps:

1. Open the **Start** menu, point to **Programs**, point to **Netscape Communicator**, point to **Utilities**, and click **Netscape Mail Notification**. The Mail Notification icon appears on your taskbar (see Figure 3.3).

2. Right-click the icon, and a Properties sheet appears. Click **Options**. The Options dialog box shown in Figure 3.4 opens. (If you double-click the icon instead of right-clicking, Netscape Messenger opens.)

3. Under Frequency, enter a number in the **Check for Mail Every** text box. The default is every minute, which is fine if you have a dedicated Internet connection. However, if you don't have a dedicated connection, you'll probably want to enter something a little more reasonable, like 30 or 60.

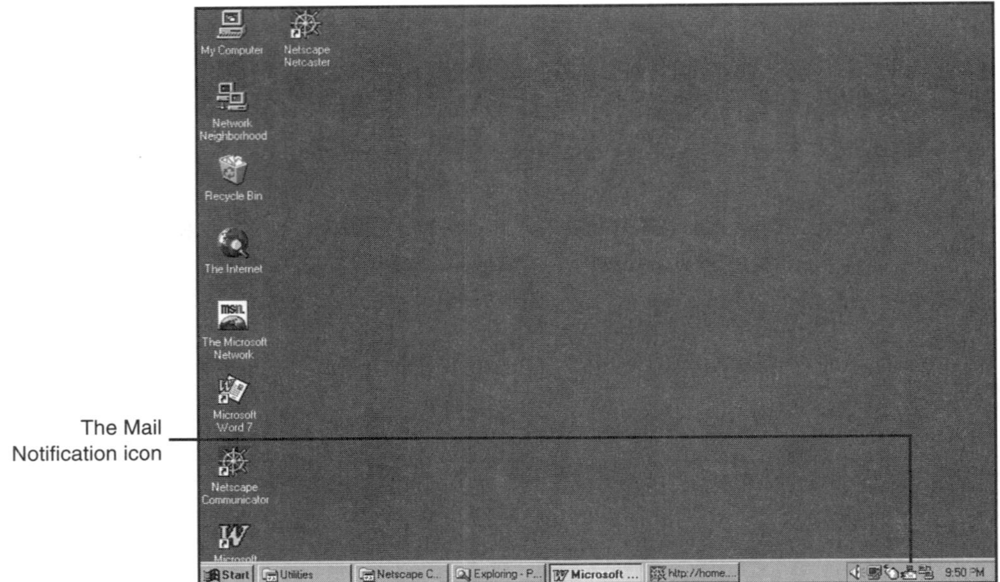

The Mail
Notification icon

Figure 3.3 Netscape's Mail Notification icon appears on the taskbar.

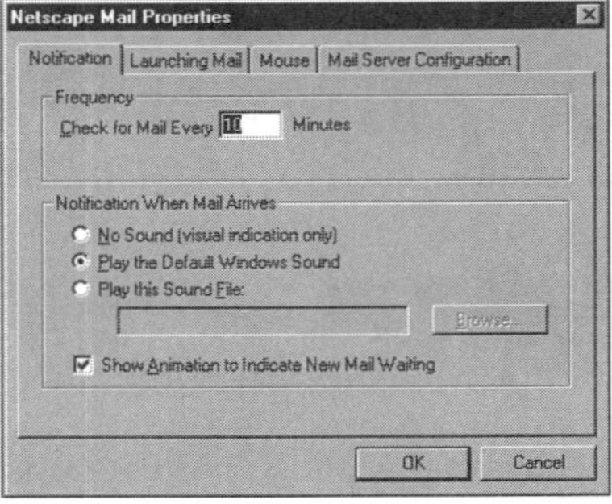

Figure 3.4 Mail Notification properties.

4. (Optional) You can change how Mail Notification lets you know when you get a new message. You can have it play the Windows default sound, another sound file of your choice, or no sound at all. Click whichever option suits your fancy.

5. Click **OK** to close the Netscape Mail Properties dialog box.

This is really all you need to know to run Netscape Mail Notification. After you turn it on, it runs quietly in the background until you receive a new message. At that point, you can launch Messenger to read the new message.

Opening an E-Mail Message

Your new mail is placed in the Inbox. To view the messages, click the **Inbox** folder. Messages appear in the Inbox window. Unread messages appear in bold text and are marked with an envelope icon, as shown in Figure 3.5 (there will also be a green diamond in the third column marking unread messages). Click the message you want to open, and its contents appear in the bottom pane. If necessary, scroll down to read the complete message.

There Is No Bottom Window   If the bottom pane is not visible in Messenger, click the blue triangle icon at the left end of the status bar.

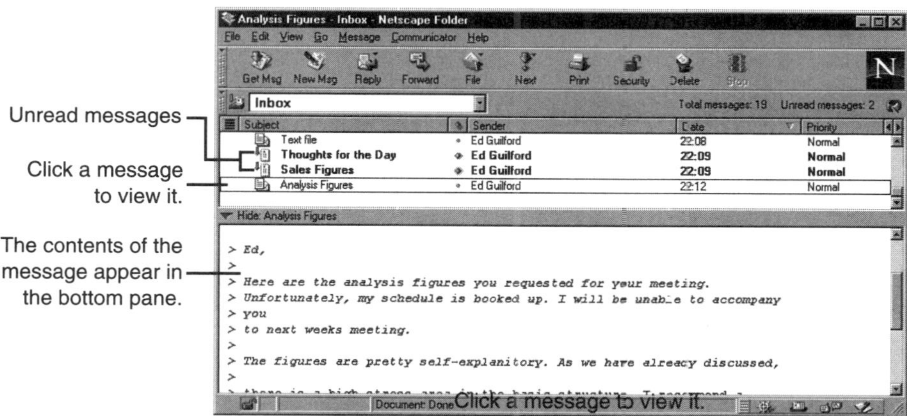

Figure 3.5   Unread messages in the Inbox appear in bold.

Order, Please   By default, Netscape Messenger displays messages in the order in which they were received. You can select a different sort order using the **View**, **Sort** command. If you want Netscape Messenger to use a different sort order all the time, you can configure it to do so. See Lesson 1 for help.

Can't See Enough?   If you're having trouble viewing part of a message or the message list, you can adjust the size of either of the panes by dragging its border.

To view the next message in the list, simply click it. You can quickly open the next unread message by clicking the **Next** button.

If you read a message that you want to note for some particular reason, you can flag it so that you can easily find it again. To do so, click within the flag icon column (next to the Priority column header) in the message pane. A flag icon appears, marking the message.

What Flag Column?   The flag column may not be visible. If you can't seeit, maximize the Messenger window. If you still can't see the flag column, click the left arrow at the right end of the column headings until the flag column appears.

If you want to print the open e-mail message, open the **File** menu and select **Print**.

Files Attached   If a file is attached to your message, you must follow the steps in Lesson 6 to retrieve the file.

To save the contents of the message in a text file, open the **File** menu and select **Save As**. The Save As dialog box appears. Change to a different folder if necessary, type a name for the new file, and click **Save**.

Responding to E-Mail Messages

You can reply to or forward any message you receive. When you reply to a message, Netscape Messenger automatically fills in the address of the originator in your new message. All you have to do is type your reply and then send the message. You can reply to all the recipients of the original message (using the **Reply to All** command) or just the sender.

When you reply to a message, Netscape automatically includes the text of the original message for reference. As explained in Lesson 1, you can customize Netscape Messenger so that the original text is not included if you want. Or, if you like to include the original text most of the time, you can just delete any text you don't want to include in a particular reply.

You'll learn how to forward a message in just a minute. To reply to a message, follow these steps:

1. Click the message to which you want to reply.

If It's Already Open...   If the message you want to reply to is currently open, skip to step 2.

2. Click the **Reply** button on the toolbar (or choose **Reply** from the **Message** menu). In the menu that appears, choose **Reply To Sender** or **Reply To Sender and All Recipients**. Netscape Messenger opens a Compose window and updates the appropriate header information, filling in the To:, Cc:, and Subject: lines as necessary. The text from the original message appears in the message area. When you reply to a message, each line of the original message is marked with an arrow (>) as shown in Figure 3.6.

Where's the Original Text?   By default, Netscape Mail does not show you the contents of the original message in the reply window (the recipient will still see the text). To view or edit the original text, open the **File** menu and select **Include Original Text**, or click the **Quote** button.

Delete That!   If you want to delete any of the lines from the original message, just select them and press **Delete**. In addition, if you want to respond to a message point-by-point, you can type your reply between the lines of the original message. Place the cursor at the end of an original line and press **Enter** to create a blank line on which you can type.

3. Type your message under the copy of the original message.

4. Send your message as usual by clicking the **Send** button.

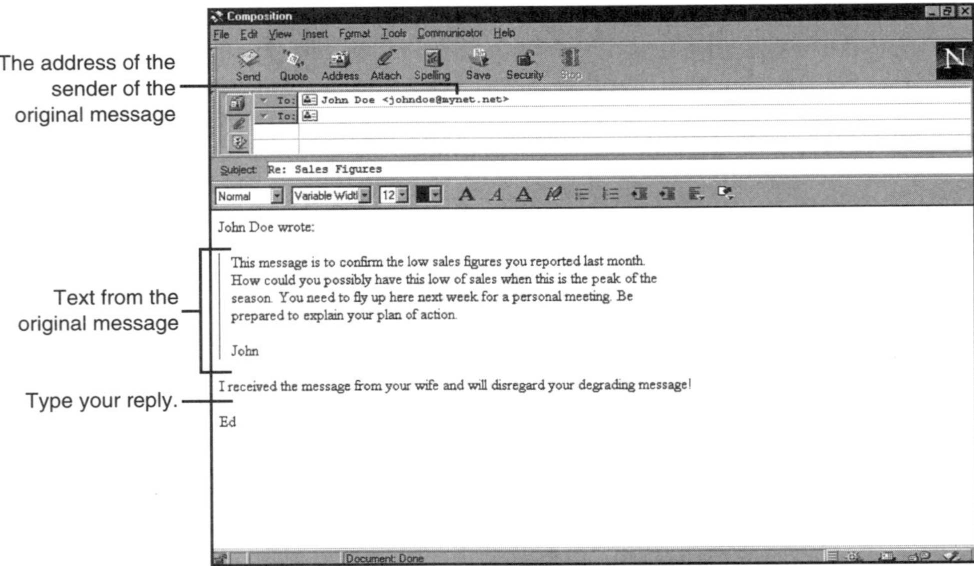

Figure 3.6 Replying to an e-mail message.

Forwarding a Message Instead

When you forward a message to someone else, Netscape Messenger sends a copy of the original message to the person you indicate and allows you to add your own message if you want. You can forward the original message as a quotation (by using the **Forward Quoted** command), in which case the contents of the original message appear preceded by > symbols.

Follow these steps to forward a message to someone else:

1. Click the message you want to forward. If the message you want to forward is currently open, skip to step 2.

2. Open the **Message** menu and select **Forward** or **Forward Quoted**. Notice that, when you forward a message, its text is not copied into the window. If you want to see the original text, click the **Quote** icon in the toolbar.

Quick Forward To forward a message quickly, click the **Forward** button at the top of the Mail window as a shortcut to step 2.

3. Type your message.

4. Send your message as usual by clicking the **Send** button.

In this lesson, you learned how to retrieve messages, open them, and reply to them. In the next lesson, you'll learn how to organize your incoming and outgoing e-mail messages.

Organizing Your E-Mail

In this lesson, you learn how to organize the e-mail messages you send and receive.

Arranging Your Messages

By default, Netscape Messenger arranges your e-mail messages in the order in which they were received (by date). This arrangement may not be very useful if you're trying to locate a single message in a long list, especially if you can't remember exactly when you received it.

Messenger provides you with seven options you can use to determine the sort order. To arrange your e-mail, select the folder whose messages you want to arrange. Then open the **View** menu, select **Sort**, and choose from the following options:

By Date	Sorts messages by the date on which they were created.
By Flag	Sorts messages according to whether or not they are flagged.
By Priority	Sorts messages by the priority that was set by the message sender.
By Sender	Sorts messages according to who sent them.
By Size	Sorts messages based on their sizes.
By Status	Sorts messages by their status.
By Subject	Sorts messages by subject.
By Thread	Sorts messages according to their thread.
By Unread	Separates unread messages from those you have read.

What's a Thread?   A thread is a collection of messages that follow a particular subject. The thread begins when you receive a reply to a message.

These options are grouped as option buttons: When you select one, you automatically deselect all the others. In other words, you can't use these options in combination, such as By Sender arranged within Date.

Ascending sorts messages in ascending order. If you sort messages by date, newer messages appear at the top of the list, and older messages appear at the bottom. If you sort messages by subject, those whose subjects begin with the letter A are listed last, and those subjects that begin with Z are placed at the top of the list. If you do not select this option, messages are automatically arranged in descending order.

New Messages on Top   To sort your list so that new messages appear at the top, make sure the Ascending option is selected.

You can also sort your messages by clicking the buttons at the top of the message list, as shown in Figure 4.1. To sort messages by date, click the **Date** button; to sort by sender, click the **Sender** button.

Click here to arrange messages by sender.

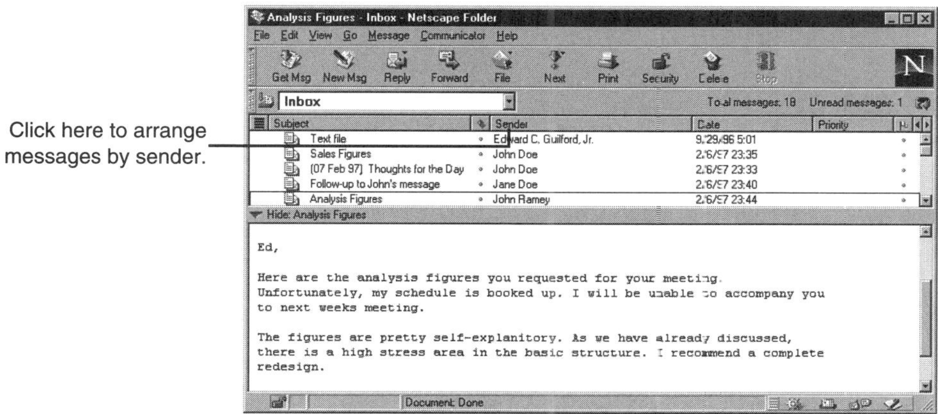

Figure 4.1   Messages arranged by sender.

Creating Folders

Once you start using Netscape Messenger, it's easy to accumulate a number of messages in a short time. With all this correspondence building up, you're quickly going to need some way to organize it.

By default, all incoming messages are placed in the Inbox folder. Likewise, outgoing messages (messages you send) are placed in the Sent folder. As you'll see in a moment, you can create additional folders in which you can group related messages.

Although there's no limit to the number of folders you can create, you won't want to create so many that they become unmanageable. After you create the folders, you can copy or move messages from the Inbox into your folders.

To create a folder, follow these steps:

1. Just above the window that contains your message is a box with the word "Inbox" in it. This tells you that you are viewing the contents of the Inbox folder. Click the drop-down arrow in this box and select **Mail**. The Netscape Message Center opens (see Figure 4.2).

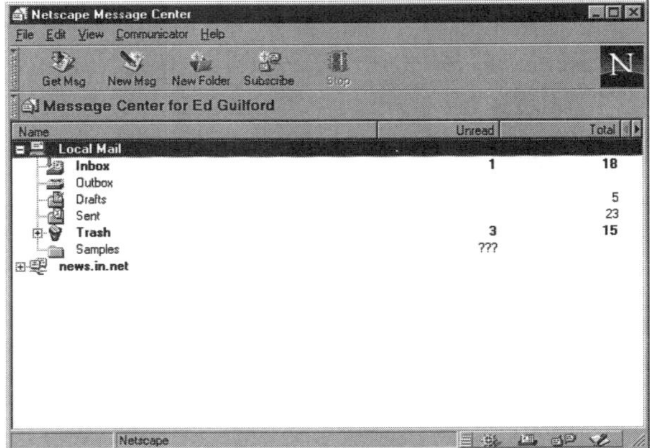

Figure 4.2   The Netscape Message Center shows all your folders.

2. Open the **File** menu and select **New Folder**.

3. Type a name for your new folder. (You can include spaces.)

4. From the drop-down list, choose the folder under which you want your new folder placed.

5. Click **OK**, and your new folder appears in the folder list along with the other folders. Figure 4.3 shows the new folder in the list.

Your new folder is ready to use. You can now copy or move messages into this folder by following the steps in the next section.

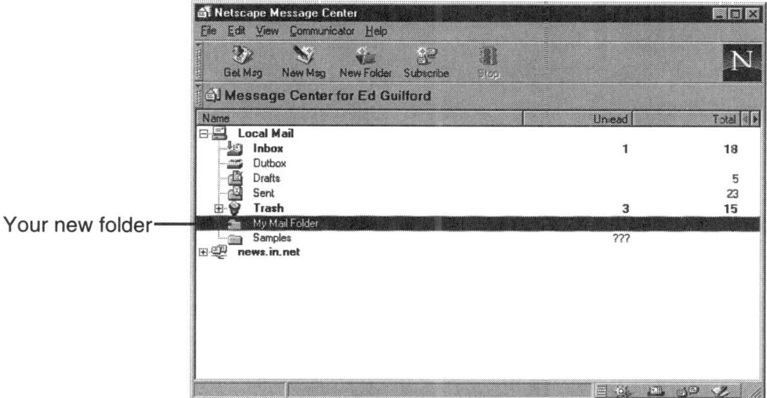

Figure 4.3   Your new folder appears in the folder list.

Unwanted Folders   You can delete a folder you no longer want. First delete or move any messages that are in it. Then select the folder and press the **Delete** key.

What's in a Name?   If you don't like the name of a folder, you can change it. To do so, select the folder, open the **File** menu, and select **Rename Folder**. Then type the new name in the dialog box and click **OK**.

Selecting Messages

In order to copy, move, or delete a message, you must select it first. When you select a message, its name becomes highlighted. You can select just one or several messages at a time by using the following methods:

- To select one message, click it.

- To select multiple adjacent messages, click the first message in the group, press and hold the **Shift** key, and then click the last message. Those two messages and all the messages between them become highlighted.

- To select messages that are not listed next to each other, press and hold the **Ctrl** key and click each message you want to select. Figure 4.4 shows multiple nonadjacent messages selected.

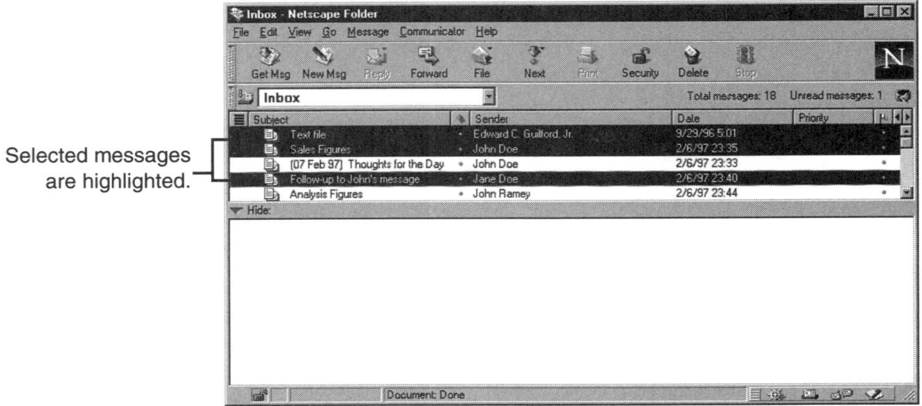

Figure 4.4 You can select any messages you want.

The Edit menu offers three additional options for selecting messages. Open the **Edit** menu and choose **Select Message** to see a submenu with the following options:

Thread When messages are connected by subject, they are shown in a thread. In a thread, the messages that pertain to the original message (such as replies and follow-ups) appear indented under the first message. Choose this option to select the original message and any additional threaded messages.

Flagged As you learned in Lesson 3, you can flag messages of particular note by clicking in the flag column next to the message name. If you choose this option, you can quickly select those flagged messages.

All Messages This option selects all the messages in the current folder.

250

Copying, Moving, or Deleting Messages

To copy or move messages, simply select them and open the **Message** menu. Point to either **File Message** or **Copy Message,** and a list of available folders pops up (see Figure 4.5). Click the desired folder, and the messages are either moved or copied (depending on which option you chose).

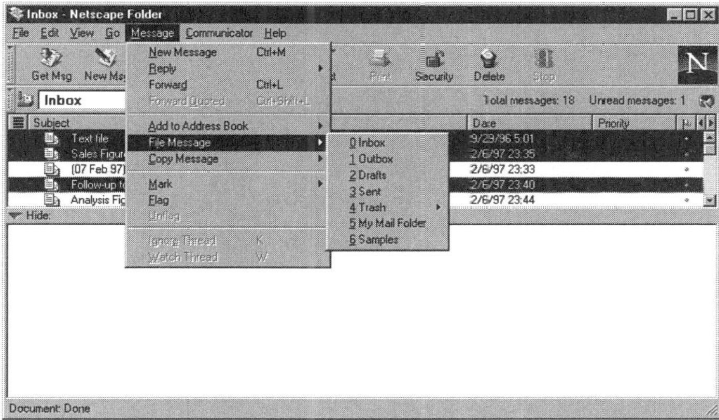

Figure 4.5 Select a folder from the menu to file a message.

Another View If you are viewing a message in its own window, you can use the same commands to copy or move it to a new folder.

To delete messages, select them and press **Delete**. The messages disappear from the list and are placed in the Trash folder. If you accidentally delete a message, you can move it from the Trash folder back into a regular folder. When you're sure that the Trash folder contains only messages that you want to get rid of permanently, open the **File** menu and select **Empty Trash Folder**.

Compressing Folders

When you add messages to a folder, it gets bigger. However, when you delete a message or remove a message from a folder, the folder does not change in size. (Think of the folder as a row of chairs. When a person vacates his chair, the chair is not removed, so the row stays the same size.) Because empty space remains where messages used to be, you are essentially wasting space on your hard drive.

You can compress a folder to remove this wasted space. When you compress a folder, its contents are rearranged so that there are no empty spaces between messages. The resulting folder takes up less room on your hard disk. As you might think, you can read and use the messages in a compressed folder as you would normally.

To compress a folder, open the **File** menu and select **Compress Folders**. The messages are rearranged so that empty spaces are removed.

In this lesson, you learned how to arrange your messages, locate a particular message, and delete unwanted messages. In the next lesson, you'll learn how to create an address book of people to whom you frequently send messages.

Managing Addresses with an Address Book

In this lesson, you learn how to save the e-mail addresses you use frequently so that you don't have to retype them.

Opening an Address Book

E-mail addresses are often complex combinations of long user names and bizarre domain names, such as jkasterask@EDS.decMeca.bzzark.com. If you get any part of the address wrong or change any character from uppercase to lowercase (or vice versa), your e-mail will not reach its destination. The best defense against unruly e-mail addresses is to enter them once into an address book so you can reuse them as needed by selecting from a list or using a nickname that's easy to remember. Luckily, Netscape Messenger provides you with an address book that's ready to use. To open your address book, simply select **Address Book** from the **Communicator** menu. The address book opens, as shown in Figure 5.1. Notice that by default, your Personal Address Book opens. You can change the address book displayed by opening the drop-down list in the **in** box.

You can create smaller mailing lists within your address book. For example, if you wanted to keep your personal addresses in a private area of the address book, you could create a mailing list called Personal Addresses. Each mailing list appears on-screen with an icon that looks like two address cards one on top of the other (as shown in Figure 5.2).

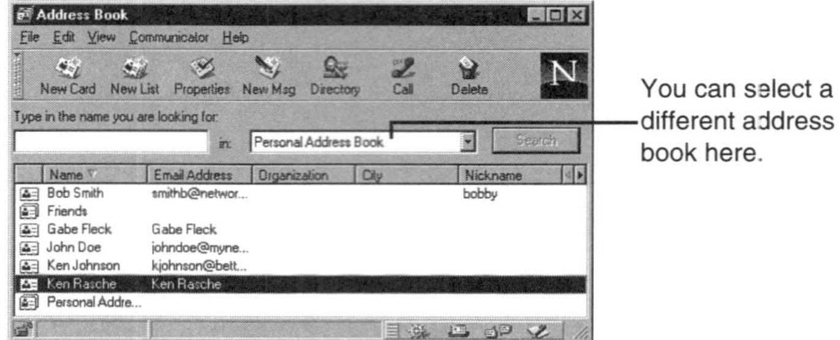

Figure 5.1   The address book.

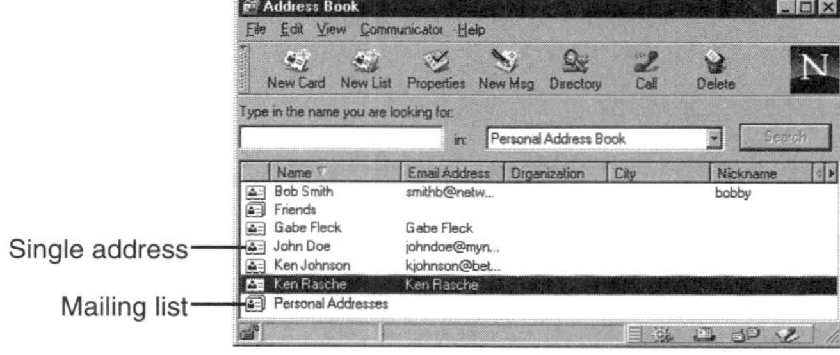

Figure 5.2   Create a separate mailing list for personal e-mail addresses.

To create a mailing list within your address book, follow these steps:

1. Open the **File** menu and select **New List** (or click the **New List** icon on the toolbar). The Mailing List dialog box opens (see Figure 5.3).

2. In the **List Name** text box, type a name for your mailing list.

3. (Optional) There's no need to use the Nickname field in this context. However, you can enter a description for your new mailing list in the **Description** text box.

4. Type the name of the person you want to add to the list. Messenger helps you by filling in the rest of the name when you begin typing.

5. Press **Enter** to add the name to the list. The cursor moves down one line so you can add another name.

6. When you finish adding names, click **OK**. Your new mailing list appears in the main address list (refer to Figure 5.2).

7. Click **OK**.

Figure 5.3   Create a mailing list.

If you add someone to the mailing list who doesn't have an entry in your address book, a generic entry is added. This entry will just have the name listed in the e-mail address field. Obviously, this entry will have to be edited to change the e-mail address. You will learn how to do that later in this lesson.

Adding an Address

You can add an address to your address book in several ways. To add an address *manually*, follow these steps:

1. Open the **File** menu and select **New Card** (or click the **New Card** button on the toolbar). The New Card screen shown in Figure 5.4 appears.

2. Type the person's name in the **First Name** and **Last Name** text boxes.

3. (Optional) Type the name of the person's organization in the **Organization** text box.

4. (Optional) Type the person's **Title** text box.

5. In the **Email** text box, enter the person's e-mail address.

6. (Optional) In the **Nickname** text box, enter a short nickname for this person (using no capital letters and no spaces). You can later enter this name in the To: text box of the message window, and the user's address will appear.

7. (Optional) Type any notes you want to add in the **Notes** text box.

8. (Optional) If you want to enter some more detailed information, click the **Contact** tab and fill out the form.

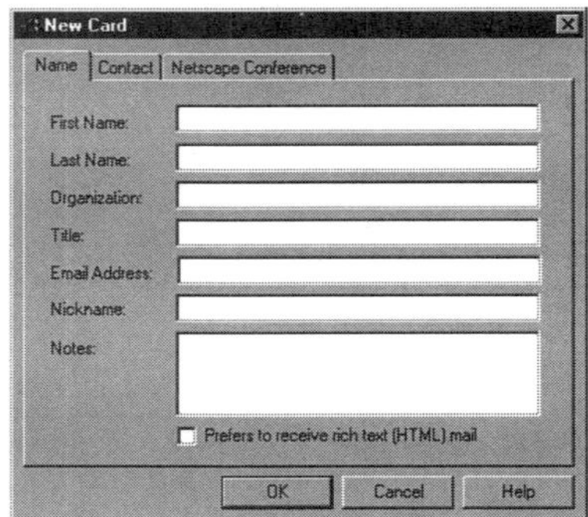

Figure 5.4 Enter the new address in the New Card dialog box.

9. (Optional) If you know the person's Netscape Conference address, click the **Netscape Conference** tab and enter the address in the text box. (You will learn more about Netscape Conference in Part 5.)

10. Click **OK**, and the user is added to your Personal Address Book.

Quick Entry   You can add the address of anyone who has sent you an e-mail message by opening that message, opening the **Message** menu, pointing to **Add to Address Book**, and clicking **Sender** or **All**.

As I mentioned earlier, you can move copies of particular entries into smaller mailing lists. Having smaller lists of related entries makes it easier to locate the person you're looking for. To copy an entry to a mailing list, double-click the mailing list to open it, move to an empty line, and start typing the name you want to add. When you finish adding names to your address book, click the **Close** button to close it.

Using Your Address Book

Now that you have your addresses neatly organized into an address book, you need to know how to use them to send e-mail messages. Follow these steps to find out:

1. From Netscape Messenger, click the **Compose** button. A blank message window appears.

2. Click in the **To:** text box and type the nickname of the person to whom you want to send your message (see Figure 5.5). When you click in another field, the person's e-mail address appears.

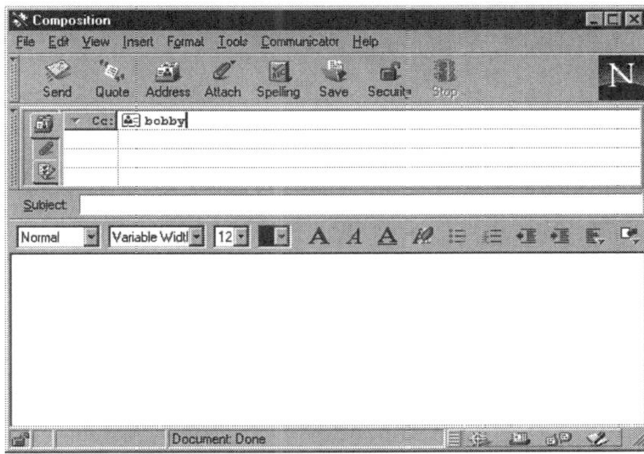

Figure 5.5 Type the nickname of the person to whom you want to send your message.

3. If the person doesn't have a nickname, or if you can't remember it, click in the **To:** text box and click the **Address** button on the toolbar. Select the person's name from the list in the Select Addresses dialog box shown in Figure 5.6. Then click the **To:** button. Repeat to add additional persons to the To:, Cc:, or Bcc: lists. When you're done, click **OK**.

4. Enter a subject, type your message, and send it as usual.

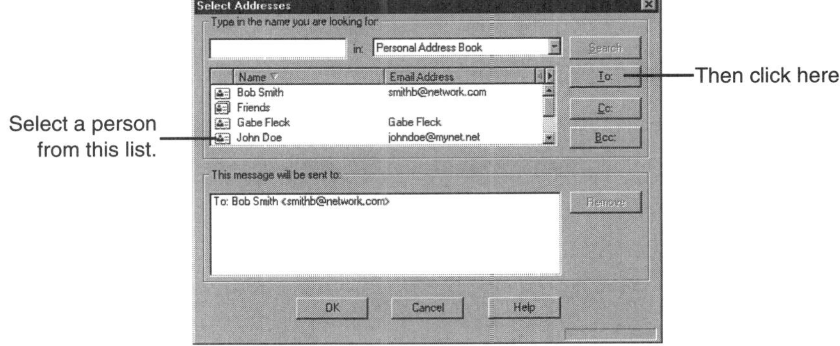

Figure 5.6 You can select a person from the Select Addresses dialog box.

Changing an Address

If someone switches jobs and changes his e-mail address, you'll need to change his entry in your address book. Thankfully, changing an address is easy.

1. Open the Address Book by opening the **Communicator** menu and selecting **Address Book**.
2. Right-click the entry you want to change.
3. Select **Card Properties** from the shortcut menu.
4. Make changes to the entry as needed, and click **OK** when you're finished. If you have copied the entry to other parts of the address book, those aliases will automatically be updated as well.

Deleting an Address

If you have an entry in your address book that you no longer need, you can remove it by following these steps:

1. Open the Address Book by opening the **Communicator** menu and selecting **Address Book**.
2. Select the entry you want to remove.
3. Press **Delete** (or click the **Delete** icon in the toolbar). The entry is removed from the address book.

Importing an Address Book from Another Program

If you have already invested the time to set up an address book in another mail program, Netscape Messenger has a way to use it. Follow these steps:

1. Open the **Communicator** menu and select **Address Book**.
2. Open the **File** menu and choose **Import**.
3. Locate the file that contains the address book from the other program (you may have to consult the program's documentation to find out the name of the address book file).
4. Click **Open.** The name entries are added to your address book.

In this lesson, you learned how to add, copy, and delete address book entries. In the next lesson, you'll learn how to attach files to an e-mail message.

Attaching Files to E-Mail Messages

In this lesson, you learn how to send files with an e-mail message and how to download files from messages you receive.

Sending a File with a Message

You can send just about any type of file over the Internet with an e-mail message. For example, you might send someone a spreadsheet file, a sound file, or a report complete with graphic images.

Of course, sending a file with a message doesn't do any good unless your recipient can actually do something with it. Your recipient needs some way of reading the contents of the file. For example, if you send a Lotus 1-2-3 spreadsheet file as an e-mail message, your recipient must have a copy of Lotus 1-2-3 (or some other program that can read 1-2-3 files) in order to view and use the information in the file.

When you send an attached file over the Internet, that file has to be converted into ASCII (text codes). Likewise, when your recipient gets the file, it needs to be converted back to its original format before it can be used. There are several ways to convert files for transmittal over the Internet, each of which has its pros and cons.

Common Methods for Converting a File for Transmission

Many e-mail programs handle the problem of sending a file over the Internet by placing a MIME (Multipurpose Internet Mail Extension) header in the e-mail message just before the file's data to show that what follows is not text. The MIME header also indicates the file's type (such as a bitmap graphic or a word processing document). This process works okay as long as the recipient's e-mail program recognizes the MIME header and sends the data that follows the header to the indicated program for translation. For example, if the MIME header indicates that the attached file is a bitmap, the e-mail program automatically sends the file for translation to a program that can handle bitmap files (such as Paint). So, if you receive a MIME-encoded message that contains a bitmap, Netscape Messenger wakes up your Paint program (or whatever program is associated with bitmaps), and Paint translates the encoded bitmap and displays it in the Paint window.

Unfortunately, if the recipient of such a message uses an online service, it's unlikely that his e-mail program will be able to make sense of the MIME coding. For example, WinCIM (the e-mail program used on CompuServe) does not recognize MIME information. So if you were to send a MIME-encoded file to a CompuServe address, the recipient would have to have a special program to decode the file.

The most dependable process for sending files over the Internet is called uuencoding. The process of uuencoding converts the information in the file into ASCII (plain text) so that it can be sent over the Internet. At the other end, the recipient (or the recipient's e-mail program) decodes the e-mail message, converting the attachment back into a usable file.

You can uuencode any file yourself with a uuencoder such as WinCode. Fortunately, though, when you attach a file to a Netscape Messenger message, it is automatically uuencoded. So you don't have to do the uuencoding yourself.

If you are sending a large file, you might want to compress it. Compressing a file makes it smaller, which means it can be transferred to the Net more quickly, thus decreasing your connect time. The most popular type of compression is called ZIP. ZIP was developed by PKWare and is the de facto standard for file compression on the Net. WinZip is a popular program that will compress and uncompress ZIP files. You can download WinZip from www.winzip.com.

Yet Another Way Another method of sending files over the Internet is BinHex. The theory behind BinHex and uuencoding is much the same, but the methods and results are somewhat different. BinHex is a method used often among Macintosh computers, but it's not very common in the Windows arena.

Including a File in an E-Mail Message

To send a file in an e-mail message, follow these steps:

1. Open the **File** menu, point to **New**, and select **Message**.

2. Complete the **To:** and **Subject** fields as usual.

3. Click the **Attach** button, and a menu appears.

4. Click **File**.

5. In the dialog box that appears, locate and select the file you want to send, and then click **Open**. You're returned to the Message Composition window, and the file name you selected appears at the top of the list, as shown in Figure 6.1.

Click this tab to see the attached files.

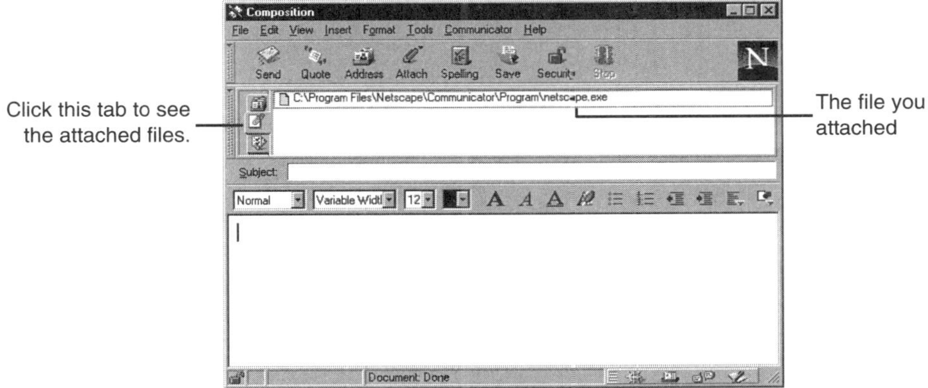

The file you attached

Figure 6.1 The attached file is listed here.

6. (Optional) Repeat steps 4 and 5 to attach additional files to your message.

7. (Optional) To include a message (information about the file's contents, for example), type it in the message area.

8. Send the e-mail in the usual manner.

Just as you can send a file, you can send a copy of the Web page you are currently viewing in Netscape Navigator. To do so, follow steps 1–3 above. Next, click **WEB Page**, verify that the address you see in the box is the address of the

Web page you want to send, and click **OK**. Then proceed with steps 6–9. When Messenger finishes capturing the Web page (you can tell by looking at the status area at the bottom of the message window), you can send your message.

Pictures, Too?   When you send a Web page to someone, keep in mind that the graphics included in the page are not always sent with it. For better results, use Navigator to view the page first, and then send it using Netscape Messenger.

Using a File Sent with a Message

If you receive a message with a uuencoded file attached to it, Netscape Messenger can automatically decode it, but you must have the program you need to open the file. For example, if someone sends you an Excel spreadsheet file, you'll need a copy of Excel (or a program that reads Excel files) in order to open and use the spreadsheet.

If someone sends you a file using MIME or BinHex encoding, you'll need to retrieve that file using an e-mail program that supports MIME or BinHex. Fortunately, all Internet e-mail programs (including Netscape Messenger) do.

When you receive a message with an attachment, it will look similar to the one shown in Figure 6.2.

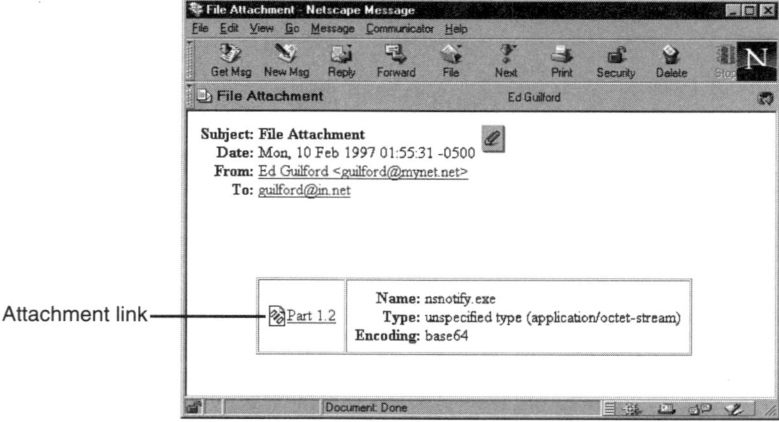

Figure 6.2   A file attached to an e-mail message.

To use the file, follow these steps:

1. Open the message that contains the file by clicking it.

2. Click the **Attachment** link. If a program is associated with this file's extension, Navigator automatically launches that program. The program then displays the contents of the file within its window.

Good Association   You set up an association between a program and a particular file extension using options in the Applications category of Navigator's Preferences dialog box. See Part 1 Lesson 18 for details.

3. If no program is currently associated with the file's extension, you'll see the dialog box shown in Figure 6.3. Click the **Save File** button to save the file to the hard disk. Then select a directory in which to save the file and click **Save**. Once the file is saved to your hard disk, you can load the file into the appropriate program anytime you want.

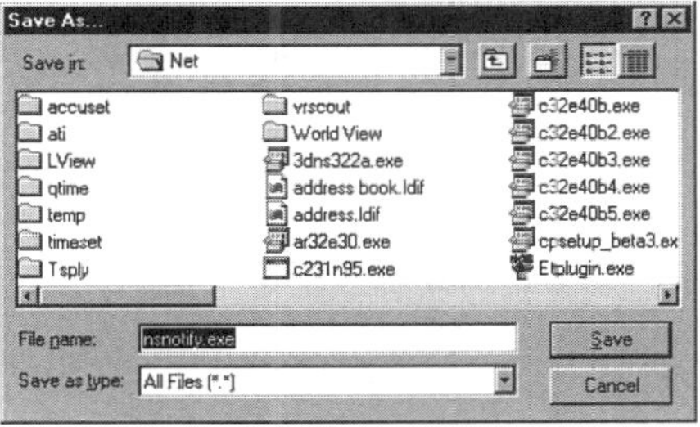

Figure 6.3   You can save an unassociated file to the hard disk for later use.

In this lesson, you learned how to attach files to Netscape Messenger messages and how to open files attached to messages you receive. In the next lesson, you'll learn how to add graphics and HTML tags to your messages.

Spicing Up Your Messages with Graphics and HTML Tags

In this lesson, you learn how to add flair to your messages using rich text, graphics, and HTML.

The Basics of Rich Text

You may ask yourself, "What is rich text and what will it do for me?" Rich text is simply text with style. In the past, most e-mail packages only allowed you to send messages using plain text—not much formatting whatsoever, just boring text. Now, with the recent popularity of the Web and the improved functionality of desktop publishing, people don't want to settle for just plain text. Because e-mail has become such a popular method of corresponding for both business and pleasure, people are demanding the ability to add flair to their messages.

Luckily, Netscape Communicator gives us that ability. With Communicator, you can change the font, make text bold or italic, and even change the color. But Communicator didn't stop there. You can also include graphics in your e-mail to give it extra zing. And as a bonus, you now have the ability to add HTML tags to your messages. If a user opens a message with an HTML link embedded in it, he just has to click it, and Navigator will launch automatically and take him to the link.

There is one catch to all this, however. Only people with Netscape Messenger or another HTML-compatible e-mail program will be able to read the fancy text and graphics. Therefore, the important thing to do is to consider your audience before you spiff up your message too much. If they don't have compatible e-mail programs, you could be wasting your time.

The Formatting Toolbar

Now that you know Netscape Messenger has all these new capabilities, you might as well learn how to use them. Formatting text works much the same in Messenger as it does in the popular word processors out today. The first thing you need to do is open Netscape Messenger and bring up a Message Composition window. Follow these steps:

1. Open Netscape Messenger (it is not necessary to connect to the Internet yet). If you are already in Navigator, you can just click the **Mailbox** icon in the Communicator taskbar. If you are not running Navigator, open the **Start** menu, point to **Programs**, point to **Netscape Communicator,** and click **Netscape Messenger**.

2. Open a Message Composition window by clicking the **New Msg** icon in the toolbar (or by opening the **File** menu, pointing to **New**, and selecting **Message**).

Take a look at the toolbar just above the message area (see Figure 7.1). This is called the Formatting toolbar. This little toolbar gives you all the functionality to create a dynamite message.

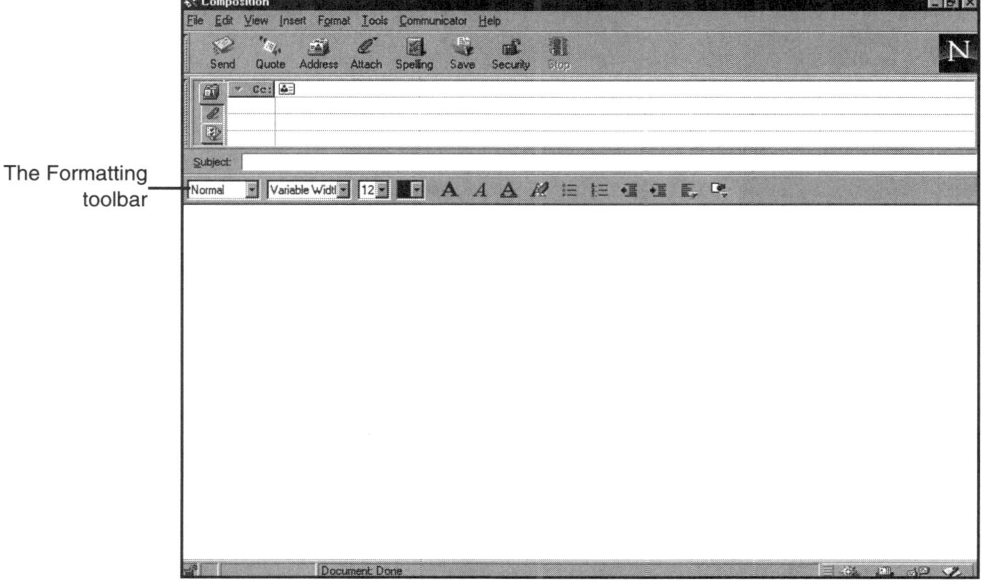

Figure 7.1 The Formatting toolbar.

Table 7.1 provides a brief description of each of the items on the Formatting toolbar.

Table 7.1 The Formatting Toolbar

Item	Name Keyboard Shortcut (If Applicable)	Description
Normal	Paragraph Style	Displays a drop-down list with which you can change the overall style of a paragraph (e.g., normal, heading, list item, description).
Default Font	Font	Displays a drop-down list with which you can select the font for your text.
+C	Font Size	Displays a drop-down list with which you can change the size of your font.
	Font Color	Displays a drop-down list with which you can change the color of your text to add emphasis.
A	Bold Ctrl+B	Makes the text **bold**.
A	Italic Ctrl+I	*Italicizes* your text.
A	Underline Ctrl+U	Underlines the text.
	Bullet List	Adds a bulleted list.
	Number List	Adds a numbered list to your message.
	Decrease Indent Ctrl+Shift+M	Moves indenting one step left.
	Increase Indent Ctrl+M	Indents text one step.
	Change Alignment	Displays a drop-down list from which you can choose left, right, or center alignment.
	Insert Object	Displays a drop-down list you can use to add graphics and HTML tags to your message.

Adding Character Formatting to a Message

Just changing the character formatting can make a big difference in a message. Follow these steps to add some character formatting to your message:

1. You should already have a Message Composition window open (if not, follow the steps in the section "The Formatting Toolbar" to open one).

2. Type the text **The quick brown fox jumped over the lazy dog.**

3. Click anywhere in the sentence, open the **Style** drop-down list, and select **Heading 1**. The sentence becomes bold, and the font changes to a larger size (see Figure 7.2).

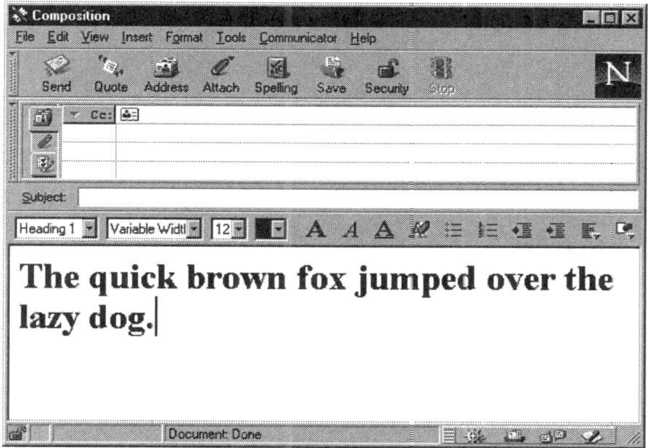

Figure 7.2 The Heading 1 style.

4. Select **Normal** from the **Style** drop-down list to change the text back to its original size.

5. Highlight the word **quick,** click the **Font** drop-down arrow, and select **Arial**.

6. Highlight **quick** again, click the **Font Size** drop-down arrow, and select **14**.

7. Highlight the word **brown,** click the **Font Color** drop-down arrow, and select **Brown**.

8. Highlight the word **jumped** and click the **Bold** button.

9. Highlight the word **lazy** and click the **Italic** button.

10. Highlight the word **dog** and click the **Underline** button. Your example should look like Figure 7.3.

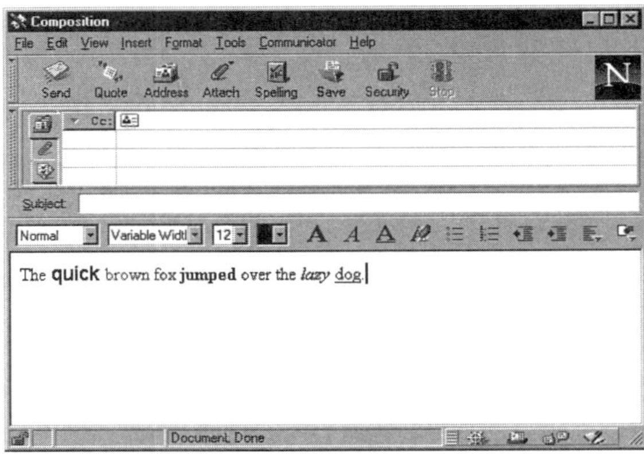

Figure 7.3   Your sentence is more exciting with formatting.

Adding Paragraph Formatting

Now that you've had some fun changing the font and style of your text with the
Formatting toolbar buttons, you can add some formatting to your paragraphs.
Follow these steps:

1. Using the previous example, click at the end of the sentence and press
   Enter twice to create an empty line.

2. Click the **Bullet List** button and type **This is the first bullet.** Notice that
   the sentence is automatically preceded by a bullet character.

3. Press **Enter** to move to a new line. The next line also begins with a bullet.
   Type **This is the second bullet.**

4. Press **Enter** to create another new line. Suppose you don't want a bullet on
   this line, though. Click the **Bullet List** button to clear the bullet. Then press
   Enter again to create another line.

5. Now add a numbered list. Click the **Number List** button and type **We're
   number one.**

6. Press **Enter**. Notice that the next line automatically starts with a number
   sign (see Figure 7.4). Type **They're number two.** You may be thinking that
   those numbers signs really aren't getting your message across. However,
   when the intended receiver gets your message, the number signs will be
   replaced with the correct numbers (see Figure 7.5).

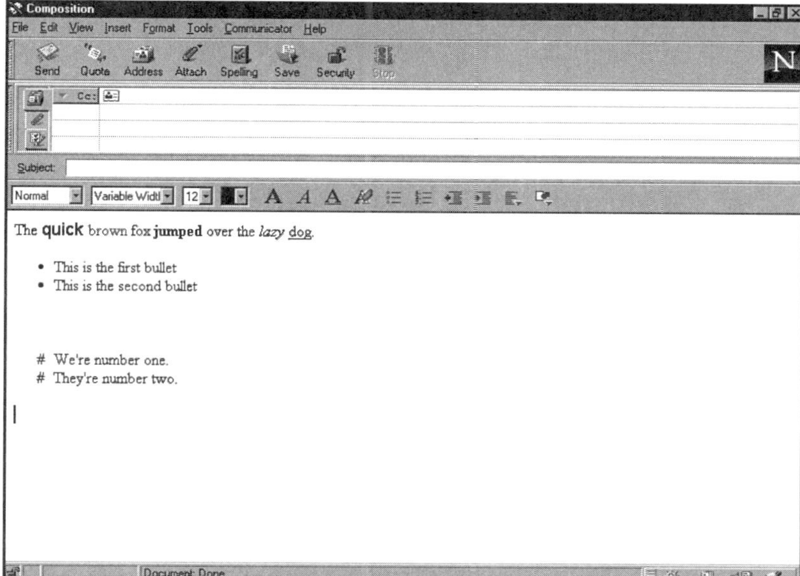

Figure 7.4   The numbered list shows up with number signs while you are composing your message.

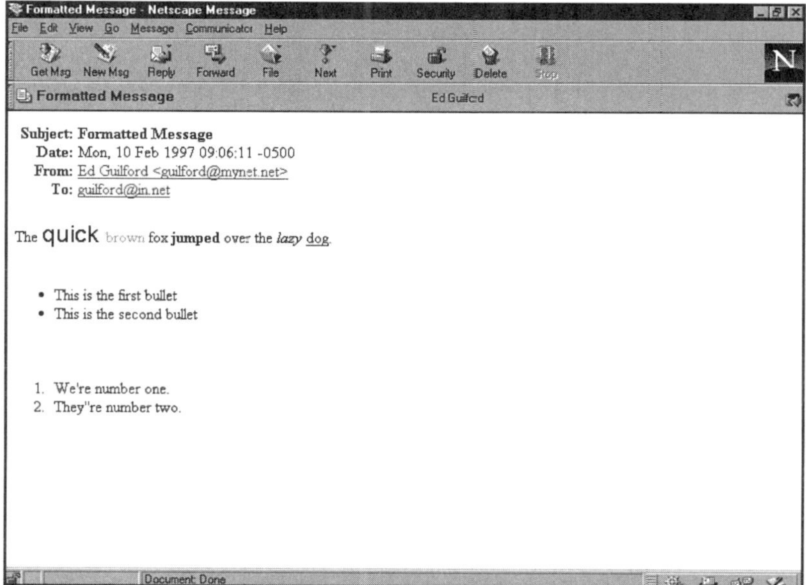

Figure 7.5   When the message is sent, the number signs are replaced with real numbers.

7. Press **Enter** to create a new line. Click the **Number List** button to end the numbered list. Then press **Enter** again to make a new line.

8. Click the **Increase Indent** button to move the text to the right one step. Type **This text is indented for emphasis.**

9. Press **Enter**. As you can see, the next line is automatically indented to the same level. Click the **Increase Indent** button again to indent the text further to the right. Type **This text is indented further.**

10. Press **Enter** to create the next line. Click the **Decrease Indent** button twice to move all the way back to the left. Then type **This text is not indented at all.** Your message should look like the one in Figure 7.6.

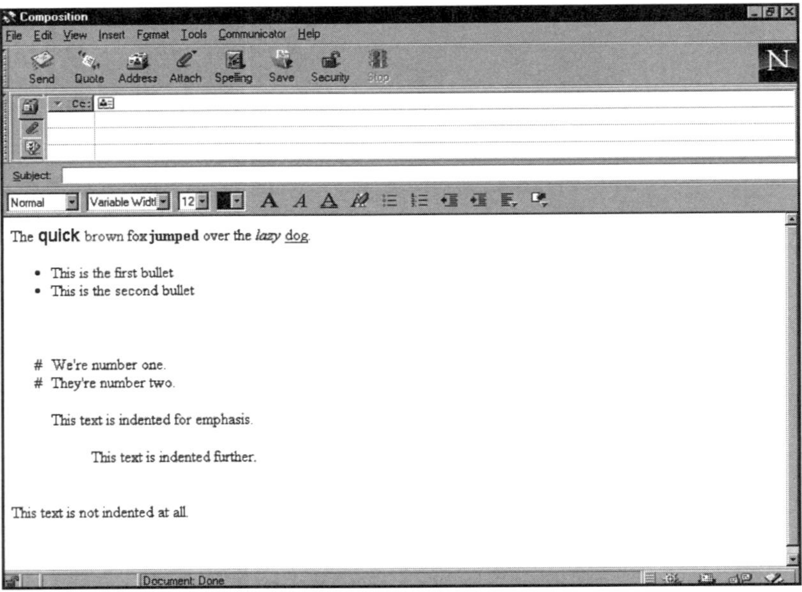

Figure 7.6   An indented example.

11. Press **Enter** to move to a new line and type **This text is centered.** Click the **Alignment** button and select the **Center** icon.

12. Press **Enter** and type **This text is aligned right.** Then click the **Alignment** button and select the **Align Right** icon.

13. Press **Enter** one more time and type **This text is aligned left.** Click the **Alignment** button and select the **Align Left** icon.

14. If you want, you can send the message to yourself to see what it looks like after it's sent. To do so, type your e-mail address in the **To** box and click the **Send** button. If you're not that interested in seeing it, click the **Close** button. A dialog box asks if you want to exit without saving the changes. Click **Yes.**

Your example should look like the one in Figure 7.7. Obviously, this example would not make a very interesting mail message. But you can see that you could use a variety of combinations to really add flair to a message.

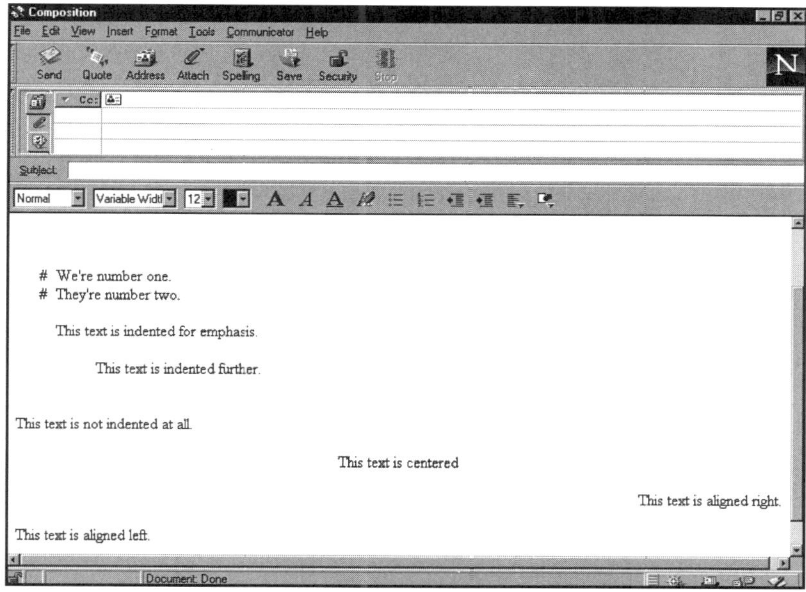

Figure 7.7 Changing the alignment of your paragraphs.

Adding HTML Tags to Make Your Message Look Like a Web Page

As you can see from the previous examples, there is a lot you can do with what used to be simple e-mail messages. Now, you can take it one step further by adding HTML tags to your message. Follow these steps for an example:

1. Open a new message by clicking the **New Msg** button.

2. Don't worry about the To or Subject fields; just skip down to the Message area.

3. The easiest way to add HTML to a message is to copy it from a Web page. You can also create your own HTML tags, but you will learn more about that in Part 6. Connect to the Internet and open Navigator. Then go to the Netscape home page at **home.netscape.com**.

4. Right-click a link and select **Copy Link Location**.

5. Go back to the Message Composition window and right-click in the message area. Select **Paste Link** from the shortcut menu.

6. The link appears in your message (see Figure 7.8). Right-click the link and select **Browse To** to try it out. Navigator opens and takes you to the location specified by the link. When the recipient gets this message, he will only have to click the link. Navigator will then open automatically and take him to the specified location.

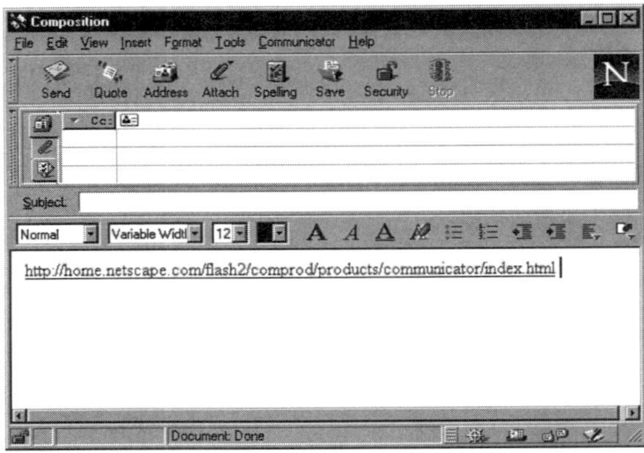

Figure 7.8   A hypertext link embedded in a message.

7. Switch back to the Navigator window. Right-click a graphic and select **Save Image As** from the shortcut window. Choose a location for the file and click **Save**. (If you already have a graphic saved somewhere on your system, you can skip this step.)

8. Switch to the Message Composition window, click the **Insert Object** button, and select the **Insert Image** icon. The Properties dialog box shown in Figure 7.9 appears.

9. Click the **Choose File** button and select the graphic you saved in step 7. Then click the **Open** button.

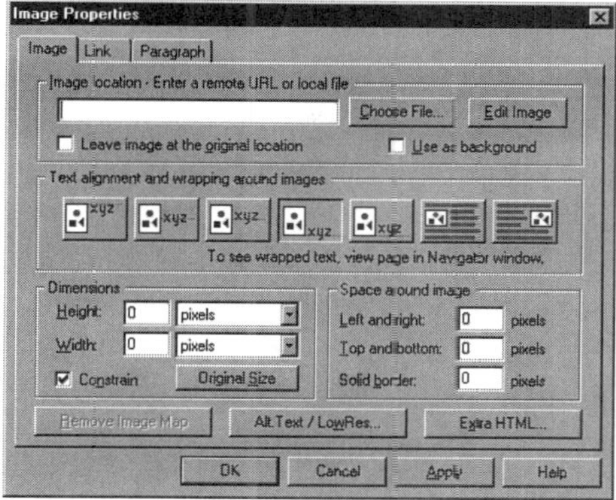

Figure 7.9   Use this dialog box to select your image.

10. Click **OK**, and the image is added to your message. If the image is large, you may get a message telling you that the image is being added to the message. When it is finished, the message disappears, and an image appears in your message (see Figure 7.10)

What About Drag and Drop?   The easiest way to copy a graphic from a Web page is with drag and drop. Open Navigator and find the graphic you want to copy. Then, create a new message in Messenger. With both your Messenger and Navigator windows visible, click the graphic in Navigator and drag it over to your new message.

11. For readability, it is often nice to add a horizontal line to separate text. Click the **Insert Object** button from the toolbar and click the **Horizontal Line** icon. A horizontal line is added to your message.

12. Finally, you can add a table to put the finishing touches on your message. Click **Insert Object** from the toolbar and click the **Table** icon.

13. The New Table Properties dialog box opens. You could change the number of rows and columns, but for this example, just click **OK** to insert a 1 × 2 table.

14. The table appears in your message with nothing in it. You can click in each table cell and insert text or objects. When you finish, your message will look something like Figure 7.11.

15. You can send the message to yourself if you want to see what it will look like, or you can close the Message Composition window and discard the changes.

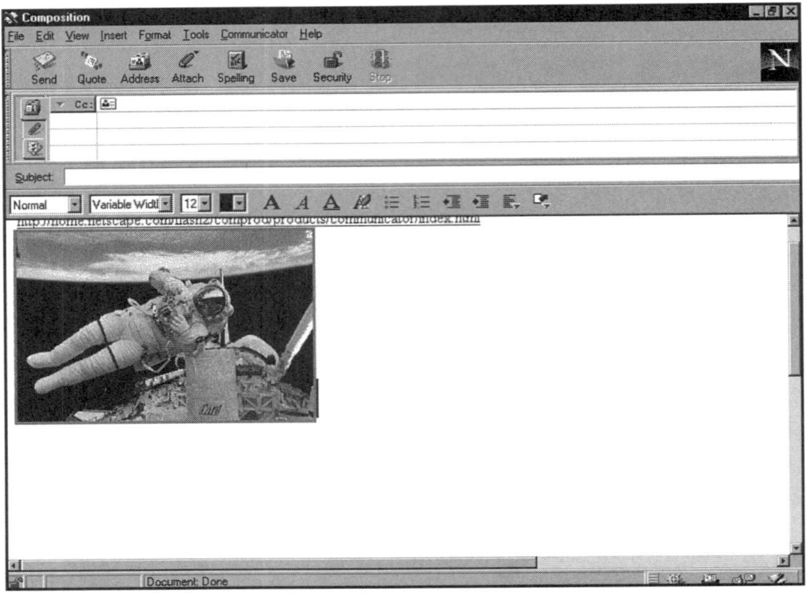

Figure 7.10 A picture is worth a thousand words.

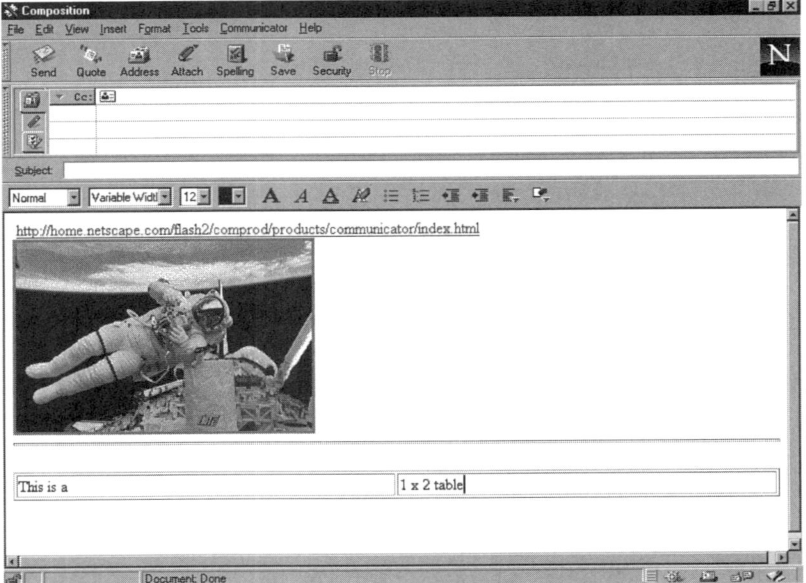

Figure 7.11 A message with HTML formatting.

I Got an Error!   When you send a message formatted with HTML to a new recipient, you may get a message telling you that the address is not registered as understanding HTML messages. If you're sure the recipient can read HTML messages, click the option to send in HTML only. If you're not sure, choose one of the other options.

CAUTION

I Want More   If you want to learn more about HTML and what you can do with it, see Part 6.

TIP

In this lesson, you learned how to add spice to your messages using formatting and HTML. In the next lesson, you will learn how to search through your messages.

Using the Search Tool to Find Messages

In this lesson, you learn how to use the search tool to search for messages.

Using the Search Tool to Find Messages

E-mail is fast becoming a craze. People are sending each other messages at a phenomenal rate. The way it's going, it doesn't take too long to have more than a hundred messages in your inbox. Suppose you want to find a message someone sent you last month about the new product he was developing. You remember the name of the product, but you can't remember the subject line. It is going to take you all day to read through all those messages. Luckily, you don't have to. Netscape Messenger has included a powerful new search tool with this release.

Follow these steps to open the search tool:

1. From the Message center, select the folders you want to search.

2. Open the **Edit** menu and select **Search Messages**. The Search Messages dialog box appears (see Figure 8.1).

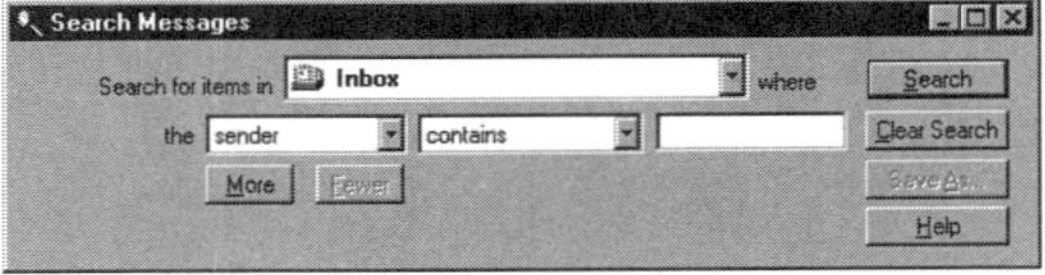

Figure 8.1   Searching for a message.

3. Select where you want to search from the **Search for Items in** drop-down list. You can search either all folders or just the folders you selected in step 1.

4. Choose which field you want to search from the drop-down list.

5. In the next drop-down list, indicate how you want to search. The list will change depending on what you are searching for. For example, if you are searching for the date, this list will contain **is**, **isn't**, **is before**, or **is after**.

6. The last field will either allow you to type in text or turn into a drop-down list, depending on the type of search you are doing. Experiment with the available options to see all the different searches that are you can do (see Figure 8.2).

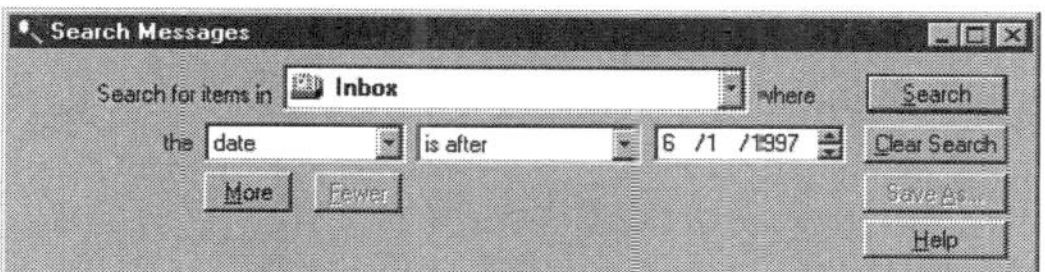

Figure 8.2   There are a variety of searches you can try.

7. You can specify more criteria by clicking the **More** button. Then fill in the new criteria as necessary (see Figure 8.3). If you need even more, click the **More** button again.

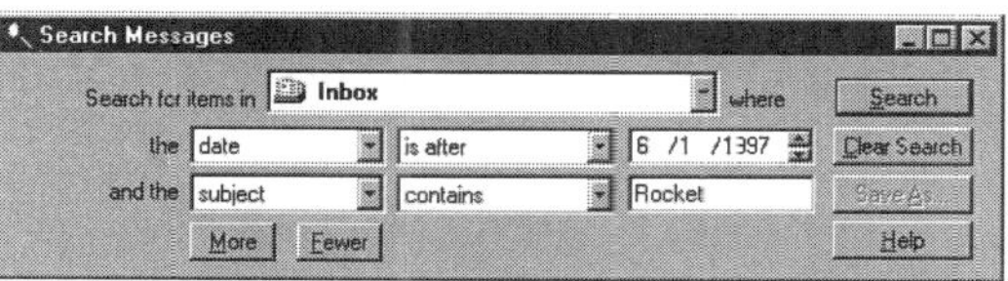

Figure 8.3   More search options.

8. Click **Search**. Netscape Mail searches the list and displays a list of the messages that match the search criteria (see Figure 8.4). Double-click a message to open it.

Empty-Handed   If Netscape Mail doesn't find a match, it displays the message **No matches** in the Search status bar.

CAUTION

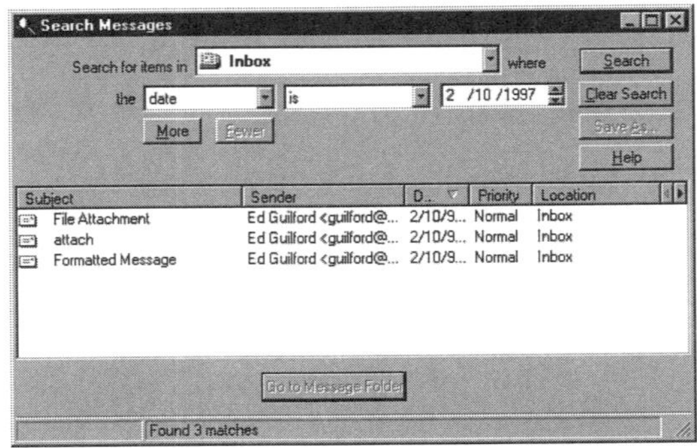

Figure 8.4 The results of your search.

Searching for E-Mail Addresses

Have you ever wondered what happened to your long lost friend in Peoria? Perhaps you can't remember the e-mail address of your sales contact at a company you deal with. Fortunately, you're in luck. Netscape Messenger has provisions for searching some large databases to find e-mail addresses.

By default, Messenger can search the Bigfoot, Four11, InfoSpace, WhoWhere, and Switchboard databases. Each of these databases contains millions of e-mail addresses to search from. The best part is that they are provided freeof charge. (You can also search these sites using Navigator by connecting to www.bigfoot.com, www.four11.com, www.infospace.com, www.whowhere.com, or www.switchboard.com.)

So what are you waiting for? Follow these steps to search:

1. From your Inbox, open the **Communicator** menu and select **Address Book**. Your address book opens (see Figure 8.5).

2. Enter a name or part of a name in the text box labeled **Type In the Name You Are Looking For**.

3. Click the drop-down arrow in the **In** box.

4. Select one of the directories from the list.

5. Click the **Search** button. Messenger searches the database and displays the results in the lower pane (see Figure 8.6).

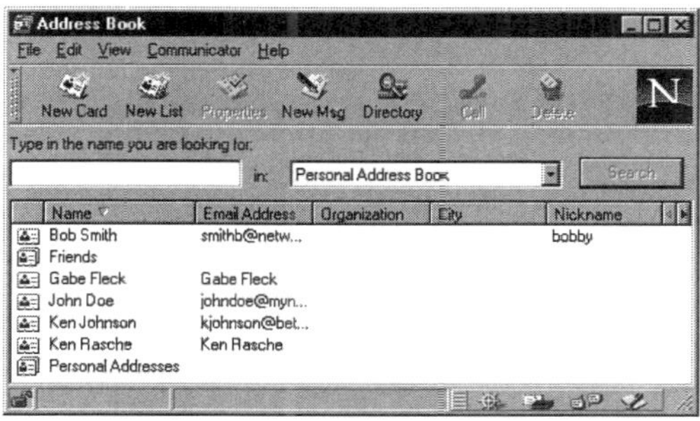

Figure 8.5 Your address book.

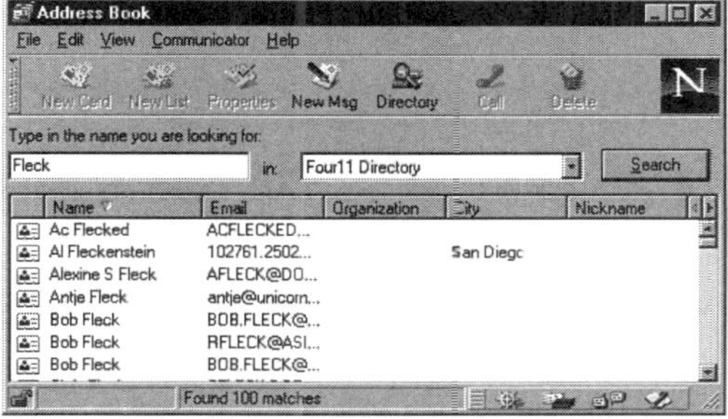

Figure 8.6 The results of your search.

When you find the address you are looking for, click the name and click the **New Msg** button. The name then appears in the **To** box.

In this lesson, you learned how to search for messages and people using Netscape Messenger.

Netscape Collabra

The Basics of Netscape Collabra

In this lesson, you learn how to use Netscape's built-in newsreader.

What Are Newsgroups?

Bulletin boards (the cork kind that you can quickly cover with notices, ticket stubs, and whatnots) are pretty much all over the place: at work, in your kid's classroom, at the grocery store, and even at the library. They all serve the same purpose: to provide a central spot for the exchange of information.

On the Internet, bulletin boards are called *newsgroups*. Most of the newsgroups on the Internet are *UseNet* newsgroups. Each newsgroup focuses on a particular interest. No matter how strange or seemingly insignificant your interests or hobbies might be, there's almost certainly a newsgroup that addresses it.

TERM **UseNet** Short for *user's network*, UseNet defines the standards by which information is exchanged within a newsgroup.

You read the messages posted in a newsgroup just as you might scan through the brochures, notices, and want ads posted on a local bulletin board; then you add your own comments or questions. Later, other people come along and read your messages, and they can reply to your posting, offering advice, opinions, or answers as appropriate. Collabra also includes search engines to help you find what you're looking for.

Setting Up Netscape Collabra

To read the messages posted in an Internet newsgroup, you need a newsreader program. Luckily, Communicator comes with its own newsreader, Netscape Collabra.

What About Navigator? Unfortunately, you can't use Navigator to read newsgroup messages. Newsgroups follow an entirely different set of standards than Web pages do, so you'll have to use Collabra to browse your favorite newsgroup.

CAUTION

To use Netscape Collabra, you first have to tell it the name of your Internet provider's news server. Hopefully, you already have this information. (If not, give your provider a call first to get it.) Then follow these steps:

1. If you have Navigator or Messenger open, click the **Discussion Groups** button in the Communicator toolbar to open Collabra. Otherwise, open the **Start** menu, point to **Programs**, point to **Netscape Communicator**, and click **Netscape Collabra**.

2. Open the **Edit** menu and select **Preferences**.

3. Under **Mail & Groups**, click the **Groups Server** category to see the options shown in Figure 1.1.

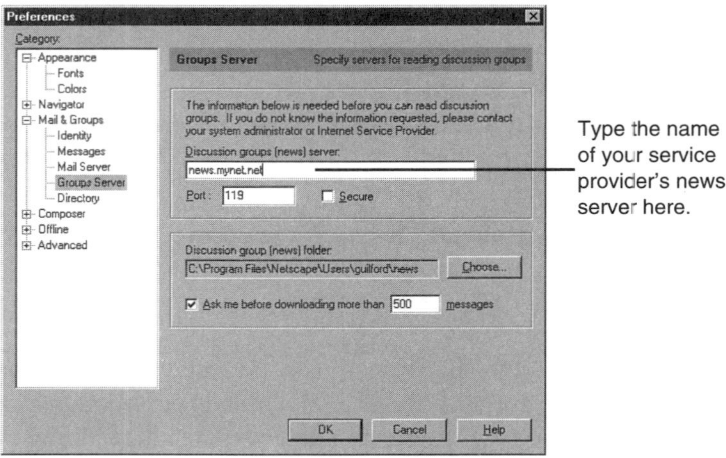

Figure 1.1 Setting up Netscape Collabra.

4. Type the name of your Internet provider's news server in the **Discussion Groups (News) Server** text box.

5. (Optional) In the **Discussion Group (News) Folder** text box, enter the path to the folder in which Netscape stores your list of newsgroups. Click the **Choose** button to browse for a folder.

6. (Optional) You can change the number of messages before Collabra notifies you. You might want to lower it to around 300 or so to keep your download time short.

7. Click **OK** to enter the settings. You're now ready to use Netscape Collabra.

Displaying the List of Available Newsgroups

Although there are more than 10,000 newsgroups on the Internet, your service provider probably subscribes to only the top 1,000 or so. When you start Netscape Collabra, it downloads a list of available newsgroups from your service provider. You can then *subscribe* to any of the newsgroups you find listed there.

My Service Provider Doesn't Carry the Newsgroup I Want   If your Internet service provider doesn't subscribe to the newsgroup you want, contact the service and ask them to add the newsgroup. If you don't get a favorable response, you may want to try a different Internet service provider or subscribe to a dedicated newsgroup provider.

Subscribe   To gain access to the messages in a newsgroup. After you subscribe to a newsgroup, its messages are downloaded to your PC so that you can access them. The message list is updated each time you start Collabra.

To display the available list of newsgroups, follow these steps:

1. Connect to the Internet and start Collabra.

2. Click the folder that represents your service provider's news server. In Figure 1.1 it would be **news.mynet.net**.

3. If necessary, click the plus sign (+) in front of your service provider's folder. Netscape Collabra displays only the newsgroups to which you've already subscribed. (At this point, there aren't any.)

What Are These Messages?   You may already have a few text messages from your service provider. To view any of those messages, double-click it.

CAUTION

4. Open the **File** menu and select **Subscribe to Discussion Groups** to display the list of available newsgroups. After a few minutes, Netscape Collabra displays your provider's list of available newsgroups (see Figure 1.2).

5. (Optional) If you would like to search for a particular newsgroup, click the **Search for a Group** tab. Type the text you would like to search for in the **Search for** text box, and then click the **Search Now** button.

6. (Optional) To see a list of the newsgroups that have been added recently, click the **New Groups** tab.

See the next section to learn how to subscribe to the newsgroups that interest you.

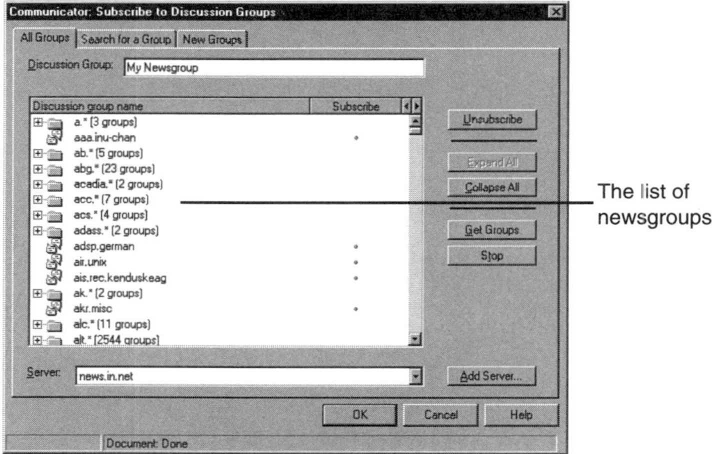

Figure 1.2   Netscape Collabra displays a list of available newsgroups.

I Can't Read the Name   If the first column is too small to read the name of the newsgroup, click the right arrow in the column headings. The first column will expand to show more of the name.

TIP

Subscribing to Newsgroups

When you find a newsgroup that interests you, you *subscribe* to it so you can read the messages that are posted to it. How can you tell which newsgroups you're interested in? As you may have noticed, newsgroups use abbreviated names such as comp.lang.basic, which can make it difficult to figure out what a particular group is about. This list of common abbreviations should help:

alt	Alternative topics (unusual stuff, possibly offensive)
comp	Computer-related topics
misc	Miscellaneous topics
news	Newsgroup-related information
rec	Recreational topics—hobbies, sports, and so on
sci	Science topics
soc	Social issues
talk	Discussions focused on controversial topics (talk show information)

Most of those topics are further divided into subtopics. For example, the comp group consists of many computer-related newsgroups, such as comp.dcom (data communications) and comp.ai (artificial intelligence). In addition, these sub-groups are often divided into specialized groups, such as comp.dcom.fax, which focuses on sending computer data via fax or fax modem.

When you find a newsgroup you want to review, you subscribe to it by clicking the dot that appears after the newsgroup's name in the Subscribed column. A check mark appears next to each group to which you've subscribed (see Figure 1.3).

Just the Ones I Want, Please   After you subscribe to a few newsgroups, Netscape Collabra displays only the subscribed newsgroups. This can be very helpful: The shorter the newsgroup list is, the easier it is for you to locate information you want.

When you finish subscribing to newsgroups, click **OK** to close the dialog box.

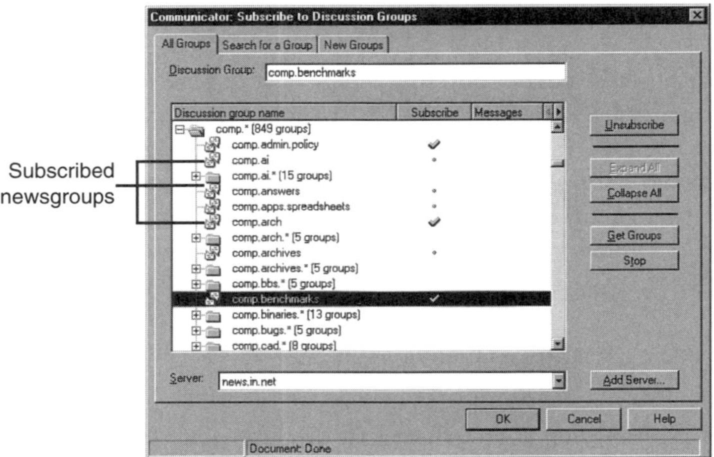

Figure 1.3   Subscribing to newsgroups.

Want to Unsubscribe?   After you've read a few messages in a newsgroup, you may decide that it's not for you. To unsubscribe, highlight the group you want to unsubscribe from and hit the **Delete** key. Collabra displays a dialog box, asking if you're sure you want to unsubscribe. Click **OK**.

In this lesson, you learned how to set up Netscape Collabra and how to subscribe to newsgroups. In the next lesson, you'll learn to read and reply to newsgroup messages.

Reading and Responding to Newsgroup Messages

In this lesson, you learn how to read and reply to newsgroup messages.

Reading a Message

To view the messages in a particular newsgroup, double-click the newsgroup's name (see Figure 2.1). A list of the messages in that newsgroup appears. You must subscribe to a newsgroup in order to view its messages and reply to them. Follow the instructions in Lesson 1 to find and subscribe to newsgroups.

Hey, It's Empty! Next to the name of each newsgroup are two numbers. The first is the number of messages you haven't read yet, and the second is the total number of messages in that newsgroup. (You may have to adjust the size of the pane in order to see both numbers.) If you do not see any numbers at all, there are no messages in that particular newsgroup.

CAUTION

When you select a newsgroup, its messages appear in the panel in the top half of the screen, as shown in Figure 2.2. To display the contents of a message, click the message. Netscape Collabra displays its contents in the lower pane. If necessary, you can access an earlier message to which your message relates by clicking one of the numbers next to **References**.

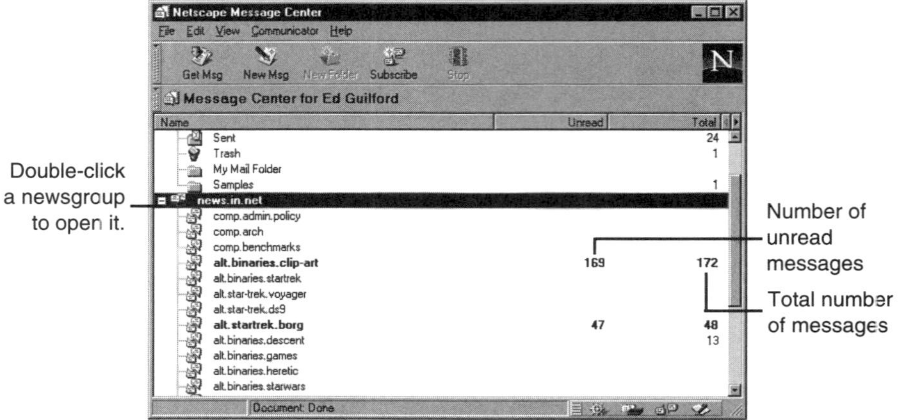

Figure 2.1   Opening a newsgroup.

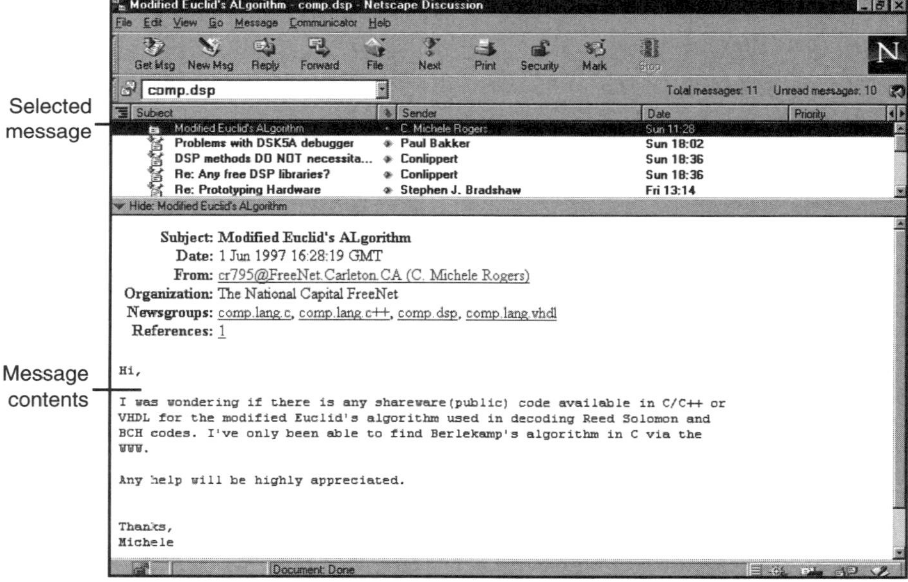

Figure 2.2   Reading a message.

Messages in a newsgroup do not appear in chronological order; instead, they follow a *thread*. A thread is a collection of messages that follow a particular discussion. A thread starts when someone replies to a comment or question. Then someone else comes along, reads the first message, reads the reply, and adds his comments. When he tacks his comments onto the reply, a single thread forms, connecting the three messages. As additional comments or questions are added, it creates a continuous discussion that anyone can trace by following the thread of the conversation. Netscape Collabra marks a thread by indenting later comments that form the thread under the original comment that started it all.

My Message Expired!   Because so many messages are posted to newsgroups, Internet providers don't have enough disk space to keep them around forever. How long messages are kept depends on your Internet provider, but it usually ranges from one week to one month. If you like a message you are reading and want to keep it, select **File**, **Save As** to save the message to your hard drive.

In Order   You can sort messages in a newsgroup in a number of ways. To change the sort order, open the **View** menu, select **Sort**, and select **by Date**, **by Flag**, **by Subject**, **by Sender**, **by Size**, **by Status**, **by Thread**, **by Unread**, or **by Priority**.

After you read one message, you can click another one to view it. Alternatively, you can use one of these options from the Go menu to jump from one message to another more easily:

Next Message   Displays the next message in the list.

Next Unread Message   Displays the next unread message in the list. (You can also click the **Next** button.)

Next Flagged Message   Displays the next flagged message in the list.

Next Unread Thread   Displays the next unread thread in the list.

Next Category   Displays the messages in the next category.

Next Unread Category   Displays the messages in the next unread category.

Next Group   Displays the messages in the next newsgroup in your list of subscribed newsgroups.

Next Unread Group   Displays the messages in the next unread newsgroup in your list of subscribed newsgroups.

Previous Message   Displays the previous message in the list.

Previous Unread Message   Displays the previous unread message in the list.

Previous Flagged Message   Displays the previous flagged message in the list.

First Flagged Message   Displays the first flagged message in the list.

Flagging a Message

If you're short on time but you know you want to read a message you've come across, you can flag the message for later viewing. To flag a message, follow these steps:

1. Select the message you want to flag.

2. Open the **Message** menu and select **Flag**. The message appears with a small red flag in the Flag column.

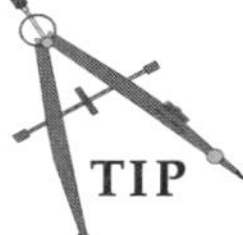

Fast Flag   You can also flag a message by clicking in the flag column (the one marked with a red flag).

To return to a flagged message, open the **Go** menu and select **First Flagged Message**, **Next Flagged Message**, or **Previous Flagged Message**. When you select First Flagged, for example, the first flagged message in the newsgroup list is highlighted so that you can read it. If you select Next Flagged, the highlight moves to the next flagged message in the list.

If you want to unflag a message, select it, open the **Message** menu, and select **Unflag**. You can also click the red flag in the flag column to remove the flag (unflag the message).

Searching for a Message

Netscape Collabra has a powerful search tool that will help you find a message based on search criteria you set up. To perform a search, follow these steps:

1. Open the **Edit** menu and select **Search Messages**.

2. Choose an option from the **Search for Items** drop-down list. You can choose to search the current newsgroup, all subscribed newsgroups, or all searchable newsgroups.

3. From the drop-down list next to **The**, select an area to search. You can choose **Sender** or **Subject**.

4. In the next box, choose **Contains**, **Is**, **Begins with**, or **Ends with**.

5. In the next box, type the text you want to search for.

6. If you would like to do a multi-level search, click the **More** button and repeat steps 3–5.

7. Click the **Search** button to begin the search. Eventually, Netscape Collabra displays a list of messages that match your search criteria.

8. Double-click a message to view it.

Replying to a Message

Before you post any message to a newsgroup, make sure that you've taken the time to familiarize yourself with the focus of its discussions. In addition, you should read all the messages in a thread so that your comments don't repeat what's already been said.

Read the FAQs   You should search for messages with the letters "FAQ," which is short for *frequently asked questions*. In these messages, you'll find answers to the most commonly asked questions within that newsgroup. Make sure you always read the FAQs before posting a question, to avoid duplicating an earlier effort.

When you're confident that you have something new (and relevant) to say, you can post a public or private reply. A *public reply* appears with the other messages in the newsgroup. A *private reply* is basically an e-mail message sent directly to the originator of the message.

Follow these steps to reply to a message:

1. Select the message to which you want to reply by clicking its name.

2. Open the **Message** menu and point to **Reply**. Select **To Sender** (to e-mail your reply), **To Sender and All Recipients** (to e-mail your reply to all of the original recipients), **To Group** (to post a public reply), or **To Sender and Group** (to post a public reply and send an e-mail message).

3. If you want to include the text of the original message, open the **File** menu and select **Quote Original Text** (or click the **Quote** button on the toolbar). The text of the original appears, preceded by a blue vertical line down the left edge of the message (see Figure 2.3). In order to keep your message short, you should repeat only the parts of the original message that the reader needs to get the gist of it. Select and delete the extraneous parts of the original message.

4. Type your reply after the original message's contents (as shown in Figure 2.3).

5. Click **Send** to send your reply. If you decided to post your reply instead of mailing it, your reply appears with the other messages in the newsgroup. At that point, it is available for viewing.

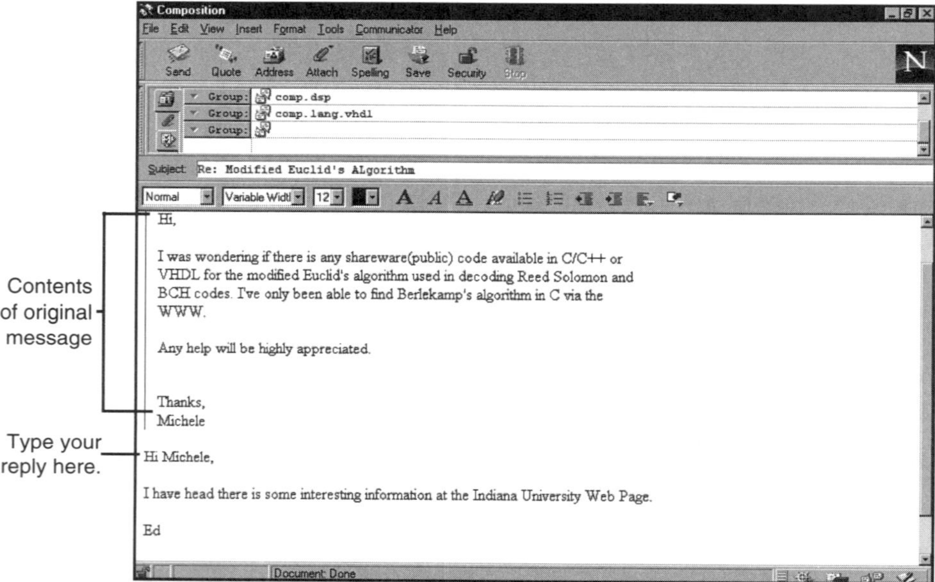

Figure 2.3 Posting a reply.

Watch What You Say! Do not use CAPITAL LETTERS in your message. On the Internet, using CAPS is considered shouting. Also, if you want to avoid being *flamed* (verbally abused), don't insult anybody personally or attack a particular topic as being "too silly." Instead, keep your comments pertinent to the topic being discussed, and avoid repeating what has already been said.

CAUTION

Starting a New Thread

If you'd like to introduce a new topic to a newsgroup, you can do that by starting your own thread (discussion). Before you start a new thread, make sure that your topic has not yet been covered under some other thread.

When you're ready to start a new thread, follow these steps:

1. Open the newsgroup to which you want to add your thread.

2. Click the **New Msg** button on the toolbar.

3. In the **Subject** text box, type a subject for your discussion (see Figure 2.4).

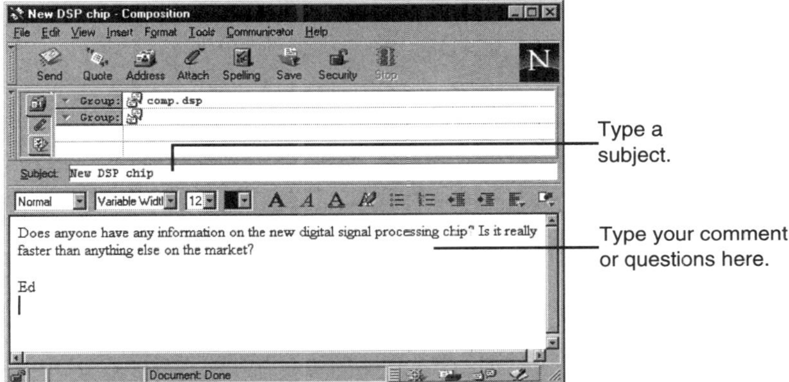

Figure 2.4 Posting a new thread.

4. Type your comment or question in the large text box.

5. Click **Send**, and your message becomes available for viewing. Check back every so often to see if your new thread has had any responses.

In this lesson, you learned how to read and reply to newsgroup messages. In the next lesson, you will learn how to attach files to your newsgroup messages and how to download files that other people have attached to their messages.

Attaching and Detaching Files in Newsgroup Messages

In this lesson, you learn how to attach files to your newsgroup messages, as well as how to download files that other people have attached to their messages.

Understanding Attached Files

Not everything you find within a newsgroup is text discussion. Often, a user will upload (send) a file to the newsgroup to share its contents with other readers. For example, in a music-related newsgroup, members might trade MIDI sound files. A photography group might trade graphic files instead. (Of course, once you download such a file from the newsgroup, you must have the appropriate program to view its contents. For example, to view a graphic file, you might use a graphic viewer such as LView.)

Being able to use a file downloaded from a newsgroup is only part of the story. The real story starts when the file is uploaded to the newsgroup. You see, the Internet was really designed for the transmission of textual data—data that consists of letters and numbers without fancy text enhancements such as bold, italic, and underline. But data files, such as graphic and sound files, are not simple text files; they contain special codes and not just text. So in order to transmit such files over the Internet, you have to convert into text (ASCII) using a process called *uuencoding*. The process of uuencoding converts the information in a data file into ASCII (plain text). At the other end, the recipient (or in this case, the recipient's newsreader program) decodes the file, converting it back into usable data.

If uuencoding sounds very complex, that's because it is. In some cases, you need a special uuencoding program to encode your files before you upload them to the Internet. For the most part, though, uuencoding a file for uploading is handled automatically by Netscape Collabra. However, when downloading a file, you may have to decode the file manually, depending on the file's type.

Which Uuencoder Should I Use?   Because you'll need a uuencoder to decode some of the files you grab from a newsgroup, you should get a copy of WinCode, a popular uuencoding program. You can find WinCode at various software sites on the Internet. See Part 1 Lesson 10 for information on downloading files from the Internet.

Downloading Attached Files

Many files that you find in newsgroups are divided into parts, because a lot of newsgroup servers limit the size of messages. In such a case, you'll find references like these in the descriptions for several messages:

> eagle.gif (0/3)
>
> eagle.gif (1/3)
>
> eagle.gif (2/3)
>
> eagle.gif (3/3)

In the 0/3 file, you'll find a description of the eagle.gif graphic. The other three files make up the eagle.gif file itself; it's divided into three parts.

There's Only One File!   Sometimes a file is small enough that it can be contained in one message. So don't fret if you don't find multiple messages for a single file as described here.

To download (receive) a file attached to a newsgroup message, double-click the first part of the file (the one with $1/x$ in the description). Netscape Collabra automatically grabs all the parts of the file and decodes it.

If the file is a GIF or a JPEG graphic, the contents of the file appear in the message area, as shown in Figure 3.1. To use the file in a program, right-click it and select **Save Image As** from the shortcut menu. Netscape Collabra saves the file to disk, where you can load it in the appropriate program.

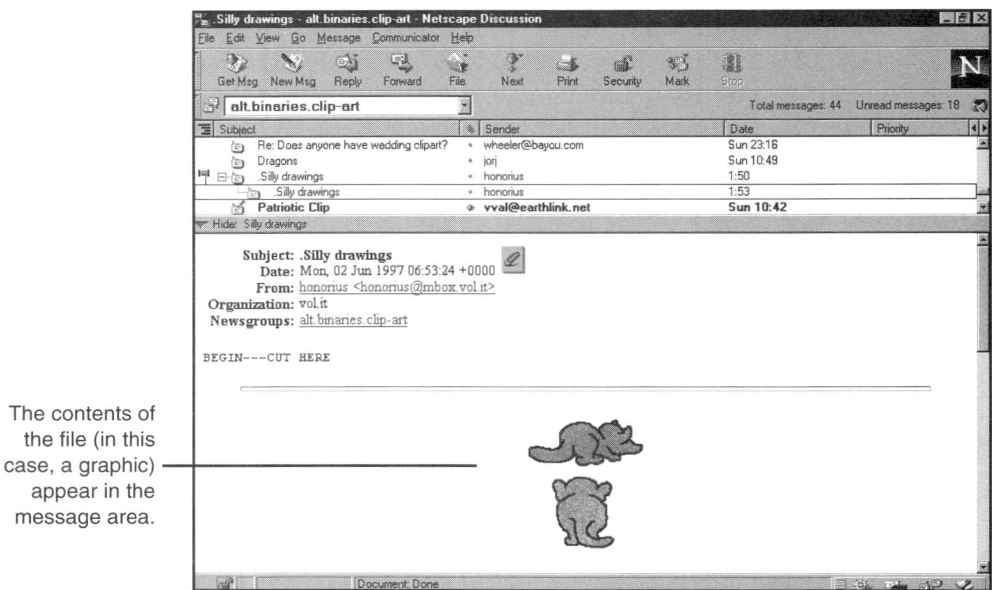

The contents of the file (in this case, a graphic) appear in the message area.

Figure 3.1 The contents of the file appear in the message area.

If the file is not a graphic, it may appear as an attachment (as shown in Figure 3.2) or in its uuencoded form (Figure 3.3).

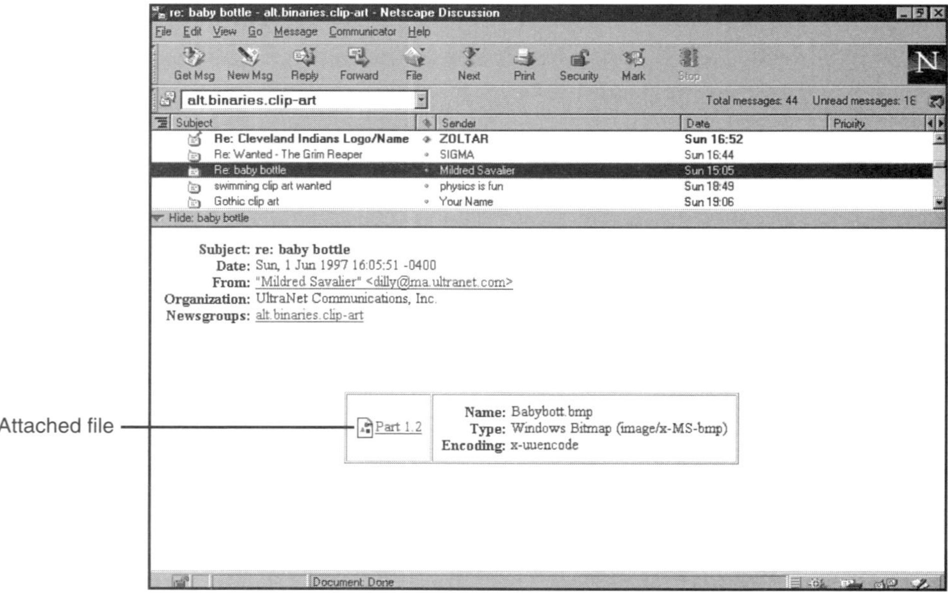

Attached file

  Figure 3.2 Some files appear in attachment form.

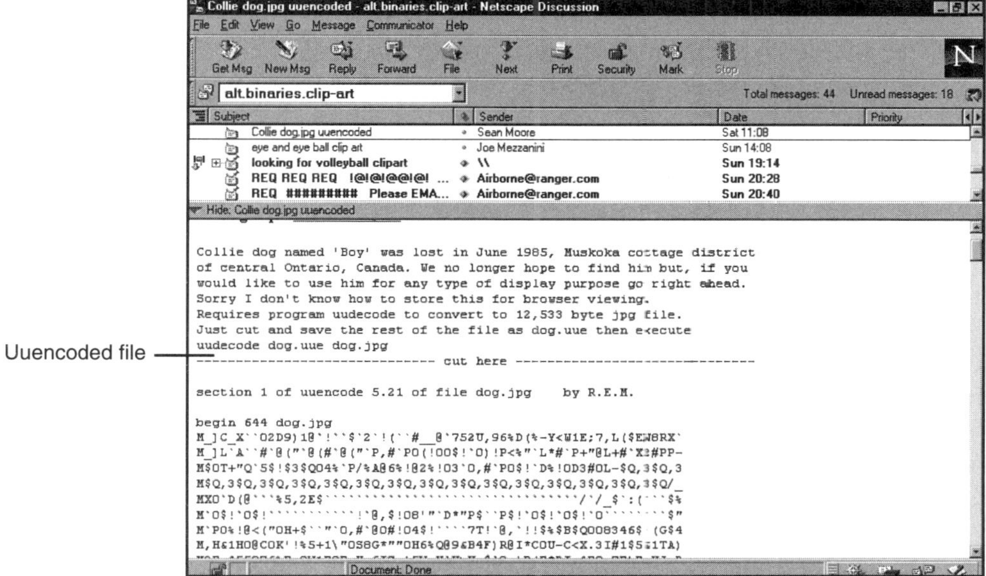

Uuencoded file

Figure 3.3   Some files appear in encoded form.

If the file appears as an attachment (as in Figure 3.2), follow these steps to save it to your hard drive so you can open and view it:

1. Right-click the file link in the attachment.

2. Click **Save Link As** from the shortcut menu.

3. Choose a storage location for the file and click the **Save** button. Netscape Collabra decodes the file automatically so it is ready to be used with whatever application it was designed for.

If the file appears as it does in Figure 3.3, it is encoded. You will have to save the file to disk and then decode it. Follow these steps to do that:

1. Open the **File** menu and select **Save As**.

2. Select a directory in which to save the file, and then type a name for it using the .UUE extension (as in FILE01.UUE).

3. If the file was broken into parts (if it appears as more than one message in the newsgroup window), repeat steps 1 and 2 for each file part (each message).

4. When you have saved all the parts to disk, start WinCode.

5. Open the **File** menu and select **Decode**.

6. Change to the directory that contains the uuencoded file(s).

7. Select the file(s) you want to decode. If the file is split into several parts, select all of them.

8. Click **OK**, and WinCode decodes the file. When it finishes, you can load the file into the appropriate program for use.

Uploading Files to a Newsgroup

In addition to downloading files from newsgroups, you can upload (send) files. To upload a file to a newsgroup, you simply attach the file you want to share to your newsgroup message.

When you attach your file and send the message, Netscape Collabra automatically uuencodes the file for transmission. As you learned earlier, the file is decoded at the user's site when he downloads your file from the newsgroup.

To upload (send) a file to a newsgroup, follow these steps:

1. Follow the usual steps for posting a message (described in Lesson 2).

2. Before you click the Send button, click the **Attach** button on the toolbar.

3. Choose **File** from the drop-down list that appears.

4. In the Enter File to Attach dialog box (see Figure 3.4), select the file you want to send with your message and click **Open**.

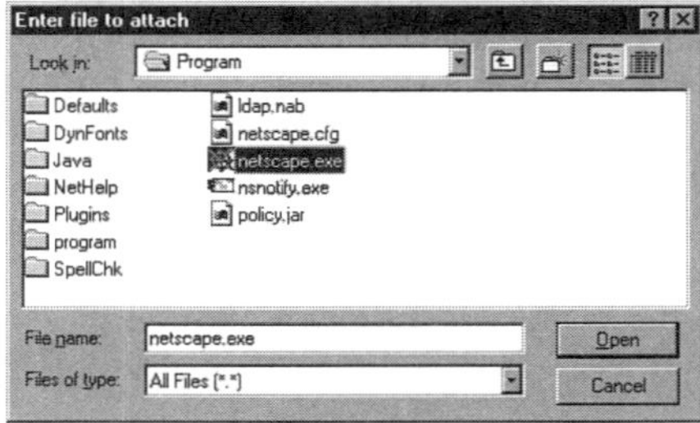

Figure 3.4   Select the file you want to attach to your newsgroup message.

5. The name of the file you selected appears in the Attachments tab of the message window. Click **Send** to send your message. Netscape Collabra automatically uuencodes the file, splits the file into several messages if necessary, and then sends them.

In this lesson, you learned how to download and upload files in newsgroups. In the next lesson, you will learn how to work with discussion groups.

Working with Discussion Groups

In this lesson, you learn to create and manage discussion groups.

What Are Discussion Groups?

Many companies have the need to set up groups to discuss certain aspects of their company. For example, it might be nice to have an engineering discussion group in which engineers could share problems and ideas, or a financial discussion group that could collect financial information. Unfortunately, it is difficult to start a newsgroup, and it's almost impossible to keep a newsgroup private within your company. Of course, e-mail works to some extent, but true discussion groups could really enhance productivity.

To answer this need, Netscape bought Collabra and developed Collabra Server (Collabra Share first introduced this interface). With Collabra Server, your company can set up and administer discussion groups on virtually any topic. They also have the option of keeping the discussion groups accessible to members of your company only, making it possible to discuss almost anything.

More than likely if your company is using Collabra Server, it also has an *intranet*. An intranet is similar to the Internet, but it is local to the company. Intranets are the hottest craze in company information transfer. On the intranet, the company sets up pages specific to its organization. Each member of the company can access the intranet using Navigator.

If your company is using Collabra Server or is planning to use it in the future, this lesson will help you get started in working with discussion groups.

Configuring Collabra for Your Company Server

In Lesson 1, you configured Collabra to receive newsgroups from your Internet service provider. You may need to change this setup slightly to configure Collabra to talk to your company's discussion group server. If you are unsure what that is, talk to your system administrator to get the necessary information; then follow these steps:

1. If you have Navigator or Messenger open, click the **Discussions** button in the Communicator toolbar to open Collabra. Otherwise, open the **Start** menu, point to **Programs**, point to **Netscape Communicator**, and click **Netscape Collabra**.

2. Open the **File** menu and select **New Discussion Group Server** to see the options shown in Figure 4.1.

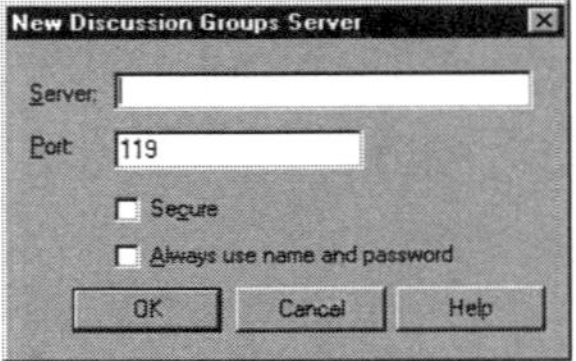

Figure 4.1 Choosing your discussion groups server.

3. Type the name of your company's discussion group server in the **Server** text box.

4. If your company uses a secure server, check the **Secure** check box.

I'm Not Sure If It's Secure A secure server encrypts all messages posted to it so that no one can read a message in a discussion group unless he or she has authorization. Check with your system administrator to see if your company has a secure server.

CAUTION

5. (Optional) For added security, you may want to check the **Always Use Name and Password** check box. When this option is checked, Collabra asks for a password from anyone entering a discussion group.

6. Click **OK** to enter the settings. You're now ready to use discussion groups.

Displaying the List of Available Discussion Groups

Displaying discussion groups is very similar to displaying newsgroups. Follow these steps:

1. From the Netscape Message Center, highlight your discussion group server (see Figure 4.2).

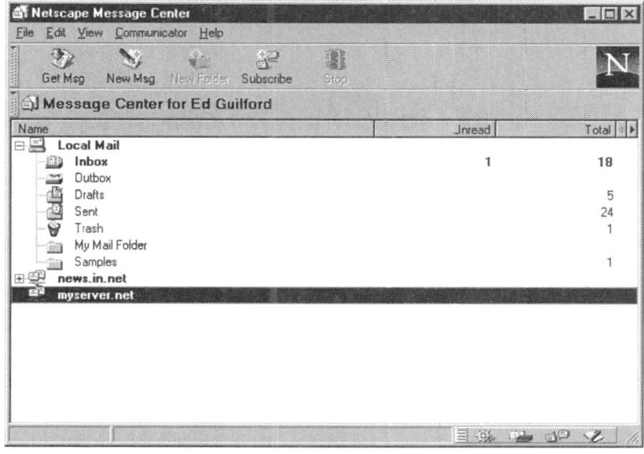

Figure 4.2   Select your discussion group server.

2. Click the **Subscribe** button on the toolbar, and the Subscribe to Discussion Groups dialog box opens (see Figure 4.3). Unless your company is very large, there probably won't be many groups listed here.

3. Click any groups to which you want to subscribe, and then click the **Subscribe** button.

4. Click **OK** to close the dialog box. The groups you subscribed to are listed under your discussion group server.

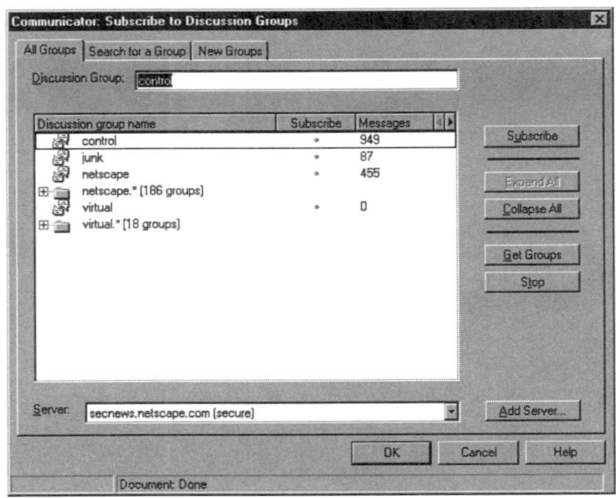

Figure 4.3   Subscribe to any available discussion groups.

Searching for a Discussion Group

If you have a large company, hundreds of discussion groups might be available. Obviously, you don't want to spend all day scrolling through the list of groups looking for one you are interested in. Fortunately, Collabra includes a search engine. Follow these steps to use it:

1. From the Netscape Message Center, highlight your discussion group server and click the **Subscribe** button on the toolbar. The Subscribe to Discussion Groups dialog box opens.

2. Click the **Search for a Group** tab to see the options shown in Figure 4.4.

3. Type a search string in the **Search For** text box.

What About the Server?   Most small- to medium-sized companies will have only one Collabra server. If your company has more than one, you can change the server you are searching by using the **On Server** drop-down list.

CAUTION

4. Click **Search Now**, and Collabra displays a list of discussion groups that match your search criteria.

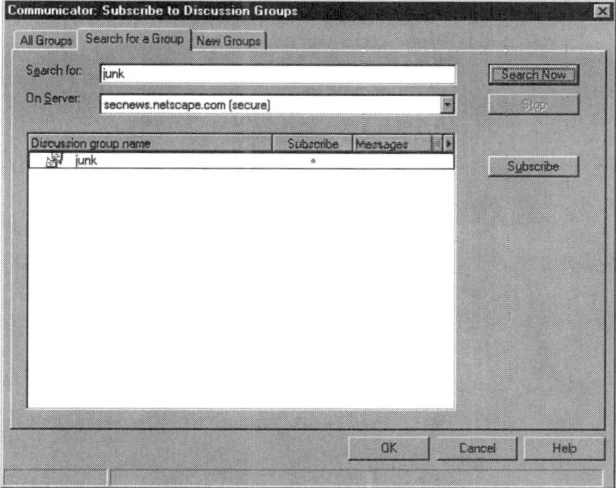

Figure 4.4 Searching for discussion groups is easy in Collabra.

5. If you find the group you are looking for, select it and click the **Subscribe** button.

6. (Optional) Repeat steps 2 through 5 to search for groups using other search criteria.

7. Click **OK** to close the Subscribe to Discussion Groups dialog box.

Once you have found and subscribed to a discussion group, you can read and post messages to it just like you did in newsgroups. See Lesson 2 for more information.

Adding a New Discussion Group

One thing that sets discussion groups apart from newsgroups is that you have the ability to create new discussion groups relatively easily. You are limited only by your company's policy on what or how many discussion groups you can create. Check with your system administrator for rules on creating new discussion groups. If he or she approves your new group, follow these steps to create it:

1. Open the Netscape Message Center and highlight your company's discussion group server.

2. Open the **File** menu and select **New Discussion Group**.

3. If you get a dialog box asking for your user name and password, type them and click **OK**.

4. Enter the name of the discussion group you are creating and click **OK**.

After you create a new discussion group, you can use it just like any other discussion group.

In this lesson, you learned how to add your company's discussion group server to your Collabra setup and how to create your own discussion group.

Netscape Conference

Holding Virtual Meetings with Netscape Conference

In this lesson, you learn the basics of using Netscape Conference.

What Is Netscape Conference?

Have you ever wished that you could talk to your sister in Alabama, your parents in California, or your brother in the next town without paying long distance charges? With Netscape Conference, you can—as long as you take the time to get them all set up with an Internet account. For business applications, it makes even more sense; you can put away your plane tickets and discuss this month's sales figures from your desk.

Netscape Conference enables you to take part in real-time audio conferencing and data sharing. You use Netscape Conference as you would a telephone: You talk into a microphone attached to your PC's sound card, and Netscape Conference sends your voice over the Internet to your family or colleagues. Netscape Conference includes speed dialing and call-screening features, and it even has a mute button!

There's One Catch   You can use Netscape Conference only if the person you want to call also has a copy of Netscape Conference (which is included with Netscape Communicator).

New with this version of Netscape Conference is a "Collaborative Browsing" tool . With Collaborative Browsing, you can lead your friends around the Web. You click a link, and Navigator takes both you and your friend to the same site.

Netscape Conference also includes a chat tool (with which you "talk" by typing what you want to say) and a Whiteboard (through which you can share text and graphical data). In addition, there's a phone book that you can use to store the e-mail addresses for the people you talk to often. And if your friends aren't home, Netscape Conference gives you a way to leave them voice messages.

Won't I Need a Sound Card?   If you do not have a sound card, you can still use the chat tool (which allows you to type messages you want to send) and the Whiteboard (which lets you transfer graphics and annotate them during a virtual meeting).

Setting Up Netscape Conference

Netscape Conference comes with a wizard to help you set up the program the first time you use it. Follow these steps to see how it works:

1. Connect to the Internet.

2. Open the **Start** menu, point to **Programs**, point to **Netscape Communicator**, and click **Netscape Conference**.

3. The Setup Wizard brings up a welcome screen. Click **Next** to continue.

4. The next screen goes over the minimum requirements for Netscape Conference. Read the requirements and click **Next**.

5. The next screen allows you to set up your business card (as shown in Figure 1.1). Your business card enables other people on the Net to identify you. Fill out the form and click **Next**.

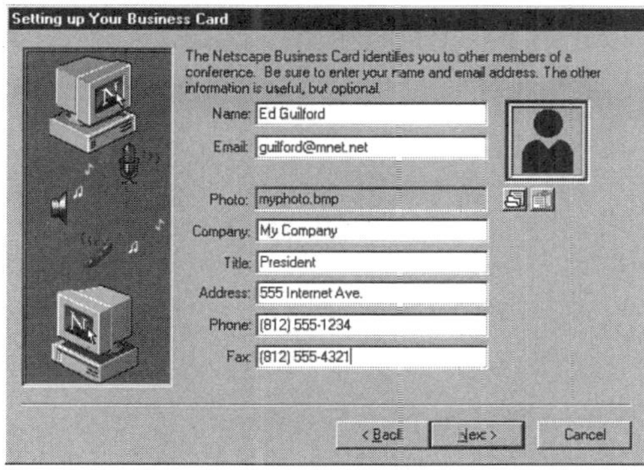

Figure 1.1   Enter the information for your business card.

Photogenic?   If you have a photo image file, you can include it with your business card. To do so, click the folder icon (next to the Photo field) and select the file that contains a digital version of your photograph.

6. The next screen asks you to specify which server you want to use for conferencing. You can use the default Netscape server. Leave the box next to **List My Name in Phonebook** checked. (This way, others can find you if they want to call.) Then click the **Next** button.

7. Select the type of connection you have (see Figure 1.2) and click **Next**.

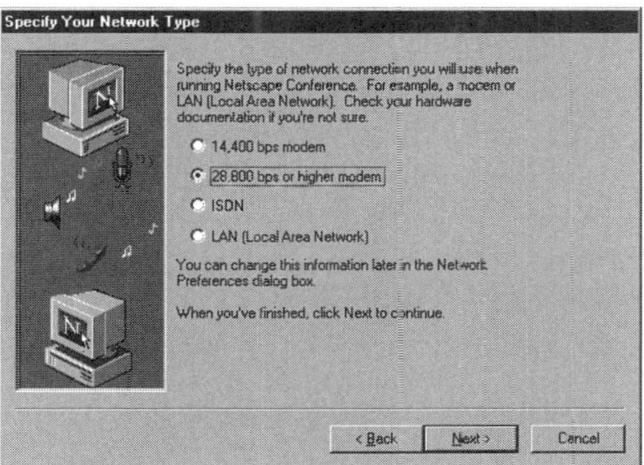

Figure 1.2   Select your connection type from this list.

8. The next screen asks you to confirm your sound card. If you only have one sound card (most people do), the default choices should be fine. Click **Next** to continue.

9. The next screen explains the audio test. Make sure your microphone is connected to your computer and click **Next**.

10. Follow the instructions to perform the microphone test. When you finish, click **Next**.

11. Congratulations! You've finished with the setup. Click the **Finish** button to open Netscape Conference.

I Need to Change My Setup   This setup procedure is a one-time process. The next time you run Netscape Conference, the program window appears immediately, and you can start making phone calls. If you want to change settings later, you can run Setup Wizard again by opening the **Help** menu and selecting **Setup Wizard**.

Starting a Conference

To start a conference, you send an invitation to the person with whom you want to talk. In order to send the invitation, you need that person's e-mail address. If you don't know the person's address, there's a chance that you can obtain it from Netscape—that is, if the person you're looking for is logged on to Netscape Conference. When you start Netscape Conference, it automatically registers you on the Netscape conference server. The Web Phonebook keeps a list of everyone who is currently running Netscape Conference, which makes it easier to find someone to conference with.

The person with whom you want to conference must also have Netscape Communicator. In addition, in order to receive your invitation, he must be connected to the Internet and must be running Netscape Conference.

What's the Attendant?   The Netscape Conference Attendant is a program that monitors incoming calls without running Netscape Conference. If Netscape Conference Attendant is running and you receive an invitation to a conference, you will be notified. If you accept the invitation, Netscape Conference starts automatically. To run Netscape Conference Attendant, open the **Start** menu, point to **Programs**, point to **Netscape Communicator**, point to **Utilities** and click **Netscape Conference Attendant**. While the attendant is running, a phone icon is displayed on the taskbar.

To start a conference, follow these steps:

1. Connect to the Internet and start Netscape Conference. The Netscape Conference main screen appears (see Figure 1.3).

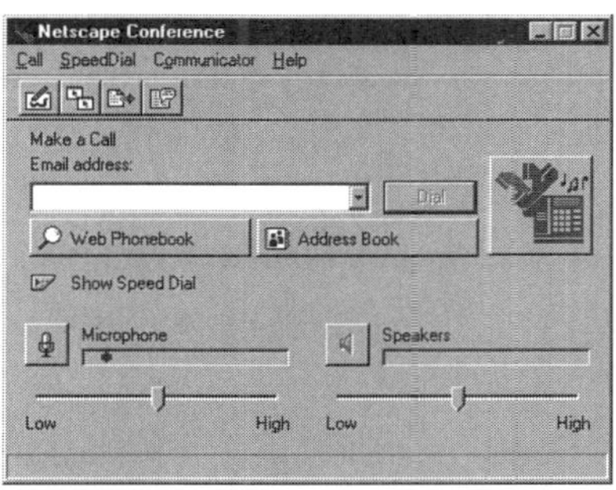

Figure 1.3   Netscape Conference main screen.

2. Enter the address of the person you want to invite, using one of the following methods:

- Enter his e-mail address directly into the **Type In Email Address** text box. If the person's e-mail address is in your address book, click the **Address Book** button to open your address book. Then double-click the name of the person you want to invite.

- Click the **Web Phonebook** button to see a list of everyone registered on Netscape's server. Netscape Navigator opens, displaying the Conference Phonebook page (see Figure 1.4). You can type a name in the box and click the **Search** button, or you can click **View All Entries** to browse through the list. When you find the person you want to call, click his name, and Netscape Conference dials him automatically.

- Click one of the Speed Dial buttons. To add an address to a Speed Dial button, click one of the **Speed Dial** buttons and add the information to the dialog box that appears. If the Speed Dial buttons are not visible, click the arrow beside **Show Speed Dial** (see Figure 1.5).

Netscape Conference sends an invitation to the person you selected. If that person is currently connected to the Internet and is running Netscape Conference—and if he isn't involved in a conference—he receives your invitation. When you receive an invitation, the computer beeps, and a dialog box appears, asking if you want to accept the invitation.

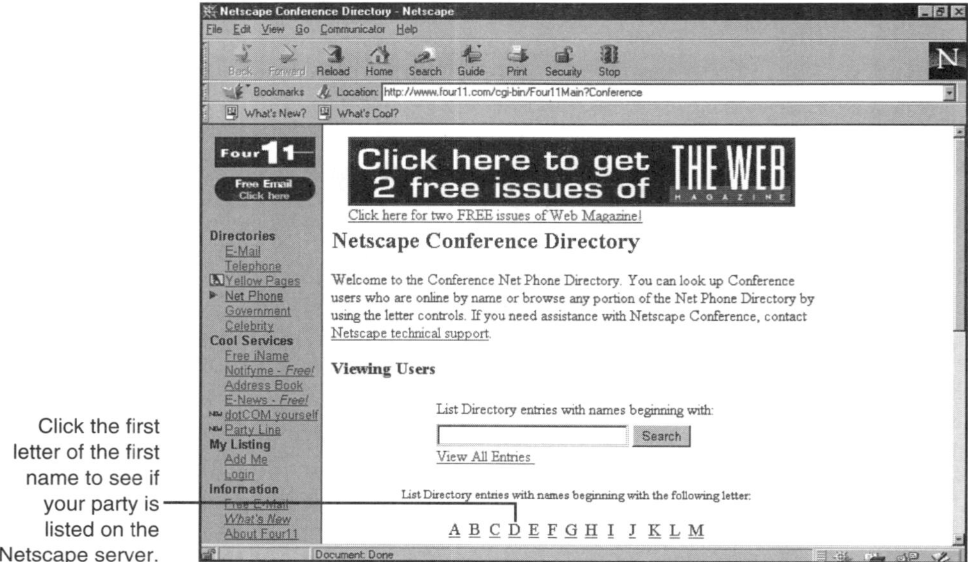

Click the first letter of the first name to see if your party is listed on the Netscape server.

Figure 1.4 Netscape's Conference Phonebook.

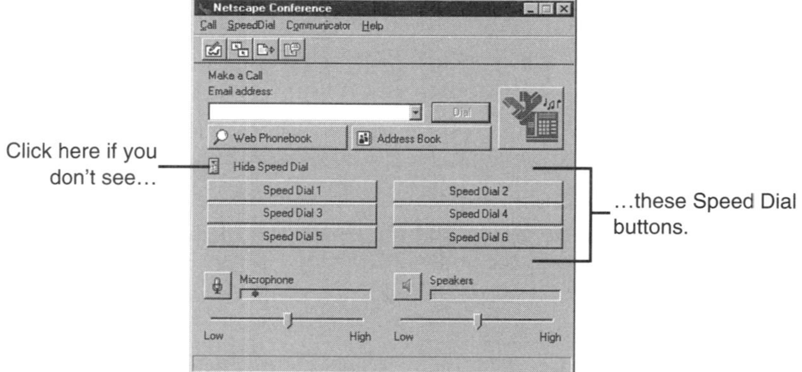

Click here if you don't see...

...these Speed Dial buttons.

Figure 1.5 The Speed Dial buttons.

3. Repeat step 2 to invite others to join your conference.

4. If the person accepts your invitation, your connection is established. You can talk into your PC's microphone, and you can hear the other person's voice through your speakers.

5. When you want to leave the conference, open the **Call** menu, select **Hang Up**, and click **Yes**, or just close the Netscape Conference window.

Trouble Hearing?   If you have trouble hearing what's being said, drag the slider under **Speakers** to the right to increase the volume.

CAUTION

Receiving a Call

Receiving a call is easy: Simply connect to the Internet and start Netscape Conference. To make sure you can receive calls, follow these steps:

1. From Netscape Conference, open the **Call** menu, and you will see the screen shown in Figure 1.6.

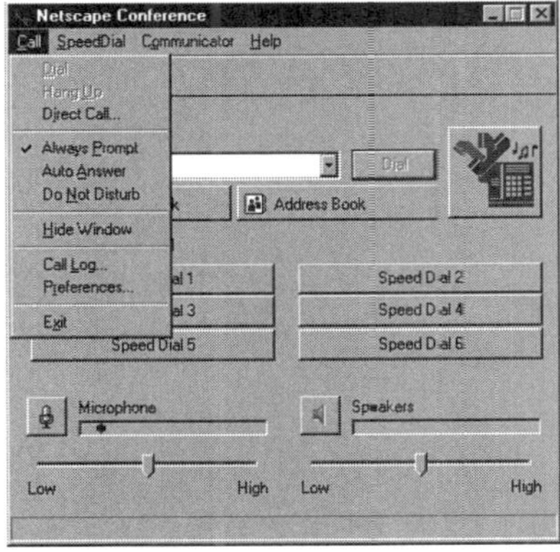

Figure 1.6   The Call menu.

2. Choose from these three options:

- **Do Not Disturb.** This option runs Netscape Conference but doesn't accept any incoming calls. Use this option if you want to start a conference, but you don't want to receive any calls from others.

- **Always Prompt.** Choose this option to have Conference ask if you want to receive a prompt before you answer a call. With this option checked (this is the default), you will see a dialog box telling you who is calling and asking if you want to receive the call. It's like having Caller ID! You don't have to accept the call from your boss, but you can keep the line open for your friends.

- **Auto Answer.** In this mode, Conference answers all incoming calls. If you want to talk to anyone who calls you, choose this option.

Once you accept a call, you can continue your conference.

In this lesson, you learned the basics of Netscape Conference. In the next lesson, you'll learn how to use the Whiteboard to share documents during a conference.

Sharing Documents Using the Whiteboard

In this lesson, you learn how to use Netscape Conference's Whiteboard to share files during a conference.

What Is the Whiteboard?

The Whiteboard is the "overhead projector" for your conference. You can post an image to the Whiteboard and use the tools to draw, zoom, and mark up the image for emphasis. You can even draw arrows to an important part of the image (like this month's increased sales, for example). The only problem with the Whiteboard is that you may notice a slight drop in performance of your voice transfers while Whiteboard is running. However, that's a small price to pay if you can avoid unnecessary travel expenses.

Another feature of the Whiteboard is that you and the person you are calling can mark up the image simultaneously. You won't have to bang elbows marking up a piece of paper. Your caller can mark one part of the image while you mark up another.

The Whiteboard contains two distinct layers:

- **Image Layer**   Images loaded to the Whiteboard exist on this layer.
- **Markup Layer**   When you make marks on the image using the tools on the toolbar, those marks exist on this level.

It's like placing a clear piece of plastic on your overhead. This enables you to erase your markups without reloading the image. (And no more spitting on paper towels to wipe off those overheads.)

Loading an Image

Whiteboard gives you the option of loading an image you have on your hard drive or capturing an image from your desktop. First, let's look at loading a previously created image. If you already have an image in TIFF, GIF, JPEG, or BMP format, you can use it. Follow these steps:

1. During a conference, click the **Whiteboard** button. The Whiteboard program starts.

2. To load an image, open the **File** menu and select **Open**, or click the **Open File** button. Change the file type if necessary, and then change to the directory in which the file is located. Select the file and click **Open**.

3. The image is not loaded at first. Instead, there is a dotted box with a crosshair in the upper-left corner (see Figure 2.1). This dotted box represents the size of the image. Position the box where you want the image to appear on the Whiteboard, and then click the left mouse button. Your image is then inserted there.

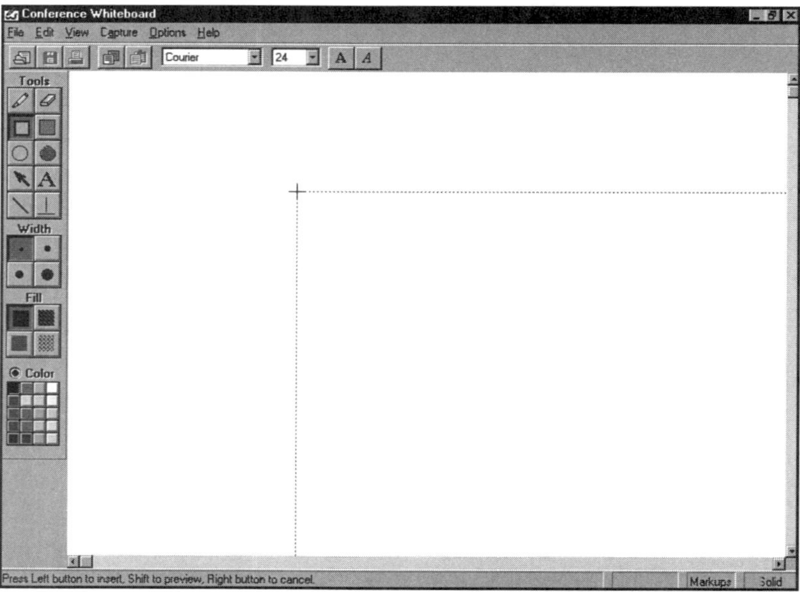

Figure 2.1   Inserting an image in the Whiteboard.

4. After an image loads, it is automatically sent to the other attendee. If necessary, you (or the others) can mark up the image with the toolbar tools described later.

Loading an Image with Screen Capture

Most of the time, you won't have an image file just waiting to be opened in the Whiteboard. Luckily, Whiteboard has a convenient utility that enables you to capture all or a portion of your desktop. Follow these steps to capture an image:

1. From the Whiteboard, open the **Capture** menu and select one of these three options:

   - **Window**   This option captures the contents of a window on your desktop. If you want to include only the contents of the window, click in the window. If you want to include the entire window (the title bar, toolbars, menus, and so on), click the title bar. The outline of the captured area appears in the Whiteboard (see Figure 2.2). Click the left mouse button when you have captured the area you want.

Figure 2.2   This is the area that will be displayed after capture.

   - **Desktop**   This option captures your entire desktop. This might be a useful option if you were trying to teach your mom how to run her new computer.

   - **Region**   This option allows you to capture a region from your desktop. After you select this option, a crosshair appears. Click the spot on your desktop where you want the upper-left corner of the region. Then press and hold down the button and drag your mouse to the lower-right until a box encloses the region you want to capture. Release the mouse button to capture the region.

The Whiteboard Is in the Way   If the Whiteboard window gets in the way of what you want to capture, you can hide it during the capture. To do so, open the Whiteboard's **Options** menu and click **Hide on Capture**.

2. After you capture the image, you can place it on the Whiteboard. It is now ready to be marked up.

Marking Up the Image on the Whiteboard

The Whiteboard contains a wide variety of tools you can use to add emphasis to your image. The following steps walk you through a short example of what you can do with the drawing tools. (See Table 2.1 for an explanation of the drawing tools.)

1. Open the Whiteboard and insert an image using one of the previously mentioned techniques.

2. Select the **Circle** tool, and then select a larger width to add emphasis. Click somewhere on the Whiteboard and drag a circle around an item (see Figure 2.3).

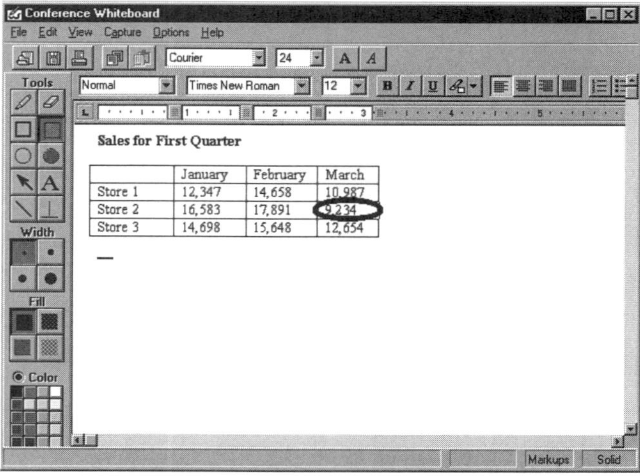

Figure 2.3   Circle an item using the Circle tool.

3. Select the **Eraser** tool and drag it over the circle you just drew. Notice that only the circle disappears, not the text from the image.

4. Select the **Rectangle** tool. Click where you want the upper-left corner of the rectangle, and then drag the mouse to the lower-right corner. Release the mouse button, and a rectangle appears on the image.

5. Select the **Pointer** tool and place an arrow on the Whiteboard. You can use this tool to point out important figures in your presentation.

6. Select the **Text** tool and click below the pointer. Then type some text to add to the Whiteboard (see Figure 2.4).

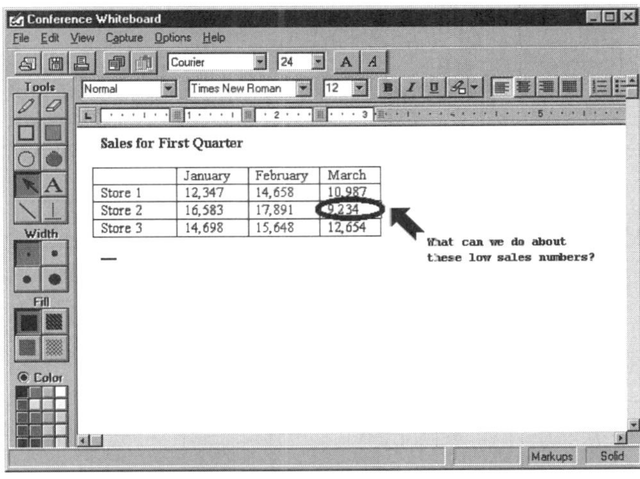

Figure 2.4   Emphasizing an important figure on the Whiteboard.

7. If you think you might want to keep the markups for a future meeting, or if you want to include them in your minutes, you can save the contents of the Whiteboard. Open the **File** menu and select **Save As**. Choose a name for the file and click **Save**.

8. When you finish making your point, open the **Edit** menu and select **Clear Markups**. Notice that the image remains on the Whiteboard, and you can use it to make another point.

9. When you finish marking up this image, open the **Edit** menu and choose **Clear Whiteboard**. The Whiteboard is erased—ready for you to open the next image.

10. To close the Whiteboard, open the **File** menu and select **Close** (or click the **Close** button).

Table 2.1   The Drawing Tools

Tool	Name	Description
	Freehand Line	Draws lines, curves, and other shapes freehand.
	Eraser	Erases markups or parts of the image (depending on the Options menu setting).
	Rectangle	Draws a perfect rectangle.
	Filled Rectangle	Draws a rectangle filled with color.
	Circle	Draws an ellipse. To draw a perfect circle, press and hold the **Ctrl** key while drawing.
	Filled Circle	Draws an ellipse filled with color.
	Pointer	Draws an arrow.
	Text	Inserts text.
	Line	Draws a straight line.
	Perpendicular Line	Draws a line that is perpendicular to one of the sides of the window.
	Width	Enables you to change the width of the lines you draw.
	Fill	Enables you to select the fill pattern for filled-in shapes.
	Color	Enables you to change the color of the objects you draw.

CAUTION

Too Chatty Be choosy when using the Whiteboard. Every time you start to draw on it, the Whiteboard becomes the focus for all the other attendees. This means that if someone is trying to type a message in the Chat window, she will be interrupted mid-sentence because her PC will bring the Whiteboard to the front of all open windows. If she tries to return to the Chat window and you continue to draw, you'll continue to interrupt her. So be courteous and use the Whiteboard only when you know that you "have the floor."

In this lesson, you learned how to use the Whiteboard. In the next lesson, you will learn how to have a written conversation using the Chat tool.

Talking with Text Using the Chat Tool

In this lesson, you learn how to use the Chat tool to type your conversation.

What Is the Chat Tool?

By now, you have read about Netscape Conference and you have probably had some fun talking with people using your microphone and speakers. But what if you or the person you want to talk to doesn't have a microphone or a sound card (heaven forbid)? You can still use Netscape Conference's Chat tool.

The Chat tool allows you to carry on a conversation by typing in what you want to say. You will see what you type on the screen, and you can send it to the person you are conferencing with. You might think this is no better than e-mail, but you do have the ability to converse in *real time*. You can type someone a question, and she can answer you back right away. You can also use the other features of conference (collaborative browsing, Whiteboard, and file transfers), so you can still have a productive conference even without the convenience of voice communications.

TERM **Real Time** A feature that enables you to converse interactively. In other words, you can ask a question and receive an answer right away.

Another nice thing about the Chat tool is that you can save the conversation when you finish. This gives you a record of your call—which could come in handy for business purposes. Any agreements you make during the conference can be recalled for future reference.

Using the Chat Tool

The basics of the Chat tool are very simple, so dive right in. Follow these steps:

1. Start a conference as you did in Lesson 1.

2. Click the **Chat** button.

3. Type what you want to say in the Personal Note Pad (see Figure 3.1).

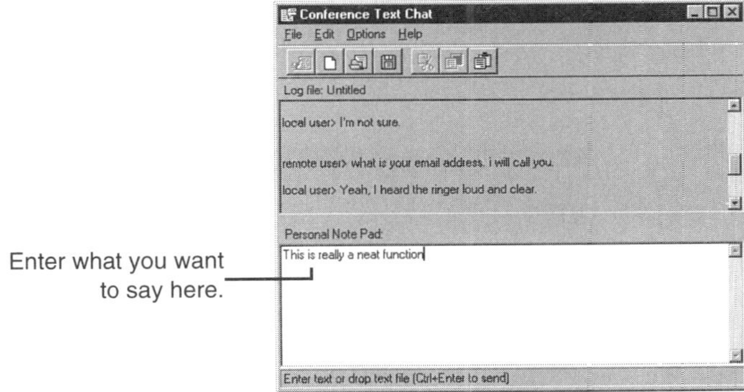

Enter what you want to say here.

Figure 3.1   With the Chat tool, you type what you want to say.

4. When you're ready to send your text, click the **Send** button (or press **Ctrl+Enter**).

5. Netscape records your conversation in the Log File portion of the window.

Importing Text into the Chat Tool

Another handy feature of the Chat tool is the ability to include text from a file. With this option, you can type part of what you want to say before you get on the Internet.

Why Should I Import?   Importing text is a good idea for several reasons. You can save valuable connect-time charges by typing what you want to say "offline." You may want to tell the caller what you've done this week or about some crazy stunts the kids have accomplished. After he reads this opening, the conversation proceeds from there.

Follow these steps to include text in your Chat window:

1. Using Notepad or another text editor, type in what you want to say.
2. Save the file. For this example, use the file name MYFILE.TXT.
3. Connect to the Internet, start your conference, and click the **Chat** icon in the toolbar.
4. Open the **File** menu and select **Include** (or click the **Include** button on the toolbar).
5. In the Include File Into Pad dialog box (see Figure 3.2), choose the file you just created and click **Open**.

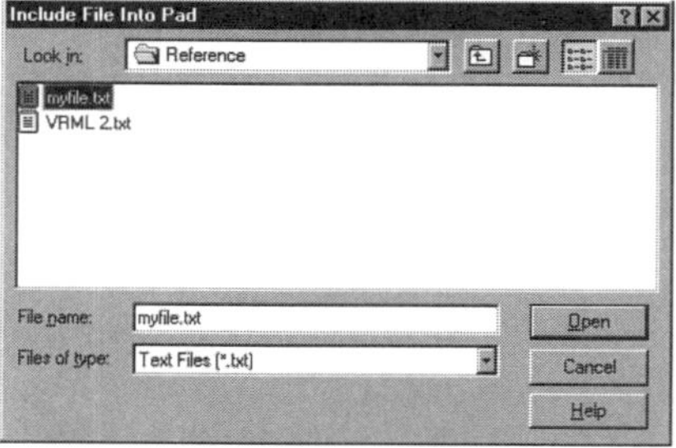

Figure 3.2   Use this dialog box to include your file.

6. The text from the file appears in the Personal Note Pad (see Figure 3.3).
7. Click the **Send** button to send the text to your caller. You can continue the conversation from there.

What About Copy/Paste?   You can also add text to the Chat tool by copying and pasting. Simply open the application that contains the text, highlight the text you want to send, and select the **Edit**, **Copy** command. Then move to the Chat tool and select **Edit**, **Paste** to copy the desired text into the Chat window.

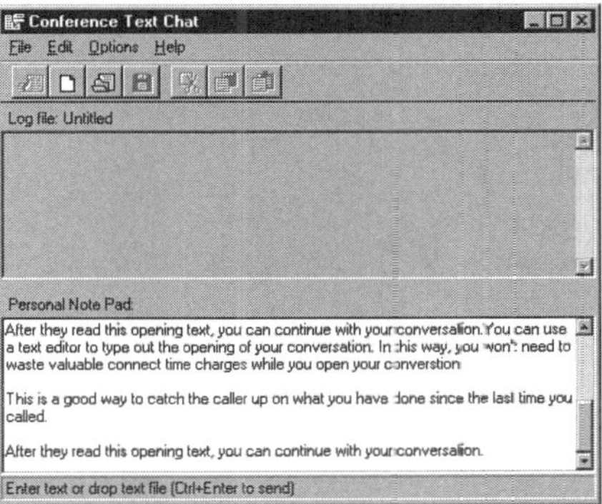

Figure 3.3   You can see the text from your file in the Personal Note Pad.

Saving a Record of Your Call

You may want to keep a record of a personal call so you can go back and read it
again later. If you make a business call, it can be invaluable to have that record.
With a record, there is no mistake on what you have agreed to. Follow these
steps to create the record:

1. After you complete your conversation, open the **File** menu and select
    Save As.

2. Type a name for the file in the dialog box and click **Save**. You now have
    a record of your call. You can open the file in any text editor to view the
    record.

3. If you want to start a new log file, open the **File** menu and choose **New**
    (or click the **New** button).

In this lesson, you learned how to use the Chat tool. In the next lesson, you'll
learn how to surf the Internet using collaborative browsing.

Surfing Together with Collaborative Browsing

In this lesson, you learn how to use collaborative browsing to allow everyone in your conference to view the same Web page.

What Is Collaborative Browsing?

Collaborative browsing sounds like a fancy term, but all it means is that you and your caller can view the same Web page at the same time. Maybe your mom doesn't know much about the Web and you want to take her on a virtual tour, or you want to look up company information while you're having a work-related conference. Whatever you use it for, collaborative browsing is a very convenient tool.

There are a few things you need to watch out for while you are in a collaborative browsing session. The performance of your conference will be degraded while you are browsing. Your voice transmissions will not be as clear during the browsing session, and it may take longer for one person in the conference to receive a Web page if you are connected to the Internet at different speeds.

Who's in Charge?   Only one person can be the leader in a collaborative browsing session. The others are along for the ride.

CAUTION

Collaborative Browsing Basics

Once you have the conference running, it's pretty easy to use the collaborative browsing feature. Follow these steps:

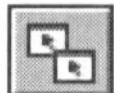

1. Start your conference and click the **Collaborative Browsing** button. You'll see a message box like the one shown in Figure 4.1.

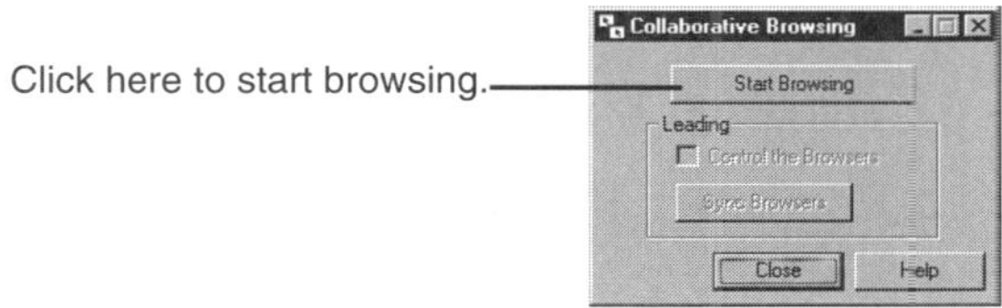

Figure 4.1 Click here to start collaborative browsing.

2. Click the **Start Browsing** button. The other member of the conference will get a message asking if he wants to join in the Collaborative Browsing session (see Figure 4.2).

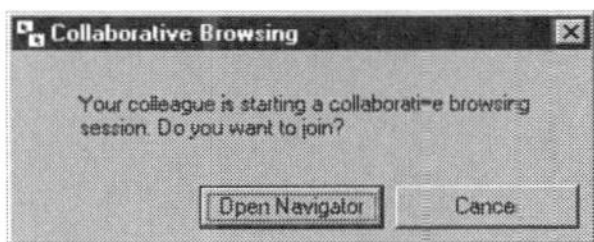

Figure 4.2 The receiver is asked if he wants to surf with you.

3. To join in, your colleague clicks the **Open Navigator** button. If he doesn't want to join in, he clicks **Cancel**.

4. Assuming the other person has joined, open Navigator and go to the page you want to show your colleague. Then go back to the Collaborative Browsing window and click the **Sync Browsers** button.

5. Navigator takes your colleague to the same page you are viewing.

I'm Tired of Leading   If you get tired of leading and want your colleague to take over, tell him to open the **Collaborative Browsing** window and click **Request to Lead**.

6. When you finish browsing, open the **Collaborative Browsing** window and click **Stop Browsing**. The person you were browsing with regains control of his browser.

As you can see, the Collaborative Browsing tool is a powerful feature. Use your imagination, and the possibilities for its usefulness are endless.

In this lesson, you learned how to surf together using collaborative browsing. In the next lesson, you will learn how to transfer files during your conference.

Sharing Files

In this lesson, you learn how to share files during your conference.

What Is File Exchange?

The File Exchange tool provides an easy way to exchange files during your conference session. Suppose you have a Microsoft Excel file that contains last month's sales figures. Since sales were up, you want everyone in the conference to receive a copy of the file. Or maybe you just got pictures back from your son's big game and you want to send a copy to his grandma. Whatever the reason, File Exchange makes it easy to send it.

The advantage to sending files this way (as opposed to sending them via e-mail) is that all recipients receive the file right away. With e-mail, some recipients may not receive the file for several hours.

Sending Files

Selecting files is easy with File Exchange. If you know what files you want to send, you can load them into File Exchange before the conference starts. Follow these steps to select the files:

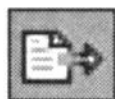

1. From Netscape Conference, click the **File Exchange** button on the toolbar. File Exchange opens (see Figure 5.1).
2. From the File Exchange toolbar, click the **Open** button (or open the **File** menu and select **Add to Send List**). The Add File to Send List dialog box opens (see Figure 5.2).

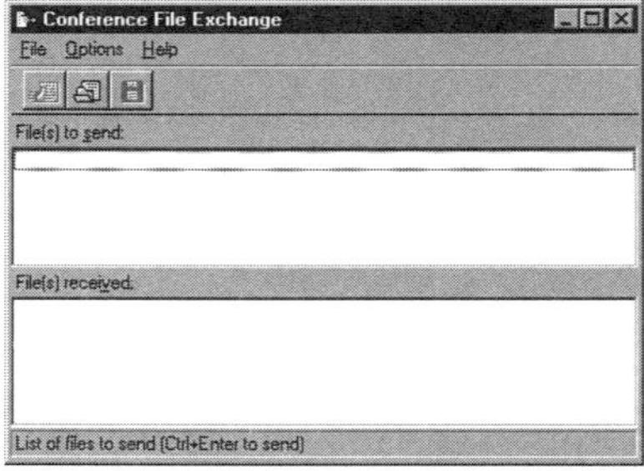

Figure 5.1   The File Exchange window.

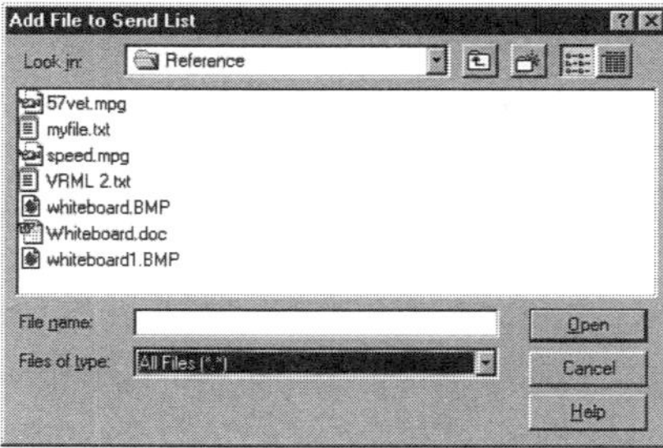

Figure 5.2   Choose the files you want to send from the Add File to Send List dialog box.

3. Click the **Files of Type** drop-down arrow and select the type of file you want to add. You can choose either **Executables** (programs) or **All Files**.

4. When you find the file you want to send, click it to select it. Then click the **Open** button. The file name appears in the File(s) to Send portion of the File Exchange window (see Figure 5.3).

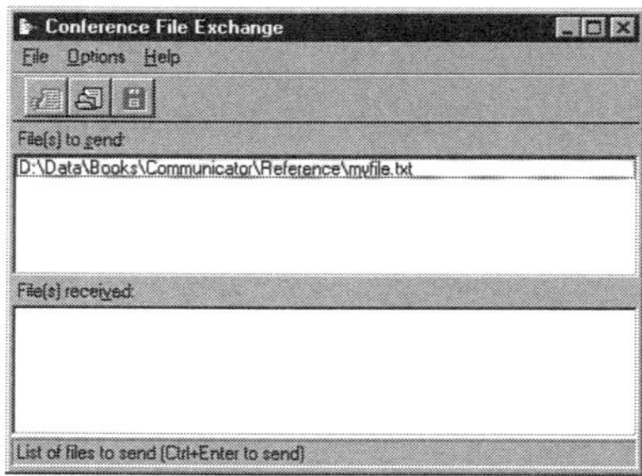

Figure 5.3   The file you selected appears in the top window.

5. If you want to send more files, repeat steps 2–4 until you have selected all of the files you want to send.

6. When you are ready to send the files, click the **Send** button.

Saving Received Files

After you receive files from another member of the conference, you will probably want to save the files to your hard drive. Follow these steps to do that:

1. From Netscape Conference, click the **File Exchange** button.

2. If any files have been sent to you, they are listed in the Files to Receive window (see Figure 5.4). Notice that the name of the sender appears beside each file.

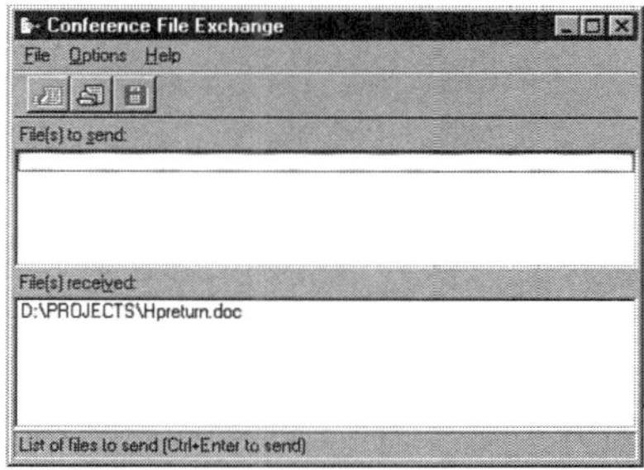

Figure 5.4   The received files are listed in the bottom window.

3. Select one of the files from the list, and then open the **File** menu and select **Save**.

4. Type a name for the file and click the **Save** button.

What's in a Name?   If you do not specify a name for the file, Netscape saves it using the same name as the sender's file.

CAUTION

Netscape saves the file to the location you specified and removes it from the File Exchange window. Repeat steps 3 and 4 to save any other files in the window.

If you have received files that you do not want to save, you can delete them. To do so, follow these steps:

1. Select the names of the files you want to delete from the Files to Receive window.

2. Open the **File** menu and select **Delete**.

3. A dialog box opens, asking if you're sure you want to delete the file. Click **OK**. Netscape removes the file from the list and your hard drive.

Setting File Exchange Options

In File Exchange, there are a number of options you can set. You can access these options from the **Options** menu. Here is a summary of your choices:

- **Compress**   Check this option and files will be compressed before they are sent over the network. This allows you to transfer files quickly.

Will Compression Hurt?   Compression will not hurt your files in any way. Compressing the file just packs the information into a smaller space to save time when you send it. When it gets to its destination, it will automatically be uncompressed.

CAUTION

- **Pop Up on Receive**   With this option checked, File Exchange automatically opens and moves to the front when files are received.

- **ASCII**   With this option checked, files will be transferred in ASCII. Choose this option if you are transferring text files.

- **Binary**   Choose this option to send files in binary format. This option should be checked if you are sending programs, images, or any other file that is not a text file.

In this lesson, you learned how to use the File Exchange program to transfer files in a conference.

Designing and Publishing Web Pages with Netscape Composer

What Can Composer Do for Me?

In this lesson, you learn how Composer can help you create your own Web pages and jazz up e-mail with graphics, links, and other objects.

What Is Composer?

When you wander the Web, pulling up pages and clicking links, it's easy to forget that behind each attractive page is a text file containing the codes that tell Navigator how to display the page. If you haven't seen these codes yet, run Navigator and open a page that interests you. Then open Navigator's **View** menu and select **Page Source**. Navigator displays the coded HTML file that it used to render the current Web page (see Figure 1.1).

In the old days, Web page developers created Web pages by manually typing all these codes into a text file and then saving the file with the .HTM or .HTML extension. Although you can still do that, many software companies have created special Web page editing programs (also called HTML editors) that take care of the coding for you. These programs act as word processing or desktop publishing programs for the Web. You type the text, format it, and add graphics and other objects; the HTML editor then inserts the necessary codes for you.

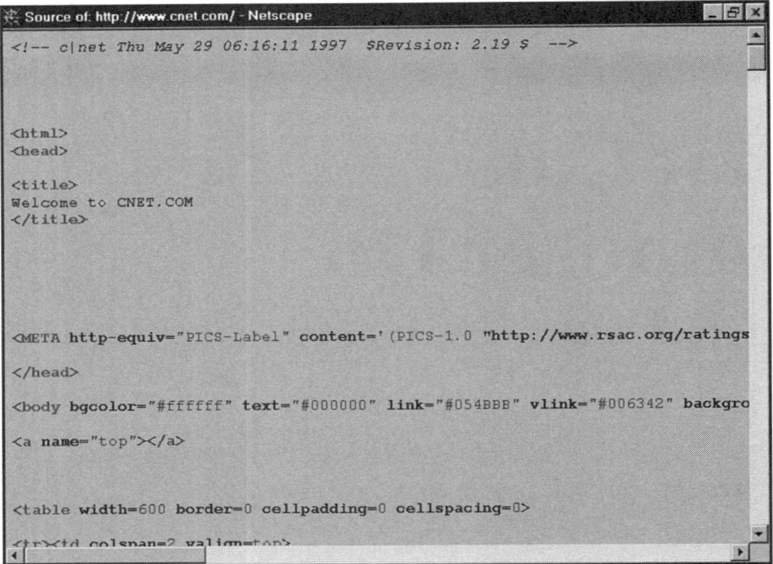

Figure 1.1   Behind every Web page is a text file that contains HTML codes.

Netscape Composer is Netscape Communicator's HTML editor. Formerly available only in Netscape Gold, Composer takes a central role in the Communicator package, providing the following enhancements:

- **Page wizards and templates** give you something to start with, so you never have to create a Web page from scratch. See Part 6 Lessons 2 and 3 for details.

- **E-mail support** allows you to enhance your e-mail messages with fancy text, bulleted and numbered lists, tables, graphics, and links.

- **Easy Web publishing** lets you save your Web pages directly to a Web server on the Internet or on your company's intranet with a single click of a button. See Part 6 Lesson 9, "Publishing Your Web Pages."

- **Spell checking** (a new tool) checks your Web pages and e-mail messages for spelling errors and typos.

Composer Plug-Ins?   Because Netscape designed Composer using open standards, third-party developers can develop plug-ins for Composer, such as grammar checkers and image editors. When you're looking for plug-ins, keep an eye out for Composer plug-ins.

Running Composer

You can run Composer in Windows 95 by selecting it from the **Start, Programs, Netscape Communicator** menu. In Windows 3.1, change to the Netscape Communicator program group and double-click the **Netscape Composer** icon.

Because Composer is an integral part of the Communicator suite, there are other more convenient methods of running Composer:

- Click the **Composer** button in the Component bar.
- Open the **Communicator** menu in any of the other Communicator components (Messenger or Collabra, for instance) and select the **Page Composer** option.
- To edit an existing page, you can open it directly in Composer. In Navigator, select **File, Open Page**. Type the URL of the page you want to open, and make sure **Composer** is selected. Click the **Open** button.
- You can start creating a Web page immediately by opening Navigator's **File** menu, pointing to **New**, and selecting **Blank Page, Page From Template**, or **Page From Wizard**. See Lessons 2 and 3 for details. (If you select the Template or Wizard option, the page opens in Navigator; you must then select **File, Edit Page** to display the page in Composer.)

However you choose to run Composer, the Composer window eventually appears. Figure 1.2 shows Composer displaying a Web page template from Netscape. Note that the Composer window contains tools you often see in standard word processing applications, including a formatting toolbar for styling text, as well as a standard toolbar for cutting, copying, pasting, and performing other common tasks. You will learn how to use these tools in the coming lessons.

Composer Does E-Mail, Too!

Composer is completely integrated with Netscape Messenger and Collabra. Whenever you display a window for composing a new e-mail message or creating a message to post in a newsgroup, the window contains the Composer toolbars. You can use the tools just as you do when creating a Web page to add bulleted lists, tables, graphics, links, and other objects to your messages (see Figure 1.3).

The standard toolbar

Composer's formatting toolbar

A Web page template from Netscape

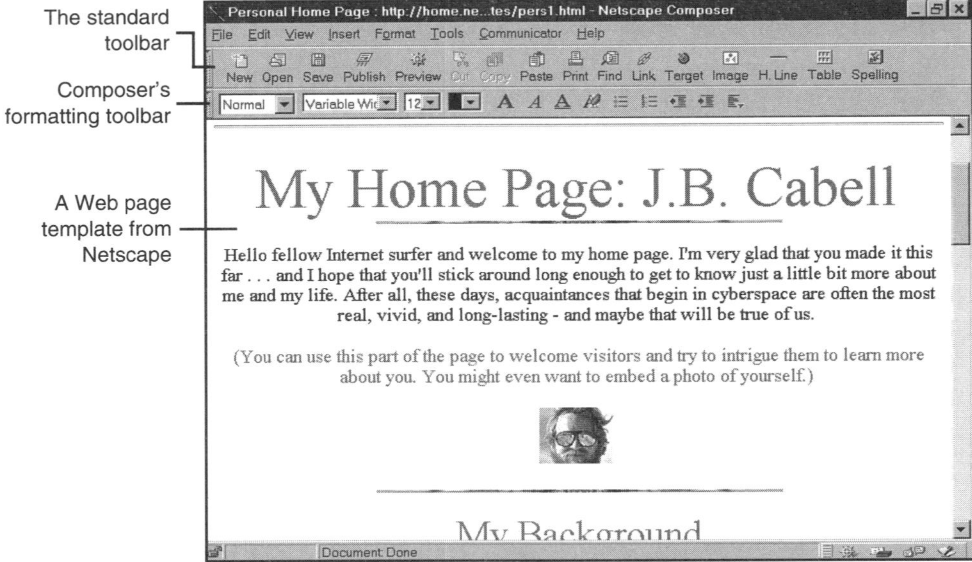

Figure 1.2 Composer's window looks like a word processor or desktop publisher.

The Composer toolbar

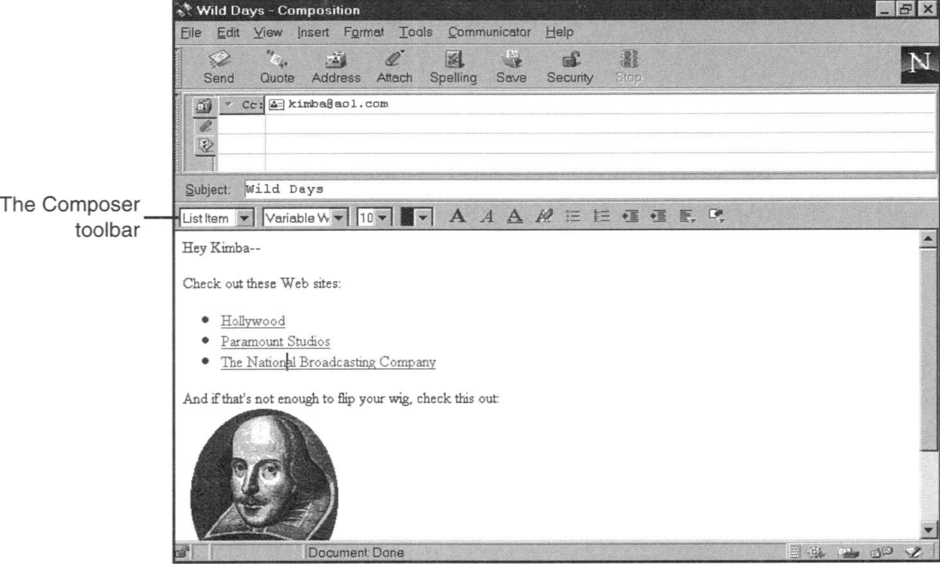

Figure 1.3 Add bulleted lists, links, and graphics to your missives.

Before You Save Web Pages

It may seem premature to discuss saving Web pages before you have even created one, but you can avoid frustration by preparing a storage area for your Web pages ahead of time. It is important that your Web page and all related files (graphics, sound clips, and so on) are stored in a single folder separate from your other files. When you go to place your page on the Web, you can simply dump all the files from this one folder into a folder or directory on the Web server. So before you start creating Web pages, use Windows Explorer or File Manager to create a separate folder for your Web page. Call it something like WebPage, WebTemp, Composer, or Practice.

Entering Preferences for Composer

Although Composer is ready to use right away, you may want to change a few settings before you begin. To change the configuration options for Composer, take the following steps:

1. Run Composer. Open the **Edit** menu, select **Preferences**, and click **Composer** (under Category). The Preferences dialog box shown in Figure 1.4 appears.

2. Click in the **Author Name** text box and type your name. This name appears in the HTML code for every Web page you create, but it is not displayed on the page itself.

3. Make sure there is a check mark next to **Automatically Save Page Every ___ Minutes**. This will help you recover a Web page if your computer crashes or you accidentally exit Composer without saving changes to a page.

4. Under **External Editors,** you can choose other programs that you want to use to edit your Web page and graphics. For example, you may want to use WordPad as your HTML Source editor or LView Pro as your graphics editor. The Source Editor opens the HTML file as a text file so you can edit HTML codes manually, which is sometimes helpful. (See Lesson 11, "Adding HTML Tags," for details.)

5. Under **Font Size Mode**, select any one of the following options to control the way Composer displays font sizes on the Font Size drop-down list:

   Show Relative Size As Points Based on Your Navigator Font Sizes displays font sizes as points (there are approximately 72 points in an inch). If you are accustomed to working with text size in terms of points, select this option.

Show Relative HTML Font Scale: –2, –1, 0, +1, +2, +3, +4 displays font sizes according to HTML standards. 0 is normal text size, –1 and –2 are smaller than normal, and +1, +2 +3, and +4 are larger than normal. If you select this option, the Font Size drop-down list displays these settings as your available font sizes, which may be a little more difficult to work with.

Show Relative HTML Scale and Absolute "Point Size" Attributes tells Composer to display both point size and relative HTML sizes on the Font Size drop-down list.

6. Ignore the Publishing options (in the Category list under Composer). Part 6 Lesson 9 provides details on how to enter Publishing preferences. Click **OK** to save your changes.

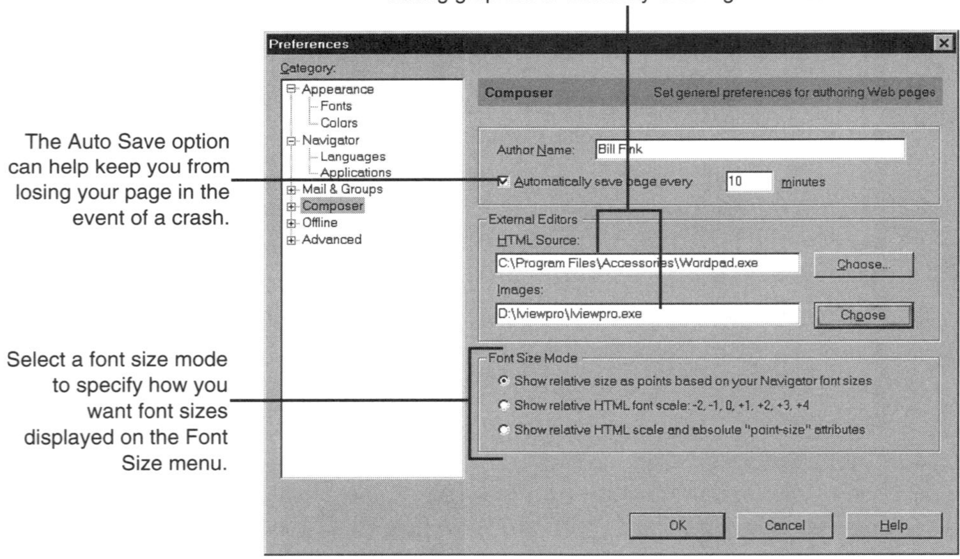

Figure 1.4   Enter your preferences for Composer.

This lesson introduced you to Composer. You learned what Composer is, how it can help you create Web pages, and how to enter your preferences. In the next lesson, you will use Composer along with Netscape's Web Page Wizard to create your first Web page.

Using the Netscape Page Wizard

In this lesson, you learn to use the Netscape Page Wizard to make simple, good-looking Web pages easily.

What's a Wizard?

Netscape Composer gives you access to the Netscape Page Wizard, an automated program that practically lays out a Web page for you. Because the wizard is designed to create one basic type of page, it's not a very flexible program and isn't well-suited to multipage sites. Still, if you want to put together a single good-looking page as quickly as possible, this is a tool for you.

Netscape Page Wizard does not come with your copy of Netscape Composer; it is located on Netscape's servers. As such, you access it via a Web page. One advantage to having the design program reside on Netscape's servers instead of on your computer is that Netscape can add features to it at any time, and everyone can use those features immediately without having to download new software. Therefore, it's entirely possible that between the time you read this section and the time you use the wizard, other features will have been added!

Running the Wizard

To have the wizard program put your page together, follow these steps:

1. Connect to the Internet and start Netscape Composer.
2. Click the **New** button in Composer's toolbar and click the **Page From Page Wizard** button.

3. A browser window opens up the three-framed document shown in Figure 2.1. Only the upper-right frame has anything in it. Scroll down to the bottom of this frame and click the **Start** button. (Because the Page Wizard runs on the Internet, you must run it from Navigator. You can then save the page you create and open it in Composer to make additional changes.)

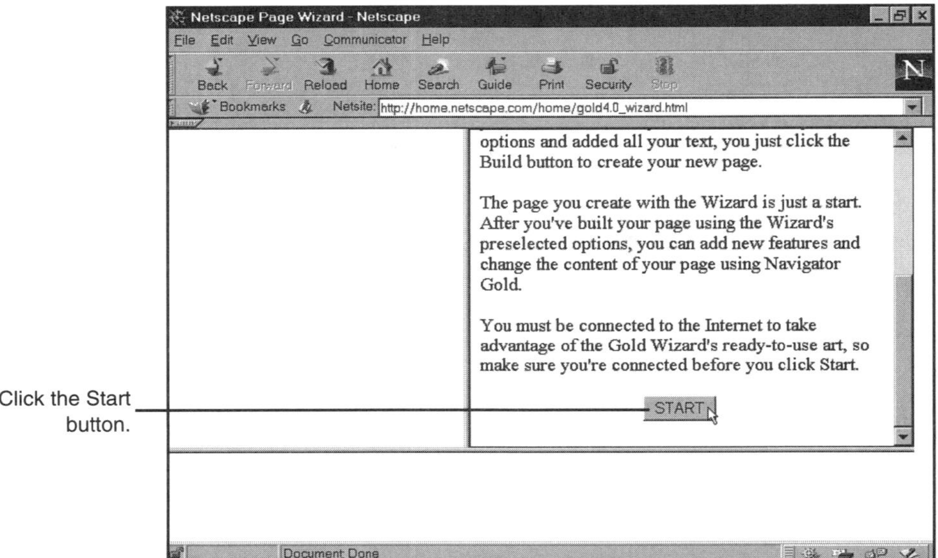

Click the Start button.

Figure 2.1   The initial screen of the wizard.

4. The upper-left frame contains instructions for using the wizard, and the upper-right frame has a preview of the page you're designing. The underlined links in the left frame are commands for the wizard. Click the **Give Your Page a Title** command.

5. A simple form with just one field appears in the bottom frame (see Figure 2.2). Select the text that is there, and then type **The Well-Meaning Zippy-Doo Page**.

6. Click the **Apply** button, and this title appears in the preview document.

Fix Your Mistakes   If you discover that you messed up your entry for any of the commands, just select that command again. The form will reappear, and you can change what you selected!

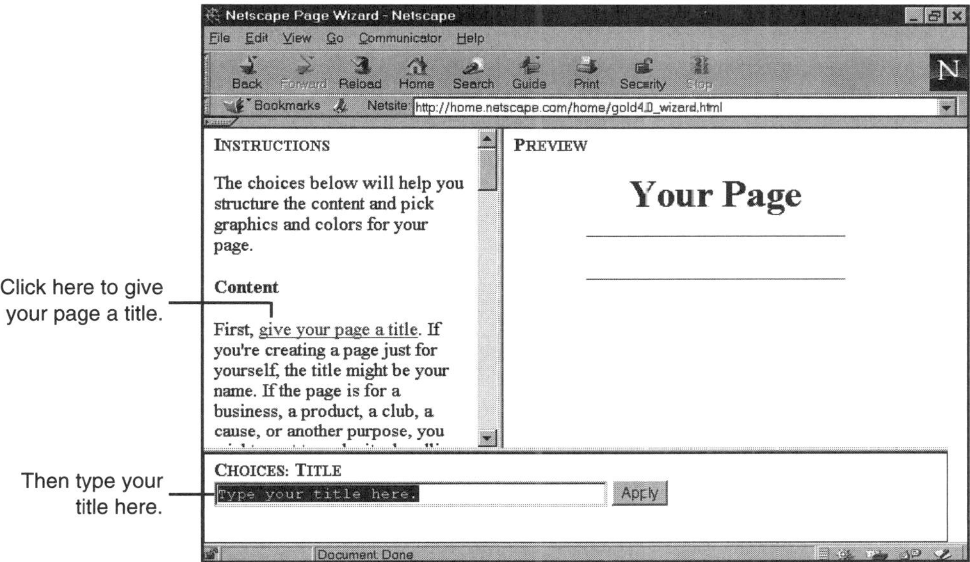

Figure 2.2   Use the wizard to choose a title.

7. A little lower in the left frame (you may have to scroll down to find it), click the **Type an Introduction** command. Another one-field form appears in the bottom frame.

8. Replace the text in this field (which can hold up to 1,000 characters) with the text **This page will keep you up to date with the latest in Zippy-Dooism, and how you can do the doo with the best of them!**

9. Click the **Apply** button, and this text appears in the preview frame.

10. In the left frame, scroll to and click the **Add Some Hot Links to Other Web Pages** command. A two-field form appears in the bottom frame as shown in Figure 2.3.

11. Replace the text in the **Name** field with **Nat Gertler, Author Supreme!**; then replace the text in the **URL** field with **http://ourworld.compuserve.com/homepages/nat/**. (Forcing the reader to type nice things about you is one of the few advantages of being a computer book author.)

12. Click the **Apply** button, and this link appears in the preview frame (see Figure 2.4). You can repeat steps 11 and 12 to add links to other pages.

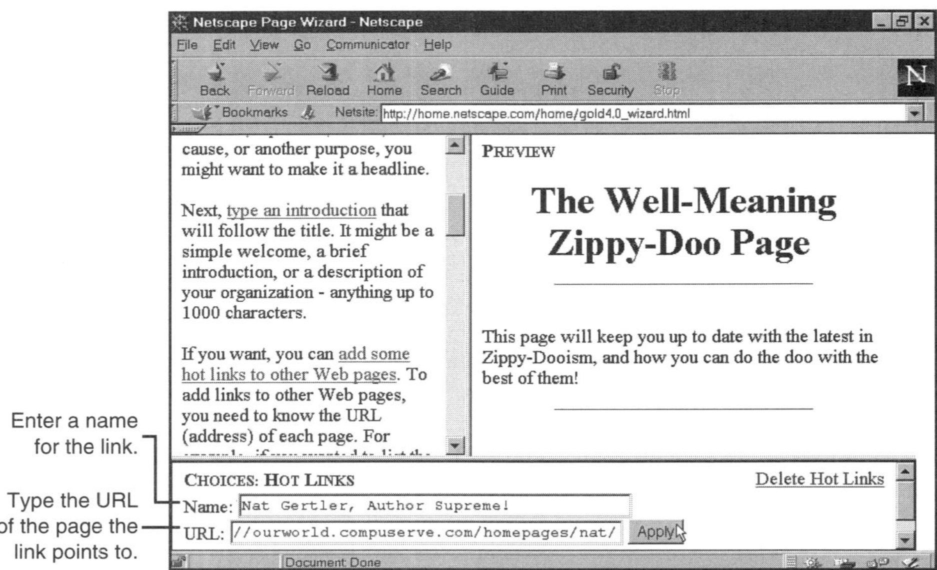

Figure 2.3 You can add links to your page.

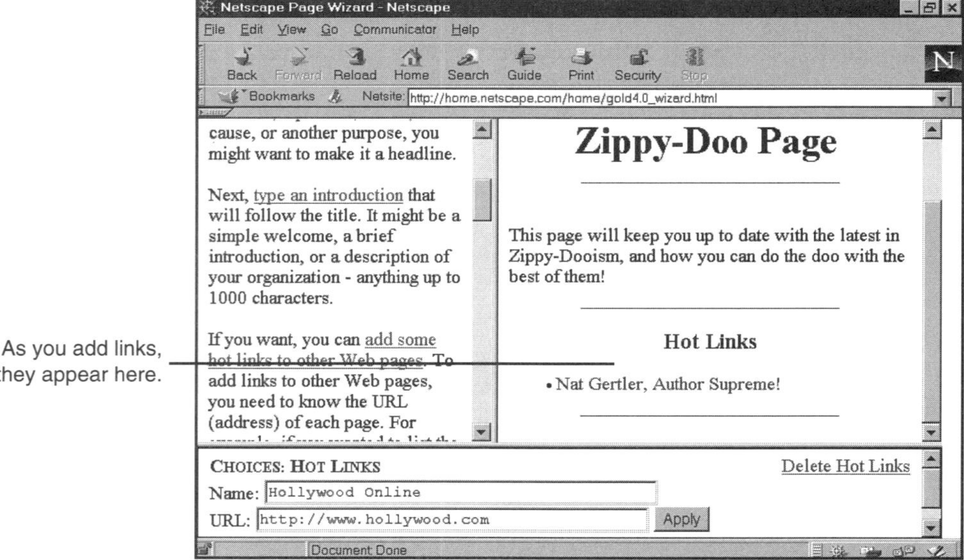

Figure 2.4 The wizard lets you add links to other Web pages.

More Links or Fewer Links   Note that if you repeat this command, you will be adding another link, not replacing the existing one. You can string together as many links to interesting sites as you want. To delete your links, click **Delete Hot Links**. In the list that appears, click to remove the check marks next to the links you want to delete.

13. In the left frame, scroll to and click the **Type a Paragraph of Text to Serve As a Conclusion** command. Another 1,000-character text field appears in the bottom frame.

14. In this field, type **For all those Zippy-Doos and those who love them: Be kind to each other, if anyone is watching.**

15. Click the **Apply** button, and the wizard adds that text to the preview frame.

16. Click the **Add an EMail Link** command, and another one-field form appears in the bottom frame. Type your e-mail address into the field and click **Apply** to put it on the preview frame.

17. Now that you have all the text on the page, it's time to worry about how it looks. Click the **A Preset Color Combination** command, and the wizard displays color choices in the bottom frame (see Figure 2.5).

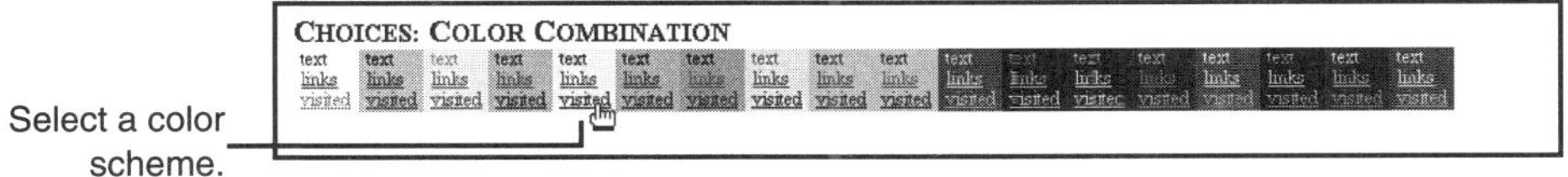

Figure 2.5   In color, this looks a lot more, well, colorful!

18. Click one of the squares with dark text on a bright background. The preview frame immediately takes on the color combination used in that square. (The background of the preview frame becomes the selected background color, most text becomes the color of the word "text," and the links become the color of the word "links.")

19. Skip over the next few commands, which let you set the background and text colors individually. Click the **Choose a Bullet Style** command, and the bullet style choices shown in Figure 2.6 appear in the bottom frame.

20. Click the *bullet* (a typography term for a highlighting mark) with the white star on a blue background. The selected bullet appears in front of the link (or links, if you added several) in the preview frame.

21. Click the **Choose a Horizontal Rule Style** command. A column of separation lines appears in the bottom frame (see Figure 2.7).

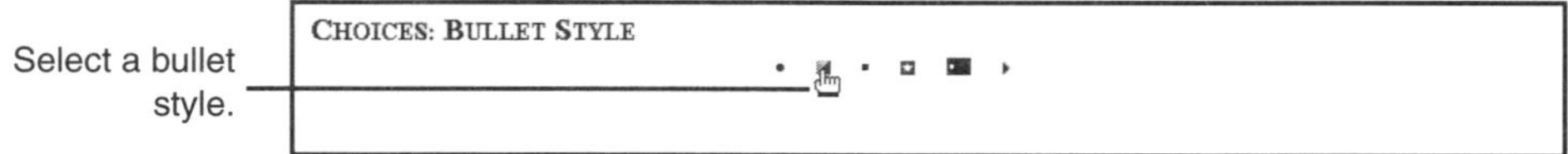

Select a bullet style.

Figure 2.6   The bullet styles from which you can choose.

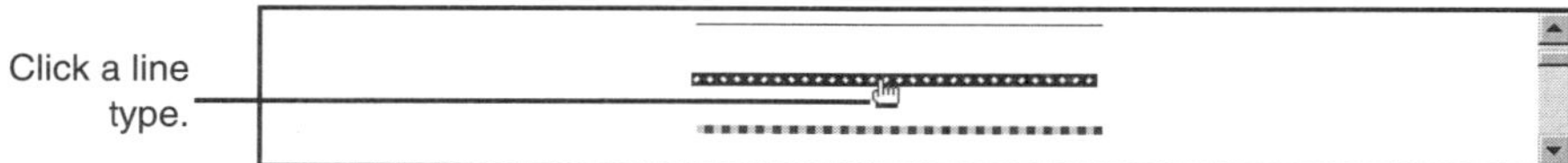

Click a line type.

Figure 2.7   Pick a style for your horizontal rules.

22. Click the line made up of alternating black and gray boxes, and it appears in the preview frame, separating the sections of your page.

23. Scroll to the bottom of the left frame, and you will see several buttons. Click the **Build** button, and your finished page appears, taking up the entire window, as shown in Figure 2.8.

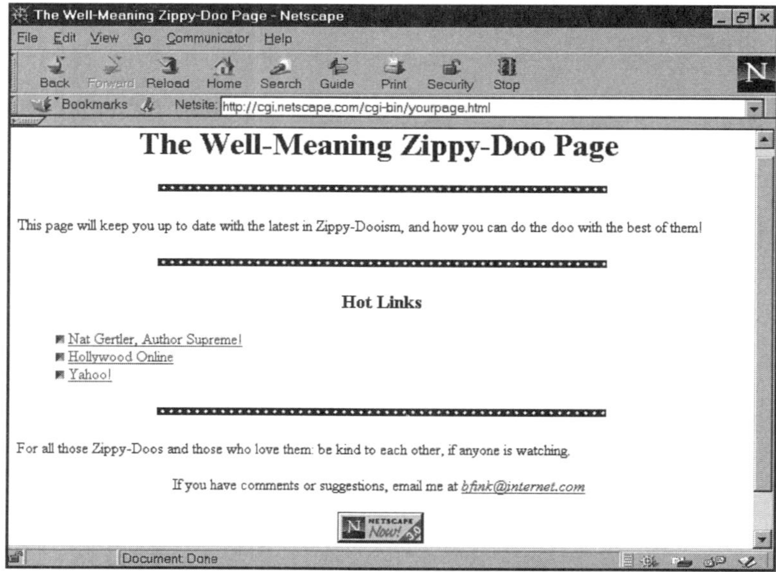

Figure 2.8   Your finished masterpiece!

The good news is that your page is now complete. The bad news is that it is still on Netscape's computer, and you have to move it to your computer before you can publish it. (You might also want to edit it before you publish it—adding things that the wizard didn't take care of, for example, or deleting the built-in advertisement for Netscape that's at the bottom of the page.)

Copying a Page to Your Computer

The method you use to save the page that the wizard generated will also work with *any* page that you find online. It does a lot more than the File, Save As command (which saves only the HTML file to your hard disk). This command saves not only the HTML file, but also all of the page's graphics files (such as the bullets on the Wizard-composed pages or the illustrations on other pages). It also translates all of the links for local items on the page, so that those links will work when the page is on your hard disk.

To copy the page to your computer, follow these steps:

1. Click inside the frame that contains the completed Web page. Open the **File** menu and select the **Edit Page** command. (If one of the other frames is selected, it will appear in Composer.)

2. Composer runs, displaying the page you just created. Click the **Save** button, and the Save As dialog box appears.

Copy? Right!   You don't have to worry about the copyright on Netscape-created bullets and horizontal rules that the wizard put on your page. Netscape put them there for you to use!

3. In the Save As dialog box, type a name for the file in the **File Name** text box and select the drive and folder in which you want the page stored. Then click **Save**.

Use a Separate Folder   It's a good idea to save each Web page in its own folder. This keeps the HTML file and all related graphic files separate from other files on your hard drive.

4. A Saving Document dialog box appears, listing each text and graphics file as it downloads, and counting off the number of files it has left to download. When the download is complete, the page appears in your editor window, ready for you to edit (see Figure 2.9).

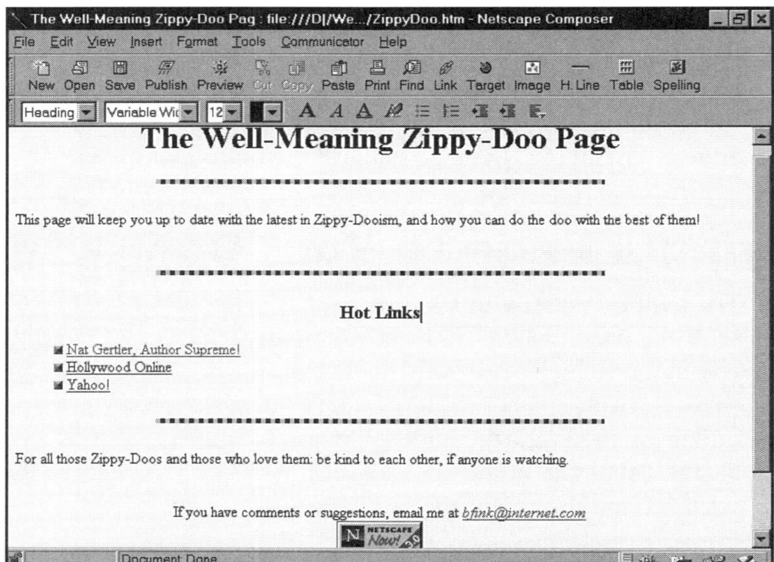

Figure 2.9   You lay the groundwork with the wizard, and then you tweak your page in Netscape Composer.

Because you can save any Web page to your hard drive, if you find a page with a layout you like, you can copy it. Of course, you have to be sure to replace all the text and images with your own (or get permission to use the existing elements). But you can take advantage of a useful structure that already exists.

Publishing Your New Page   If you're ready to place the Web page you created on the Web, skip ahead to Part 6 Lesson 9, "Publishing Your Web Pages." The remaining lessons in this part discuss other ways to create Web pages and modify existing pages.

In this lesson, you used the Netscape Page Wizard to automate the creation of a basic Web page. In the next lesson, you will learn how to create Web pages using existing Web pages called *templates*.

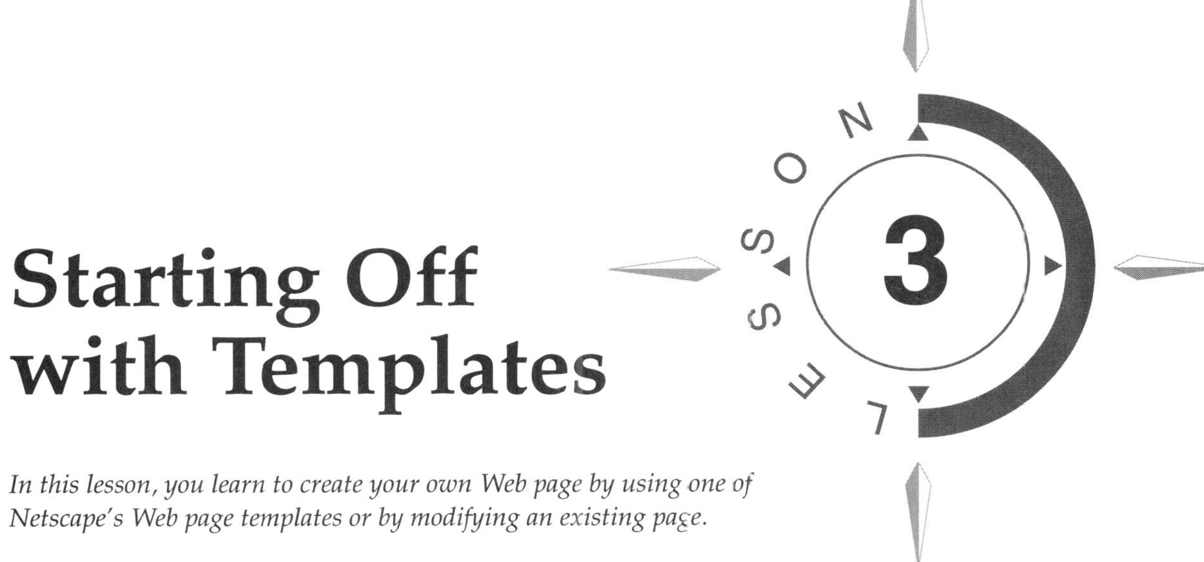

Starting Off with Templates

In this lesson, you learn to create your own Web page by using one of Netscape's Web page templates or by modifying an existing page.

Creating Your Own Web Page Using a Template

Web page templates are nothing more than existing Web pages that you can modify and use as your own Web pages. Netscape has a collection of templates grouped by category: Personal/Family, Company, Small Business, Department, Product/Service, Special Interest Group, Interesting and Fun.

You can open any of these templates in Netscape Composer and use Composer's tools to edit the text, add graphics, add your own links, change the background, and modify the page in any way you want. To use one of these templates, take the following steps:

1. Run Navigator or Composer. Open the **File** menu, point to **New**, and select **Page From Template**. (In Composer, you can click the **New** button and then the **From Template** button.) The New Page from Template dialog box appears.

2. Click the **Netscape Templates** button. Navigator opens the Netscape Web Page Templates page.

3. Scroll down the list and click a link for the template you want to use. Navigator opens the template and displays it. (If you don't like the template, click the **Back** button and try a different link.)

4. Open the **File** menu and select **Edit Page**. Navigator automatically saves the template and all associated graphic files to your hard drive and opens the template in Composer (see Figure 3.1).

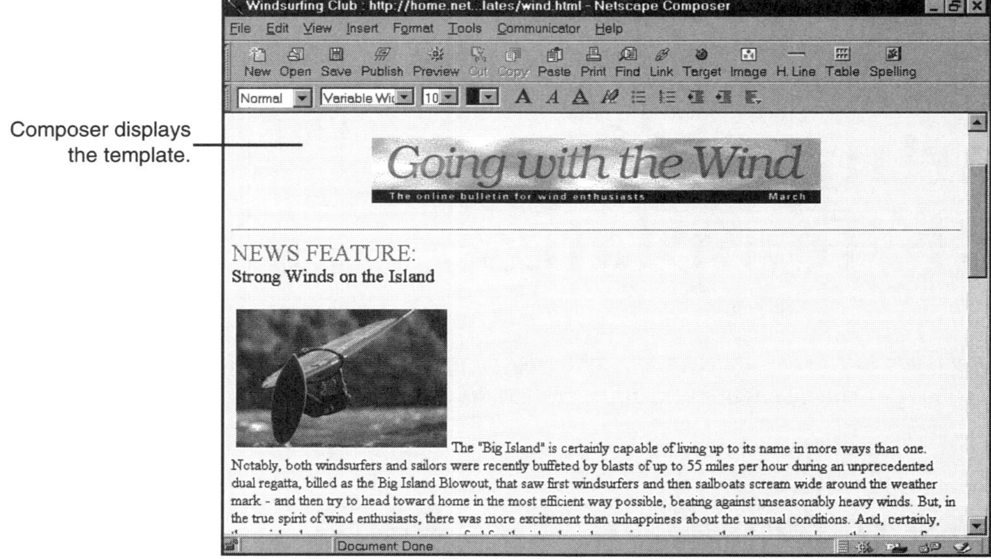

Composer displays the template.

Figure 3.1   You can start editing the template.

5. Enter your changes and change any formatting as desired. The following section, "Making Some Quick Adjustments," provides instructions on some changes you can make. Other lessons in Part 6 go into greater detail.

6. When you finish making changes, delete or replace any text, sample logos, links, images, and other objects that you do not want to appear on your page.

7. Open the **File** menu and select **Save**. Use the Save As dialog box to save the Web page to your hard drive. You will learn how to place your pages on the Web in Lesson 9 of this part.

Every Page Is a Template   Don't restrict yourself to using only Netscape's templates. Any page on the Internet can act as a template. If you find a Web page you like while wandering with Navigator, open Navigator's **File** menu and select **Edit Page**. You can then edit the page in Composer and save the page to your hard drive or to your Web server.

Making Some Quick Adjustments

The general steps in the previous section didn't explain how to edit a template once you found one you like. Later lessons in this part provide the details you need to insert your own links, format text, make your own tables, insert graphics, and so on. However, those lessons are a long way down the road, so read the following list to learn how to make some of the more common adjustments. Figure 3.2 shows all of the tools you need to make these changes.

- You can transform a line of text into a heading. Drag over the text, and then select one of the Heading styles from the Paragraph Style list.

- To the right of the Paragraph Style list are three Font lists: Font, Font Size, and Font Color. Use them to change the look of selected text.

- The three buttons marked "A" let you make selected text Bold, Italic, or Underlined. The fourth button enables you to remove all formatting from the text.

- To create a numbered or bulleted list, click the appropriate button and type the list. Or, select existing paragraphs and click one of the buttons to transform the selected text into a list.

- Use the Indent buttons to indent text or remove indents.

- Use the Alignment button to center text or move it to the left or right.

- The upper (standard) toolbar contains some buttons that should be familiar: Cut, Copy, and Paste. Use these buttons to delete or move selected text.

- On the right side of the standard toolbar are five buttons that let you insert a link, target, image, horizontal line, or table. If you click one of these buttons, a dialog box appears, telling you what to do next.

Anchor versus Link   You already know that a link points to another page on the Web. A link can also point to an *anchor*, a marked location on the current page or on another page. The Insert Target (Named Anchor) button on the standard toolbar allows you to mark a location on a page. When you insert a link, you can then point the link to this anchor. See Part 6 Lesson 6 for more information about links.

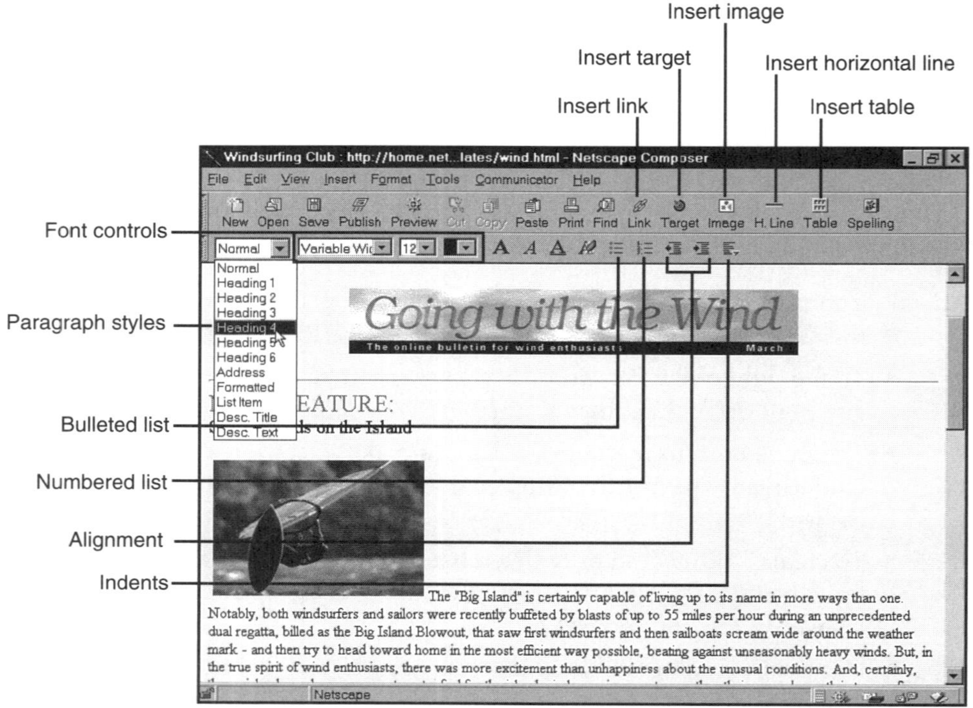

Figure 3.2   The toolbars contain the tools you need to make some quick changes.

Finding Other Good Web Page Samples

Netscape's Web page templates provide some good ideas on what to place on your Web pages, but they won't win any design awards. If you're striving to make the best possible Web page, check out some of the award winners. The following URLs take you to online lists of the sites considered by some people to be the best the Web has to offer.

- **http://home.netscape.com/home/whats-cool.html** is Netscape's own guide to cool sites.

- **http://www.yahoo.com/Entertainment/Cool_Links/** is Yahoo!'s cool links page. This Internet directory also displays a little sunglasses graphic next to officially cool sites in its normal listing.

- **http://www.pointcom.com/categories** offers a listing of the top five percent of all Web sites, sorted into a number of categories. Figure 3.3 shows Lycos' guide to cool sites.

Plenty of other guides are available, some in the form of a service provider's list of key sites on their server, and some in the form of an individual's list of his personal favorite sites.

How Cool Is Cool? Of course, what makes a site "good" or "cool" is very subjective. You might have to bop around a bit until you find a list that tends to steer you in the right direction.

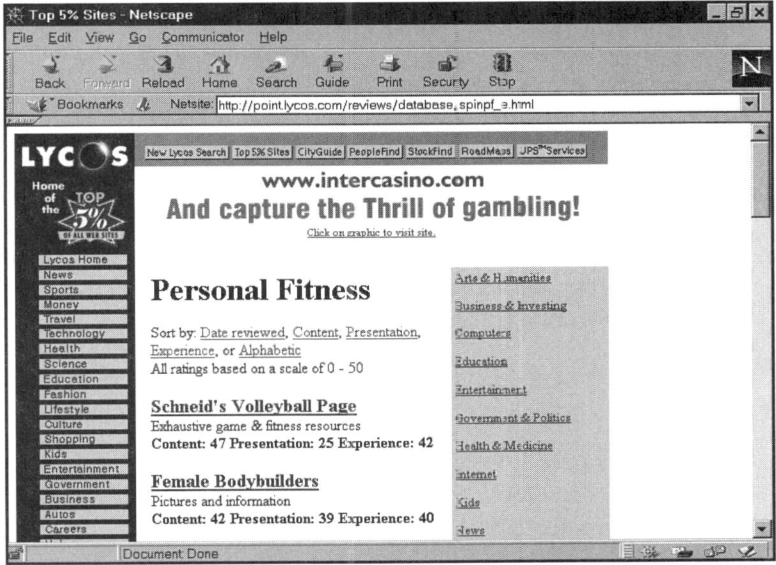

Figure 3.3 The Lycos guide to cool sites.

In this lesson, you learned how to use Netscape's Web templates and modify them to create your own Web pages. In the next lesson, you will learn how to type additional text on your page and format it.

Adding and Formatting Text

In this lesson, you see how to use Composer to start a new Web page, type headings and running text, and format the text.

Opening a Web Page

If you already have a page open in Composer, you can skip ahead to the next section to start adding text. If you closed the page to take a break, reopen it by taking the following steps:

1. Run Netscape Composer (as explained in Lesson 1). Open Composer's **File** menu and select **Open Page**. The Open Page dialog box appears.
2. Next to Open Location or File In, click **Composer**.
3. Click the **Choose File** button. The Open dialog box appears, prompting you to select a file.
4. Use the Open dialog box to select the HTML file you created. Then click the **Open** button. This returns you to the Open Page dialog box.
5. Click **Open**.

Quick Open   When you installed Navigator, Windows created a file association between HTML files and Navigator. Double-click the icon for an HTML file, and Navigator will automatically run and open the file. Then open Navigator's **File** menu and select **Edit Page**.

If you really want to start from scratch, simply run Netscape Composer. When you first start it, Composer displays a blank page in which you can start working. Here are a couple other ways you can start with a blank slate:

- Click Composer's **New** button and then the **Blank Page** button.
- Open Composer's or Navigator's **File** menu, point to **New**, and select **Blank Page**.
- Press **Ctrl+Shift+N**.

Adding Text to a Page

Whether you start with an existing page or open a blank page, Composer displays an insertion point somewhere on the page. The insertion point is a blinking vertical line, and it shows you where text will be inserted when you start typing. You can move the insertion point by clicking where you want to place it or by using the arrow keys on your keyboard.

There are basically two ways to add text to a page: You can just start typing and then format the text later, or you can select your formatting options first and then start typing. To type a title at the top of the page, you might open the **Paragraph Style** drop-down list and select the **Heading1** style, select **Center** from the **Alignment** drop-down list, and then type your title (see Figure 4.1).

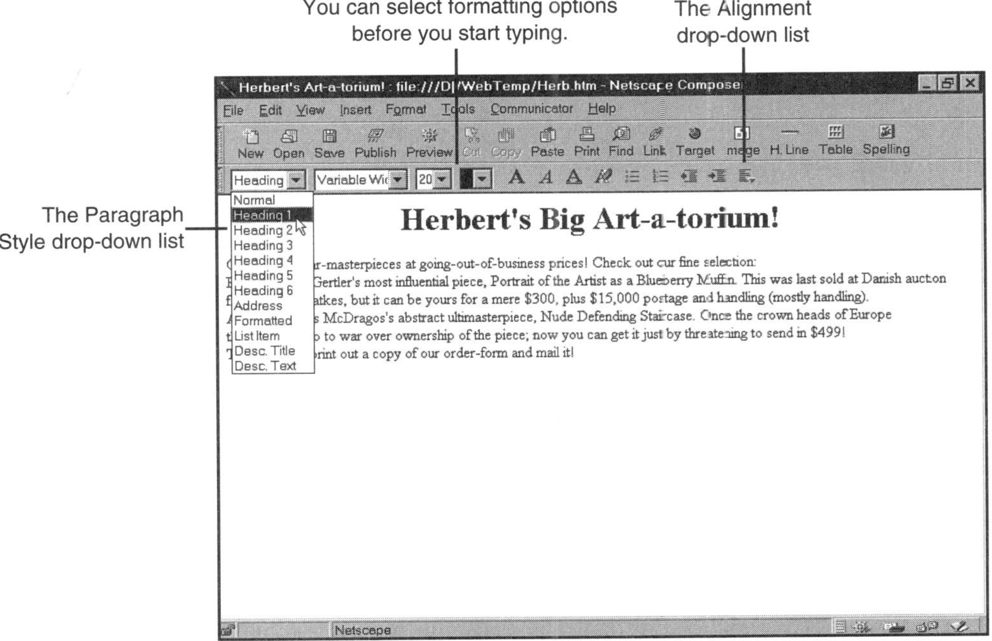

Figure 4.1 To add text, start typing.

Save Typing   The editor accepts standard cut and paste commands. This means that if you have a document that you created in another application (such as a word processor), you can copy and paste text from it onto your Web page. To do so, select the text in the document, and then select the application's **Copy** command. Then switch to your Web page, position the insertion point where you want the text inserted, and click the **Paste** button.

Text Enhancement

Now you have a dull, flat Web page—just flat text on a flat background. It's time to liven up the text a bit. Composer has several tools for enhancing your text, as shown in Table 4.1.

Table 4.1   Text Enhancement Tools

Tool	Name	Function
Variable Wid ▼	Font	Changes the text style
20 ▼	Font Size	Changes the text size
▼	Font Color	Changes text color
A	Bold	Makes text thick
A	Italic	Makes text slanted
A̲	Underline	Underlines text

To enhance your text, follow these steps:

1. Drag over the text whose look you want to change.

2. To change the font, font size, or font color, open the appropriate drop-down list and click the desired font, size, or color.

3. To add a text enhancement (such as bold), click the **Bold**, **Italic**, or **Underline** button.

To remove an enhancement, click the button again. To remove all of the styles and enhancements you've applied to text, drag over the text and then click the **Remove All Styles** button (just to the right of the underlined A).

When selecting fonts and sizes, keep in mind that each person's Web browser is in charge of assigning fonts to your text, so your fonts and sizes may appear different when viewed with other browsers. If you are creating a Web page for use on an intranet, where you know that people will be using a browser that supports additional font settings, you can get fancy with fonts. Otherwise, stick with the standard font sizes.

You can set up Composer to use relative font sizes that support HTML standards. To do so, open the **Edit** menu, select **Preferences**, click **Composer**, and select **Show Relative HTML Font Scale**. Then click **OK**. The Font Size list will then show seven relative sizes: –2, –1, 0, +1, +2, +3, and +4. These font sizes enable the visitor's browser to select the appropriate fonts and sizes.

Undo!   If you make any mistakes, pull down the **Edit** menu and select the **Undo** command to unmake the mistake!

Formatting Paragraphs

In addition to formatting individual words or characters, you can also format entire paragraphs. The paragraph formatting tools shown in Table 4.2 let you change the appearance of entire paragraphs.

Table 4.2   Paragraph Formatting Tools

Tool	Name	Function
Heading	Paragraph Style	Indicates current paragraph's format
	Bullet List	Turns text into a bulleted list
	Number List	Turns text into a numbered list
	Decrease Indent	Moves text left
	Increase Indent	Moves text right
	Alignment	Aligns text left, center, or right

The Paragraph Style list enables you to apply different predefined styles to your paragraphs. The available styles are:

- *Normal*, which gives you standard-sized text.
- *Heading 1* through *Heading 6*, which are designed for headlines and section designations. Each gives you a different size or emphasis of text, ranging from 1 (biggest) to 6 (smallest). The program automatically skips a line after the heading.
- *Address*, which usually appears in italics.
- *Formatted*, which displays a monospace font and doesn't automatically wrap at the margins. You have to insert the start of a new line by clicking where the previous line should end and then pressing Enter. This style does not automatically add an extra line between formatted paragraphs.
- *List Item*, which indents the paragraph and puts a bullet in front of it (as in this list). No line is skipped between list items.
- *Description Title* and *Description Text*, which you can use on alternating lines to create a list of items with information on each. The item name (the Title) will stay at the left edge, while the information is indented. No lines are skipped.

Unlike the text formatting tools that required you to select text before applying a format, the paragraph formatting tools require only that the insertion point be somewhere within the paragraph you want to format. Simply click anywhere in the paragraph, and then select a style from the Paragraph Style list or click one of the paragraph formatting buttons.

If you want to format several paragraphs, you can drag over them and then select the desired paragraph format. For example, to convert a series of paragraphs into a numbered list, drag over the paragraphs and click the **Number List** button. (You don't have to be too careful when dragging; just make sure you select a portion of each paragraph you want the change to affect.)

The details of how each of these changes will appear on the finished page depends on the viewer's browser and options.

Alignment   The settings that control where the text appears across the page's width. When you click the Alignment button, a list of Alignment buttons appears. Each alignment button shows a picture of how text will look when you click that button.

More Format Options via the Format Menu

Composer's toolbar provides convenient access to most of the formatting options you'll use to create your Web pages. However, Composer does have additional formatting options, which you can select from the Format menu. Simply open the **Format** menu and select the desired option (see Figure 4.2).

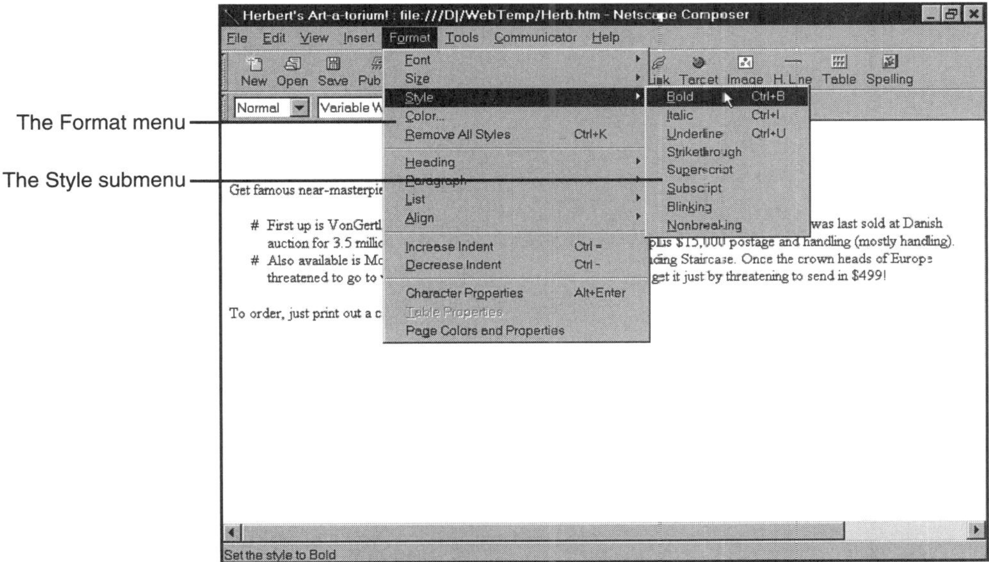

Figure 4.2   The Format menu offers additional options.

You can access most of the formatting options by displaying the Character Properties dialog box shown in Figure 4.3. To display this dialog box, first select the text you want to format, and then right-click the selected text and choose **Character Properties**.

Return to Normal   To clear all styles and return text to normal, highlight the text and click the **Remove All Formatting** button in the Formatting toolbar.

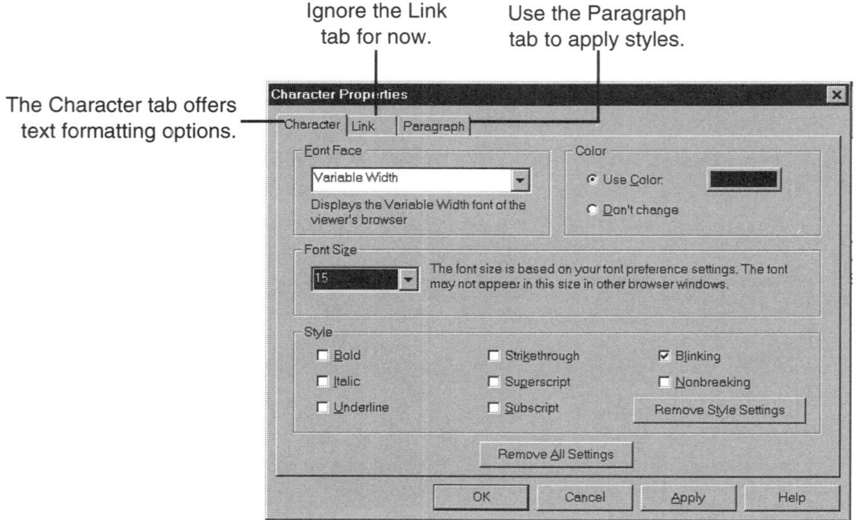

Figure 4.3 The Properties dialog box offers one-stop shopping for character and paragraph formats.

Checking Your Work

When you finish formatting the text on your page (or if you want to check your work periodically before you're done), you can click the **Preview** button to see how your page will look to people surfing the Web. To see how your page will look in a browser, follow these steps:

1. Click the **Preview** button (shown in Figure 4.4) to see how those numbered lists will actually look to someone who encounters them on the Web. A dialog box appears, asking if you want to save the changes to the file.

2. Click **Yes** and follow the trail of dialog boxes to name and save the file. A new browser window displays the page. Notice that there are actual numbers by the list, instead of number signs.

3. To close the browser window, click the **Close** (X) button.

4. Click the **Save** button (the one with a picture of a disk) to save the changes you've made to the file. Then click the **Close** (X) button to close the editor window.

The Preview button —

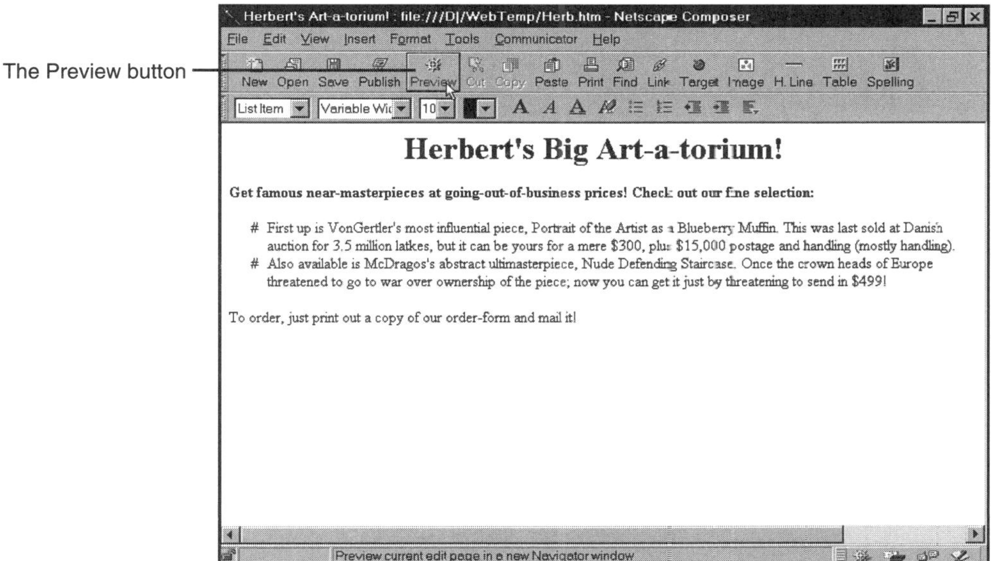

Figure 4.4 To see how your page will look inside a real Web browser, click Preview.

In this lesson, you learned how to start a Web page, add text to it, and format the text. In the next lesson, you'll learn how to use graphics to spruce up the page even more.

Adding Graphics and Changing Backgrounds

In this lesson, you learn to change the background of your page and add graphics.

Changing the Background Color

If you don't specify what color the page background should be, it will default to whatever background the person viewing it has configured for his browser. Usually, this will be a dull gray or a clean white. If you want to add excitement to the page or if you want to make sure that your colored text will be visible, you should specify a background color. To do that, follow these steps:

1. If your page is not already open in Composer, open it.

2. Open the **Format** menu and select **Page Colors and Properties**. The Page Properties dialog box appears.

3. Click the **Colors and Background** tab.

4. Click the **Use Custom Colors** option button.

5. Open the **Color Schemes** drop-down list and select a color scheme you want to start with. Each color scheme controls settings for the background, text, and links. The preview area lets you see how the page will look with the current settings (see Figure 5.1).

6. Once you have a color scheme in place, you can change colors for individual items. Click the button for the item whose color you want to change (for example, Background). A color dialog box appears, prompting you to select a color.

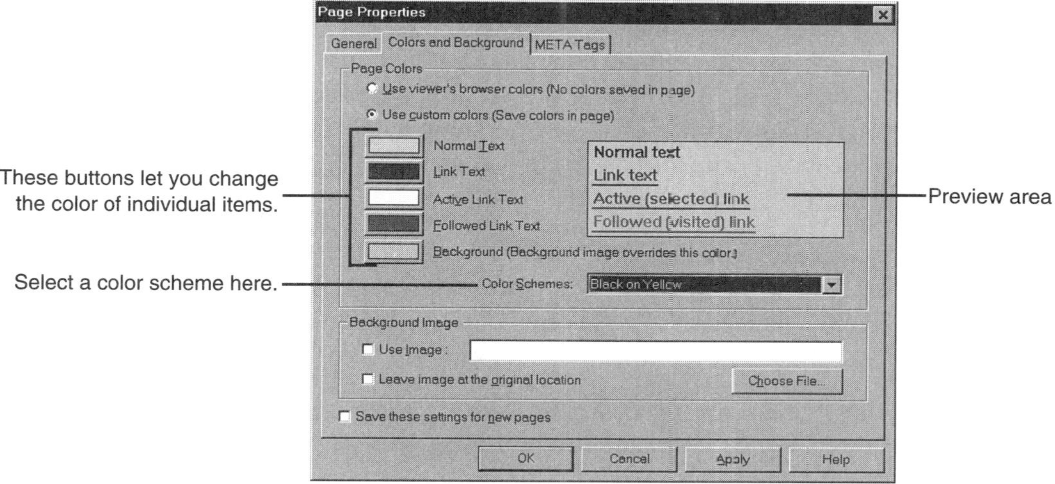

These buttons let you change the color of individual items.

Preview area

Select a color scheme here.

Figure 5.1 The Colors and Background tab of the Page Properties dialog box.

7. Select the desired color, and then click **OK** to close the Color dialog box. Repeat steps 6 and 7 to change the color of any additional items.

8. Click **OK** to save your color settings and close the Page Properties dialog box. Composer redisplays the page in the selected colors.

Setting Default Colors If you are creating two or more Web pages and you want to give them a consistent look, enter your color preferences as defaults. In the Page Properties dialog box, click the **Colors and Background** tab and check the **Save These Settings for New Pages** box. Then click **OK**. Whenever you start a new Web page, these color settings will be in effect.

Using a Background Image

If you want a fancier-looking page, you can select a GIF or JPEG image to go behind the text. If the image isn't big enough to fill the user's browser window, the browser will repeat the image horizontally and vertically to fill the space. In the following sections, you will learn how to obtain background graphics and use them on your Web page.

Getting Some Background Graphics

You can use any GIF or JPEG image as a background. If you are wandering the Web and you find a picture you want to use as a background for your own Web page, right-click it and use the Save As command to save it to your hard drive. Then take the steps in the following section to use the picture as a page background.

If you can't find a picture you want to use, go back to Netscape's Template page (select **File**, **New**, **Page From Template**), scroll down to the bottom, and click the link for Web page tools. This takes you to a page with background colors and patterns. Right-click a link and click **Save As** to save the graphic to disk.

You may wonder whether you can just lift a background from an existing page on the Web. Well, that's a little complicated. You can't just right-click the background and select Save As. (Unlike other graphics and icons that sit on the page, the background graphic is "behind" the page.) However, you can still pilfer the background. Here's what you do:

1. Open the page that contains the appealing background in Navigator.

2. Open the **View** menu and select **Page Source**. This displays the coded HTML version of the page.

3. Look near the top of the page for a code that looks something like this:

```
<body background="JPG/back4.jpg" text="#FFFFFF" link="#FFFF80"
vlink="#00FFFF">
```

   The `background="JPG/back4.jpg"` part gives you the name of the file you want. Usually, the background image is in the same directory as the HTML page, so there's no complicated directory path to worry about.

4. Drag over everything between the quotation marks. (In the preceding example, you would drag over **JPG/back4.jpg**.) Then press **Ctrl+C** to copy it.

5. Close the Source window, and then click in the **Location** text box. Drag over any document name on the right end of the URL. For example, if the URL is **http://www.softhelp.com/webauth.htm**, drag over **webauth.htm**.

6. Press **Ctrl+V** to insert what you copied from the Source window, and then press **Enter**. Navigator opens the background image as if it were a separate Web page (see Figure 5.2).

7. Right-click the image and click **Save Image As** to save it to your hard drive.

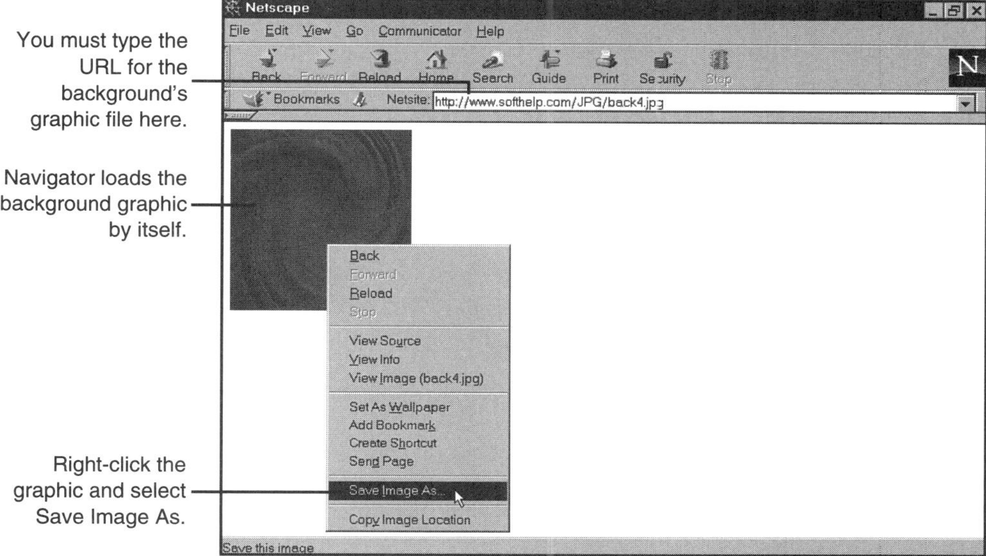

Figure 5.2 You can grab an existing page's background, but it's not easy.

Finding More Graphics   If you just can't get enough graphics, look to the
Web Designer page at **http://web.canlink.com/webdesign/**. Or, use any of
the search tools described in Part 1 Lesson 7 and search for **html web page
background**. The Web has many resources where you can pick up useful
graphics.

Adding a Background Image to Your Page

If you have a GIF or JPEG image you want to use as a page background, adding
it to your Web page is fairly easy. Take the following steps:

1. With your Web page open, open the **Format** menu and select **Page Colors
   and Properties**. The Page Properties dialog box appears, with the Colors
   and Background tab in front.

2. Under Background Image, click the **Use Image** option to place a check
   in the box. (You can choose **Leave Image at the Original Location** if you
   are using an image that is already stored somewhere on the Internet.

This saves you from having to store the background image on your Web server, but if this image is moved later, you will lose your background.)

3. Click the **Choose File** button, and the Choose Image File dialog box appears, prompting you to select an image.

4. Select the drive and folder that contains the image you want to use, and then click its file name. Click **Open**. You return to the Page Properties dialog box, and the path to the selected file appears in the Use Image text box.

5. Click **OK**, and the image becomes tiled behind your page (see Figure 5.3).

Can You Still Read It?   Not all background images or colors are suitable for the text colors you have selected. If you place dark text on a dark background, you and others will have trouble reading the text. If the background image swallows your text, use a different image or use a color instead.

CAUTION

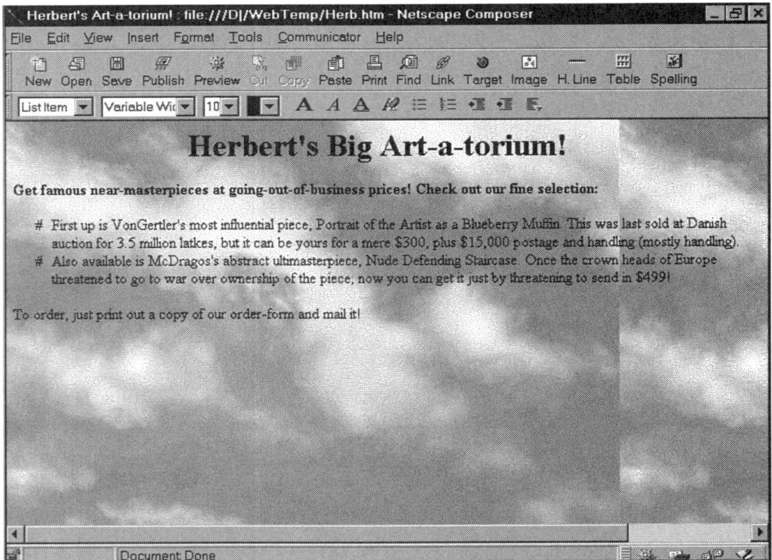

Figure 5.3   A tiled background.

Adding a Horizontal Line

The simplest non-text element that you can add to a document is a *horizontal rule,* a horizontal line that separates one section of the document from another. To add a horizontal rule to your Web page, follow these steps:

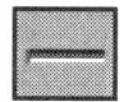

1. Click at the end of the first line of text to place the cursor there.

2. Click the **H. Line** button. The horizontal line immediately appears on its own line, below the first line of text.

3. You can drag the edges of the horizontal line to make the line thicker or longer.

4. To take more control over the line, right-click it and select **Horizontal Line Properties**. This displays the dialog box shown in Figure 5.4, which allows you to change the line's properties.

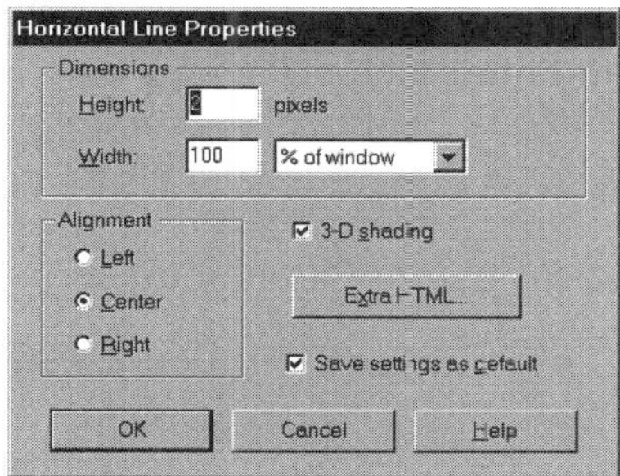

Figure 5.4   You can change additional line settings.

You may have seen more graphical horizontal lines used to divide a page. If you see a line you like, you can usually grab it by right-clicking it and selecting **Save Image As**.

If that doesn't work, open the page that has the graphical divider lines you want, and select **File**, **Edit Page** to display the page in Composer. Then select **File**, **Save**. When Composer saves the page, it saves all the graphics on that page. You can then sift through the graphic files to find the one you need.

You can also find graphical lines at Netscape's template site. See "Getting Some Background Graphics," earlier in this lesson, for details.

Is It Stealing?   It is common for people to lift background images and graphics from other pages to use on their own personal Web pages. Some sites even encourage you to use their graphics. However, if you are using graphics for commercial purposes, or if you're not sure if someone will mind, contact the person via e-mail and ask permission. Most Web pages have an e-mail link (usually at the bottom of the page) that you can click to get the author's e-mail address.

Adding an Image

Most denizens of the Web will quickly skip over your Web page if it doesn't contain some pretty pictures. Fortunately, inserting graphics in Composer is fairly easy.

If you don't have any graphics to insert, you can download sample graphics off the Web, as explained earlier in this lesson. Unlike the background image, you are not restricted to using GIF or JPEG images, so you can use any clip art images you may have obtained with other applications or images you have created and saved in Paintbrush.

To insert an image and position it on your page, take the following steps:

1. Click where you want to insert the image on your Web page. The insertion point moves to the selected position. (It's a good idea to place the image on a blank line.)

2. Click the **Image** button. If you haven't yet saved the page, the Save New Page dialog box appears. Save your file. The Image Properties dialog box then appears, as shown in Figure 5.5.

3. Click the **Choose File** button next to the Image Location text box. The Select Image File dialog box appears, prompting you to pick a file.

4. Change to the drive and folder in which the image file is stored, click the file's name, and then click **Open**. You're returned to the Properties dialog box.

5. Click one of the **Text Alignment** buttons to specify how you want text aligned with or wrapped around the graphic. The first five buttons specify vertical alignment (for example, you can align text with the top or bottom of the image). The last two buttons provide text wrapping options.

6. Under **Dimensions**, you can enter settings, but it's easier just to drag the border of the image to resize it once it is on the page.

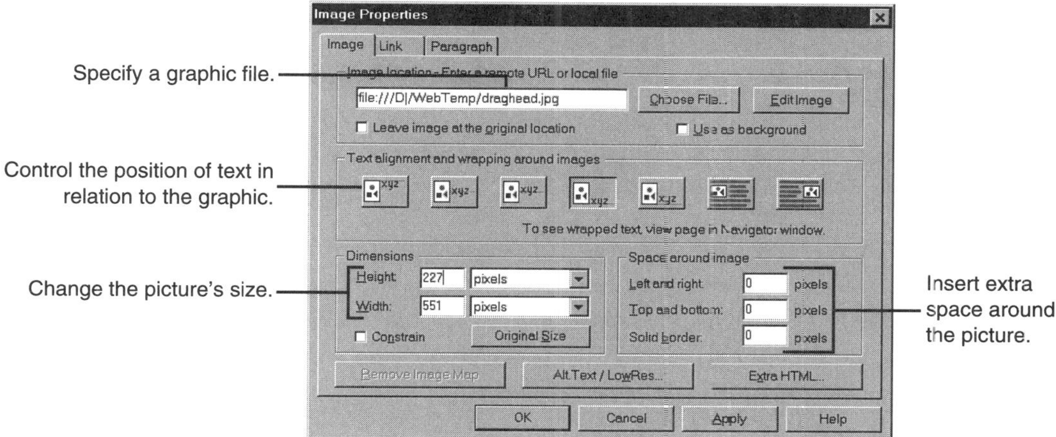

Specify a graphic file.

Control the position of text in relation to the graphic.

Change the picture's size.

Insert extra space around the picture.

Figure 5.5 The Image tab of the Image Properties dialog box.

7. Under **Space Around Image**, you can type entries to insert additional space between the image and surrounding text. (Keep in mind that a pixel is tiny—one screen dot.) The Solid Border option places a black line around the image.

8. Click **OK**, and Composer inserts the image.

Don't Expect to See It Text-wrapping isn't displayed on the editor screen. To see how your changes affect the image, click the **Preview** button.

CAUTION

To change any of the settings you entered, right-click the image and click **Image Properties**. In addition, you can change the size of an image by dragging one of its borders, and you can move the image by dragging it. You can also use some of Composer's formatting tools to change its position. For example, if the image is on a separate line, you can click the image and select Center from the Alignment list to center the image. You can even make the image a bulleted list item— although I can't imagine why anyone would want to do that.

In this lesson, you learned to use backgrounds and graphics to enhance your page. In the next lesson, you'll learn to create links the visitor can use to go from one page to another.

Creating Links

In this lesson, you learn to add links that point to other Web pages, and you learn to add targeted links that point to specific parts of a page.

Linking Your Page to Other Web Pages

No matter how good your Web page is, it's nothing without links to other Web pages. Without links, your Web page is nothing more than a dead end. Links show that you know your way around the Web, and they express your taste (good or bad) for Web pages. Take the following steps to sprinkle your page with a few links:

1. To create a text link, type the text you want to use as the link, and then drag over it. To use a graphic, insert the image, and then click it.

2. Click the **Link** button. The Properties dialog box opens, with the Link tab displayed (see Figure 6.1). You can also display this dialog box by pressing **Ctrl+Shift+L** or by right-clicking the selected text or graphic and choosing **Create Link Using Selected…**.

3. In the **Link to a Page Location or Local File** text box, type the URL of the page to which you want to link. For example, you might type **http://www.hollywood.com** to create a link to Hollywood Online. (You can quickly de-link a link at any time by right-clicking the link and selecting **Remove Link**.)

Copying URLs   URLs are long. The easiest way to enter them is tc copy and paste. In Navigator, open the page you want to point to, drag over the URL in the **Location** text box, and then right-click it and select **Copy**. Or, right-click a link and select **Copy Link Location**. Then when you're asked to enter the URL here, right-click in the text box and select **Paste**.

4. Click **OK**. The selected text appears highlighted.

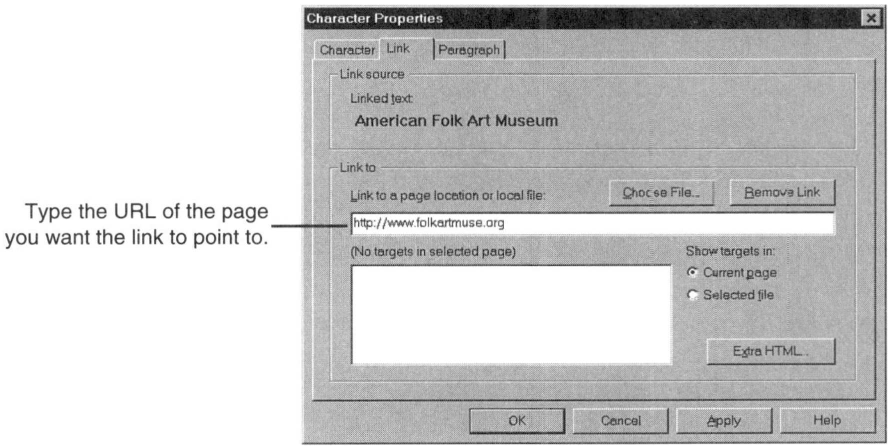

Figure 6.1 Add links to other Web pages.

Inserting a Link for Your E-Mail Address

If you want people to be able to contact you after reading your Web page, you can insert a link at the bottom of the page that points to your e-mail address. If the user has an e-mail program that's set up properly, he or she can then click the link. The e-mail program will run automatically and address a new message to you. All the person has to do is type the message and send it.

To insert a link to your e-mail address, perform the steps given in the previous section. You can use any text as the link text, such as **I Need Mail!**, **E-Mail Me**, or your e-mail address itself. Drag over the text and click the **Link** button. In the **Link to a Page Location or Local File** text box, type **mailto:** followed by your e-mail address (for example, **mailto:bfink@internet.com**). Then click **OK**.

Linking Your Page to Other Pages at Your Site

If you are creating a personal home page that's not very long, chances are that you will publish a single page. However, if you have a business or you work for a company that has several Web pages (or you just have a lot of important things to say), you can create links to your other Web pages.

To create links to other pages at your Web site, you first have to have another page to link to. Also, before you start, you have to think about where the two HTML files will be stored on the Web server. You have a few options here:

- *Store the pages in the same directory.* This is the easiest way because you need not specify a path to the Web page you want to link to. You simply enter the file's name.

- *Store the pages in the same directories* on your hard disk as they will be stored in on the Web server. If you do this, you won't have to edit the links later to point them to the correct directories on the Web server.

- *Don't worry about it now.* This is easy—until you find out later that all your links don't work (not recommended!).

When you have another HTML page on your hard drive, take the following steps to create links to these other pages:

1. Drag over the text, or select the graphic that you want to act as the link.
2. Right-click the selected item and choose **Create Link Using Selected…**. The Properties dialog box appears.
3. Click the **Choose File** button, and the Link to File dialog box appears.
4. Use the Link to File dialog box to select the page you want the selected link to point to, and then click **Open**. You're returned to the Properties dialog box.
5. Click **OK**. If you selected text as the link, it appears underlined. Deselect the text, and you'll see that it is also a different color to indicate that it is a link.
6. Click the **Save** button to save the file. Then, to test the link, click the **Preview** button.
7. When Navigator opens, click the link. The linked-to page appears. Click the **Close** (X) button to close the browser.

Linking to a Specific Place on a Page

There will be times when you want to provide a link not just to a page, but to a specific place on a page. Many people do this on long pages that are broken into sections, for example. The place on the page that you want to link to is called a *target*, and the link to it is called a *targeted link*.

Often, the place that you are linking to is on the same page as the link. This way, you can have an index at the top of the page that quickly links to any part of the page that someone wants to find.

The procedure for linking to a target consists of two steps. First, you mark the target you want to point to, and then you create a link that points to the target. (I usually mark all my targets first.)

To mark the target, take the following steps:

1. Click where you want the target placed, or select the target. (If you select text to use as the target, Composer uses that text as the target name, which saves you some keystrokes.)

2. Click the **Target** button. The Target Properties dialog box appears, as shown in Figure 6.2, prompting you to type a name for it.

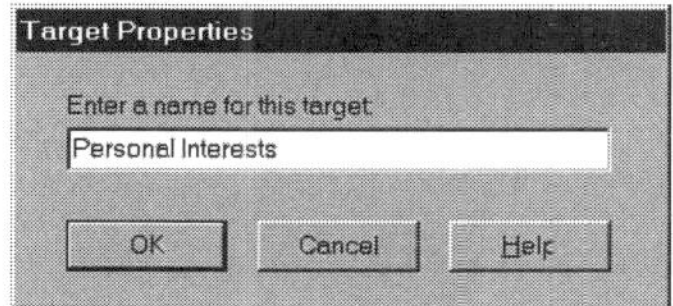

Figure 6.2 The Target Properties dialog box.

3. Type a brief but descriptive name for the target. When you create a link to the target, you must select the target from a list of marked targets; be sure you type a name you'll remember. Click **OK**, and Composer inserts a small target symbol at the insertion point or to the left of the selected text. (This is only an editor's symbol; it won't be seen by visitors who view the page.)

After you have marked at least one target in the document, you can create a link that points to it. Take the following steps:

1. If necessary, type the text that you want to act as the link. Then drag over the text to select it.

2. Click the **Link** button. The Character Properties dialog box appears, with the Link tab displayed. The Select a Named Target in Current Page field lists all the targets on the current page (see Figure 6.3).

3. Click the target name you want to link to. The selected target appears in the Link to a Page Location or Local File text box.

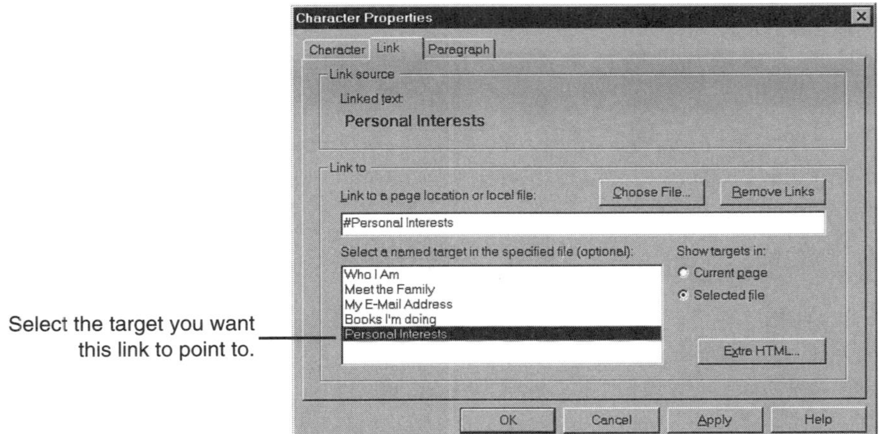

Select the target you want this link to point to.

Figure 6.3   Composer lists all the marked targets on the current page.

4. Click **OK** to accept this link.

5. Click the **Save** button.

6. Click the **Preview** button, and a browser window opens, displaying the current page.

7. Click the link that points to the target. Assuming you selected the correct target, Navigator automatically brings the target into the viewing area. (If the target and the link are on the screen together when you click the link, nothing will happen.)

The procedure for linking to a targeted location on another page of your site is similar. However, when you make the link, you have to click the **Choose File** button to select the page with the target before you can select the target from the list on the page.

Good Form   If you have a long Web page consisting of several sections, insert a link at the bottom of each section that points to a target at the top of the page so the user can quickly return to where she started. If you have a Web document consisting of several pages, insert links on the other pages that point to the home page.

Quick Edits   You can quickly edit a link or a target by right-clicking it and selecting the **Link Properties or Target Properties** option at the top of the context menu. (If the text is both a link and a target, right-click the target icon— not the text—to edit the target properties.)

Drag-and-Drop Web Page Creation

One of the coolest aspects of Composer is that you can drag and drop objects onto a Web page you're creating in Composer. If you have a shortcut on the Windows desktop that points to a Web page or a graphic on your hard drive— or even a document you created—simply drag it into the Composer window and drop it on the page.

If you open a Web page in Navigator and you want to link to it from your Web page, drag the **Location** icon from Navigator onto your page in Composer and release the mouse button (see Figure 6.4). You can even drag and drop graphics from Web pages displayed in Navigator into your Web pages! You might have to reformat them, but that is much easier than typing all these URLs.

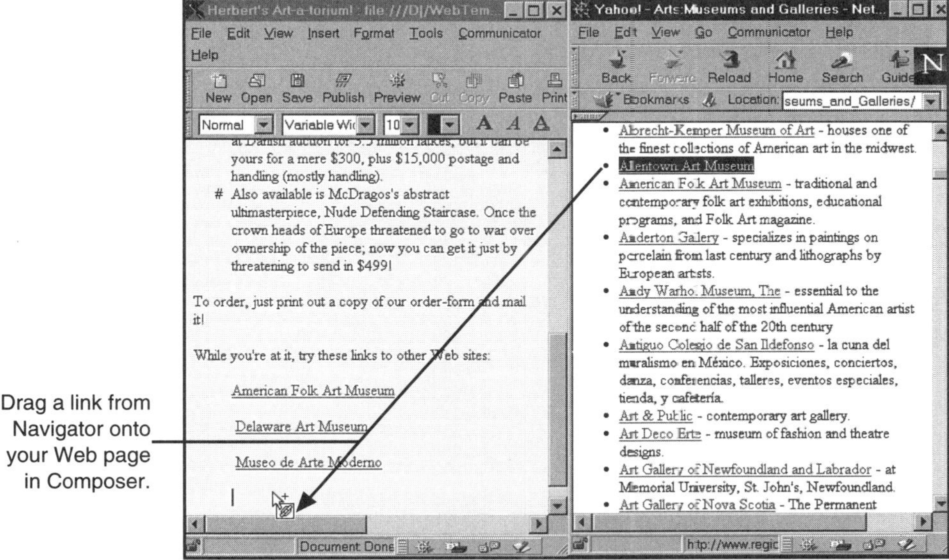

Figure 6.4   You can drag items from the Windows desktop, from documents created in other applications, or from pages on the Web into your Web page.

Changing the Color of Links

People recognize a link in text in two ways. One is that text links are usually underlined (unless the browser has been configured not to show them that way). The other is that text links show up in a different color. When you create pages, you can configure the colors for each page. Actually, you can configure the color for three distinct items:

- A link to a page or target that the viewer hasn't visited recently
- A link that has been visited recently
- The link the visitor is currently clicking

Why would you want to change those colors? Some folks want to change them just to make their pages prettier. But it can really be important to change them if you create a page that has a background color or background images. You have to make sure that your links will show up well against that color.

To set link colors, follow these steps:

1. Open the page that contains the links whose color you want to change.
2. Open the **Format** menu and select **Page Colors and Properties**. The Page Properties dialog box appears.
3. Click the **Colors and Background** tab to see the options shown in Figure 6.5.

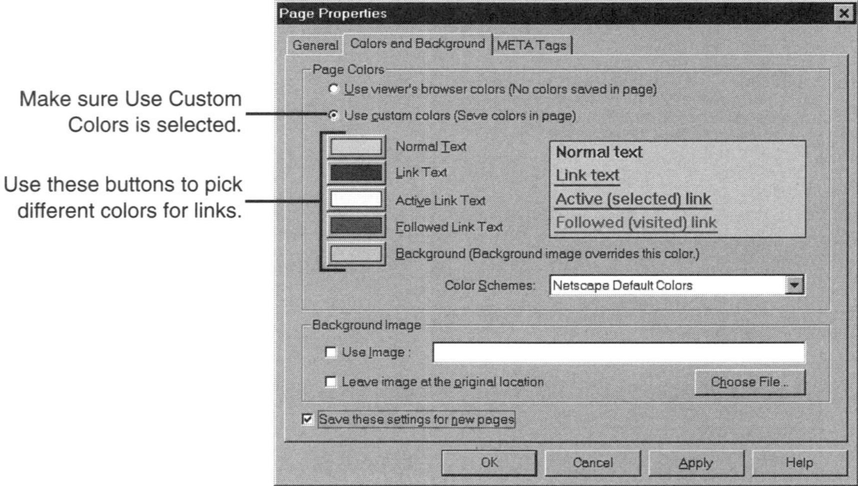

Figure 6.5   You can select link colors in the Page Properties dialog box.

4. Click the **Use Custom Colors** option button if it is not already selected. In the Custom Colors area, you will see the settings for all three link types and for the normal text color against the currently selected background color.

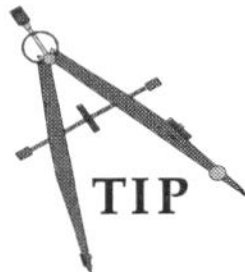

Match Your Background Color   Even if you have a background image, the text in the sample shown in the Page Properties dialog box appears against the selected background color. Because of this (and other reasons as well!), you should set your background color value to match the main color of your background image.

5. Click the **Link Text** button, and a color selection dialog box appears.

6. Click a color that will show up well against your background and click **OK**.

7. Repeat steps 4 and 5 for the **Active Link Text** and **Followed Link Text** buttons.

8. Click **OK**, and the dialog box disappears. Your settings immediately take effect in the displayed page.

9. Click the **Save** button to save these changes to your page.

As you probably noticed, there was also a button to change the normal text. If you want to change the color of most of the text on your page, it's better to use that button than to select all of the text and use the Font Color button. Some browsers will be able to show a color you select using the Normal Text button but won't be able to show a color you select with the Font Color button.

In this lesson, you learned to create links. In the next lesson, you will learn to add tables and frames.

Creating Tables and Frames

In this lesson, you learn how to use tables and frames to arrange text, graphics, and links on your Web page.

Why Use Tables and Frames?

When you are creating a Web page, you must consider your audience—those people who are going to pull up your page on their 15-inch monitors and try to navigate your site. These folks are going to expect your page to be set up in some logical way that fits on their screen. Tables and frames are useful tools in achieving a logical, appealing page layout.

Tables are especially useful for arranging text in columns and rows. With Composer, you can specify the number of rows and columns you want the table to have, and Composer creates it. All you have to do is type entries into each cell (the box formed by the intersection of a column and row). Figure 7.1 shows a table on a sample Web page.

Like tables, frames allow you to arrange text. However, frames are a little more intrusive. Instead of being an actual part of the Web page, frames control the browser window (the viewing area), chopping it into two or more rectangular sections, each of which displays a different Web page. Composer does not offer tools for easily creating frames, but you can create them by typing HTML frame codes, as explained later in this lesson.

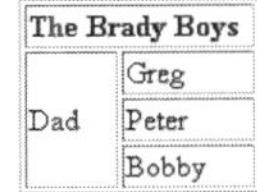

Figure 7.1   Tables make it easy to arrange text in rows and columns.

Why Not Use Frames?   Frames are difficult to create and manage in Composer. In addition, some older browsers are not capable of displaying frames, so you always have to either create an alternative frameless page or include a note indicating that to view this page, the user needs a browser that supports frames. In addition, it's tempting to overuse frames, and it's difficult to design useful frames. Before you work with frames, look around the Web for good and bad examples of frames.

Inserting a Table

Creating a table in Composer is a breeze. You simply click the Table button and specify the number of rows and columns you want the table to have. Composer creates the table, inserting all the complicated HTML codes for you. Take the following steps to create your table:

1. Position the insertion point where you want the table inserted. (It's a good idea to place the insertion point on a blank line.)

2. Click the **Table** button. The New Table Properties dialog box appears, as shown in Figure 7.2, allowing you to specify the table's structure and appearance.

3. Type the number of rows you want your table to have, and then tab to the **Number of Columns** text box and type the desired number of columns.

4. Select an alignment option to control the position of the table in relation to the window: **Left**, **Center**, or **Right**.

5. (Optional) To add a caption above or below the table, click **Include Caption** and pick the desired location.

6. (Optional) Type the number of pixels you want to use for the following table attributes:

   Border Line Width: This setting controls the width of the lines that make up the table. You can enter 0 (or remove the check mark next to this option) if you don't want any lines to appear at all.

Cell Spacing: This setting controls the space between cells.

Cell Padding: This setting controls the space between the line that defines a cell and the text or object that the cell contains.

Enter the number of rows and columns.

Select a table alignment on the page.

You can set other table attributes here.

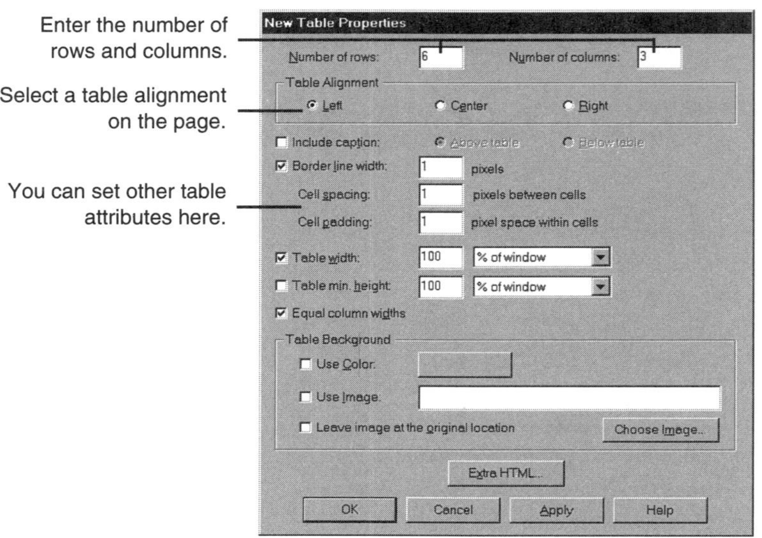

Figure 7.2   The New Table Properties dialog box.

7. (Optional) If you don't specify a table width or height, Composer creates a blank table as wide as the page, divided into columns of equal width. To specify a table width or height, select the following options:

Table Width: Click this option to turn it on. You can then use the text box and drop-down list to make the table a certain number of pixels wide or to specify the width as a percentage of the window width.

Table Min Height: This option lets you specify a minimum height for the table. You can set the table height as an absolute number of pixels or as a percentage of the window height.

8. Make sure there is a check in the **Equal Column Widths** box. This tells Composer to divide the table into columns of equal width. If this option is turned off, Composer creates columns that expand as you type—which makes the table very unmanageable.

9. (Optional) Use the **Table Background** settings to choose a color to add some shading to the cells. Or you can select a background image to use. (The table is clear by default.)

10. Click **OK**. Composer creates the table as specified and inserts it on your page (see Figure 7.3).

11. Start typing entries into the cells. (You can also insert links or graphics into cells.) To move from cell to cell, use the arrow keys or the Tab key. You can format the text in a table, as explained in Part 6 Lesson 4, "Adding and Formatting Text."

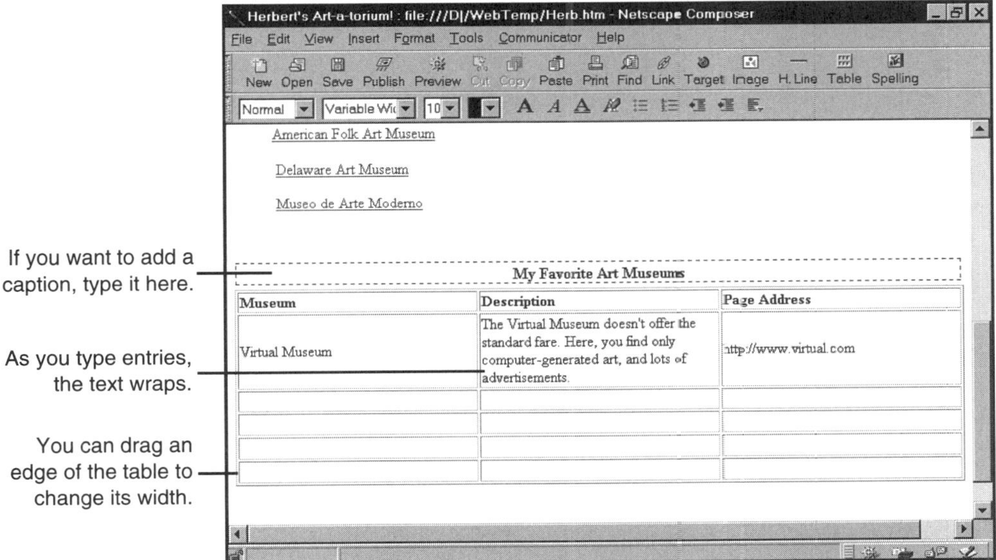

Figure 7.3 Composer inserts the table according to your specifications.

If you turned on Equal Column Widths (in step 8) and you did not specify a table width, the table appears as wide as the page and is divided into columns of equal width. If you type an entry that is wider than the cell, Composer automatically wraps the text inside the cell. If you turned off Equal Column Widths, as you type entries into the cells, they automatically expand to accommodate the text. In either case, you can drag the right side of the table to change its width.

Restructuring Your Table

The table you created in the previous section is pretty generic. All the columns are the same width, and the rows are the same height. If this works for you, fine. But you probably need something special—maybe a single cell at the top that spans an entire column, or a cell on the left that spans a couple of rows.

Whatever the case, you can change cell and row properties to create the desired effect. Take the following steps to adjust the generic table to fit your needs:

1. Click in the cell, or drag over the cells you want to reformat.

2. Right-click one of the cells, select **Table Properties,** and click the **Cell** tab. The Table Properties dialog box shown in Figure 7.4 appears.

You can make a cell span two or more columns or rows.

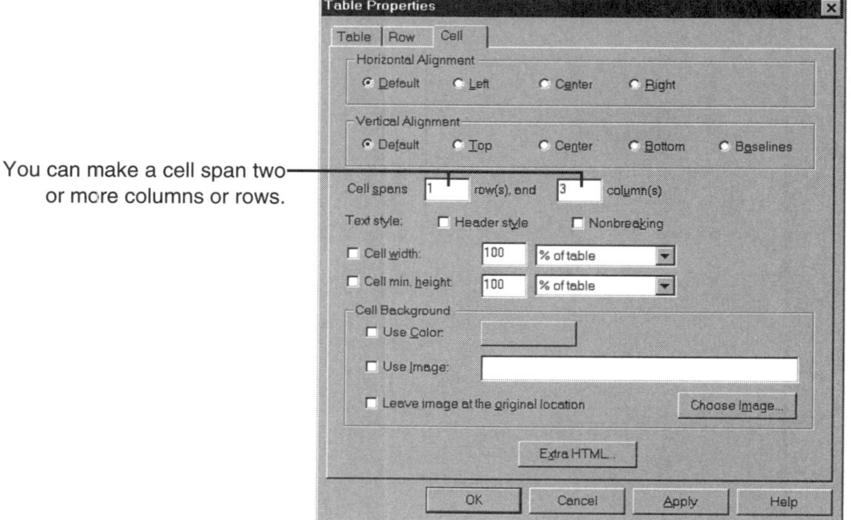

Figure 7.4   You can change the properties of individual cells.

3. Under **Horizontal Alignment** and **Vertical Alignment**, you can specify how you want your text entries positioned in relation to the cell.

4. To have a cell span two or more columns, enter the desired number of rows or columns you want the cell to span in the **Cell Spans** text boxes. For example, if you have a three-column table and you want a cell at the top that spans all three columns, type **3** in the **Cell Spans____Columns** text box.

5. Under **Text Style**, you can choose **Header Style** to make the text bold and centered in the cell (this is useful if you have a wide cell at the top of the table that spans several columns). **Nonbreaking** is off by default, but you can turn it on if you don't want Composer to wrap text in the cell.

6. You can use the options at the bottom of the dialog box to specify the cell height, minimum width, and color. Click **OK** when you are done.

If you chose to make a cell span two or more columns or rows, Composer does not merge the selected cell with the other cells in that row or column, so you may have to delete those cells. If the cells contain entries, use the Cut and Paste buttons to move the entries to other cells. Then right-click the extraneous cell, point to **Delete**, and click **Cell** (repeat to delete additional cells).

What About the Row Tab?   In Figure 7.4, you can see a Row tab hidden behind the Cell tab. The Row options allow you to set the text alignment and color for the currently selected row.

CAUTION

Adding and Deleting Rows, Columns, and Cells

When you first create a table, you rarely know how many rows and columns you need. You make your best guess (which is usually wrong), and then you add columns and rows as needed. You can easily add rows, columns, and cells in Composer. When inserting rows or columns, keep in mind that rows are inserted below the selected row, and columns are inserted to the right of the selected column.

To add cells, columns, or rows, follow these steps:

- To insert a row, select a cell in the row where you want the new row added. Open the **Insert** menu, point to **Table**, and click **Row**.

- To insert a column, select a cell in the column where you want the new column added. Open the **Insert** menu, point to **Table**, and click **Column**.

- Right-click a cell, point to **Insert**, and select the item you want to insert: **Row**, **Column**, or **Cell**. (If you chose Cell, the new cell is inserted to the right of the selected cell.)

To delete rows, columns, or cells, right-click the row, column, or cell you want to delete, point to **Delete**, and click **Row**, **Column** or **Cell**. Or, select the row, column, or cell you want to delete and choose the desired object from the **Edit**, **Delete Table** submenu.

Page Formatting with Tables

You can use tables for more than just grids of data. Because you can create columns in tables, you can use tables to create column-style text layouts. For example, the Web page in Figure 7.5 was created using a table.

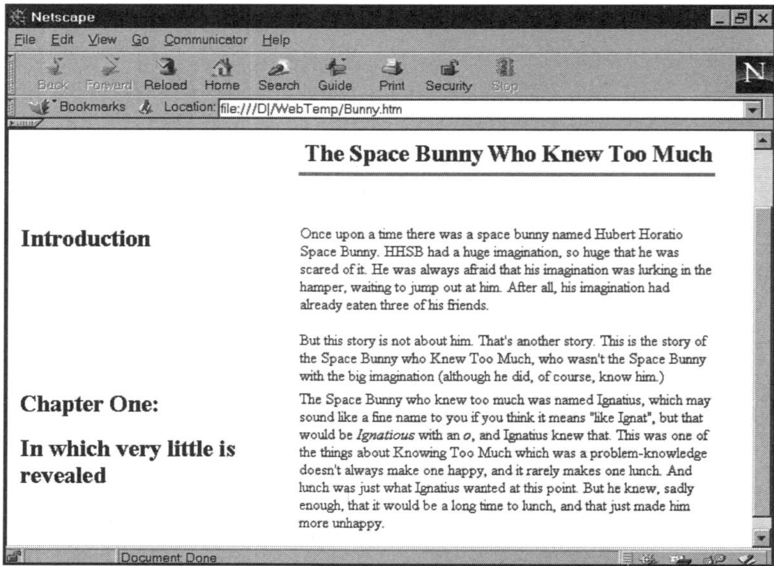

Figure 7.5   A table-based page layout.

You can create the look shown in Figure 7.5 by using a wide table. This table has three columns: a column for the titles, a column for the text, and a blank column between them. Using this blank column, you can create a nice amount of space between the titles and the text. Whenever you need to add a new title that you want to line up with the text, you just start a new row.

Adding Frames

Frames enable you to divide the browser screen so that you can display different Web pages in different sections of the screen. As I explained at the beginning of this lesson, Composer has no Insert Frame command. In fact, Composer can't even display frames. In order to use frames, you must insert the frame codes manually. (For details on working with HTML codes, see Lesson 10, "Getting Started with HTML.")

You can insert the codes by using Composer's **Insert, HTML Tag** command (which is terribly difficult) or by opening your Web page in a text editor (such as Windows Notepad) and typing the codes. Because you have to type several frame codes, the text editor option is preferred.

You can run your text editor or word processor and use it to open the Web page, or you can set up Composer to use a text editor of your choosing. To select a text editor, open the **Edit** menu, select **Preferences**, and click **Composer**. Under

External Editors, click in the **HTML Source** text box. Then click **Choose** and select the file that runs your text editor (such as C:\Program Files\Accessories\WordPad.exe). Click **OK**. To open the currently displayed Web page in your text editor, open the **Edit** menu and select **HTML Source**.

Use Your Word Processor Most word processing applications allow you to edit text files. Just be sure that when you save the file, you save it as a text file. Also, make sure you save the file using the .htm or .html extension.

Entering the Frame Codes

To create frames, you insert frame codes into your Web page. These codes tell the visiting Web browser how to divide its window into frames and which page it should load into each frame. You can do all sorts of fancy stuff with these codes (such as nesting a set of frame codes inside another set of frame codes), but we're not going to do that here. Instead, I'm going to give you the codes to enter to create a simple two-frame window. I will then show you how to modify some of the parameters inside the codes to tweak the design. If you want details on how to do more with frames, search the Internet for **html frame**.

First, create three Web pages: one file for the framing codes and two Web pages (one to display in the left pane, and the other for the right pane). To accommodate Web browsers that cannot display frames, you should enter your framing codes at the top of your main Web page file. These codes tell the browser, "If you can handle frames, here's what you do." You can then bracket the rest of the page with <NOFRAME> </NOFRAME> codes that enable a browser that cannot handle frames to display a non-framed page. If your service provider lets you use only one file as your main Web page file, be sure to enter the frame codes in that file.

Now, open your main Web page file in your text editor, and move the insertion point before any <BODY> codes; the framing codes cannot be between the <BODY> and </BODY> codes. Then, enter the following codes, as they are displayed here:

```
<FRAMESET COLS="25%,75%">
<FRAME SRC="index.htm" NAME="index">
<FRAME SRC="main.htm" NAME="main">
</FRAMESET>
<NOFRAME>
{Insert the Web Page Contents Here}
</NOFRAME>
```

Now you can go back through and revise the codes to tweak the design and work more effectively for your situation. The following list takes the codes one-by-one, explains what each code does, and shows you how to modify each code.

<FRAMESET COLS="25%,75%">   This turns frames on and divides the window into a left and right pane (see Figure 7.6). The left pane is 25% of the window width, which leaves 75% for the right frame. (You can enter different percentages.) To divide the window into a top and bottom pane instead, enter **<FRAMESET ROWS="25%,75%">**.

<FRAME SRC="index.htm" NAME="index">   This code tells the browser which Web page to load in the first frame (the left frame, in this case). In place of *index.htm*, type the file name of the Web page that you want to be displayed in the right pane. In place of *index* (after Name=), type a name for the frame—something that will be easy to remember (see the following section to learn the purpose of this name).

<FRAME SRC="main.htm" NAME="main">   This code tells the browser which Web page to load in the second frame (the right frame, in this case). In place of *main.htm*, type the file name of the Web page that you want to be displayed in the right pane. In place of *main* (after Name=), type a name for the frame.

</FRAMESET>   This code simply says, "We're done with frames."

<NOFRAME>   This code essentially tells the Web browser, "If you can't handle frames, then do the following." (Some older Web browsers cannot interpret frame codes.)

{Insert the Web Page Contents Here}   This isn't a code. I'm just telling you to insert whatever you want here to provide an alternative for browsers that cannot display frames. You can insert a simple link that points to a non-frame page, or you can insert the codes for an entire Web page.

</NOFRAME>   This is the Off code for NOFRAMES.

Setting Relative Frame Sizes with Asterisks   Instead of entering precise settings for frame sizes, you can use asterisks to set relative sizes. For example, instead of entering **<FRAMESET COLS="25%,75%">**, you could enter **<FRAMESET COLS="*,3*">**. This tells the browser to give one share of the window to the left frame and three shares to the right frame.

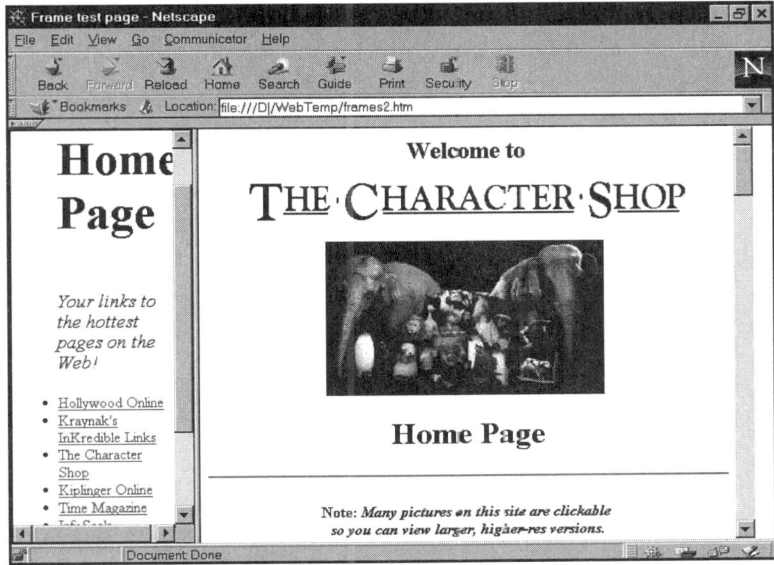

Figure 7.6   A browser window broken into two frames.

Holding Your Index Steady in the Left Frame

If you open your framed page in Navigator and try to use the index in the left pane to open pages, something very troubling will occur. When you click a link in the left pane, your index will disappear and be replaced by the page that link pointed to. The browser doesn't "know" that it's supposed to open the page in the right pane.

To fix this problem, you are going to have to add a target code that tells the browser which frame to use for displaying the linked page. For example, the following code

```
<A HREF="http://www.hollywood.com/">Hollywood Online</A>
```

displays **Hollywood Online** as a link that points to the page at http://www.hollywood.com. When you click the link, the browser opens the Holly-wood Online page in the current window. To force the browser to open the page in a specific frame, you add a target command, telling the browser which frame to use. The following code tells the browser to open the page in the frame named "main."

```
<A HREF="http://www.hollywood.com/" target=main>Hollywood Online</A>
```

Where did we get the name "main?" The name comes from the frame codes you entered in the previous section. For example, with the **<FRAME SRC="main.htm" NAME="main">** code, I named the frame on the right "main." If you replaced "main" with some other name, you will have to use that name for the target= command.

In this lesson, you learned to use tables and frames with your Web pages. In the next lesson, you will learn how to spell check your Web page in preparation for publication.

Spell Checking Your Web Page

In this lesson, you learn how to use Composer's new built-in spelling checker to check your Web pages and e-mail messages for misspellings and typos.

Checking Your Page for Spelling Errors and Typos

Few of the older Web page authoring tools or e-mail programs offered spelling checkers. Users had to rely on their own keen editing eyes, their typing skills, and their spelling proficiency to ensure that their electronic communications were as error-free as their paper messages. However, the current breed of e-mail programs and Web page editors have introduced features to help us out.

This release of Netscape Composer features its own spelling checker, which you can use to check for spelling errors and typos in your e-mail messages and Web pages. Take the following steps:

1. Create the e-mail message or open the Web page whose spelling you want to check.

2. Click the **Spelling** button (on Composer's standard toolbar or in Messenger). The spelling checker starts. If the spelling checker encounters any words that do not match the words in its spelling dictionary, the Spelling dialog box (shown in Figure 8.1) appears, displaying the word in question.

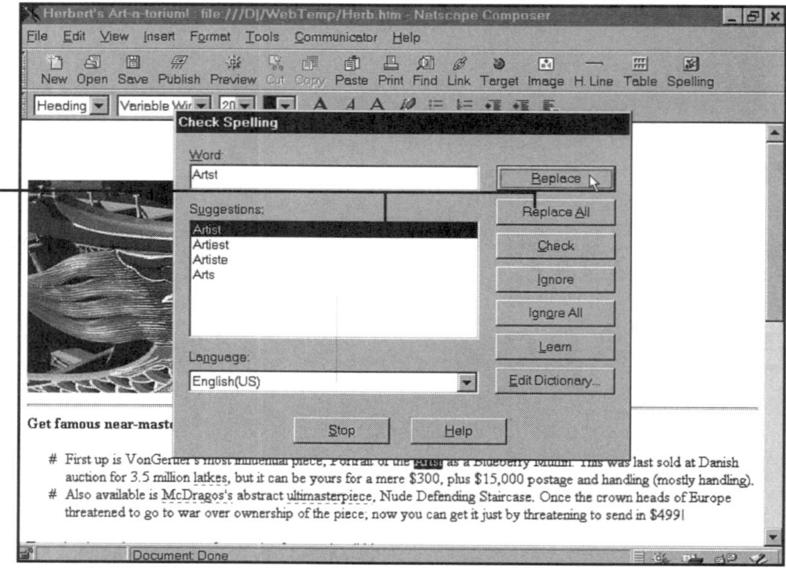

If the spelling checker displays the correct spelling, click it and select Replace.

Figure 8.1   The spelling checker can help you find and correct misspellings and typos.

3. Take one of the following steps:

- Click **Ignore** to skip over this occurrence of the word and proceed with the spelling check. If the word appears in the document again, the spelling checker will question it again.

- Click **Ignore All** to skip over all occurrences of this word in this document.

- If the word is misspelled and the spelling checker displays the correct spelling, click the correct spelling in the Suggestion(s) list, and then click either **Replace** or **Replace All** (to change only this occurrence or all occurrences in this document).

- If the word is spelled correctly, and you want the spelling checker to never question it again, click **Learn**. This adds the spelling to Composer's custom spelling dictionary.

- To stop, click the **Stop** button.

4. When the spelling checker finishes, most of the buttons become gray (unavailable). Click **Done**.

Making Sure Your Page Works

Although it's important to check your Web page for spelling errors and typos, it is even more important to check it for coding errors. A misplaced code can throw a heading off the screen, make all your text bold, or point links down dead-end alleyways. Before placing your page on the Web, check it.

The best way to check your page is to open it in Navigator. If you have the page opened in Composer, simply click the **Preview** button. Or, you can open the page directly from Navigator by opening the **File** menu and selecting **Open Page**. With the page displayed in Navigator, check the following things:

- Does the text show up well against the background? Be sure to check *all* the text if you formatted some text with a different color.

- Click your links. Do they work? If a link fails to open the correct page, you can quickly edit the link in Composer by right-clicking it and selecting **Link Properties**.

- Do the links appear in a different color from normal text? Do they change color after you click them? If they don't change color to indicate that they have been clicked, you may have set the same color for Link text and Followed Link text.

- Is your text aligned in a visually appealing layout? Although you can usually judge the layout in Composer, Navigator can sometimes reveal problems you haven't seen in Composer.

You can check links in Composer, but whenever you enter the command to follow the link, Composer automatically opens the page in a separate window (a Composer or Navigator window). Composer opens the linked page in a separate window, even if the link points to a target on the same page. For that reason, it is better to check links in Navigator. However, if you want to check a link in Composer, here's what you do:

1. Right-click the link you want to check. A context menu appears, as shown in Figure 8.2.

2. Select **Browse to...** (to open the linked page in Navigator) or **Open Link in Composer** (to open the linked page in a separate Composer window). Composer or Navigator opens the page.

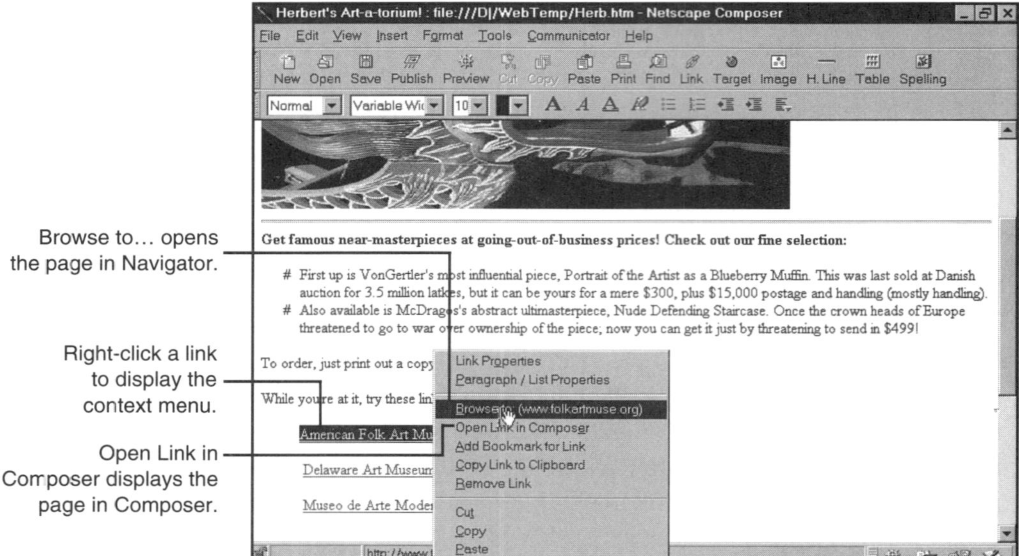

Browse to... opens the page in Navigator.

Right-click a link to display the context menu.

Open Link in Composer displays the page in Composer.

Figure 8.2   You can check your links in Composer.

In this lesson, you learned how to use Composer's spelling checker to find and correct spelling errors in your Web pages. You also learned how to check your page for other errors. In the next lesson, you will learn how to place your page on the Web.

Publishing Your Web Pages

In this lesson, you learn how to use Netscape Composer's one-button publisher to put your Web pages onto a Web server where everyone can see them!

Adding a Title, Description, and Keywords

Before you place your page on the Web, you should add a title, description, and keywords that will help Web search tools find your page and add it to their lists of Web pages. That way, when somebody searches for something that your page contains, the search tool can point them to your page. To add this information, take the following steps:

1. Run Composer and open your Web page.
2. Open the **Format** menu and select **Page Colors and Properties**. The Page Properties dialog box appears.
3. Click the **General** tab to move it up front, as shown in Figure 9.1.
4. Type a title for the page in the **Title** text box, type your name in the **Author** text box, and type a brief description of the page in the **Description** text box.
5. Under **Other Attributes**, type some unique words that describe your page in the **Keywords** text box. These are words that you think someone might use to search for your page.
6. In the **Classification** text box, type one or more words that describe the category in which your page should be included (for example, Personal Web Page or Fine Art). Some search tools, such as Yahoo!, can use this information to classify your page.
7. Click **OK**.

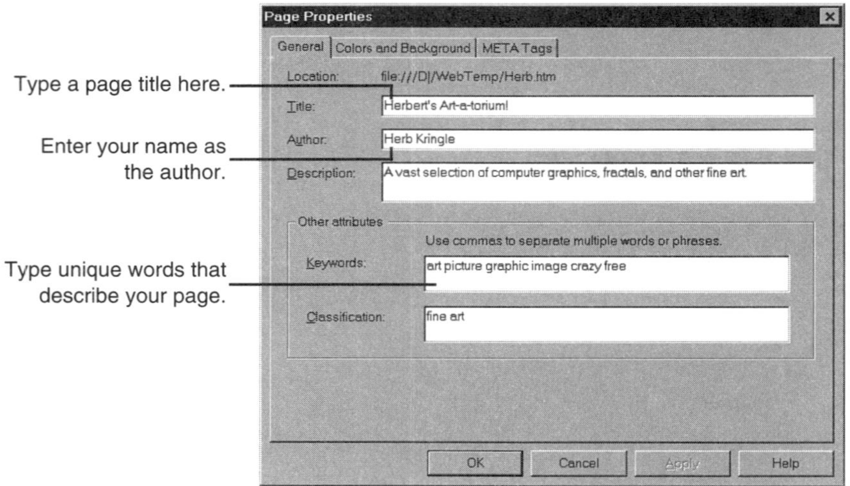

Type a page title here.

Enter your name as the author.

Type unique words that describe your page.

Figure 9.1   You can type information about your page to help people find it.

Where Are My Entries?!   None of the entries you just typed appear on your Web page, but they do appear in the coded HTML file that the Web browser uses to render the page. The title will appear in the browser's title bar when the browser opens your page. It also is used as the bookmark name, should anyone choose to add your page as a bookmark. As for the other entries, they are there just in case someone wants to know that information or search for it.

CAUTION

Getting Your Page Out on the Web

Unless you've been working directly on a *Web server* (a computer that stores Web sites where people browsing the Web can see them), you will have to take the additional step of *publishing* your Web pages.

Publish   To copy your files to the proper directory on a Web server. This is called "publishing" because it enables people to read your pages, just as publishing a book makes copies of the book available for people to read.

TERM

Fortunately, Netscape Composer has a built-in publishing feature. As long as you have stored your Web page and all related files in a single directory on your hard drive, all you have to do is enter the File, Publish command and provide some information about where you want those files sent. Composer takes care of the rest.

Before you start, you need to make sure you have somewhere to place your Web page. The best place to start is to call your Internet service provider. Most providers make some space available on their Web servers for subscribers to store personal Web pages. Call your service provider and find out the following information:

- Does your service provider make Web space available to subscribers? If not, maybe you should change providers.
- How much disk space do you get, and how much does it cost (if anything)? Some providers give you a limited amount of disk space, which is usually plenty for one or two Web pages.
- What is the URL of the server you must connect to in order to upload your files? Write it down.
- What username and password do you need to enter to gain access to the server?
- In which directory must you place your files? Write it down.
- What name must you give your Web page? In many cases, the service lets you post a single Web page, and you must call it **index.html**.
- Are there any other specific instructions you must follow to post your Web page?
- After posting your page, what will its address (URL) be? You'll want to open it in Navigator as soon as you post it.

If you are using a commercial online service, such as America Online or CompuServe, you may have to use its commands to upload your Web page and associated files. For example, CompuServe has its own Web page publishing wizard. In similar cases, you should use the tools the online service provides instead of trying to wrestle with Composer.

If your service provider does not offer Web page service, fire up Navigator, connect to your favorite search page, and search for places that allow you to post your Web page for free. These services vary greatly. Some services require you to fill out a form, and then the service creates a generic Web page for you (you can't use the page you created in Composer). At others, you can copy the HTML-coded document (in Notepad or WordPad) and paste it in a text box at the site. A couple of other places will let you send them your HTML file and associated files. Find out what's involved.

Configuring Composer's Publisher

In order to publish your page, Composer needs to know your user name, your password, and your Web site address. When you have that information, follow these steps to configure the publisher:

1. Open Composer's **Edit** menu and select **Preferences**.

2. Click the + in the box next to Composer to expand the item, and then click the **Publishing** item. The form displayed in Figure 9.2 appears.

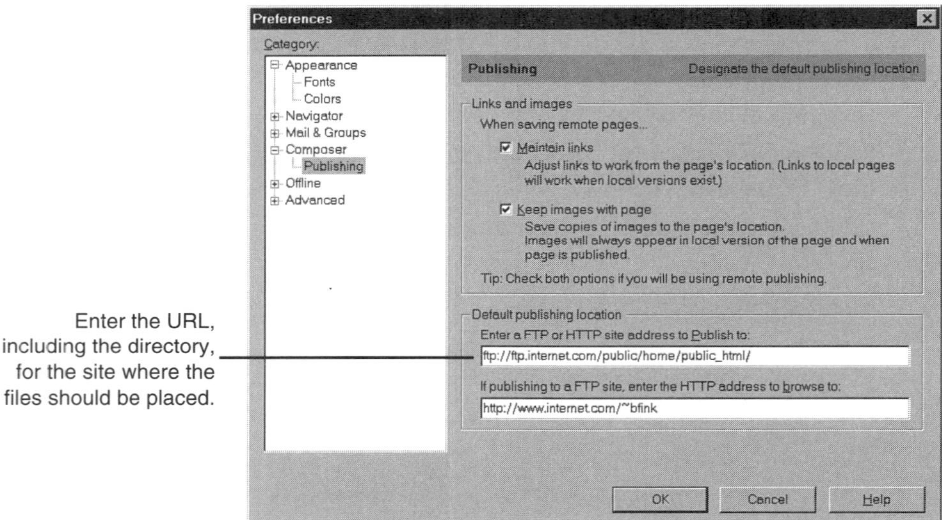

Figure 9.2   Tell the publisher where you want the page sent.

3. The Maintain Links option and the Keep Images with Page option are both turned on by default. Leave them on to ensure that your page's links will work and that any associated graphic files will be shipped with your page.

4. In the **Enter a FTP or HTTP Site Address to Publish To** text box, type the address of the FTP or HTTP (Web) site to which you want to upload your file(s). This address consists of the URL of the server plus the path to the directory, such as **ftp://ftp.internet.com/pub/users/webpages/**.

5. If you are uploading your page to an FTP server, click in the second text box under Default Publishing Location, and then type the URL you must use to open the page in a Web browser.

6. Click **OK** to save your settings.

Publishing Your Pages

You can use Composer to publish any pages you have, whether they were created with the Web page editor or with any other tool. You can even mix pages from different sources. Just make sure that all of the pages you want to publish are in the same directory on your hard drive before you begin. To publish your pages, follow these steps:

1. Establish your Internet connection, run Composer, and open the page you want to place on the Web.

2. Click the **Publish** button, and the Publish dialog box appears (see Figure 9.3).

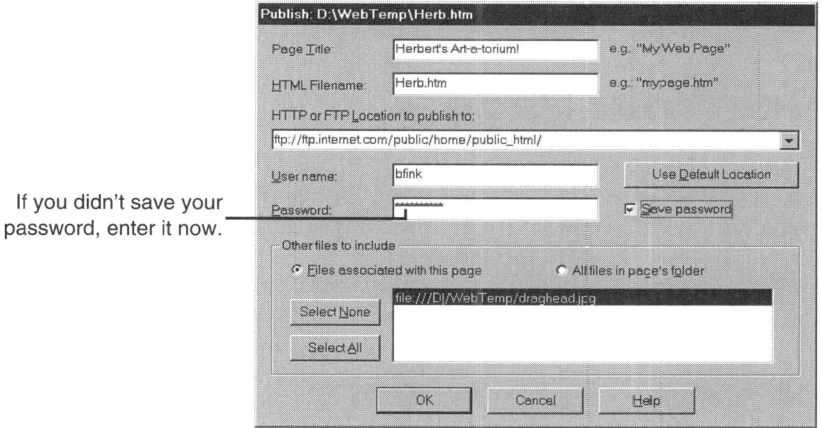

Figure 9.3 The Publish Files dialog box.

3. If the **HTTP or FTP Location to Publish to** is blank, open the drop-down list and select the desired location, or click the **Use Default** button to insert the address you entered under Preferences.

4. If this is the first time you are publishing a page, enter your user name and password in the appropriate text boxes. To have Composer save this information (for the next time you publish a page), click **Save Password**.

5. To publish just this one page, click the **Files Associated with This Page** option button, which uploads the HTML file for this page, along with all of the files for graphics on the page. To publish all the pages in the current directory, click the **All Files in Page's Folder** option button.

6. Click **OK** to start the publishing process. Composer connects to the Internet (if you are not already connected). The Publishing Page dialog box appears, listing the name of each file as it is uploaded and showing the number of files that have been uploaded in relation to the total number to be uploaded. When all the files have been uploaded, this box disappears. Congratulations! Your material is now out on the Web!

Test It Again   Once you have your page on the Web, open it and check it out again to make sure it was not corrupted during transfer, that all the graphics and lines are positioned correctly, and that your links work. If you have a different Web browser or a friend who uses a different browser, check it out in a different browser.

Publicizing Your Page

If your goal in creating a Web site is simply to take pleasure in the creation, you can keep the site a secret. However, if your goal is to have people take a look at your page, you will have to let them know that it exists.

There are many ways to spread information about your Web page. More and more often now, TV and newspaper ads include the advertiser's URL. In addition, people are putting URLs on their business cards, on letterhead, and at the bottom of e-mail messages. You might even see them on T-shirts and race cars. These are all good ways to spread the word, but they cost money. The following sections show you how to get some free publicity for your Web page.

Don't Publicize Your URL Too Early   If you publicize an URL before the site is in proper running condition (or before it's even up at all), people who visit it might decide the site is not worthwhile—and they'll probably never return. Although your site doesn't have to be perfect, you shouldn't publicize it until it is usable and useful.

Exchanging Links

No matter how esoteric in nature your site is, odds are good that sites on similar or related topics exist. If you can create a link from those sites to yours, you have a good chance of drawing in people who are surfing that link. So, consider swapping links with the authors of those related pages. You place a link to her Web page on your Web page, and she places a link on her page that points to your page.

To swap links, simply contact the author of the related page via e-mail. You might include the URL of your page in your e-mail message, along with a suggested name for the link. Then the other author can simply cut and paste that information instead of typing it. Be sure to offer the author the courtesy of adding a link to your page that points to her page. Better yet, inform the other author that you have already inserted a link to her page, and invite her to visit your page to check it out.

Registering Your Page with Search Engines

There are dozens of different search engines and World Wide Web directories designed to help people find what they are looking for on the Web and the rest of the Internet. These systems can help steer interested people toward your site—but only if the systems know about your site. A search engine or directory finds out about a Web site in either or both of two ways.

- You *register* your site by supplying the URL, the topic of your site, and other relevant pieces of information.
- The system finds your site by means of its *Web crawler program*. A Web crawler program runs unmanned, searching the Web and following whatever links it finds; as it does, it looks for new Web pages it hasn't seen before and grabs the information from them.

If you want to register with a directory, go to that directory's Web site. (Try looking up *search engines* using your favorite Web search tool, and you should find links to more Web directories.) If the directory accepts registrations, there should be a clearly marked link to a registration form. You might also try searching for "publicize Web page" or "announce Web page."

A typical registration form asks you for a description of your site, a list of keywords relating to the topic of your site, the URL, and an e-mail address for the person in charge of the site. Choose your keywords carefully, realizing that you might have to put in several words that mean the same thing or overlap in concept. If you have a Web site about growing roses, for example, you should use the keywords *roses*, *flowers*, and *horticulture* because the person searching for that information could be using any of those words as his search keyword.

Registration might not produce instant results. In fact, it may be weeks before your page appears in the directory because the managers of many directories check each site that's registered before they add it to their official lists. When your page is added, you might receive e-mail telling you that the registration went through and asking you to return the courtesy by putting a link to the directory somewhere on your site. If a directory asks you to create such a link, you don't have to put it in an obtrusive location; adding it to your page of links should be fine.

Becoming Easy Prey for Web Crawlers

You can do a number of things to increase the chances that a Web crawler program will find your site. The more people there are who have links to your site, the more likely it is that your site will be found. And it's very important that you make sure every one of your pages has links that go (either directly or indirectly) to your home page. It would be a shame if the Web crawler found a link to one of your pages and that page was a dead-end. That page would be the only part of your site to be registered.

You can also do certain things to ensure that once the Web crawler does find your site, the site will show up in other people's searches.

- Make sure that the titles on your pages are descriptive of the contents of the page that people will be interested just from reading the title.
- Make sure that the first few lines of text on your page contain appropriate keywords that someone might use on a search for such a page. Because some Web crawlers record only the first few text lines, someone using the crawler's search form will only find your page if she enters one of those words. Other directories capture the whole text of your document, but later during the search, they determine whether to list your page as a "hit" based on where the user's keywords appear in the document. Those directories recommend a document in which the words appear at the beginning before they recommend one in which the words occur at the end.

Many of the larger Web crawler sites and search engines are commercial undertakings, and they make money by selling display ads on their pages. If you're running a commercial site, you might want to consider getting some of these ads. Generally, they let you run a small graphic with a link to your page. Some of these randomly display an ad whenever someone performs a search, while others just add the graphic to the listing of the site (much like in the Yellow Pages, where your listing is free, but you can pay extra for a fancy display).

In this lesson, you learned to automatically publish your pages on the Web. The remaining lessons discuss more advanced Web page topics, including adding HTML codes manually and designing effective Web documents.

Getting Started with HTML

In this lesson, you learn what HTML is, and you learn how to edit an HTML file in a text editor and open the file for viewing in Navigator.

Facing HTML Codes Outside Composer

Composer is a great tool for creating simple Web pages from scratch. But if something goes wrong, you may need to flip the hood on your Web page and get your hands dirty with some HTML codes. You might also want to go behind the scenes of a Web page you admire to learn some of the author's techniques.

Whatever your reason for wanting to tinker with the codes behind the page, this lesson, along with Lessons 11 and 12, provide you with a better understanding of these codes and how you can use them to take control of your Web pages.

What Is HTML?

HTML stands for HyperText Markup Language. HTML is used to define the location and description of elements on a Web page (or other hypertext document). An HTML encoded document includes the text you want to display, information on how that text should be formatted (such as whether the text is a headline, whether it should be centered, and so on), the names of the pictures that will appear (but not the pictures themselves), and other important information. When you connect to a Web page, your Web browser (such as Netscape Navigator) "builds" the Web page in memory according to the HTML instructions, and then it displays the assembled Web page on-screen.

How Is an HTML File Organized?

An HTML file is a plain ASCII text file that contains only letters, numbers, spaces, and punctuation. You can edit an HTML file with any text editor (such as Notepad or WordPad, which are included with Windows) or any word processor that has a "save as text" feature (which includes most modern word processors such as Microsoft Word and WordPerfect). HTML file names usually end in the extensions .HTM or .HTML, so that computers and humans can recognize them as HTML files.

Coding in Composer   Composer makes it easy to insert HTML codes. You simply type text and insert links, graphics, and lines on your Web page, and Composer inserts the codes for you. However, Composer doesn't offer features for inserting all the Web page objects that have HTML codes. In Lesson 11, you will learn how to add codes for these objects.

Two basic types of information appear in an HTML file: *text* and *tags*. The words that appear on the Web page are the text. The tags are the special codes that tell the browser how to format the lines of text and how to include other elements on the page. The tags in an HTML file are easy to spot because they appear inside angled brackets as shown here:

```
One word will appear in <B>bold</B> type.
```

In this line, `<B>` and `</B>` are the tags. The first tag means "start bold type," and the second tag means "end bold type." So when that line appears on a Web page, it looks like this:

```
One word will appear in bold type.
```

Paired and Unpaired Tags   Most HTML tags are paired tags. You need two tags to complete the set: One tag turns the feature on, and the second tag turns it off. Some tags, however, are unpaired (such as the `<IMG>` tag, which pulls a graphic into the page).

Who Decided What the Tags Mean?

HTML isn't actually a language per se, it's more of a document type definition (DTD), or an adaptation of another language. That other language is SGML (Standard Generalized Markup Language). SGML is deceptively simple; all it really does is define markup tags, stating that they begin with a < and end with a >. HTML defines what each specific tag is supposed to do.

Netscape and Microsoft have designed their Web browsers to understand not only the standard HTML tags, but additional tags as well—some of which just aren't part of the official HTML yet, and some of which may never be. The good thing about the additional tags, called *extensions* (as in the Netscape Extensions and the Microsoft Extensions) is that they allow people to create more complex and useful Web pages. The bad thing is that you can't properly view Web pages that are designed around them unless you have a browser that understands these extensions. (To the Web browser manufacturer, this has historically been a good thing because it encouraged people to use their browsers instead of the competition's.) However, with the promised widespread adoption of HTML 3.2 (whose specifications were drafted with the assistance of both Netscape and Microsoft), these extensions might become a thing of the past.

Starting a Web Page

In order to see how an HTML page is built, let's just go ahead and start making one! Start up a text editor and open a new blank document. I'll walk you through building the document.

Many HTML pages begin with an identification command, which is called a *prologue*. For example, you might see a prologue like this:

```
<!DOCTYPE HTML PUBLIC "-//IETF//DTD HTML//EN//3.0">
```

This prologue lets the Web browser know that this is an HTML document built around specification 3.0. This line is not very important because if the line isn't there, the browser will assume it's true anyway.

A complex HTML document is comprised of *elements*, which are parts of a document in much the same way chapters and appendixes are elements of a book. A simple HTML document has only one element—itself. Therefore, to tell the browser that a document is going to be more complex and will have formally distinguished elements, you need the tag <HTML>.

Tags That Every Web Page Should Have

The first formal element of a document that contains the <HTML> tag is the head element, whose beginning is marked with the <HEAD> tag. The head element contains identifying information about your Web page, such as its title and its place in a sequence or database. Many Web pages have just one line in the head element, such as

```
<TITLE>A very empty Web page</TITLE>
```

where the words between the `<TITLE>` tag and the `</TITLE>` tag are a title for the page. This is the title that Navigator and other Web browsers put on the title bar so you can tell where you are. It's also the name you'll see when this page is stored in your bookmark or history file.

Uppercase or Not?   You don't have to type tags in uppercase letters; the `<title>` tag works the same as the `<TITLE>` tag. But if you type them in all uppercase, it's easier to distinguish the tags from the text when you're working in your HTML file.

CAUTION

Notice that when the `<TITLE>` tag showed the start of the title, the end tag was the same, only with a slash after the first bracket. This is similar to the relationship between the tag to start bold text, `<B>`, and the tag to end it, `</B>`. Now that you have all the header information that you really need, you need a tag that indicates the end of the head element. As you probably guessed, that tag is `</HEAD>`. (Later, you'll add the end to the `<HTML>` section, which contains an `</HTML>` tag.)

As you enter paired tags, you will start to see that you can nest one set of paired tags inside another. For example, you might want to make text bold and italic. In such a case, you could nest the italic on/off tags between the bold on/off tags, as follows:

```
<b><i>This text is bold, italic</i></b>
```

When nesting paired codes, be careful to place them in the correct order. For example, `<b><i></i></b>` is correct, because the nested italic codes are between the codes that bracket them; `<b><i></b></i>` is incorrect, because the italic codes should be between the bold on and bold off codes.

Coding the Body of the Page

The element following the head is the body element of the HTML document, the material that will appear on your page. As you might expect, the body element begins with this tag:

```
<BODY>
```

If you're not going to have anything actually in the document, you can follow the <BODY> tag immediately with the tags indicating the end of the body of the document and the end of the HTML material.

```
</BODY>
</HTML>
```

As your first test of HTML document structure, you can put all of this together to create a Web page that has the formal element structure of a complex HTML document—with none of the contents. Type the following HTML code into your word processor or Windows Notepad, and you'll have a complete but blank HTML document.

```
<!DOCTYPE HTML PUBLIC "-//IETF//DTD HTML//EN//3.0">
<HTML>
<HEAD>
<TITLE>A very empty Web page</TITLE>
</HEAD>
<BODY>
</BODY>
</HTML>
```

Create a directory called **htmldocs** (or whatever name you want to give it), and (using a Save as Text or Text Only option if you're using a word processor) save this file as a plain text file with the file name **blank.htm**. That way, whenever you need to start a new HTML document, you have a blank one that you can just fill in!

Save Time with Composer   Whenever you create a new Web page with Composer, Composer automatically inserts the starting codes for you. If you add a title via the Page Properties dialog box, Composer adds the title codes for you, too.

Viewing Your HTML File

Even though Navigator is called a *Web* browser, you can use it to view HTML documents stored on your hard disk. To view your newly created HTML document, follow these steps:

1. Start Navigator. If it starts to dial your modem to connect to the Internet, cancel it; there's no need for you to be tying up the phone line or racking up Internet charges while you do this.

2. Open the **File** menu and select **Open Page**. The Open Page dialog box appears.

3. Click the **Choose File** button, select your HTML file, and click the **Open** button. Navigator loads the file and displays it, just as it would if the file were a page on the Web (see Figure 10.1).

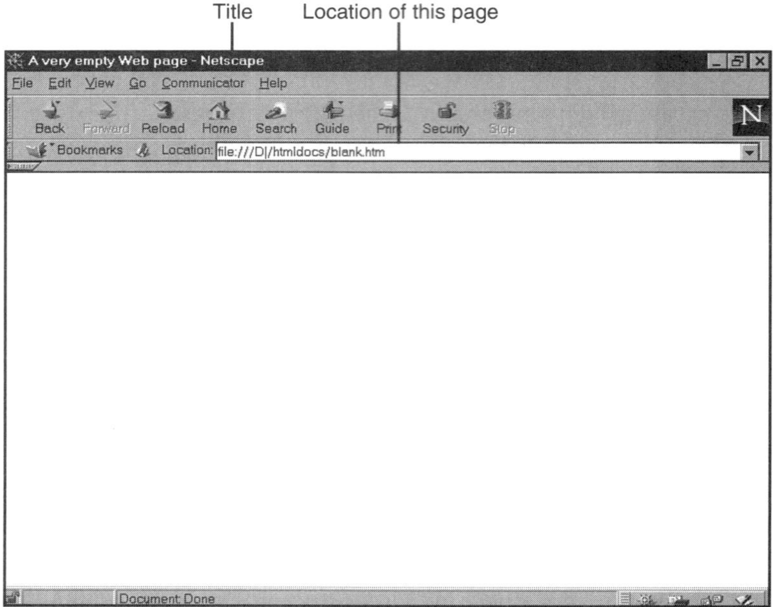

Figure 10.1   Here's your blank HTML page!

Windows 95   If you're using Windows 95, you can start your Web browser and display the file quickly by double-clicking your HTML file in Windows Explorer or My Computer.

Learning More About Tags

To learn more about the available HTML tags, check out Appendix B, "HTML Reference Section." In addition, various individuals and organizations have created online guides and references for HTML tags. To find these places, fire up Navigator and use your favorite search tool to search for **html tags**. One of the most useful references I have found is Willcam's Comprehensive HTML Cross Reference, which you can find at the following address:

```
http://www.willcam.com/cmat/html/crossref.html
```

When you connect, you are greeted by a page of HTML tags listed in alphabetical order. Click a tag, and you are taken to a page that explains what the tag does and how to type it correctly (see Figure 10.2). This page also shows which browsers support the various codes. You can even cut and paste these tags to use them in your own documents. (For more information on how to learn about HTML tags, see Part 6 Lesson 12, "Copying HTML Tags.")

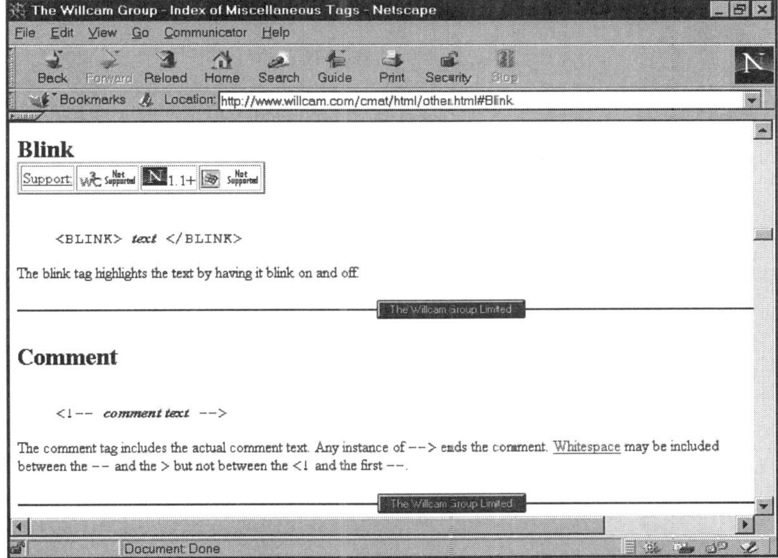

Figure 10.2 Willcam's provides a complete HTML reference.

In this lesson, you learned about HTML, and you created a simple HTML file and viewed it in Navigator. In the next lesson, you'll learn how to use Composer to add HTML tags to your Web pages.

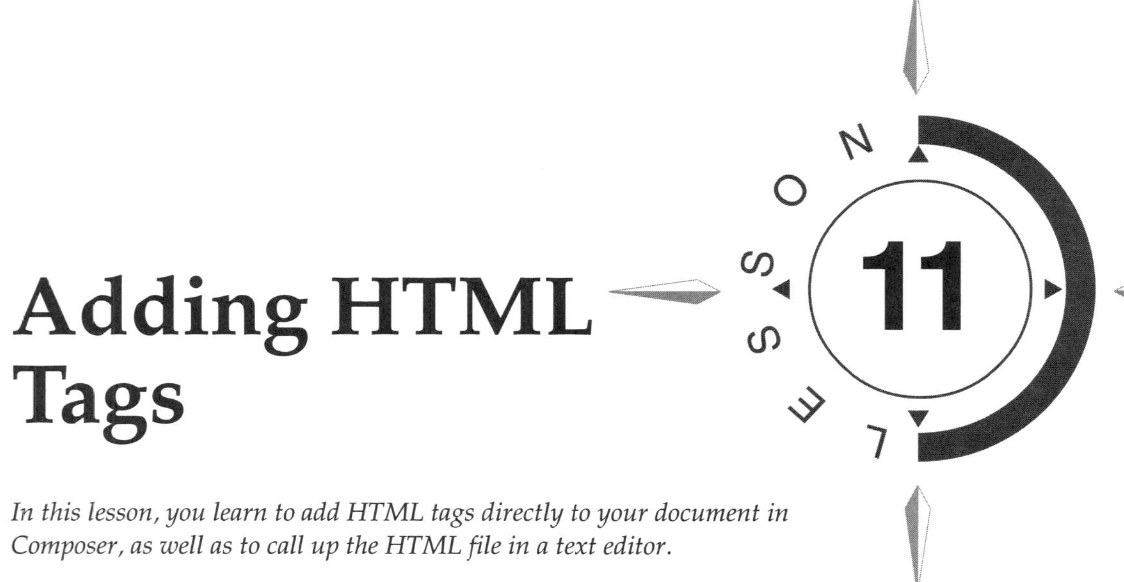

Adding HTML Tags

In this lesson, you learn to add HTML tags directly to your document in Composer, as well as to call up the HTML file in a text editor.

Inserting and Checking the Tags

Composer is very powerful, but it doesn't have tools for inserting all the HTML tags that are available. For example, Composer cannot generate the tags to include a form on the page or to render frames. However, you can use Composer to manually insert tags that it's not designed to generate automatically.

To add tags to a Web page, you use Composer's Insert, HTML Tag command. The procedure is a little complicated and time-consuming, because it takes several steps to insert a single tag, and you can insert only one tag at a time. The following steps show you how to add a simple pair of tags (<em> and </em>), which tell the browser to emphasize text (typically to display it bold and italic):

1. Open your Web page in Composer, and position the insertion point directly before the text you want to emphasize.

2. Pull down the **Insert** menu and select **HTML tag**. The HTML Tag dialog box appears, as shown in Figure 11.1.

3. Type **<EM>** into the field. (Be sure to type the closing angle bracket, or you'll get an error message.)

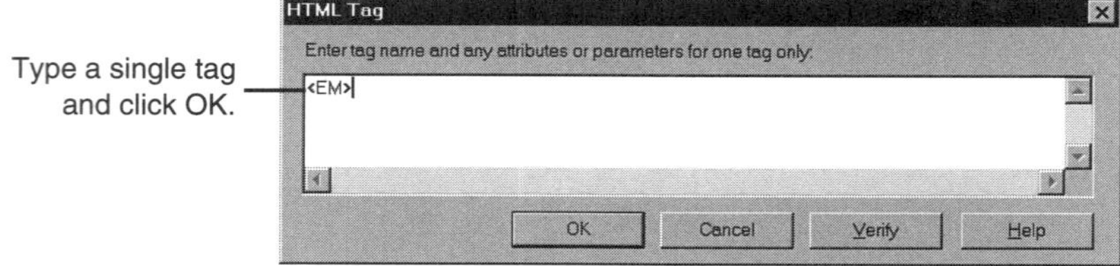

Figure 11.1 You can insert HTML tabs manually.

4. Click **OK**, and a triangular tag symbol appears in the editor to mark the position of the tag.

5. Move the insertion point to the right of the text you want to emphasize, and then choose **Insert, HTML tag** again.

6. Type </EM> and click **OK** to enter it. Another tag appears to the right of the text.

Don't Forget the Format, Style Menu Although Composer has no command for inserting the <EM> tags, you can emphasize your text by marking it with bold and italic. The Format, Style submenu also contains options for other text formatting, including Underline, Fixed Width, and Blinking text.

7. While Composer is showing you the full Web page you are working on, it's actually storing the whole thing as a file of HTML codes (sometimes called the **source**, because it is the basis for what is displayed), which is what Web browsers understand. To see the HTML source for the page, open the **View** menu and select the **Page Source** command. A source display window appears (see Figure 11.2).

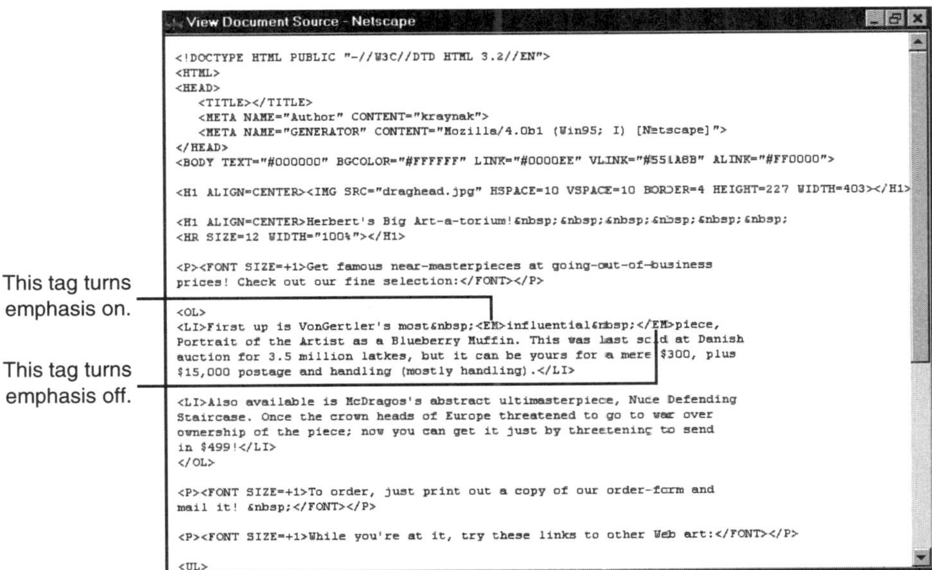

Figure 11.2 The underlying HTML source code, with your new tags inserted.

8. Verify that the tags you've added are really there, and then click the **Close** (X) button on the title bar to close the window.

9. Click the **Save** button to save the changes to your hard disk. Then click the **Preview** button to see the effect of these tags in your Web page. The browser window appears.

10. Click the **Close** (X) button on the title bar to close the browser window.

You can quickly edit a tag by right-clicking it and selecting **HTML Tag Properties**. The HTML Tag dialog box appears, allowing you to edit the tag. To delete a tag, right-click it and select **Cut**.

Editing the HTML File

If you have a large chunk of HTML code to add, adding it one tag at a time can be slow and awkward. Instead, you can tell the Web editor where your favorite text editor is, and then you can edit the source code with a single command. Follow these steps:

1. Open the **Edit** menu and select **Preferences**. The Editor Preferences dialog box appears.

2. In the Category column, click **Composer** to see the options shown in Figure 11.3.

Specify the location of your text editor.

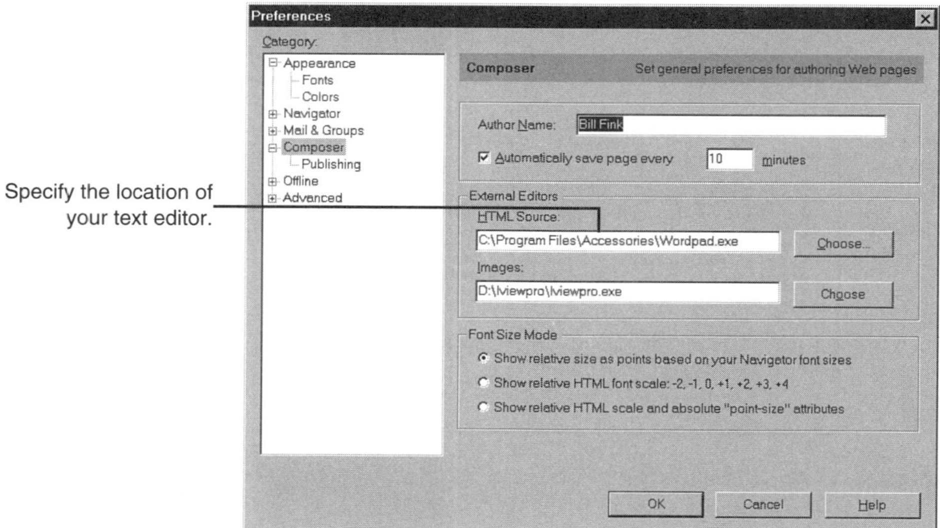

Figure 11.3   The Composer Preferences dialog box.

3. Under **External Editors**, click the **Choose** button next to **HTML Source**.

4. Locate and select your text editor (for instance C:\Program Files\ Accessories\Wordpad.exe). Then click the **Open** button.

WordPad and Notepad   You can find the WordPad text editor at C:\Program Files\Accessories\Wordpad.exe in Windows 95. You can find the Notepad text editor at C:\windows\notepad.exe in earlier versions of Windows. (This is assuming that your operating system is installed on Drive C:.)

5. Click **OK** to close the dialog box.

6. Open the **Edit** menu and select **HTML Source**. The editor you picked opens and displays the HTML source document. Figure 11.4 shows such a document open in WordPad. If you're using Notepad, open its **Edit** menu and select **Word Wrap**.

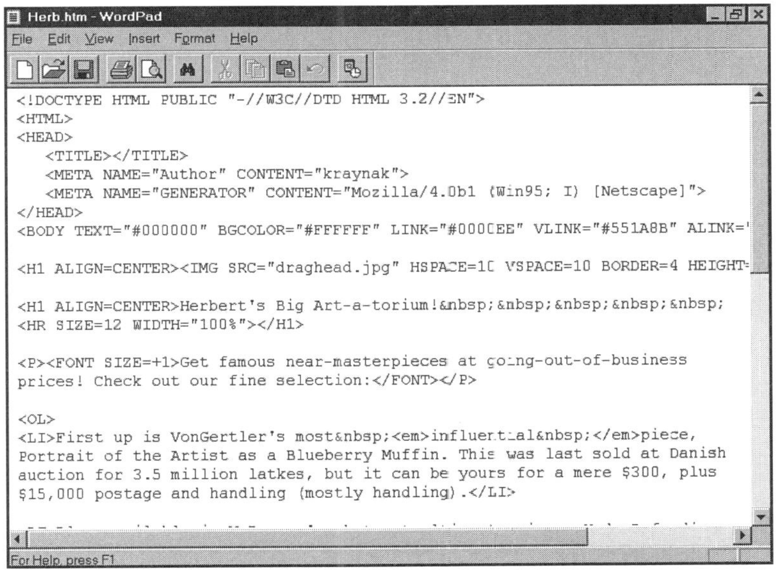

Figure 11.4   An editor (WordPad in this case) displays the HTML file.

7. Move the insertion point down to one of the blank lines and add `<P>You gotta love it, it's ART!</P>` to the document.

8. Open the editor's **File** menu and select the **Save** command to save this change.

9. Click the **Close** (X) button on the editor's title bar to close the editor.

10. You return to Composer, which displays a dialog box saying **This page has been modified by another program. Reload page to see changes?** Click the **Yes** button. Composer reloads the page, and the phrase "You gotta love it, it's ART!" appears right where you added it.

Notice that the yellow symbols that indicated where you added the tags in the previous procedure are gone now. That's because when you first added these tags, the Composer didn't check to see if it knew them, but whenever it reloads the page, it checks all the tags. Because it recognizes the tags you added, it treats them as a standard part of the document. If it had found a tag it didn't recognize, it would have shown the yellow symbol, indicating that there was an unknown tag.

In this lesson, you learned how to directly add tags to your document in Composer. You also learned how to open and edit the file in a text editor such as Notepad or WordPad. In the next lesson, you will learn how to copy tags from other Web pages to use in your Web page.

Copying HTML Tags

In this lesson, you learn to look at existing Web pages and copy useful HTML tags that you can use in your own pages.

Seeing How It's Done

One of the nice things about HTML is that nothing is a secret. If you see a page with a particularly interesting feature, and you want to know how it's done, you can find out. To view the HTML codes that make up a particular Web page, follow these steps:

1. Display the page on-screen in Navigator.
2. Open the **View** menu and select the **Page Source** command. Navigator opens up a window and displays the HTML source for that page, as shown in Figure 12.1.

The HTML source display doesn't display just the ASCII text. It also highlights the following types of elements to make them more easily distinguished.

- Keywords (exclusive parts of the HTML language) appear in bold purple.
- Quoted values within tags appear in blue.
- Attributes appear in bold black.
- Comments appear in italic.

If you can follow the flow of the text in the document, you shouldn't have any problem locating the section of code that generates the effect you are interested in. The tags are right there—you just have to know how to read them.

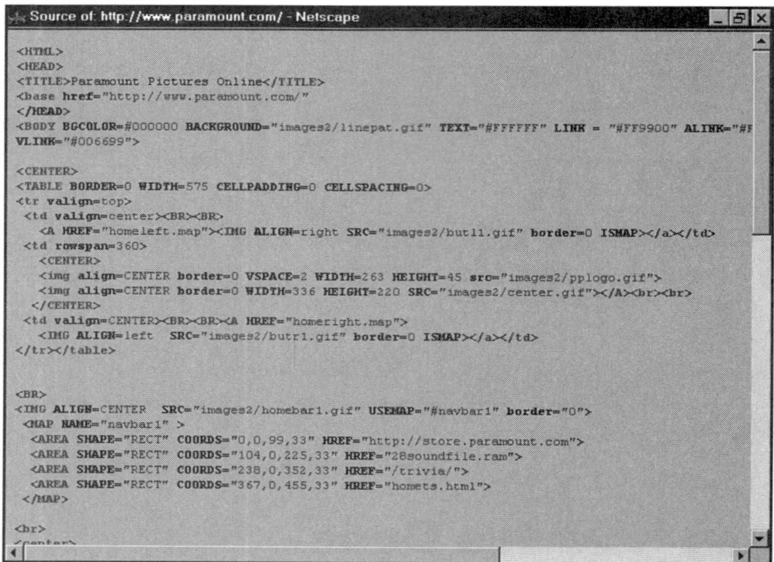

Figure 12.1   Navigator displays the HTML source in its own window.

Learning to Identify Strange Tags

When you pull up a page that has an interesting design element and you select View, Page Source, you see the code, but it may be packed and stacked so tight that you don't know where to start looking. Just keep in mind that most people are linear, and when they insert objects on their Web pages, they typically insert the codes in the same relative position as the object appears on the Web page.

Let's look at an example. Run Navigator and open a page that has an image map, a graphic that you can click to navigate the site. Figure 12.2 shows an image map at the New England Aquarium (http://www.neaq.org/index.html). You probably agree that these image maps are pretty cool, but there's no way you can create your own, right? Well, not exactly.

You can create your own image map by typing the appropriate codes in the correct format. However, you'll have an easier time if you have an example. So, open Navigator's **View** menu and select **Page Source**. Now you can see the codes used to create the image map. Figure 12.3 shows the source code for the New England Aquarium home page. You can see that the codes for inserting the image map are at the top of the HTML coded file, in relatively the same position where the image map appeared on the Web page.

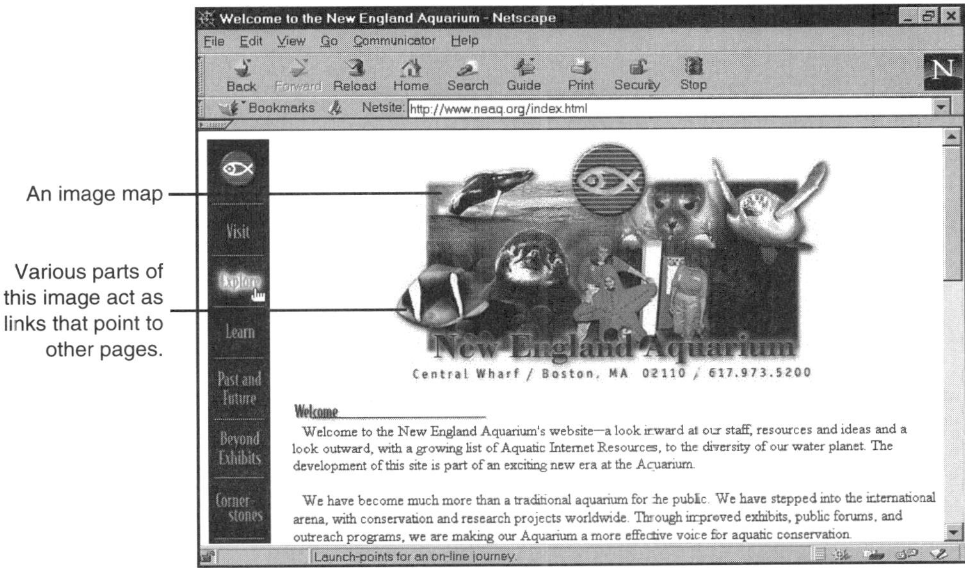

Figure 12.2   If you want to create an image map, pull one up in Navigator.

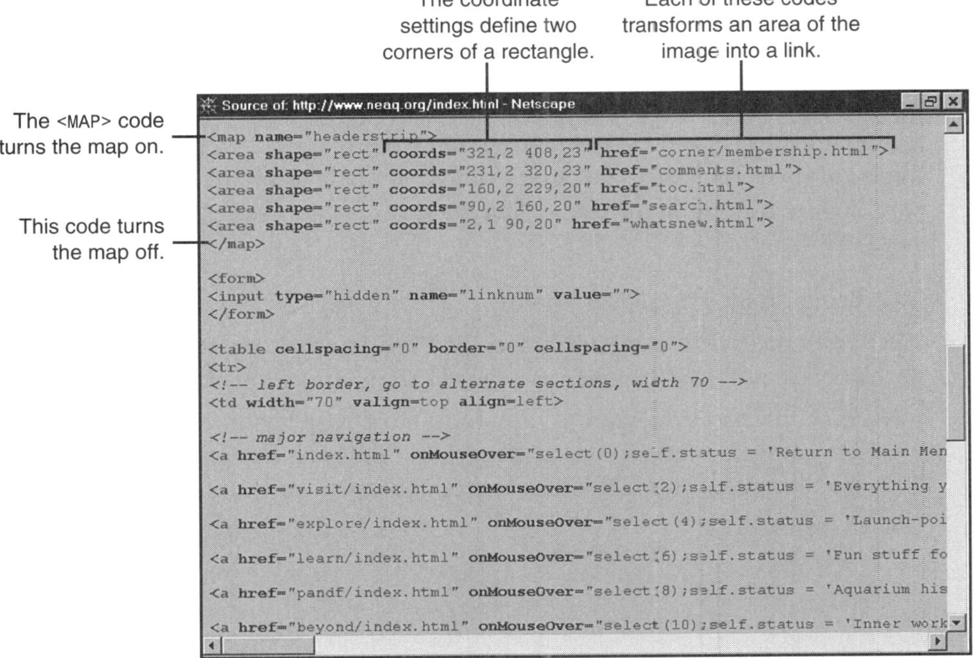

Figure 12.3   Behind the scenes of an image map.

Figure 12.3 points out some of the interesting codes that make the image act the way it does. Notice the code for inserting the image itself. Note also that the <MAP> code is paired; it requires an on and off code. You will also notice that there is a code for each area of the map that acts as a link. These codes specify coordinates on the image, and they link those coordinates to specific Web pages.

This section showed you one example of how you can learn from someone else's HTML code. There are many other ways. Whenever you look at a good page, pay attention and try to think about how it was created. If you can't figure it out, take a look at the code.

CAUTION

CGI-BIN?   There are some aspects of a Web page that you won't learn much from. For example, a link with `/bin/` or `/cgi-bin/` in the path tells you that a CGI-BIN program is being used, but it doesn't tell you how that program works. You would need to see the source code to see how it works. And even if you knew, you might have to rewrite the program for your own server (unless you happened to be running the same sort of server as the site where that Web page was stored).

Copying Someone Else's HTML Tags

Once in a while, you'll find a set of tags that is so complex you really don't want to retype it bit by bit. For example, those <MAP> codes you saw in the previous section are fairly complex. It's much easier to copy the coded text right out of someone else's page, strip out everything that made it unique to his needs, and rebuild it by putting in the things that make it fit your needs. To do that, follow these steps:

1. Bring up the page in Navigator.
2. Open the **View** menu and select the **Page Source** command. Navigator opens a window and displays the HTML source for that page.
3. Select the text you want to copy (point to the first character, hold down the left mouse button, and drag the mouse to the last character). The text you select appears as white characters on a blue background.
4. Press **Ctrl+C**.

5. Open the text editor you are using to edit your page.

6. Place the insertion point where you want to add the copied text and press **Ctrl+V**. The text—complete with codes—is inserted.

After pasting the coded text into your document, you must go through it code by code to make the code suitable for your Web page. If, for instance, you copy an <IMG> code that pulls an image into the page, you must edit the code so it points to a graphic file at your site. After making your changes, be sure to save your file and open it in Navigator to make sure everything works properly.

CAUTION

The Ethics of Borrowing Code   Back in grade school, you learned to use an encyclopedia to research a report. You probably also figured out that you could create a report just by copying paragraphs right out of the encyclopedia—but that was plagiarism and it was wrong. The same ethics apply to creating HTML documents: It is one thing to learn the structure of tags and organizational concepts from someone else's page, but it's another thing to reuse large chunks of HTML code in your own pages without permission (both ethically and legally, as there are copyright concerns at work).

If you find yourself reusing a large, barely modified section of someone else's code, or effectively copying something that made that person's page unique, you've crossed over a line. If you're ever in doubt, it's best just to ask permission. People will usually be happy to grant permission, but it really is their right to say yes or no.

In this lesson, you learned how to find cool pages, look at their HTML code, and borrow ideas. In the next lesson, you'll learn some design philosophies for setting up a Web site that consists of more than one page.

Choosing a Design Philosophy

In this lesson, you choose a target audience and decide how your Web page's information will flow.

What's a Design Philosophy?

If you're publishing a single Web page, you don't have to worry much about the structure of your Web site. However, if you plan to create a Web site with several connected pages, you should have some idea of how you want to present the site to your audience.

This includes not only what your content will be, but how you will present it. Suppose you were comparing the magazines *Ranger Rick*, *Reader's Digest*, and *Wired*, for example. Although all three magazines might have an article about rain forests, each article reads and looks quite different from the others. The writing style, the presentation of text, and the choice of graphics reflect the design philosophy of each magazine.

Choosing a Target Audience

The first step toward building your design philosophy is to figure out who you expect to visit your site. A page aimed at explaining to school children the proper procedure for feeding Jersey cows will be very different from a page aimed at explaining the same thing to farmers. You should evaluate the following factors about your intended audience:

- **Age:** If you're designing for children, you may want to lean toward shorter sentences and cleaner graphics, for example. (This is a good goal when creating pages for adults, too, but it's vital on pages for children.)

- **Computer experience:** Less experienced users will benefit from pages that can fit on a single screen and pages that contain clearly marked links. A computer is befuddling enough for most newcomers; your page should not confuse them more.

- **Reason for visiting your site:** Someone doing research is going to want a clearly organized site he can navigate quickly, without many distractions such as decorative graphics. Someone who's just out surfing the Web to see what's cool will be attracted by graphics and links that appear be mysterious and intriguing.

- **Knowledge of you:** For the same reasons you talk differently to your friends than you do to strangers, your Web site should be different for people who do and do not know you. If it's a personal page, for example, you might include information about yourself for people who don't know you, or you might include an update of what's new for your friends. If it's a commercial site, you would want to pitch advertising-type information to new customers, but include different sorts of information for existing customers.

You'll probably determine that you expect more than one type of visitor. No problem. You can design around that, particularly with different pages for different people. But you should know ahead of time what audience you expect to be dealing with.

You should also pay attention to any e-mail responses you get regarding your Web page. While such information won't reflect your entire visitor base, it might give you some clue as to what you must change at your site to make it more universally appealing.

Determining the Intended Flow

If you know how a visitor is going to go through your pages, you can try to organize the information on your Web site so that it is easy to find and is seen in reasonable context. Toward that end, the first thing you have to know is where people are going to start.

Most sites have a clear home page—the online equivalent of a front door. Other sites are designed so that people interested in different topics come in via different pages, often from links on other pages. Once you know where people are entering from, your choice of what links you put on each page can control the way in which people experience your site. The simplest site has just one HTML page. This may not be an exciting site, but if you have only a small amount of information to get out, there's no reason to complicate things.

A Controlled Site

If you want to run a *controlled* site—and make sure people see exactly what you want them to see, in the order you want them to see it—you can build a linear site with no optional paths. You might think of this as a way to present a story online, or perhaps as the Web equivalent of a slide-show presentation. The user won't get the thrill of exploring different paths, but if the content is thrilling enough, that shouldn't be a problem. Figure 13.1 shows a simple diagram of what a controlled site might look like.

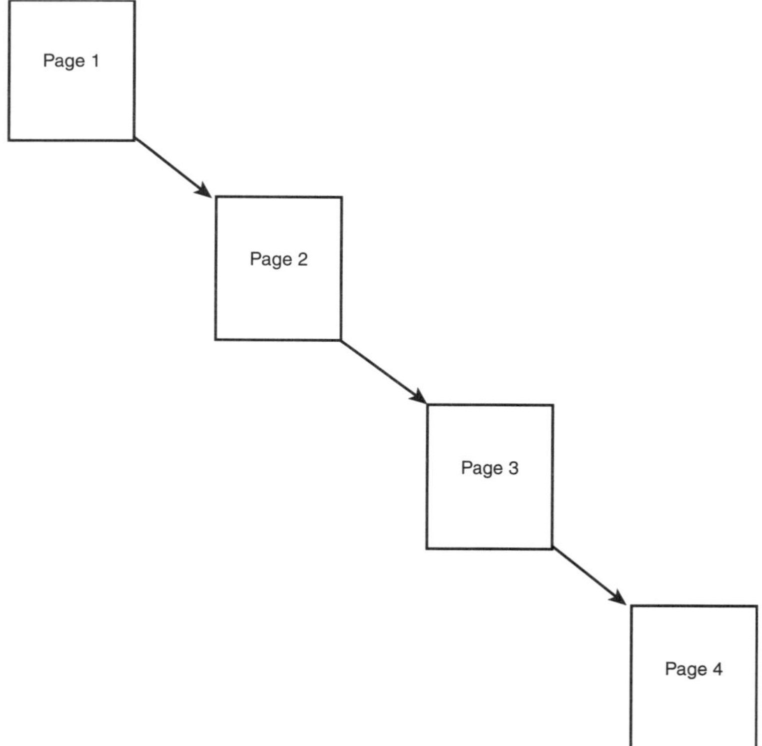

Figure 13.1 Diagram of a controlled site.

The Tree Structure

Another basic structure is a *tree* structure, in which you start at a home page (the tree's trunk) that serves as a table of contents. The links on that page take you to a number of pages (the tree's branches), each of which can be a content page or can have a more detailed table of contents with its own page links (smaller branches). Each page should have a link back to the one that it branches from, and possibly a link to the home page.

With a setup like this, it's very easy to add or remove pages because each page only has links to the page it links from and the pages it has links to. As you can see in Figure 13.2, the tree structure provides a good organized way to store large amounts of data. However, users might find it difficult to get from one piece of data to a related piece.

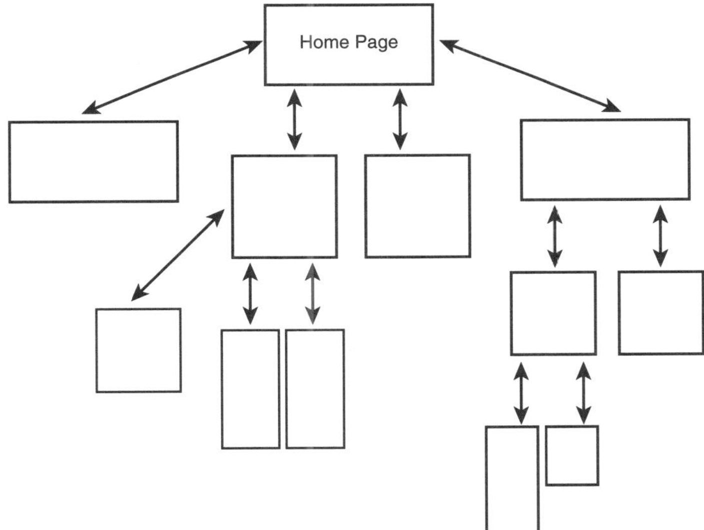

Figure 13.2   Diagram of a tree site.

An Equilateral Structure

The third basic design is an *equilateral* structure (shown in Figure 13.3), in which every page links to every other page, usually by a group of links at the top or bottom (or both) of the page. This type of structure enables quick movement from page to page. It also eliminates any worries you might have about which page the visitor is coming in on; no matter which page that is, he will be able to get to the other pages.

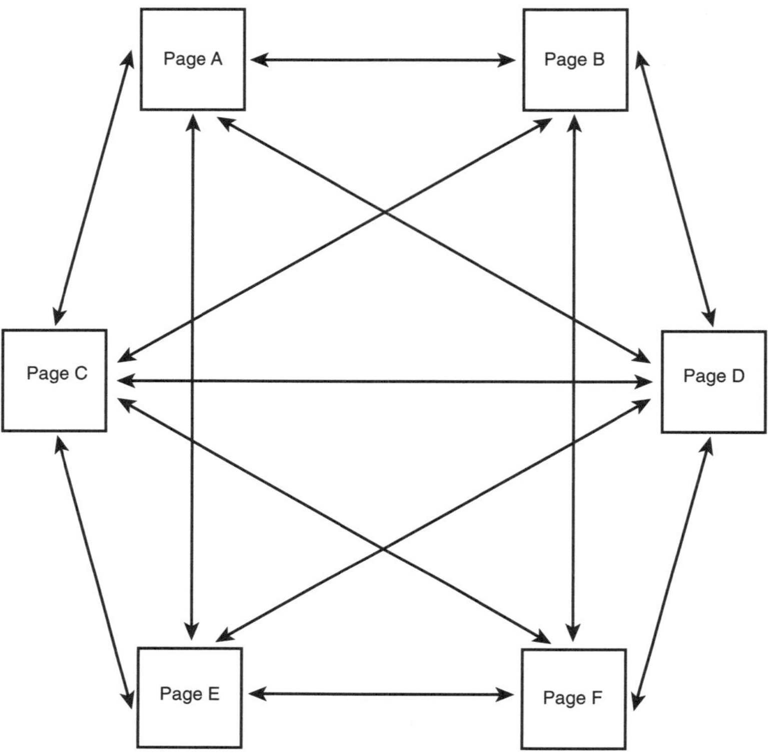

Figure 13.3   Diagram of an equilateral site.

However, the equilateral structure has certain weaknesses.

- If it contains a large number of pages, the number of links becomes unwieldy.
- To add or remove a page, you must change all of the pages.
- You have no control over the order in which the visitor moves through the information.

Frames   Using frames, you can create and maintain an equilateral site more easily. Split the page into two frames. Make one a small frame that always contains the links to all of the pages, and make the other a larger frame in which you see the current page. This way, you don't have to maintain links on every page! (For more details on creating frames, see Part 6 Lesson 7, "Creating Tables and Frames.")

Combining Structures

In reality, any reasonably complex site is going to draw from each of these designs, combining them in a way that makes sense for that site. For example, Figure 13.4 shows an equilateral set of pages on various topics, some of which serve as the starting page for a tree structure. In addition, some of those pages contain links that leap to otherwise unconnected pages for ease of access.

However you implement it, you should make sure that your basic structure is reasonably clear to the visitor. That way, he can easily find whatever he is looking for on the page.

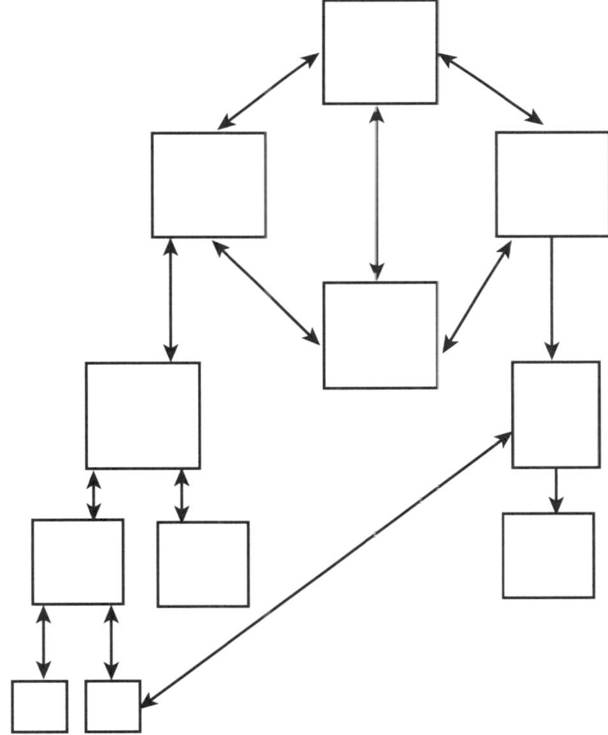

Figure 13.4   You can design a complex combination of structures.

In this lesson, you learned how to design the flow of your Web page. In the next lesson, you'll learn how to design your Web page to make it accessible to a wide audience.

Making Your Web Page Browser-Friendly

In this lesson, you learn how to make sure your Web page works correctly and is accessible to as many different Web browsers as possible.

Being Browser-Compatible

With the millions of Netscape users out there, it is easy to forget that a huge number of folks use other browsers, such as Internet Explorer and Mosaic. If you want everyone to be able to access your page, you cannot assume that they have Netscape Navigator.

The first step toward this is to make sure your Web site is not dependent on browser-specific extensions. If you design your site in such a way that a person can only navigate from one page to another using navigational information in a frame, for example, users of Mosaic, Internet Explorer, and all the dozens of other browsers (and old versions of popular browsers) won't be able to get around your site.

Does this mean that you shouldn't use any of the Netscape extensions? Not at all! You just have to understand what will happen when a non-Netscape browser encounters one of those extensions. There are three prime possibilities:

- Despite the fact that it's not Navigator, the browser will understand the tag. Many other browsers are programmed to understand the most popular Netscape extensions (such as the <CENTER> tag).
- The browser will not recognize the tag and will simply ignore it. Browsers know that anything in angle brackets is a tag, so they're smart enough not to put the unrecognized tag on the screen as text.

- The browser will recognize the tag, but will not recognize the attribute within the tag. In this case, the browser will just act as though the attribute isn't there at all.

If the unrecognized tag or attribute is necessary for your page to work, you have a problem. If it just helps the page look better, providing a visual bonus in some way, it's not going to cause problems if it's not understood.

Image Attribute Problems

Suppose you want to design a page with an illustration on the right that the text wraps around. You would use the Netscape extension attribute ALT=LEFT in an <IMG> tag placed on a line above the text itself. The result in Netscape would look something like Figure 14.1.

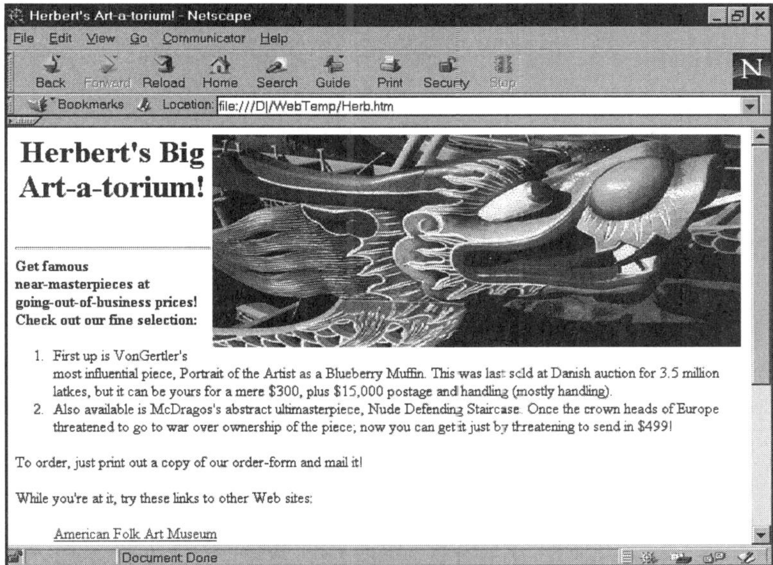

Figure 14.1 Text wrapped around an image in Navigator.

If a browser that doesn't understand the ALIGN attribute displays this page, it ignores the ALIGN=LEFT attribute and puts the image at the current location of the insertion point. Figure 14.2 shows the same page as it would look in an incompatible browser that didn't understand ALIGN.

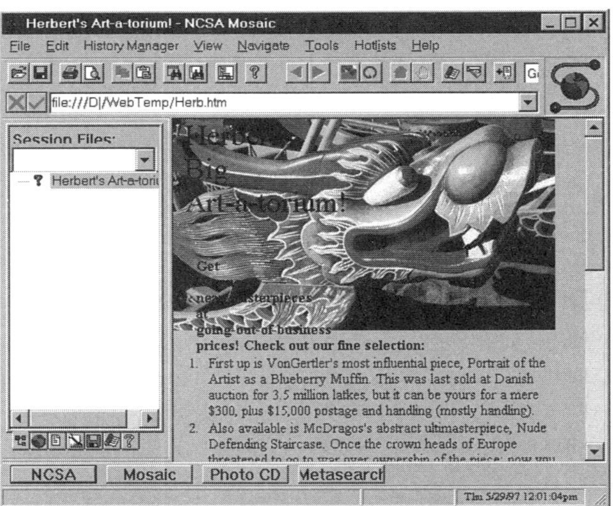

Figure 14.2   The same page as it looks without internal alignment.

If you're not sure how your page will look in a browser that doesn't understand the tags and attributes in question, there's a simple way to find out. Just remove those tags and attributes and see what your page looks like in Netscape without them.

Tags Within Tags

One other issue to pay attention to is how different browsers treat multiple simultaneous text formatting. For example, consider the following line of HTML code:

```
Some things are <B>bold <I>and</I> others are not</B>.
```

Some browsers will display that line correctly as

Some things are **bold *and*** others are not.

However, some browsers are unable to mix certain formatting characteristics and will have to turn off one type of characteristic to display another. In those browsers, the same line might look like this:

Some things are **bold** *and* **others are not**.

Or even like this:

```
Some things are bold and others are not.
```

With that in mind, if you want to be able to predict what your page will look like, you should avoid nesting or overlapping text highlights.

Frames

Another feature you have to worry about when designing your Web page is frames. Although the newer versions of most Web browsers support frames, some of the older versions are incapable of rendering frames. To give these older Web browsers access to your page, you should enter the <NOFRAMES> code to provide a non-framed version of your page.

For example, on my own home page, I use a narrow frame that includes an index of links to all of the main pages of my site (see Figure 14.3). However, in the same file, I also include a <NOFRAMES> tagged section that displays a standard list of links. As a result, people without frames can still navigate the site.

Figure 14.3   Nat's home page as it looks in Navigator.

You place the <NOFRAMES> code immediately after the </FRAMESET> code and before the section that you want the user of the frameless browser to be able to view. Then place a </NOFRAMES> code immediately after that section, as shown in Figure 14.4.

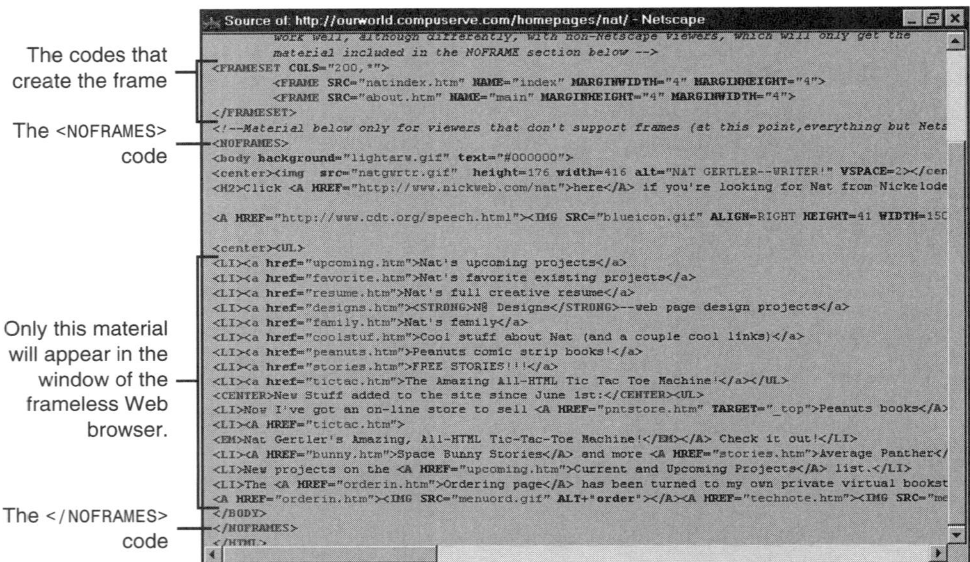

Figure 14.4   The coding behind Nat's home page makes the page accessible to browsers that cannot render frames.

Nongraphical Browsers

In these days of Web pages full of font tricks, graphical links, and eye-searing backgrounds, it is easy to assume that everyone surfing the Web is doing so with a powerful, picture-friendly computer. That assumption is wrong.

Many people use nongraphical terminals to access the Web. This is most common on college campuses, where the students may be using terminals attached to larger computers as opposed to using personal computers. The Web looks very different to these people, as Figure 14.5 attests.

There are also people out there who are using graphical browsers but have the automatic loading of graphics turned off. For the most part, these are people who have only slow Internet access. This group includes people in more rural areas of the U.S., who may not have available the array of high-speed local dial-in access points that more urban folks do. It also includes people in many foreign countries, where the general level of technology is lower.

```
Telnet - telnet.iquest.net
Connect  Edit  Terminal  Help
                                        Nat Gertler, Writer! home page (p1 o

   NAT GERTLER--WRITER!

Click here if you're looking for Nat from Nickelodeon!

   [LINK] NAT GERTLER (that's me!) writes comic books, computer books,
   prose fiction, magazine columns, and much more. (And yes, I'm
   available for new writing assignments; leave me e-mail if interested.)
      x Nat's upcoming projects
      x Nat's favorite existing projects
      x Nat's full creative resume
      x N@ Designs--web page design projects
      x Nat's family
      x Cool stuff about Nat (and a couple cool links)
      x Peanuts comic strip books!
      x FREE STORIES!!!
      x The Amazing All-HTML Tic Tac Toe Machine!

   New Stuff added to the site since June 1st:
      x Now I've got an on-line store to sell Peanuts books!
-- press space for next page --
  Arrow keys: Up and Down to move. Right to follow a link; Left to go back.
 H)elp O)ptions P)rint G)o M)ain screen Q)uit /=search [delete]=history lis
```

Figure 14.5   Nat's home page again—this time without graphics.

There are even some people browsing the Web whose main method of access is not the screen. There are blind Web surfers out there who use special tools that turn the words of the Web into either Braille or speech. You can choose to deal with these low-resolution citizens of the Web in one of three ways:

- You can ignore these people. This is a particularly viable option if what your page is about is so graphical in nature that there is no way to represent it in text. It's a particularly bad choice, however, if the academic audience is one of your target groups.

- You can make a completely separate version of your site that is designed to be text-only, and then include a link (a text link, of course) that lets these people access that page from your home page.

- You can carefully design the page so that it makes sense whether or not the pictures are visible.

The last option is a lot easier than you might guess. If you follow the guidelines outlined next, you should be well on your way.

- Avoid using graphics with vital words or large amounts of words on them. It's a bad idea to be sending all those words as a picture anyway because, while it may allow you to create all sorts of fancy lettering designs, it will also be a lot slower than plain text.

- When you do use graphics, take advantage of the ALT attribute in the <IMG> tag. This attribute lets you supply some text information that will be visible to those who can't see the image. This way, the text-only surfer will at least know what the picture he can't see is a picture of. When you are using the image as a link, the ALT attribute text will also serve as an alternate link to the same location.

- Don't assume that the character formatting will be displayed in a given manner. Most dumb terminals have some way of highlighting text, whether it's showing the text in reverse colors, making it appear brighter, or making it underlined. However, those terminals are less likely to have italics and almost definitely will not have different sizes of lettering. As such, instead of typing this line in your document

```
the books that I have in my collection are in italics
```

you might want to use a line that says this:

```
the books that I have in my collection are displayed <EM>like this</EM>.
```

That way, the user will be able to recognize the highlighting in whatever way it appears on his screen.

- Don't use *mapped* graphics. A mapped graphic allows a user to follow different links by clicking different parts of the graphic. (This function can be achieved either by using a CGI-BIN program or by using the Microsoft extension USEMAP.)

Checking for Proper HTML Codes

It's very easy to make minor mistakes when entering HTML code. After all, it's a combination of typing (where it's easy to make an error) and programming (which requires some logic).

A lot of errors will show up quickly when you test your pages. If the page doesn't look the way you expected, that's a sign that there is something wrong.

However, most browsers are forgiving of certain types of mistakes, which is great when you're looking at a flawed Web site—but bad when you're trying to find the flaws in your own. After all, you can't count on other people's browsers ignoring the same errors that yours does.

Missing Half of a Pair of Items

Possibly the most common error is leaving out one of the items of what is supposed to be a pair. One example would be missing one of the quotation marks around URLs in an HREF attribute. Another would be missing one of the angled brackets of a tag. Navigator's source display has built-in features that can help detect both of those errors.

To find a missing angle bracket or quotation mark in your HTML source, follow these steps:

1. Display your page in Netscape Navigator.
2. Pull down the **View** menu and select the **Page Source** command.
3. Look for a lot of words in bold (see Figure 14.6).

   As you saw before, categories of items appear in different colors, and keywords and their attributes appear in bold text. This will instantly help you detect a missing closing bracket because the source code display assumes that everything after the first word between brackets is an attribute. When you suddenly see a whole lot of words in bold that aren't *supposed* to be attributes, you know that the source display found an opening bracket and assumed that everything was supposed to be an attribute up until the *next* closing tag.

4. Look for light blue blinking text.

   The source display also has automatic detection for missing quotation marks. When it finds a place where it thinks a quotation mark is missing, it displays all of the text between the quotation mark that it did find and the next quotation mark in blinking light blue text.

Another pairing error would be a missing tag that is needed to make up a paired opening and closing tag set, such as <CENTER> and </CENTER>. Paired tags like these are called *elements*, and you should always make sure that both tags are in place (except with the <P> tag, where </P> is optional). You need the ending tag even if you want the tag to affect the entire page. In that case, you put the closing tag just before the </BODY> tag at the end of the file.

A common cause of this pairing error is forgetting to put the slash in the closing tag, which leaves you with two opening tags and no closing tag! Some HTML-oriented editors (including Composer) automatically put the closing tag in for you when you insert the second tag, in which case it's okay if you forget about it.

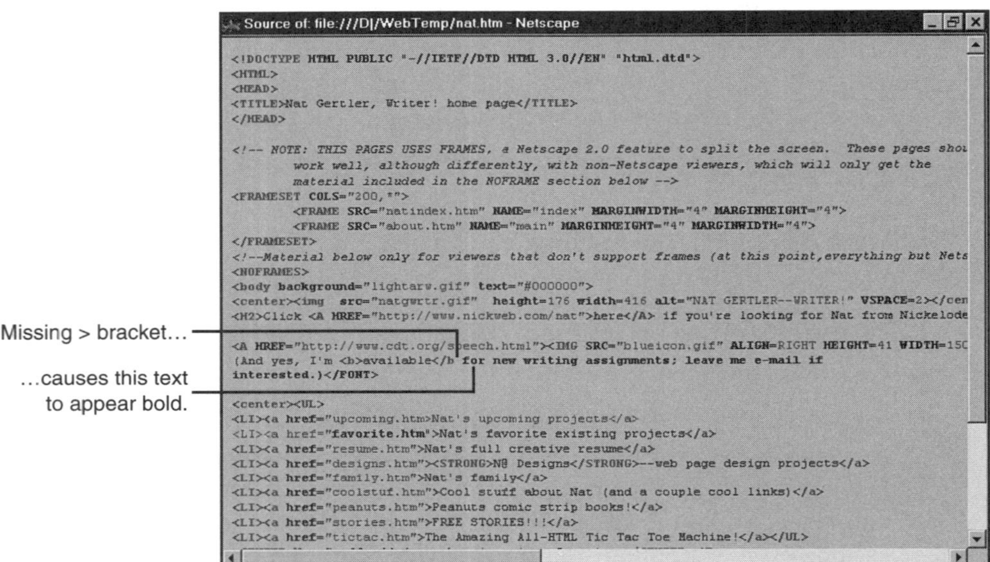

Figure 14.6   The source display reveals coding errors.

Get Help   Place your e-mail address at the bottom of your Web page so people can notify you if your links are out of date or if your page has problems when displayed in their Web browsers.

Other Tag Errors

Another common error is using the wrong tag. This is particularly easy when you're using some of the smaller tags such as <DD>, <DT>, <TR>, and <TD> (which you use to build lists and tables).

When building tables and lists, you also have to be careful to get all the tags in the right order. You have to remember that the <TABLE> tag comes before the first piece of information about the table, and the </TABLE> tag comes after the last piece. Similarly, `<TR>` comes before the first entry for the row, and `</TR>` comes after the last. `<TD>` comes before the information for each cell, and `</TD>` comes afterward. As such, your table specification should end with `</TD></TR></TABLE>`, which mark the last cell, the last row, and the end of the whole table in that order.

Avoid Errors with Composer   You can prevent most coding errors by using Composer to create your Web page. When you highlight text and then choose a formatting option, Composer automatically inserts both the on and off code for the selected format. Enter HTML codes manually only when you need to (such as to create frames or insert an image map).

Creating Readable Source Code

Making sure your source file is readable is second in importance to avoiding errors. Not only is this polite to the people who might want to look at your code and figure out how you did your tricks, but it will also help you a lot when you go to change your pages six months later and have to figure just how they work! If you can't figure it out, well, you won't be the first person to look back and think, "This stuff works? I must've either been a genius or a madman when I did this!"

You can do three things to make your HTML source code more readable:

- *Comment everything that is unusual or unclear.* If you're using complex constructions, using strange HTML extensions, or calling a CGI-BIN program, you should definitely add a comment. You type comments in the following format:

```
<!-- your comments here -->
```

- *Insert carriage returns into your file.* As you may remember, those carriage returns will be ignored on the displayed page. But they will sure make the file a lot easier to view. You shouldn't have more than about 80 characters on a line, and you should put a blank space between different sections and elements of your document so it's easy to see where one section ends and another begins.

- *Indent your tables and complex list structures.* Each list item should be on a new line with a tab before it. If you create a list within a list, indent the inner list by another tab.

  How you indent tables depends on their size and content. If you have a small table, where the contents of each row can fit on a single line, you should probably indent the whole table one level and put each row on one line. However, if you have a complex table with extensive information on each row, you should put each row element (designated by the <TR> and </TR> tags) on its own line indented by a tab, and you should put the contents of each of the cells that make up the row on its own line indented one tab further. That way, it's easy to see where each row starts and ends.

These are all just guidelines. The most important thing is that the file be readable to you. You're the best judge of what it will take to do that.

Figures 14.7 and 14.8 show the difference that using carriage returns, comments, and indents can make. These two files will generate the exact same Web page. But which would you rather try to maintain?

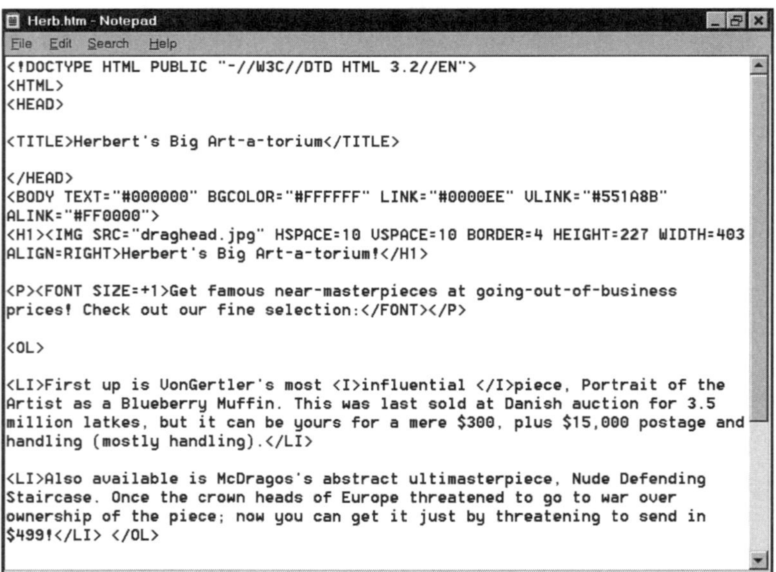

Figure 14.7   An HTML source that uses carriage returns, comments, and indents.

Figure 14.8   Without carriage returns, comments, or indents, the same page runs right off the screen. Yikes!

Test Your Links

You should check all the links on your Web site at regular intervals. If a user clicks your link to a file and that file no longer exists, the user will see an error message like the one shown in Figure 14.9.

Basically, you need to check the internal links only when you make changes to your Web site. That's the only time that any internal link can change. To check links, you simply make sure you have not renamed or eliminated something that one of the links points to.

However, you need to check your external links more frequently. URLs are changed or disconnected more often than phone numbers. People change URLs for all sorts of reasons. For example, sometimes they remove old files that they think are no longer needed. Sometimes they move their site from one server to another looking for either cheaper storage or faster delivery. And sometimes they just get rid of their Web site altogether. Whatever the reason, if you're lucky, the old URL will still have a small file that displays a link to the new site (see Figure 14.10). Test that link. If it works, use the new address in place of the old one.

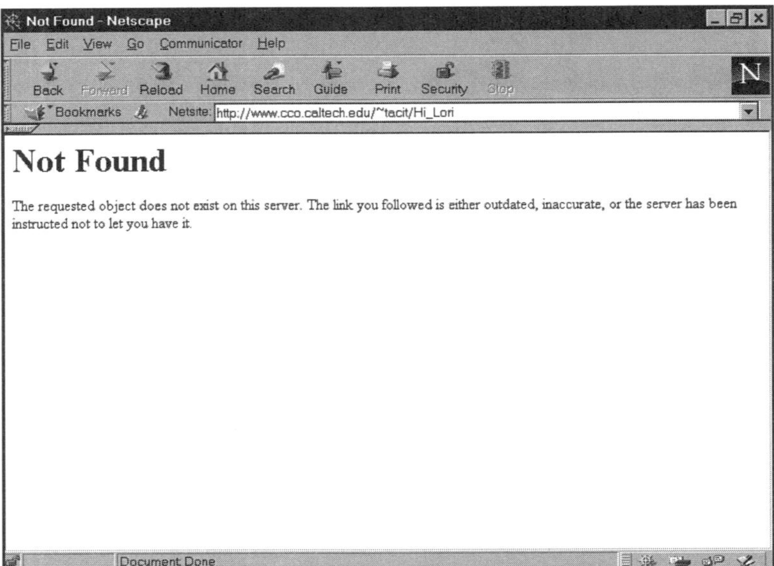

Figure 14.9 When you follow a link to a file that doesn't exist, you usually see this error.

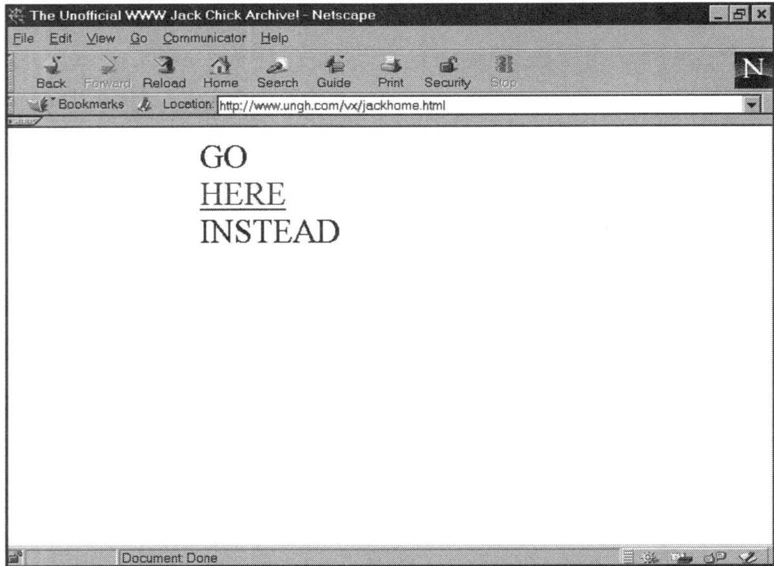

Figure 14.10 A forwarding link.

Even if you don't find a forwarding link, you still have some options. If you were linking to a specific file, try dropping the file name, entering just the directory path as the URL. If you don't see a home page or any files listed, try removing subdirectories from the path until you find something.

If you get all the way back to where you're trying the domain name as the URL and that doesn't bring anything up, or if Navigator tells you that the domain name is not listed, that doesn't mean that the site isn't out there somewhere. Check the search engines or directories to see if it's registered. Even if you can't find it now, try again in a few weeks.

Whatever you do, don't just leave a dead link on your Web site. People will forgive a dead link or two, but the more dead links you have at your site, the more it makes your site seem useless.

Do Unto Others...   The corollary to all this is that if you change URLs, be sure to notify everyone you know who has links to your page so that people can find you. Also, put up a forwarding link at your old site if at all possible.

In this lesson, you learned how to make sure your pages work correctly for everyone who wants to view them. In the next lesson, you'll learn how to make your pages load fast and take up less disk space on the server.

Designing for Speed, Space, and Readability

In this lesson, you learn how to make a smaller, faster Web page that's easy for visitors to read.

The Importance of Speed and Compactness

Your Web site can run into two limitations: speed and space. If your Web site cannot get information out on the screen fast enough, the user will become disinterested and will go someplace else.

On one hand, size and speed complement each other: Smaller HTML and image files travel across the Net more quickly than larger ones. On the other hand, sometimes you have to choose between doing something that will transfer quickly and something that will take up less space. Sometimes you can't have both. In any case, efficiency is not something to be ignored.

Making Your Pages Load Fast

Four primary factors contribute to how quickly your Web page appears on a visitor's screen:

- The speed of the visitor's connection
- The speed of the Internet (For all its bandwidth, the Internet can become overcrowded and slow during periods of heavy use.)

- The speed of your server (where your pages are stored)
- The size of the files that make up your page

The last two are the only factors you can control. If you find that it's taking a long time for your page to come up, while similar pages elsewhere are coming up lickity-split, it's time to put your site on a new server. Cheap Web space is no bargain if it's so slow that no one sticks around to see your site.

However, most of the work that you will do to keep your site swift will be focused on the last category. File size is something that you have to keep in mind from the moment you start putting your pages together.

It's very easy to put together a Web site that looks wonderful on your hard disk, where everything comes up instantly. It's not much more difficult to make a page that looks great when viewed from a corporate T1 communications line (a very fast connection).

T1 A type of communication line used for high-speed data communications, which is like a direct tap into the trunk of the phone system. T1 is too pricey for home use, but it is commonly used by corporations and universities.

Suppose your page has 10 images that are 35,000 bytes each, as well as a 10,000-byte background image and a 40,000-byte main HTML file. That adds up to 400,000 bytes. Under *ideal* conditions, a 14,400 modem downloads fewer than 2,000 bytes per second, which means it would take three and a half minutes for that page to appear fully! The less-than-ideal conditions that frequently afflict the Internet can easily double that time.

A Rough Estimate When the Internet is busy, a 14,400 modem will receive about a thousand bytes (or 1 kilobyte) of data per second. Windows Explorer lists file sizes in kilobytes. If you add up the sizes Windows Explorer lists for the HTML file and all the graphic files on that page, the number you get is approximately the same as the number of seconds it will take to download that page.

When you're designing a Web page, you should be concerned with two speed measurements: how long it will take for the user to see anything, and how long it will take for him to see the complete page. If there is text on the page, the user usually starts seeing that text immediately; the graphics take longer, appearing in stages (see Figure 15.1).

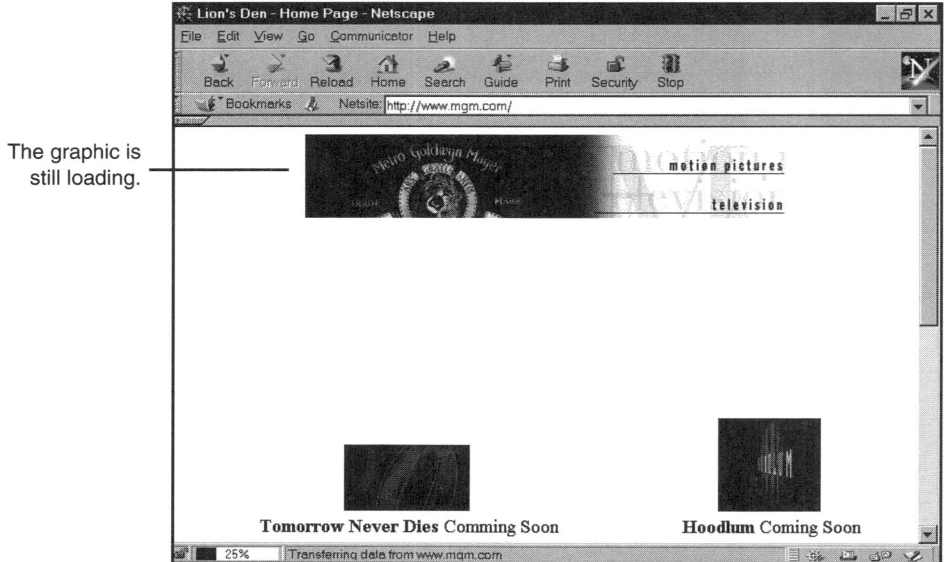

The graphic is still loading.

Figure 15.1 The text appears immediately, but the graphics take more time.

When Text Comes Later The exception is that if you are using a background graphic, some browsers won't display the text until after the background has loaded. This is a good argument for not using background graphics, particularly on pages with a lot of text.

Suppose, for example, that you have a book online. You probably don't want to include the entire book in a single HTML file. A better solution is to put small portions, such as individual chapters, into separate HTML files.

Trying to reduce your file size by removing comments, carriage returns, and tabs that you used to make the source file readable is not worthwhile (unless you have some extremely large comments). Those things generally constitute only a small percentage of your file's size.

Speedy Graphics Tricks

The images on a page will slow down the speed at which the page appears. Not only does it take time for the graphic to download to the machine, but the visitor's computer has to read the HTML file, find all the `<IMG>` tags, and request each image file separately.

A picture may be worth a thousand words, but on the Internet, many picture files are as big as a file with 10,000 words or more. Here are some things to think about that can help you keep a lid on the size of your Web pages.

Reduce the Number of Graphics

Many useful Web pages have no graphics at all. They might not be visually exciting, but they present the information effectively. In place of graphics, you can use different typestyles and sizes to jazz up your page. You can even color the text in Composer. As long as the browser your visitor uses supports colored text, it will be able to display the enhanced text. And if the browser can't display the enhancement, the user will still be able to see the text (and click it if it is a link).

Make Your Images Smaller

Many people design their images to be as large and as impressive as possible. Large does not always equal impressive, though, particularly when the person who wants to look at the image has to wait for it.

Before you settle on your image size, give it some careful thought. A smaller image downloads faster and is usable in a wider range of browser configurations. By reducing the height and width of your picture by just one third, you can cut your download times in half.

If the image is one that came to you at a certain size, there are plenty of graphics tools that you can use to resize it, such as LView Pro, Photoshop, Graphic Workshop, Conversion Artist, or Collage Image Manager.

Think Small   If the image you have is 200 pixels wide by 200 pixels high, and you use the HEIGHT and WIDTH attributes with the <IMG> tag to show it as 100 by 100 pixels, you're wasting a lot of time downloading detail you don't show. Instead, resize the image file, shrinking it down to the largest size at which it will actually be displayed.

You can make a large image available to anyone who wants to see it, without forcing the uninterested visitor to wait while the image downloads. For example, let's say you have a 100-kilobyte picture called **BIGPIC.JPG**:

1. Use your graphic program to create a small version of BIGPIC.JPG, perhaps 50 pixels wide and 100 pixels high.

2. On your page, include the following line:

```
<A HREF="bigpic.jpg"><IMG SRC="SMALLPIC.JPG">Click here to see
BIGPIC.JPG (100K) full size.</A>
```

(Including the size gives the user an idea how long it will take to display the picture.)

3. When you publish your site, be sure to include both BIGPIC.JPG and SMALLPIC.JPG.

If you don't mind having a Netscape-only page, you can forego the process of making a smaller file from the big image. Instead, you can just include the following line in your HTML source:

```
<IMG SRC="bigpic.jpg">Right-click on this image to see BIGPIC.JPG
(100K) full size.
```

Any Navigator user can right-click the file bigpic.jpg and select View Image from the shortcut menu to see the image full-size, in a page all its own.

Choose the Right File Type

An image with only a few colors should always be a GIF file. If you save these sorts of images as JPEG, they are usually larger and don't reproduce well. (You can increase the JPEG compression rate to make the JPEG image smaller, but that distorts it even more.)

The question gets tougher for images with a lot of colors. Generally, a GIF file is smaller than a good JPEG for an image with a lot of sharp, clear angles and curves to it (particularly computer-generated images). JPEG is better for photographs, complex scanned images such as paintings, and ray-traced 3-D graphics.

If you're unsure which to use, try storing the file as both. Then see which is smaller and which looks better on the page. Most good modern art programs (including Photoshop and Graphics Workshop) can read the file as one and save it as the other.

Reduce Your Color Depth

Usually, the fewer colors you use in a GIF, the less space it will take up. This is true even if you store your picture in GIF's 256-color mode.

Color Mode   The GIF file includes a setting for a maximum number of colors that can be used in the image. You have eight modes to choose from: 256 colors (also known as 8 bits), 128 (7 bits), 64 (6 bits), 32 (5 bits), 16 (4 bits), 8 (3 bits), 4 (2 bits), and 2 (1 bit).

However, a big advantage to using fewer colors comes from the fact that you can use one of the lower color modes, sometimes referred to as *bit depths*. Avoid using the 2-color mode, because it doesn't work with some browsers. Ideally, with so many choices, you should use the smallest mode that has at least as many colors as you actually use, because fewer color modes use less space to describe a color.

Reuse Your Images

Graphical browsers don't automatically start a download every time they see the <IMG> tag. First, the browser checks to see if it has downloaded the image for that URL recently. If it has, it knows that the image is already stored on the hard disk, and it loads the image from there, which is much faster than loading from the Net.

You can use this to your advantage. You can put your logo or your menu buttons on every page, and feel comfortable that they will only actually download once. Just make sure that you're always pointing to the same image file; don't make additional copies of that file for use on different pages.

Figure 15.2 shows an example of the kind of image you can use on several of your pages. As you can see on Netscape's home page, buttons give the user instant access to the "foyers," if you will, of Netscape's various services. Even though this graphic appears on all of Netscape's main pages, it is loaded into the browser only once—when the user links to www.netscape.com. Because the graphic for the button bar on every other Netscape page is the same graphic, the browser doesn't have to request it from the server again; it just recalls the graphic from the local cache, which saves several seconds of download time.

This concept applies even if you want to use smaller versions of the logo on later pages, or even on the same page (see Figure 15.3). Instead of making a smaller version of your logo, you can just use the HEIGHT and WIDTH attributes with the <IMG> tag to manipulate the size at which the image appears on the page. This will not look quite as good as having the image reduced by a really good art program, so you should compare the two and see whether it makes enough of a difference to worry about.

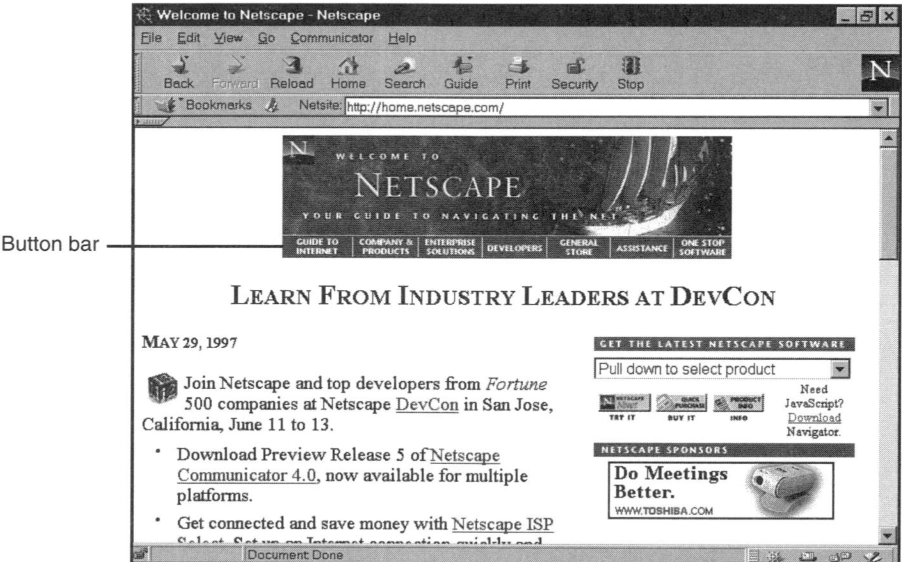

Figure 15.2 Netscape's corporate button bar.

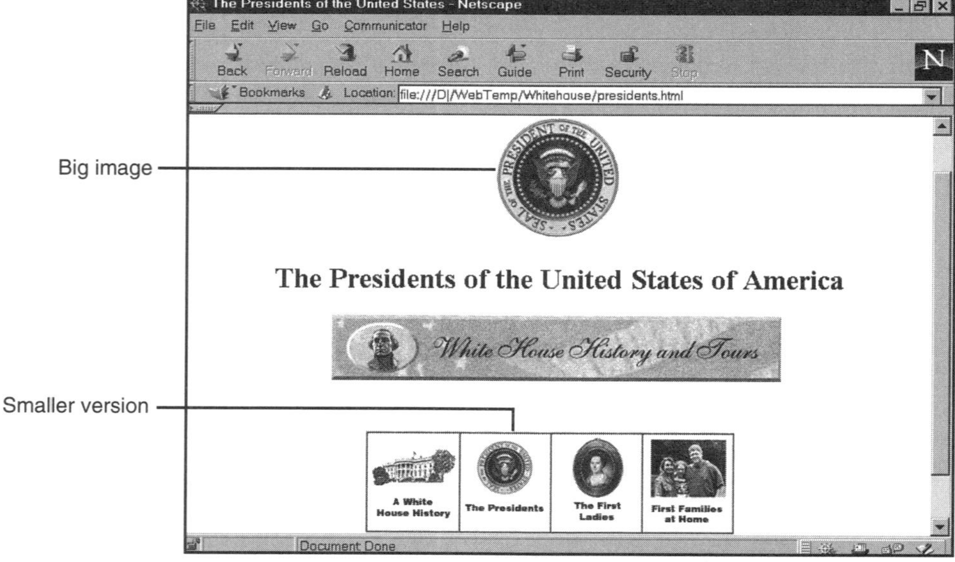

Figure 15.3 You can reuse a big image as a smaller image on the same page.

Combine Images

If you have multiple images with a similar palette that are supposed to appear next to each other, you should try combining them into a single larger image. Not only can this lead to some compression savings, but it also reduces the number of downloading processes the browser has to start.

The collage in Figure 15.4 is stored as a single image instead of as separate images. This way, the images aren't downloading at the same time, with the time being split fairly randomly among the images.

Anticipating Images   If you link from a page that contains a lot of text and no new images to a page that contains an average number of images, you can preload some images for the second page while the reader is reading the first page—but you display the images so small that no one can see them!

At the very bottom of your first page, add the `<IMG SRC="image.gif" HEIGHT=1 WIDTH=1>` tag. This will load the image.gif file (or whatever name you use) and display it as a single pixel. That way, when you go to the next page, this image is already in your buffer! (Avoid the temptation to set `HEIGHT` and `WIDTH` to 0; this may cause some browsers to display the image in an unpredictable format.)

Figure 15.4   You can combine multiple images into a single tiled image.

Working with Limited Disk Space

Most of the techniques you can use to speed up your images will serve you well when you're trying to work with limited disk space. Keeping your images at a minimum, keeping them small, and reusing them will keep you from eating up disk space unnecessarily. You can also try the tricks covered in the next two sections.

Display Images Stored on Other Servers

If there's an image on someone else's page that you'd like to have on yours, it doesn't have to take up any of your limited site space. You can direct your visitor's browser to get the image off of the other site's server and display it in your page. You can even use an image stored at a remote location as a background for a page or table.

To do this, follow these steps:

1. Get the permission of the site owner to point to his file. Not only is this polite, but there are legal concerns about using someone's image without his permission.

2. Get the URL of the image you want to use. To do this, right-click the image and select **Copy Image Location**.

3. Paste that URL into the SRC attribute of your <IMG> tag.

That's all there is to it. And there's another bonus: If you're providing a link to the site you're borrowing the image from, it will speed things up for the visitor when he follows that link, because that image will already be in his buffer. (The reverse is also true: If the visitor gets to your site by following a link from this other site, your page will appear faster.)

To use an image stored on a remote server as your page background, open Composer's **Format** menu, select **Page Colors and Properties**, and click the **Colors and Background** tab. Click **Use Image**, and type the URL that points to the image in the **Use Image** text box. Make sure the **Leave Image at the Original Location** check box is selected, and then click **OK**.

The Image's Owner Still Has Control   You don't have any control over an image located on another server. The person who runs the other site can remove it at any time without warning, and you'll be left with a symbol for an unloadable image on your page. (This can, however, serve as your own visual warning that the site has closed down.) You might want to keep a spare copy of that file somewhere (not taking up server space obviously) just in case you need it.

Take Advantage of Other Server Space

Your entire site does not have to be on one server. If you're running out of space on one server or another account, there's no reason that you can't put some of your pages or some of your image files on any other server or account space that you can lay your hands on. With many online services and Internet access providers giving out free Web space to all of their customers, you may have several sites available. Unless the visitor looks at the URLs, he will have no way of knowing that he's switching servers as he moves among pages. (And even if he found out, why would he care?)

Designing Your Page for Readability

You have no doubt encountered Web pages that have made you question the author's ability to distinguish colors. You have probably wondered if some authors have even looked at the monstrosities they have created: black text on a dark purple, marbled background, white text against a light gray brick texture, patterns that make you see double.

Whatever the case, you don't want to repeat these errors in your own page design. The following sections provide style guidelines to help you design pages that people will be able to read and use.

Text Colors

The ability to set the colors of the text in your Web pages can be used or abused. If you choose the right colors, your pages look great and can even evoke a certain mood. If you make poor color choices, however, your pages will be indecipherable.

If your sole objective is readability, your best bet is not to set the text or background colors at all. By letting the visitor's browser configuration control the font and background colors, you can be sure that your page will appear in colors the visitor is comfortable with.

If you do choose to set the text color, you should also set the background color. Otherwise, you might choose a text color that exactly matches the visitor's default background color, and your text will be invisible. Don't assume that everyone uses gray as the background color. The key to ensuring that your colors are visible is *contrast*. Be sure that there is a big difference between your text colors and the background color.

Here's a quick rule of thumb for checking contrast:

1. Take the text color code you're using (for example, "#A310F2") and jot down the first, third, and fifth characters after the number sign (in this example, A, 1, and F).
2. If you have a letter A, change it to 10. Then change B to 11, C to 12, D to 13, E to 14, and F to 15. Then, in the example, you have 10, 1, and 15.
3. Add these numbers (10 plus 1 plus 15), and it equals 26. That is a brightness value for this color.
4. Repeat steps 1–3 with your background color (for example, the brightness for the dark gray color #777777 would be 7 plus 7 plus 7, or 21).
5. Subtract the smaller of the two brightness numbers from the larger of the two: 26 minus 21 equals 5. This result is your contrast value.

For readable text, you really want a contrast of at least 15 (although a higher contrast would be better). Knowing that, you can see the colors we considered in the previous example aren't going to look good together.

Note that it doesn't make a difference which color is brighter and which is darker. Even though we're used to reading black text on a white background, having bright text on a dark background can be quite effective (see Figure 15.5). In fact, bright text seems to pop out from a black background and can really grab the reader. You wouldn't want to create huge documents like this, though, because after a while it can tire the eyes. But for something that's going to take only a few minutes to read, it's fine.

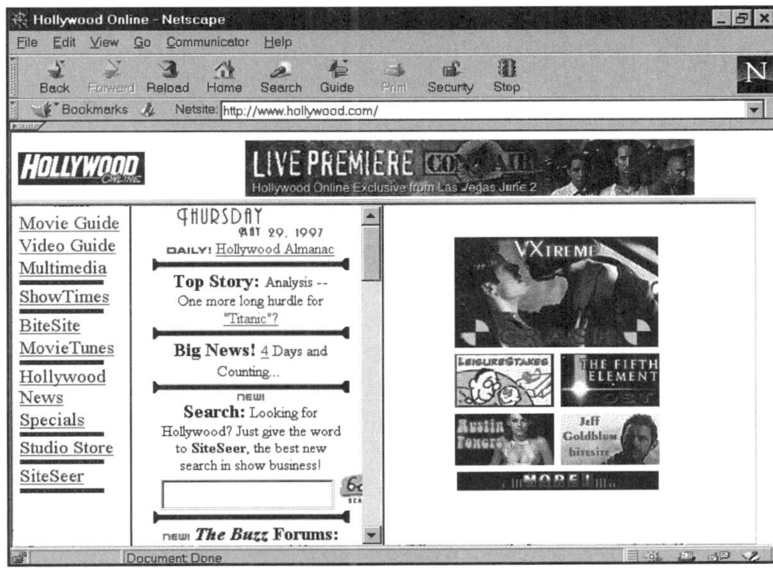

Figure 15.5   White text stands out on a black background.

Backgrounds

If you're setting a background *color*, the only real concern for readability is its contrast with the text. Yet you should choose your background color for its emotional effect. Blue tends to be calming, red is exciting, and white looks businesslike. Other colors have other subtle effects.

However, if you want to use an *image* as a background, a lot of other concerns surface. Remember that your text has to contrast with all of the background; you wouldn't want to put black text on a mostly-white-but-some-black background because the background parts that are black will make the black text unreadable.

You should make sure that you don't have much contrast within the background image. Otherwise, it will be too busy and distract from the text.

When you use a small image as a background, it is repeated vertically and horizontally. You might want to add some border space around the image so the images don't run together at the edges.

Subtle Beauty Subtle backgrounds that contain one or two colors with minor variations in darkness can look very nice. However, when displayed by a browser on a system configured for few colors (16 or even 256), two colors with minor variations can be interpreted as the same color.

When used properly, the repetition of images enables you to create some interesting designs. If you create an image whose left edge is designed to connect to its right, and its top to its bottom, you can create what looks like a single endless image. You have to be careful that the images line up cleanly, however. Otherwise, the visitor will be able to detect where the images don't line up, and will see clearly where one copy of the image ends and the next begins. Some people don't mind this, but for others, it's very distracting. Figure 15.6 shows a repeating pattern that works. This pattern is so smooth that you can't tell where the squares line up.

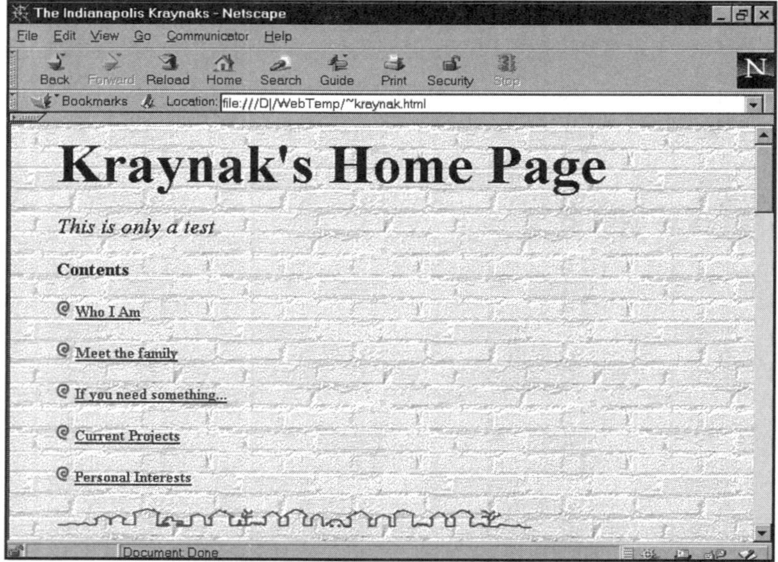

Figure 15.6 Some patterns (such as this brick wall pattern) look seamless when repeated in the background of your Web page.

Create Your Own Design You can find several predrawn background images on the Web, but if none of these appeals to you, create your own design. You'll need a graphics program, such as LView Pro, which can save the graphic as a GIF or JPEG file. You can then add the background image to your page in Composer, as explained in Part 6 Lesson 5, "Adding Graphics and Changing Backgrounds."

Vertical Bars

If you create a very wide image for a tiled background, you can be sure that it won't repeat horizontally. Using that image as the background, you can create vertical lines and patterns that don't repeat across the page.

You can achieve one professional-looking effect by building a table element for the entire page and placing a single background image behind the table to add visual effects to the borders. Figure 15.7 shows a GIF version of a light gray background. This image appears to have a vertical border about one-quarter of the way over from the left of the image (which is actually the left border of the text area of your Web page). The separate column in the left margin of the table creates a clearly separate border for comments or headers.

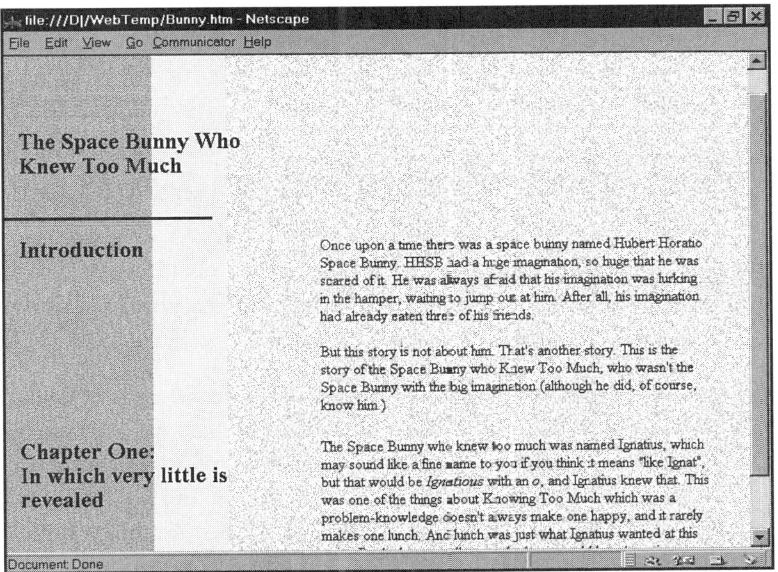

Figure 15.7   The background image is a thin horizontal line, colored at the left end and white across the rest.

Although you could use the <IMG> tag to place an image inside a single table cell, you couldn't display text on top of it. The only way to put text on top of an image is to make the image the background for the page. So when drawing your background image, you have to picture in your mind where your table cell boundaries will appear, or use the rule guides in your drawing program to keep track of the width of columns whose border effects you're currently drawing.

Plan Ahead   Make sure that your image (it should be a GIF) is very wide, so that people with large display areas won't see the image start to repeat. An image 1,000 pixels wide should work for most users. Of course, if you think it's possible that someone with one of those huge UNIX workstations might open his browser window to full size, you should make it 1,800 pixels wide.

Although you see two sections in Figure 15.7, this is actually a three-column table: The second column serves as a margin between the first and third. You can easily create this effect on your Web page by inserting an extra, narrow column in your table. The first column should be at least 30 pixels narrower than the colored area in the middle of your GIF background, but just wide enough for any comments you want to include in it. Create a second column with a width of 30 pixels to leave some space between the text in the margin area and the text in the third column (the text for the main body of the document).

Keeping Text Within Two Margins

The next obvious step is to figure out how to do a right margin. Unfortunately, the answer is that you really can't. You always know that the left margin starts at the first pixel. Because you don't know how wide the browser window is, you don't know where the right margin is.

The most common example of what happens when you make assumptions about the width of the browser screen concerns the variability of the user's browser size. Suppose a page designer is working under the assumption that his page will be viewed on a 640×480 screen, and he creates a page with a background GIF that's 640 pixels wide. If the user has a higher resolution screen, 640 pixels does not fill the width of the browser window. As a result, the GIF starts repeating horizontally and to the right.

If you really want to keep text between two designed margins, you need to use tables. To do that, follow these steps:

1. Figure out what you consider the narrowest possible browser width anyone will be using. (The minimum resolution for Windows users is 640 pixels wide; for users of old black-and-white Macintoshes, the resolution is 512 pixels wide.)

2. Create a table with three columns, each a fixed pixel width, where the three columns combined are no wider than the narrowest browser.

3. Create a background GIF that puts one color or pattern behind the first column, another color behind the second, and another (or a repeat of the first) behind the third. Then fill out the right and lower portions of it (in whatever manner you want) to at least the thousandth pixel across, so that people with wider browsers won't see the GIF repeat horizontally.

Using Proper, Readable Text

Proofread your text. Bad spelling, incorrect punctuation, and unfinished sentences make your work hard to read—and make you look unintelligent or uncaring. Spell check your page using Composer's built-in spelling checker, as explained in Part 6 Lesson 8. You might also consider taking a break and rereading the page later. A spelling checker is great for catching typos, but if the typo does not result in a spelling error (you type "to" instead of "too"), the spelling checker won't catch it.

Do not use text highlights (such as bold and italic) for large amounts of text. Highlights are like spices. Trying to read ten straight paragraphs in bold italic type with the font size cranked up to 5 is like sitting down to a dinner of nothing but spices. Also, don't type in all uppercase. On the Net, that's the equivalent of SHOUTING!!!!

Preformatted text is a good way to quickly put non-HTML formatted text into an HTML document. There are times when you have a good layout reason to use it. However, if you're using it just so you don't have to convert it to HTML, you should reconsider. Preformatted text doesn't take full advantage of the page width in the way that standard HTML text does. In addition, its monospace format makes it harder to read.

In this lesson, you learned to make economical, efficient Web pages designed for readability. In the next lesson, you will find out where to go to learn about Web programming.

Learning About Web Programming

In this lesson, you get a basic understanding of CGI, Java, and Shockwave, tools that are widely used to make Web pages "interact" with users.

When you decided to tackle HTML in order to create your own Web pages, you probably didn't count on having to become a programmer to do it. Well, good news; you don't. However, for all its complexities, HTML simply cannot do some things, such as search through a database of documents for the one that contains specified information, or display a scrolling stock ticker. In order to include such items in your Web pages, you're going to need to use some kind of programming tool. This lesson highlights a few of the more popular programming languages and tools.

CGI Programming

The *Common Gateway Interface* (CGI) enables you to use a Web page as an interface that lets the user control a program running on a Web server. CGI controls how the information gets from the user to the program; the actual program can be written in any language that will run on the server.

The most common examples of CGI programs on the Web are on-screen forms. If you fill out a form and click the button that indicates you're done, you might see the information being sent to the server in a very complex URL. When the Web server processes that URL, it takes the form information out and runs it through the program named in the URL (the name probably appears just after /CGI-BIN/, the traditional directory used for storing these programs). Figure 16.1 shows a page that was created from a form sent to the Web server. Notice that the URL at the top contains the information from the form.

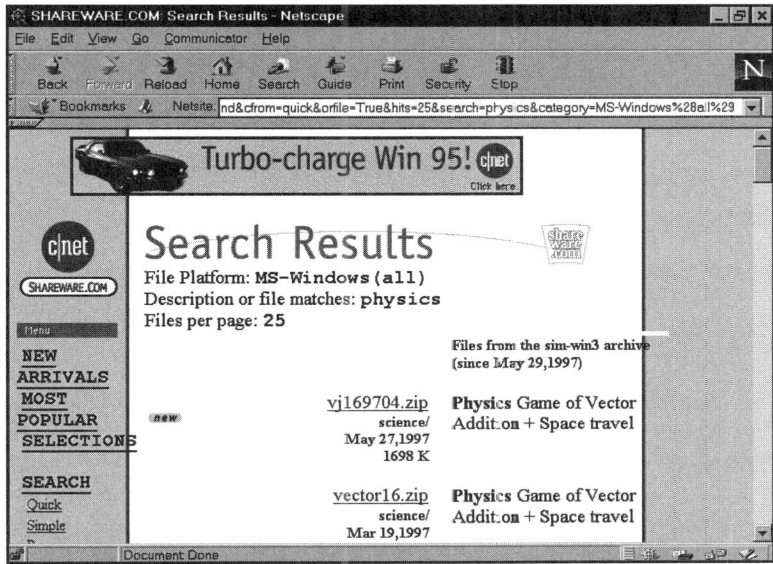

Figure 16.1 A Web page created from the information entered in a form.

For example, if you go to the Web search site Yahoo!, you'll find a very simple form: one field into which you type the text you want to search for, and a button you push to start the search. If you type **kittens** into the field and click the button, your browser sends to the server a request for an URL that ends with /search?p=kittens. When the server gets that URL, its CGI program sees it. The CGI program knows that it has to start the program search, and tell the program that **kittens** is the value for the field the program calls P. The Search program searches its database of Web sites for the word **kittens** and creates an HTML page listing all of the sites it finds. The server then sends this page out to you.

Not all Web providers allow you to run CGI programs on their systems. There are two main reasons for this:

- CGI programs use up processor time, which may slow down other activities carried out on the server.
- The provider runs the risk of a breach in security. If you can run programs on the provider's server, you might be able to gain access to and damage other people's files.

You should check with your Web provider before you start working on any vast CGI projects.

If you want to learn more about CGI programming, check out the book *Teach Yourself CGI Programming with Perl in a Week*, published by sams.net. It covers not only CGI, but also Perl, a popular programming language for Web applications.

Java

As you learned in Part 1 Lesson 14, Java is the most popular programming language for the Web. While CGI programs are run on the Web server, Java programs are interpreted by the browser and then run on the Web user's machine. The first Java-compatible browser was HotJava (created by Sun Microsystems, who also created the Java language). Since its creation, a number of major Web browser manufacturers (including Netscape and Microsoft) have elected to support Java.

With Java, you can add all sorts of nifty animations, games, and programs to your pages, making your pages more active. You have probably unknowingly experienced Java applets in your Web wanderings. Web page authors commonly use Java applets to create scrolling ads, windows that display changing images, and even tiny animations that welcome you to the page.

Using Java or JavaScript on your own computer gives you numerous advantages:

- You don't have to worry about whether your Web server will let you run the program.
- You don't have to worry about security concerns. (Java has built-in security features.)
- You can use real-time programs with animations and interaction; you're no longer limited to things that can be presented to the user via an HTML page.

People are using Java applets to create a lot of fun additions to their pages. Some of them are animations. Others have little games built into their pages. Figure 16.2 shows Karl Jeacle's Java Mortgage calculator.

A Java program is called an *applet* because it's a small application. Web page authors insert the applets into their Web pages using either the <APP> or <APPLET> tag.

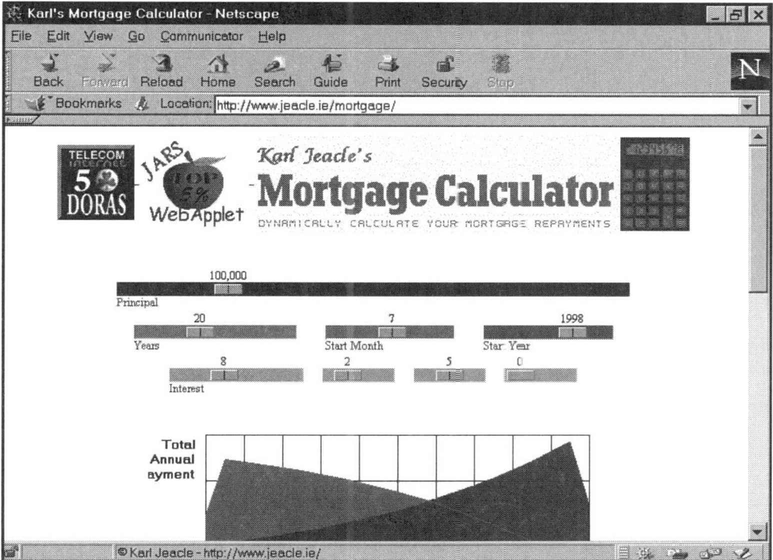

Figure 16.2   You can use this Java applet to figure out how much you should be saving for retirement.

How Java Works

Most computer languages are *compiled*, which means that a compiler program translates the file that the programmer created into a file of *machine language* commands that the processor chip can understand. That machine language file is all that you need to run the program. Other computer languages are *interpreted*, which means that each needed command in the programmer's file is translated into machine language commands as part of running the program.

Java is an interesting combination of the two. The programmer's file, written in the Java language, gets compiled not into machine language, but into an intermediate language. This file with the intermediate language is stored on the Web server and downloaded to your computer when you load a page with a Java applet on it. Then the Java interpreter (which is built into Netscape Navigator) very efficiently turns these commands into machine language.

The reason for this two-step process is simple: Java programs have to be able to run on many different types of computers, which use very different machine languages and have different ways for programs to interact with the screen and the mouse. The compiler takes care of most of the translation work, making the program compact and efficient, but it does not resolve the machine differences. That leaves only one—very important—last step for the user's computer (and browser) to take care of.

The Java-related language called JavaScript is an interpreted language that can be included on Web pages through use of the <SCRIPT> tag. A program written in JavaScript would look a lot like a Java program that does the same thing. The advantages to using JavaScript include the following:

- You don't need a compiler to write programs; you only need a JavaScript-compatible browser, because the browser acts as the interpreter.
- With Java, the browser has to download the HTML file for the Web page, see the tag with the program name in it, and then download the Java program. With JavaScript, only the HTML file has to be downloaded because the program script is in that file.

Of course, there are also disadvantages to using JavaScript.

- JavaScript programs run slower than Java programs, because with JavaScript, the browser is controlling both the Web page and the Java interpreter.
- You can't hide all of your programming tricks from the user. If he wants to see how your program works, all he has to do is use his browser's View Document Source command!
- JavaScript programs work only with Web browsers that are JavaScript-compatible.

Writing Your Own JavaScript

The best way to start learning about Java is to try your hand at writing some JavaScript. Plenty of resources on the Web provide instructions and sample JavaScript scripts. Many of these sites even encourage you to copy the scripts to modify and then insert into your own Web pages.

After you paste the script into your Web page, you can adapt it. Sample scripts commonly include a list of *parameters*, codes you can change to modify the script (see Figure 16.3). For example, if an applet shows a spinning top, you can replace the graphic of the top with a different graphic (such as a globe or your head). Or, you can use the script as is (if you get permission) and add a credit to the creator. Changing these parameters is much easier than writing JavaScript from scratch.

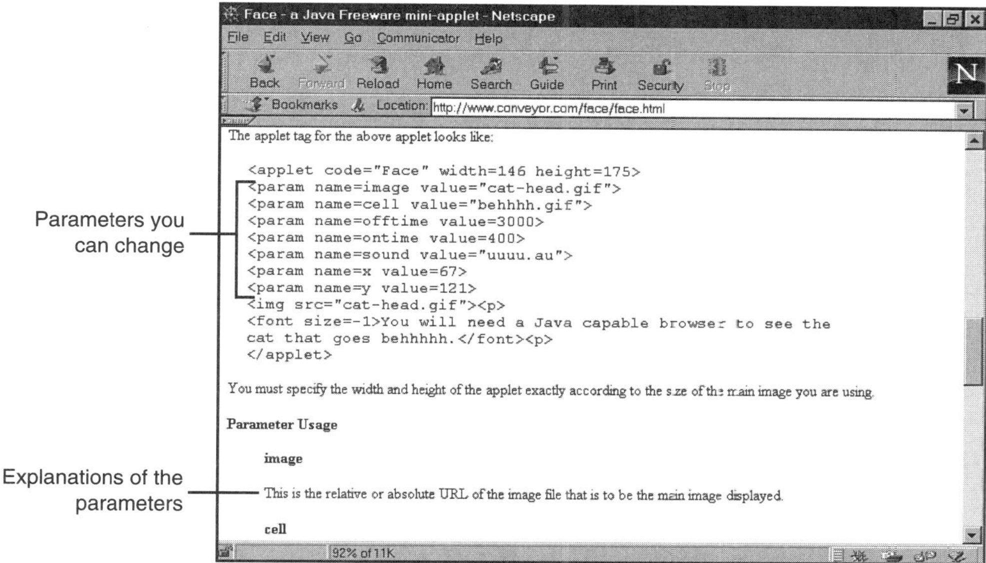


```
<applet code="Face" width=146 height=175>
<param name=image value="cat-head.gif">
<param name=cell value="behhhh.gif">
<param name=offtime value=3000>
<param name=ontime value=400>
<param name=sound value="uuuu.au">
<param name=x value=67>
<param name=y value=121>
<img src="cat-head.gif"><p>
<font size=-1>You will need a Java capable browser to see the
cat that goes behhhh.</font><p>
</applet>
```


Parameters you can change

Explanations of the parameters

Figure 16.3 You can adapt the JavaScript script for your own use.

Learning More About Java

Java was created by Sun Microsystems in an attempt to create a C-like language that would suit the needs of online programs. To learn more about creating your own Java programs and to download the Java Development Kit (which includes all the things you need to do so), check out Sun's Web site at http://java.sun.com.

If you really want to learn more about Java and JavaScript, look for one of these other available books.

- *The Complete Idiot's Guide to JavaScript, Second Edition* by Aaron Weiss (Que, ISBN 0-7897-1136-2)

- *Java by Example* by Clayton Walnum (Que, ISBN 0-7897-0814-0)

- *Java!* by Tim Ritchey (New Riders Publishing, ISBN 1-56205-533-X)

- *Teach Yourself Java in 21 Days* by Laura Lemay and Charles Perkins (sams.net, ISBN 1-57521-030-4)

There are also plenty of resources on the Web for learning about Java and JavaScript. Check out the following sites for more information:

Brewing Java: A Tutorial
http://sunsite.unc.edu/javafaq/javatutorial.html

Gamelan
http://www.gamelan.com

Candle Web's Live Java
http://www.vaxxine.com/candleweb/java/java.html

Applet Library
http://www.applets.com/cgi-bin-applets/

JavaSoft
http://www.javasoft.com

Java World
http://www.javaworld.com/

The Web Development Cyberbase
http://www.hamline.edu/personal/matjohns/webdev/java/

JARS
http://www.jars.com

Creating Interactive Programs with Shockwave

In Part 1 Lesson 19, you probably downloaded the Shockwave plug-in and visited a few interactive Shockwave sites. These sites are pretty impressive, making Web pages perform like interactive CDs.

If you want to make your own site interactive with Shockwave, it's going to cost you. The company that makes the Shockwave plug-in also makes the software that developers use to create these interactive presentations and make them suitable for the Web. And this software, Authorware, isn't cheap—$1,999 the last time I checked. The entire package, Authorware Interactive Studio, includes Authorware® 3.5, Director® 5.0, Backstage™, Designer Plus (Windows), SoundEdit™ 16, Deck II™ (for Macintosh), Sound Forge XP (for Windows), and Macromedia xRes™ SE.

To learn more about Macromedia's products, visit their Web site, located at http://www.macromedia.com.

Making Your Own VRML Worlds

The Web is evolving into a virtual world, complete with online shopping malls, schools, and museums. And VRML is making this virtual world more three-dimensional and interactive. In Part 1 Lesson 15, you had a firsthand look at some virtual worlds, using Navigator's Live3D plug-in.

If you want to transform your own Web site into a three-dimensional interactive world, you are going to need a specialized authoring program. The following list includes some VRML authoring tools, along with page addresses where you can learn more about each tool:

Pioneer
http://www.caligari.com:80/

Liquid Reality
http://www.dimensionx.com/products/lr/index.html

WebSpace Author
http://webspace.sgi.com/WebSpaceAuthor/index.html

Virtual Home Space Builder
http://www1.paragraph.com/products/i3dfamily/vhsb/

Open Inventor
http://www.sgi.com/Technology/Inventor.html

Portal
http://www.well.com/user/jack/portal.html

Huge Files If you visited some VRML worlds in Part 1 Lesson 15, you know that these VRML files are huge and can take a long time to download over a modem connection. Before you invest all your time and money into making a cool virtual site, consider that the world won't be easily accessible to half the Web surfers out there.

Working with ActiveX and VBScript

ActiveX and VBScript (Visual Basic Script) are Microsoft's answers to Java. They are programming tools used to create and place active content in Web pages that can play on any platform. Microsoft's Internet Explorer 3.0 was the first Web browser to support ActiveX controls and VBScript, but Navigator 4.0 now offers that support.

As with Java applets, creating ActiveX controls requires a good bit of programming knowledge and a copy of Microsoft Visual Basic. However, you can start out by tinkering with sample scripts. One excellent repository for sample scripts is VBScript Central at http://www.inquiry.com/vbscentral/. For additional samples, use a Web search tool to search for **vb script example** or **vb script sample**.

In this lesson, you learned about various tools you can use to make your page more animated and interactive. Appendix B contains additional resource material that you may find helpful when creating your own Web pages.

Appendixes

Obtaining and Installing Netscape Communicator

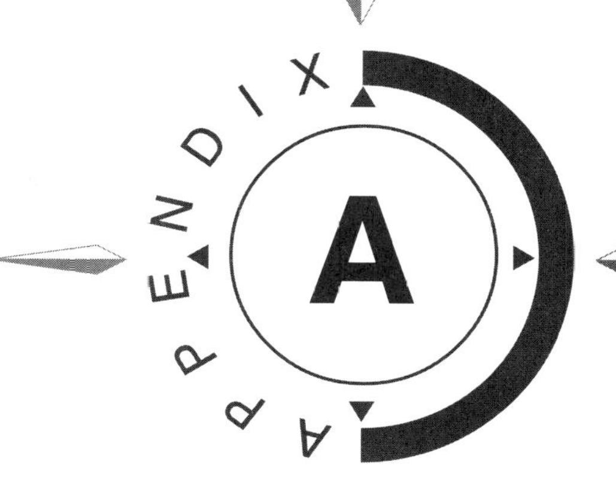

Before you can use any of the components that make up Netscape Communicator, you must obtain a copy of the software and install it on your computer. The following sections tell you where to get a copy of the program, how to install it, and how to use it to connect to the Internet.

Obtaining a Copy of Netscape Communicator

You can obtain a copy of Netscape Communicator from three different sources. The easiest way is to walk into your local computer software store and purchase a copy. You get a disk or CD and a manual that tells you how to install Communicator and start using it.

The second way to get a copy is to buy one from Netscape. You can do this by calling a Netscape sales representative at (415) 937-3777, or if you have a Web browser (Internet Explorer, Mosaic, or an old version of Navigator), you can order the software at Netscape's Web site by filling out the appropriate form and giving them your credit card number (it's pretty safe and secure to do this). If you order from the Web site, either you can have Netscape mail you a copy of Navigator, or you can copy (download) the Communicator installation file directly from Netscape. See "Downloading Netscape Communicator with Your Web Browser," later in this appendix for details.

Another way to get a copy of Communicator is to download it from Navigator's FTP site. *FTP* (short for File Transfer Protocol) is a set of rules that govern the way files are transferred across the Internet. You will need an FTP program to do this, which your Internet service provider should have provided. If you use this method to obtain a copy of Communicator, you are legally obligated to register the program and pay for continued use of it. See "Using FTP to Download Communicator," later in this appendix, for details.

Nothing's Free   Even if your Internet service provider included a copy of Communicator with its startup files (which you may have downloaded after logging in the first time), you still must pay to register Communicator and any other *shareware* programs you decide to keep. See "Registering Communicator," near the end of this appendix, for details.

Which Version of Netscape Communicator Should You Get?

Netscape Communicator comes in several flavors. The standard edition includes Netscape Netcaster (for transforming your desktop into a Webtop), Netscape Navigator (Netscape's Web browser), Messenger (the e-mail program), Collabra (for reading and posting messages in newsgroups), Conference (for carrying on real-time phone calls and having virtual meetings), and Composer (for publishing your own Web pages). The Professional edition includes all those components plus Calendar (an electronic day planner), AutoAdmin (for controlling Communicator centrally on a network), and IBM Host-On-Demand (for intranets). Unless you are a network administrator yourself, or you really need an electronic day planner, stick with the standard (non-professional) edition, which this book covers.

Communicator is designed to run on several different platforms, including Windows 95, Windows 3.1, OS/2, Mac OS, and UNIX (for network users). Make sure you get the appropriate version for your operating system.

Windows 95 and NT   Because more and more users are moving from Windows 3.1 to Windows 95 or NT, developers typically offer the Windows 3.1 version of their software long after the Windows 95 and NT versions are shipped. Don't be surprised if the Windows 3.1 or Macintosh versions of Communicator are not available.

In addition, Communicator is offered in a full version that comes complete with plug-ins for playing media files (see Part 2) or a trimmed-down version, which includes all the Communicator components without the extra plug-ins. The added plug-ins include the following valuable tools:

- Cosmo Player, which allows you to play in 3-D, interactive, virtual worlds with Navigator.
- QuickTime (for playing QuickTime video clips) and NPAVI32.DLL (for playing AVI video clips).
- LiveAudio and Netscape Media Player, which can play most of the audio clips you will encounter on the Internet.

Get the full version; it's worth the added time it takes to download the additional plug-ins.

Downloading Netscape Communicator with Your Web Browser

If you have a Web browser—any Web browser that can display forms, you can download Netscape Communicator from Netscape's Web site. (Most Web browsers can handle this operation, including Internet Explorer 3.0, Mosaic, a previous version of Netscape Navigator, and the Web browsers used in online services, such as America Online and CompuServe.) After connecting to Netscape with your browser, you specify the product you want (Netscape Communicator) and your operating system. Netscape provides a list of links you can click to download the Communicator installation file.

The following steps show the basic procedure for electronically downloading products from Netscape. The procedure might differ a little when you perform the operation, because Netscape occasionally changes the procedure.

1. Connect to the Internet and run your Web browser. Most Web browsers are set up to load a home page connecting you to the company's Web site.

2. Click in the **Location** or **Address** text box (typically right above the page display area) and type **http://www.netscape.com**. Press **Enter**.

3. Your Web browser loads and displays Netscape's home page. Click the link for downloading Netscape Communicator. (You may have to search for this link; it may appear as a button, as highlighted text, or in a drop-down list.)

4. When you click the right link, your Web browser should load the form shown in Figure A.1 (you might have to scroll down the page to see it). Use the form to specify the product you want (Netscape Communicator - All Components plus Plug-ins), your operating system, the desired language, and your geographical location. Then click the **Click to Display Download Sites** button.

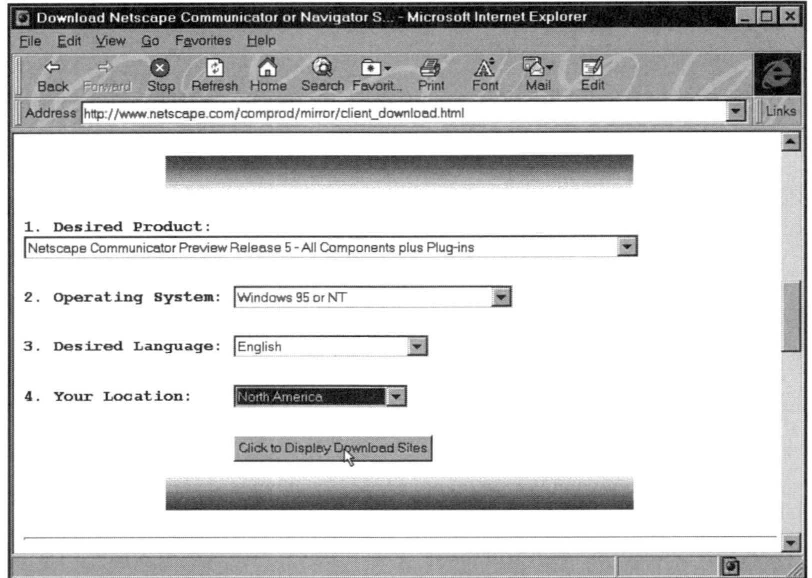

Figure A.1   Enter the requested information, and then click the Download Sites button.

5. Netscape displays links to several sites from which you can download the Communicator installation file. Scroll down the page for a list of download sites.

6. Click the link for the download site nearest you. For example, if you live in the Midwest, you might click the **Download** link for Washington University in St. Louis. What happens next depends on which Web browser you're using.

7. Take the required steps to download the file using your Web browser:

   With an old version of Navigator, you simply click the link, and then follow the dialog boxes to download the file.

   With Mosaic, hold down the Shift key while clicking the link, and then follow the dialog boxes to complete the task.

   With Internet Explorer, right-click the link and select Save Target As. Use the dialog boxes to save the file.

8. Wait until the file transfer is complete (it may take a while over a modem connection), and then close your browser and disconnect from the Internet.

Keep in mind that this copy of Communicator is a trial version. If you decide to continue using Communicator after the trial period, you need to register your copy. Or, you can purchase a software subscription that allows you to use Communicator and download any updates to it for a complete year. See "Registering Communicator" (near the end of this appendix) for details.

Using FTP to Download Communicator

If you don't have a Web browser, you can download Communicator from Netscape's Internet site using a special FTP program. Your Internet service provider probably included such a program in your package. In the following steps, you'll learn how to download Netscape Communicator using the FTP program WS_FTP. If you use a different FTP program, the steps will vary a little. Take the following steps:

1. Connect to your Internet service provider in the usual manner and start WS_FTP.

2. If necessary, click **Connect**, and the Session Properties dialog box shown in Figure A.2 appears.

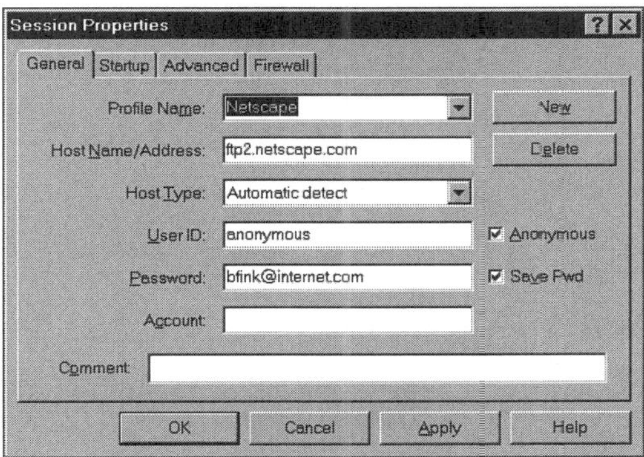

Figure A.2   Set up a connection to Netscape's FTP site.

3. Click **New**.

4. In the **Profile Name** text box, type **Netscape FTP**.

5. In the **Host Name** text box, type **ftp5.netscape.com**.

I Can't Connect! If you have trouble connecting to Netscape's FTP site, try a different address, such as ftp2.netscape.com, ftp3.netscape.com, or ftp4.netscape.com.

CAUTION

6. Select the **Anonymous Login** check box, and type your e-mail address in the **Password** box.

7. Click **Save** and click **OK**.

8. After you connect to the Netscape FTP site, change to the **pub/communicator/4.0/4.0b5/windows** directory. (Just double-click a directory name to change to it; the directories on the Netscape site should be shown on the right side of the WS_FTP window.)

The Directory Name Is Different File and directory names commonly change on the Internet. You may have to look for the directory that contains the file you need. In addition, if you're looking for a different version of Communicator (say for the Mac), the file will be in a different directory.

TIP

9. On your Local System (shown on the left side of the WS_FTP window), change to the temporary directory in which you want to store the file, as shown in Figure A.3.

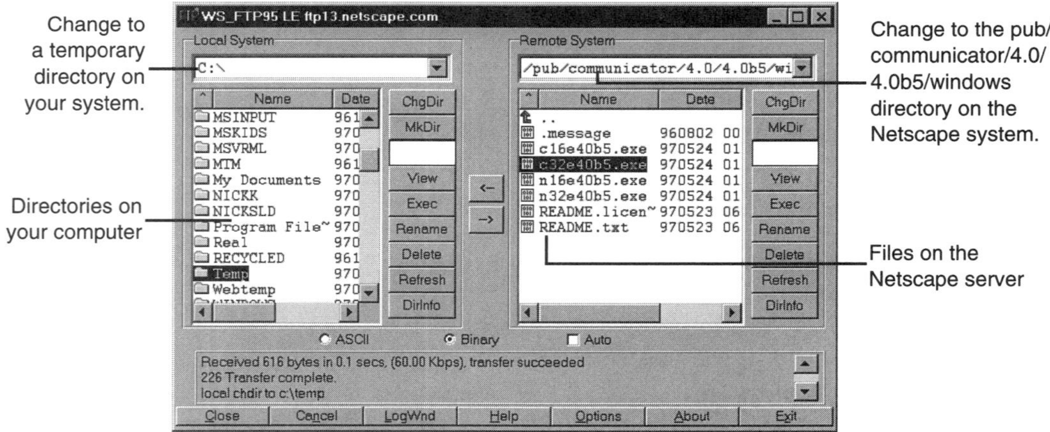

Figure A.3 Set up your directories for the download.

10. Double-click the **c32e40.exe** (for Windows 95) or **c16e40.exe** (for Windows 3.1) file to download it to the temporary directory. (Again, the file name may differ slightly; for example, if Netscape improves Communicator and offers it as version 4.1, the file name may appear as c32e41.exe.)

11. After the file is completely downloaded (it may take a long time depending on the speed of your modem or network connection and the amount of traffic at the FTP site), click **Cancel** to cancel the connection. Then click **Exit** to exit WS_FTP. Finally, disconnect from the Internet.

If you use Windows 95, you're ready to install Communicator now. Jump to the section "Installing Communicator" to proceed. If you use Windows 3.1, follow the steps in the next section before installing Communicator.

FTP with Your Web Browser If you have a Web browser, you can use it to connect to an FTP server and download the files you need. To connect to Netscape's FTP site, type **ftp://ftp.netscape.com** in the **Location** text box and press **Enter**. You can then click links to change from one directory to another, just as if you were using File Manager or Windows Explorer. For details on performing FTP file transfers with Netscape Navigator, see Part 1 Lesson 10, "Downloading Files."

Downloading Win32s

If you use Windows 3.1, you'll need to download the Win32s file in order to get Netscape Navigator to work properly. Follow these steps:

1. Connect to your Internet service provider and start WS_FTP.

2. Click **Connect**, and the Session Profile dialog box appears.

3. Select **Microsoft** from the **Profile Name** drop-down list.

"Microsoft" Is Not an Option If your FTP program doesn't include a setting for Microsoft's FTP site, add one as described in the previous section. Use the address ftp.microsoft.com.

4. After you connect to Microsoft, double-click the **/Softlib /MSLFILES** directory to change to it. You may have to click **ChgDir**, type **/Softlib / MSLFILES**, and click **OK**. (Be sure to type the path exactly as shown here; in FTP land, capitalization matters.)

5. On your Local System, change to the temporary directory in which you want to store the file (see Figure A.4).

6. Double-click the **pw1118.exe** file to copy it to your hard drive.

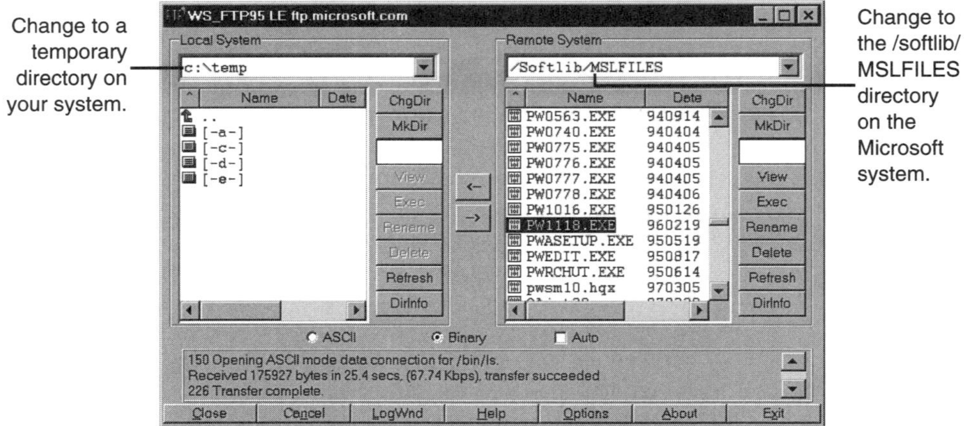

Figure A.4 Choose your directories.

See the section "Installing Win32s" for help installing the win32s.exe program *before* you install Communicator itself.

Getting Netscape Communicator Up and Running

Before you can use Communicator, you must install it on your hard drive. The process is fairly simple. The following sections provide instructions for installing WIN32S (if you're using Windows 3.1) and Netscape Communicator, and for running Netscape Communicator for the first time.

Installing Win32s

If you use Windows 3.1, you should have downloaded the pw1118.exe file, which you need to install before you install Communicator. (If you use Windows 95, skip this section.) The pw1118.exe file is compressed (zipped), which means that the separate files that make up the program have been compressed into one single file that's smaller and easier to download. To install it, you decompress the file and then begin the installation process.

What If I Use Windows 95? If you use Windows 95, you should *not* install Win32s. Install Win32s only if you're installing the 16-bit version of Communicator (for Windows 3.1).

CAUTION

474

Follow these steps to install Win32s:

1. If you haven't already done so, open File Manager and copy the pw1118.exe file to a temporary directory.

2. Double-click the **pw1118.exe** file, and it decompresses its files into the temporary directory.

3. Double-click the **wb2s120.exe** file to decompress its files.

4. Double-click the **setup.exe** file.

5. When you see a message telling you to close your other Windows programs, do so and click **Continue**.

6. The Win32s Setup Target Directory dialog box (shown in Figure A.5) requests confirmation that it has found your Windows directory. Verify the directory name and click **Continue** to proceed with the installation.

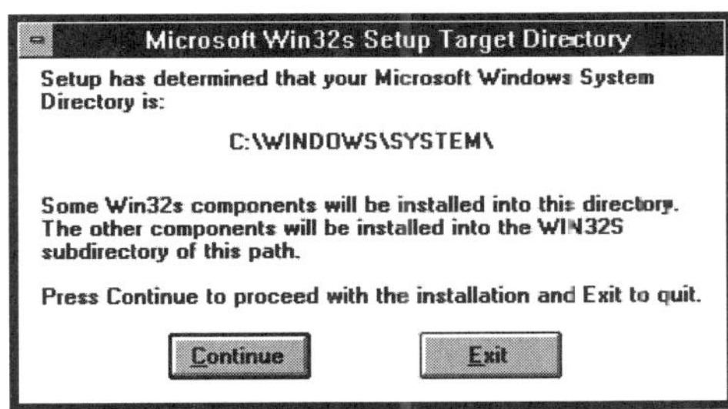

Figure A.5   Make sure that Win32s found your Windows directory.

7. Click **OK**, and Win32s is installed in the SYSTEM subdirectory of Windows 3.1.

8. In the Freecell Setup dialog box (which appears next), click **Continue** to load Freecell, a game you can use to test Win32s.

9. Verify the Freecell path and click **Continue**. Then click **OK**.

10. Click **Continue** to restart Windows.

11. Double-click the **Freecell** icon (located in the WINAPP32 program group) to start the game. If it starts, Win32s is set up correctly. Exit Freecell.

Nothing Happens   If you can't get FreeCell to work, there is a problem with your Win32s setup. Try installing it again, making sure that it correctly identifies your Windows directory.

CAUTION

Installing Communicator

Installing Netscape Communicator is fairly easy. You double-click the file you downloaded from Netscape's FTP site, and then you follow the on-screen instructions to complete the operation. If you have installed programs before, go ahead and install Communicator. If you need help, the following steps lead you through the process.

Follow these steps to install Netscape Communicator:

1. Open **File Manager** or **Windows Explorer** and double-click the Communicator file you downloaded earlier in this introduction (for example, c32e40.exe). This starts the setup program.

Windows 3.1 Setup File   In Windows 3.1, running the Netscape installation file decompresses the file. You will then have a Setup.exe file. Double-click that **Setup.exe** file to run the installation.

CAUTION

2. A dialog box appears, asking if you want to continue with setup. Click **Yes**. The InstallShield Self-extracting Exe dialog box appears, showing the progress.

3. When you see a warning telling you to close your other Windows programs, do so and click **Next**. A Welcome dialog box appears.

4. Read the welcome message, and then click **Next**. A license agreement appears. Read it and click **Yes**. (If you click No, you can't use Communicator.)

5. The Setup Type dialog box (shown in Figure A.6) appears, asking if you want to run the Typical or Custom installation. Click **Typical**. (The Custom installation allows you to install only selected components.)

6. The installation program displays the destination directory. If the destination directory is okay, click **Next**. If you want to change it, click **Browse**, select the desired directory, click **OK**, and then click **Next**.

What If It Doesn't Exist?   If the directory you want to use doesn't exist, you'll see a message asking if you want the setup program to create it. Click **Yes**.

CAUTION

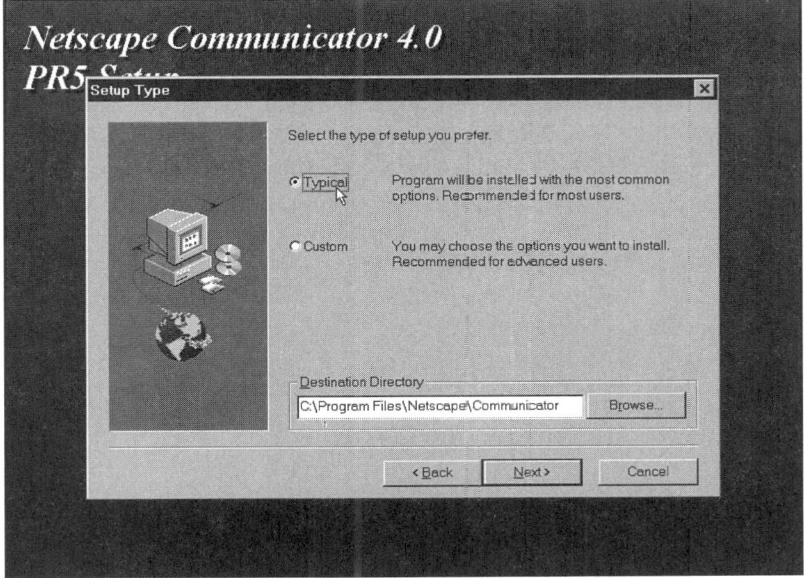

Figure A.6   Follow the Typical installation to install all components and plug-ins.

7. The Select Program Folder dialog box appears, indicating that icons for running Communicator will be placed in the Netscape Communicator folder. Click **Next**.

8. The Start Copying Files dialog box appears, showing you all of the installation preferences you selected. Click **Install**.

9. A series of dialog boxes appears, showing the progress of the installation. Eventually, the Question dialog box appears, asking if you want to view the Readme file, which contains information about this release. (You can click **Yes** to read the file now, or you can click **No** for now but open the file later in a text editor such as WordPad.)

10. When the information dialog box appears telling you how to run Communicator, click **OK**.

11. The Restarting Windows dialog box appears, indicating that you must restart Windows to complete the installation. Exit any programs you have running, and then click **OK**.

When you install Netscape Communicator, the installation program places a Netscape Communicator icon on the Windows desktop, which you can use to run Communicator. It also creates a submenu of Communicator applications on the Programs submenu of the Start menu.

Running Netscape Communicator for the First Time

You might think that you can run Netscape Communicator and start using it immediately. Actually, it's not quite that easy. When you first start Communicator, you'll have to answer a few questions and read the standard license agreement. The following steps show you what to expect.

1. The installation program placed the Netscape Communicator icon in several convenient locations. Look on the Windows desktop or on the Start, Programs, Netscape Communicator menu (in Windows 95), or look in the Netscape Communicator program group in Windows 3.1. Double-click the icon to run Communicator.

2. The first time you run Communicator, the Profile Setup Wizard appears, as shown in Figure A.7. You can use profiles to enter different settings for different users, assuming you share your computer with other people or share Communicator on a network. If the Profile Setup Wizard does not appear, you can run it by selecting **Start**, **Programs**, **Netscape Communicator**, **Utilities**, **User Profile Manager**. Click the **Next** button.

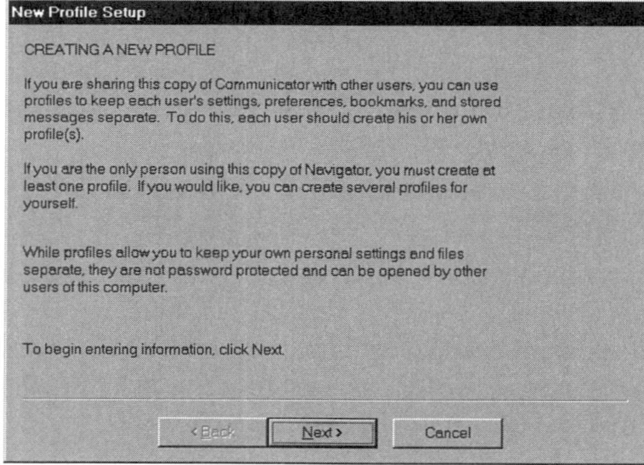

Figure A.7   Profiles are useful if you share your computer with others or work on a network.

3. The next dialog box asks you to enter your name. Type your name.

4. Tab to the **Email Address** text box and type your e-mail address (if you have one). If you are unsure, ask your Internet service provider. Click **Next**.

5. The next dialog box asks you to enter your profile name. Type a name that will uniquely identify your profile (such as your last name). (Optionally, you can specify the folder in which you want to save your profile and preferences.) Click **Next**.

6. The Mail and Discussions Groups Setup dialog box appears, prompting you to type information about how to connect to your service provider's e-mail and news server. Tab to the **Outgoing Mail (SMTP)** Server text box and type the address for the outgoing mail server; for example, you might type **mail.internet.com**. (See Part 3 Lesson 1, "Setting Up Netscape Messenger," for details.) Click **Next**.

7. The next dialog box asks you to specify login information for the mail server. Type your user name, and then enter any additional settings required to check your server for incoming mail. Click **Next**.

8. The next dialog box prompts you to enter your news server's address. Type the address specified by your service provider (such as **news.internet.com**. (See Part 4, "Netscape Collabra," for details on how to select a news server.)

9. Click the **Finish** button. The License Agreement may appear.

10. If the License Agreement appears, read the license agreement and click **Accept**. If you click **Do Not Accept**, Netscape Communicator will not run.

Registering Communicator

If you purchased a copy of Communicator, you don't have to worry about registering it; however, if you do register it, you'll get a couple of perks. For example, Netscape will notify you of upgrades and provide tech support if you get into a jam. If you didn't purchase Communicator, you can make yourself "legal" by registering Communicator at Netscape's Web site. The following steps show you the basics, but keep in mind that the process may differ if Netscape chooses to change it later:

1. Connect to the Internet and run Netscape Communicator. When you run Netscape Communicator, you are actually running the Web browser component, Netscape Navigator.

2. Open Navigator's **Help** menu and select **Register Now**. Navigator opens the Registration Information page, which explains some of the perks you get for registering.

3. Click the **Next** button at the bottom of the page. The next Registration screen prompts you to enter the registration information.

4. Type the requested information into the various text boxes, as shown in Figure A.8 (enter your e-mail address twice). Click **Next**.

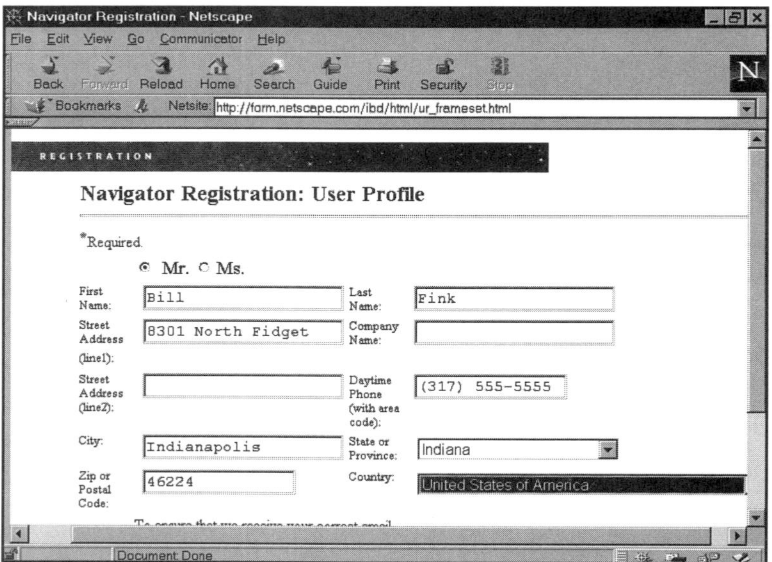

Figure A.8   To register, you must enter the requested information.

5. Another form appears, asking you the standard registration questions, such as what you do for a living and whether or not you have employees working for you. Type the requested information and click **OK**.

6. The last registration screen provides a link for learning more about In-Box Direct, a program that lets you subscribe to publications on the Internet. If you're curious, click the link. If you're not, ignore it, and you're done with the registration.

At the time this book was being written, Communicator was not for sale. Netscape was "giving away" Communicator for a trial period. However, by the time you get around to registering your copy of Communicator, you may have to purchase a license for it or buy a subscription for it.

A Word About Security   Netscape secures most of its forms, preventing unauthorized access to the information you enter. If you attempt to enter information at an insecure site, Communicator displays a warning, asking if you want to continue. To learn more about these security warnings and how to control them, see Part 1 Lesson 13, "Digital Passport, Cookies, and Other Security Topics."

HTML Reference Section

Table B.1 lists all of the HTML tags and attributes supported
by the Netscape Navigator browser. Listed under each tag are
the attributes that can be used within the brackets of the tag. For attributes
that take variables (such as SIZE=3 or HREF="www.me.com"), you'll see the
following standard variables:

- *alignment* is used to relate an image to the surrounding text or to relate
  text to the surrounding area. Possible values are ABSBOTTOM, ABSMIDDLE,
  BASELINE, BOTTOM, LEFT, MIDDLE, RIGHT, TEX⁻TOP, and TOP. (Not all tags or all
  browsers support all settings.)

- *color* represents a number sign followed by a six-digit hexadecimal value,
  where the first two digits indicate the amount of red, the second two the
  amount of green, and the third two the amount of blue (example: #80F700).
  In Netscape, *color* can also be set to one of 140 different color names, but
  that feature is not fully supported by any other browser.

- *framesize* indicates the size of a frame and can stand for any number
  of formats. If it's a number, it represents a pixel measurement. If it's a
  percentage, it represents a percentage of the whole page width. If it ends
  with an asterisk, it represents a share of the space remaining after the pixel-
  and percentage-measured frames have been accounted for. For example, if
  you have one width listed as 2* and one listed as just *, the space left over
  will be divided so that the first column (the one with 2*) gets twice as
  much width as the other column (the one with just *).

- *URL* is a uniform resource locator. This can indicate the location of a directory (http://www.fish.com/recipes/), a file (http://www.fish.com/recipes/sandwich.htm), or a targeted position in the file (http://www.fish.com/recipes/sandwich.htm#ingredients). An URL can also be relative to the current position (recipes/sandwich.htm) instead of being a full path.

- *pixels* is a measurement of screen size in pixels. This is just a standard decimal number (such as 20).

Any other variables are described in their individual entries. A variable followed by *,...* can have more than one of the same variable separated by commas. A tag can generally have any number of attributes as long as they don't conflict with one another. The attributes can be in any order.

The "Other Browsers?" column of this table indicates whether this tag is supported by current revisions of popular non-Netscape graphical browsers. The possible values in this column are **none** (Netscape-only tags), **all** (generally supported tags), and **some** (tags supported in certain non-Netscape browsers, but not all). Take this information into account when considering whether to include these tags in your pages.

Note that, while this list is accurate as of the time of this writing, new revisions are in the works for most of the popular browsers, and some tags that few of them currently support will soon be supported by more. (Of course, nongraphical browsers will be unable to handle any tag requiring a graphic display and will interpret font-altering tags differently.)

Table B.1 Netscape HTML Tags and Attributes

Tag *Attributes*	*Description*	*Other Browsers?*
`<!--text-->`	Comment (text is ignored)	all
`<!DOCTYPE>`	Header information about file format	all
`HTML`	Indicates an HTML file	all
`PUBLIC`	Indicates a readable document	all
`"standard"`	Indicates the HTML standard in use	all
`</tag>`	Ends the effect of the indicated tag	all
`<A HREF="URL">`	Marks the start of a link to a document	all
`METHODS="method,..."`	(Advanced) Lists functions document supports	some

Tag Attributes	Description	Other Browsers?
REL="*value,...*"	(Advanced) Lists relationship of link	some
REV="*value,...*"	(Advanced) Reverses relationship of link	some
TARGET="*frame*"	Puts the document in the listed frame	some
TITLE="*text*"	Gives a name for the page linked to	some
URN="*URN*"	(Advanced) Resource Name of document	some
<A NAME=*name*>	Names a location, for use as a target	all
<ADDRESS>	Text format for mailing addresses	all
<APPLET>	Loads a Java applet	some
ALIGN=*alignment*	Locates applet display within text	some
ALT="*text*"	Text for display by non-Java browsers	some
CODE="*URL*"	(Required) Indicates the program file	some
CODEBASE="*URL*"	Directory the program files are in	some
HEIGHT=*pixels*	(Required) Applet display area	some
HSPACE=*pixels*	Horizontal space from applet to text	some
NAME="*name*"	Names applet for intertask messages	some
VSPACE=*pixels*	Vertical space from applet to text	some
WIDTH=*pixels*	(Required) Applet display area	some
<AREA>	Describes one link on a mapped image	some
COORDS="*pixels,...*"	Left, top, right, bottom of link area	some
HREF="*URL*"	Location to link to	some
NOHREF	This area isn't a link	some
SHAPE="RECT"	Rectangular map area	some
TARGET="*frame*"	Links to indicated frame	some
<B>	Makes text bold	all
<BASE>	Changes defaults for URLs in document	all
HREF="*URL*"	The new base for relative URLs	all
TARGET="*frame*"	Specifies default frame for links	none
<BASEFONT>	Changes default for fonts in document	some
SIZE=*number*	Sets default font size (1–7)	some
<BIG>	Increases text size	some
<BLINK>	Causes text to blink	some
<BODY>	Starts the page content	all
ALINK="*color*"	Sets active link color	all
BACKGROUND="*url*"	Sets an image as page backdrop	all
BGCOLOR="*color*"	Sets background color for page	some
LINK="*color*"	Sets unvisited link color	all
TEXT="*color*"	Sets default text color	all
VLINK="*color*"	Sets visited link color	all

continues

Table B.1 Continued

Tag Attributes	Description	Other Browsers?
 	Starts a new text line	all
CLEAR=ALL	Starts next line below any images	some
CLEAR=LEFT	Starts new line below image on left	some
CLEAR=RIGHT	Starts new line below image on right	some
<CAPTION>	Sets a caption for a table	some
ALIGN=BOTTOM	Puts caption below table	some
ALIGN=TOP	Puts caption above table (default)	some
<CENTER>	Centers text and images across page	all
<CITE>	Text format for citations	all
<CODE>	Text format for program code	all
<DIR>	A directory list	all
<DIV>	Creates a division of text	none
ALIGN=*alignment*	(Required) Positions text across page	none
<DD>	Descriptor in definition list	all
<DL>	A definition list	all
COMPACT	Reduces list size	none
<DT>	Defined term of a definition list	all
<EM>	Emphasizes text (italic)	all
<EMBED>	Puts area for a plug-in onto page	some
ALIGN=*align*	Positions area relative to text	some
BORDER=*pixels*	Sets border color	some
HEIGHT=*pixels*	Area size	some
SRC="*url*"	(Required) Indicated document file	some
WIDTH=*pixels*	Area size	some
<FONT>	Changes font attributes	some
COLOR=*color*	Changes font color	some
SIZE=*number*	Changes font to size *number* (1–7)	some
SIZE=+*number*	Increases font size (up to 6)	some
SIZE=-*number*	Decreases font size (down to –6)	some
<FORM>	Structures a data input form	all
ACTION="*URL*"	Location to send data to	all
METHOD=*protocol*	Selects transfer protocol (GET or PUT)	all
ENCTYPE=*MIMEtype*	Format for data	all

Tag Attributes	Description	Other Browsers?
`<FRAME>`	Sets the attributes for a frame	some
`MARGINHEIGHT=pixels`	Space at top and bottom of frame	some
`MARGINWIDTH=pixels`	Space at side edges of frame	some
`NAME=frame`	Gives the frame a name	some
`NORESIZE`	Prevents frame borders from being moved	some
`SCROLLING=YES`	Frame has scroll bars	some
`SCROLLING=NO`	Frame doesn't have scroll bars	some
`SCROLLING=AUTO`	Frame has scroll bars if needed	some
`SRC="URL"`	Page to put in frame	some
`<FRAMESET>`	Breaks screen into frames	some
`COLS="framesize,..."`	Sets the width of frame columns	some
`ROWS="framesize,..."`	Sets height of frame rows	some
`<Hnumber>`	Headline text format level *number* (1–6)	all
`ALIGN=alignment`	Positions headline across page	some
`<HEAD>`	Introduces text that describes the page	all
`<HR>`	Horizontal rule line	all
`ALIGN=alignment`	Positions line across page	all
`NOSHADE`	Flat line rather than shaded line	all
`SIZE=pixels`	Thickness of line	all
`WIDTH=number%`	Line width, as percentage of space	all
`WIDTH=pixels`	Line width	all
`<HTML>`	Identifies document as being HTML	all
`<I>`	Italic font	all
`<IMG>`	Inserts an image (graphic)	all
`ALIGN=alignment`	Positions image relative to text	all
`ALT="text"`	Text is displayed if graphic can't be	all
`BORDER=pixels`	Thickness of border around graphic	some
`HEIGHT=pixels`	Vertical size of image on page	all
`HSPACE=pixels`	Horizontal space between image and text	some
`ISMAP`	This image maps to multiple links	some
`LOWSRC="URL"`	Displays this image before SRC image	none
`SRC="URL"`	(Required) Image to be displayed	all
`VSPACE=pixels`	Vertical space between image and text	some
`WIDTH=pixels`	Horizontal size of image	all
`USEMAP="URL"`	File describes links for this image	some
`<INPUT>`	A form field	all
`ACCEPT="type,..."`	File types OK in file submission field	none

continues

Table B.1 Continued

Tag Attributes	Description	Other Browsers?
`ALIGN=`*alignment*	Positions image field relative to text	all
`CHECKED`	Check box or option button is selected	all
`MAXLENGTH=`*number*	Maximum characters user can enter	all
`NAME="`*name*`"`	Gives field a name	all
`SIZE=`*number*	Size of field in characters	all
`SRC="`*URL*`"`	Image file for button on form	all
`TYPE=CHECKBOX`	Check box (yes/no) field	all
`TYPE=FILE`	Field for submission of file	none
`TYPE=HIDDEN`	Field not seen by user	all
`TYPE=IMAGE`	Form submission button with graphic	all
`TYPE=PASSWORD`	Text entry field; text isn't displayed	all
`TYPE=RADIO`	An option select field (option button)	all
`TYPE=RESET`	Button that clears all fields	all
`TYPE=SUBMIT`	Form submission button	all
`TYPE=TEXT`	Single-line text field	all
`TYPE=TEXTAREA`	Multiple-line text field	all
`VALUE="`*text*`"`	Default value for field	all
`<ISINDEX>`	Indicates page is a searchable index	all
`ACTION="`*URL*`"`	Program to send search request to	none
`PROMPT="`*text*`"`	Text appears on search form	some
`<KBD>`	Text in keyboard format (monospace)	all
`<LI>`	Start of new item on list	all
`TYPE=1`	(Default) Arabic numbers (1, 2, 3, etc.)	some
`TYPE=a`	Lowercase letters (a, b, c, etc.)	some
`TYPE=A`	Uppercase letters (A, B, C, etc.)	some
`TYPE=CIRCLE`	Use circle as bullet (unordered list)	none
`TYPE=DISC`	Use dots as bullet (unordered list)	none
`TYPE=i`	Lowercase Roman numerals (i, xiv, etc.)	some
`TYPE=I`	Uppercase Roman numerals (I, XIV, etc.)	some
`TYPE=SQUARE`	Use square as bullet (unordered list)	none
`VALUE=`*number*	Sets entry counter for an ordered list	some
`<LINK>`	Shows relationship to another document	all
`REL="`*value,...*`"`	(Advanced) Lists relationship of link	some
`REV="`*value,...*`"`	(Advanced) Reverses relationship of link	some
`TITLE="`*text*`"`	Gives a name for the page linked to	some

Tag Attributes	Description	Other Browsers?
`<LISTING>`	Text format with a fixed spacing (`<PRE>` is a better choice)	some
`<MAP>`	Describes what areas of image are links	some
`NAME="name"`	(Required) Names the map	some
`<MENU>`	A menu list	all
`<META>`	Holds information to identify page	all
`CONTENT="text"`	(Required) The information being held	all
`HTTP-EQUIV="text"`	Relates info with HTTP response field	all
`NAME="text"`	Name for the information	all
`<MULTICOL>`	Splits display into columns without using frames or tables	some
`COLS=number`	(Required) Number of columns	some
`GUTTER=pixels`	Sets space between columns	some
`WIDTH=number`	Specifies width of individual columns	some
`<NOBR>`	Insert no line breaks into text	some
`<NOFRAMES>`	Browsers with frames skip this section	all
`<OL>`	Ordered (numbered or lettered) list	all
`START=number`	First value on list	some
`TYPE=a`	Lowercase letters (a, b, c, etc.)	some
`TYPE=A`	Uppercase letters (A, B, C, etc.)	some
`TYPE=i`	Lowercase Roman numerals (i, xiv, etc.)	some
`TYPE=I`	Uppercase Roman numerals (I, XIV, etc.)	some
`TYPE=1`	(Default) Arabic numbers (1, 2, 3, etc.)	some
`<P>`	A text paragraph	all
`ALIGN=alignment`	Positions text across page	some
`<PARAM>`	Passes parameters to an applet	none
`NAME=name`	(Required) Name of attribute being set	none
`VALUE=value`	(Required) Value attribute is set to	none
`<PLAINTEXT>`	Treat rest of document as text	some
`<PRE>`	Text format with fixed spacing	all
`<SAMP>`	Text format for text samples	all

continues

Table B.1   Continued

Tag Attributes	Description	Other Browsers?
`<SCRIPT>`	A Java script	some
`LANGUAGE="JAVASCRIPT"`	Indicates script language	some
`<SELECT>`	A menu field on a form	all
`MULTIPLE`	Allows more than one selection	some
`NAME="text"`	Name for the field	all
`SIZE=number`	Number of items visible at a time	all
`<SMALL>`	Use a smaller font	some
`<SPACER>`	An area of white space	some
`ALIGN=alignment`	Positions white space across page	some
`HEIGHT=pixels`	Sets white space height for Block	some
`SIZE=pixels`	Size for horizontal or vertical	some
`TYPE=type`	Horizontal, Vertical, or Block	some
`WIDTH=pixels`	Sets white space width for Block	some
`<STRIKE>`	Display text with a line through it	some
`<STRONG>`	Highlighted text (usually bold)	all
`<SUB>`	Subscript text	some
`<SUP>`	Superscript text	some
`<TABLE>`	Create a grid	some
`ALIGN=alignment`	Position text within the cell	some
`BORDER`	Display a border on the table	some
`BORDER=pixels`	Display a border of a certain thickness	some
`CELLPADDING=pixels`	Distance between cell frame and contents	some
`CELLSPACING=pixels`	Distance between cells	some
`WIDTH=number%`	Table width as percentage of space	some
`WIDTH=pixels`	Table width	some
`<TD>`	Table cell contents	some
`ALIGN=alignment`	Horizontal position of text in cell	some
`COLSPAN=number`	Number of columns this cell covers	some
`NOWRAP`	No line breaks in cell	some
`ROWSPAN=number`	Number of table rows this cell covers	some
`VALIGN=alignment`	Vertical position of text in cell	some
`<TEXTAREA>`	A multiline text field in a form	all
`COLS=number`	(Required) Field width, in characters	all
`NAME="name"`	(Required) Names the field	all
`ROWS=number`	(Required) Field height, in characters	all
`WRAP=OFF`	(Default) No word wrap	none
`WRAP=PHYSICAL`	Word wrap affects display and data	none
`WRAP=VIRTUAL`	Affects display but not sent data	none

Tag Attributes	Description	Other Browsers?
`<TH>`	Table header cell (cell with bold text)	some
`ALIGN=`*`alignment`*	Horizontal position of text in cell	some
`COLSPAN=`*`number`*	Number of columns this cell covers	some
`HEIGHT=`*`number`*`%`	Cell height as percentage of table	some
`HEIGHT=`*`pixels`*	Cell height	some
`NOWRAP`	No line breaks in cell	some
`ROWSPAN=`*`number`*	Number of table rows this cell covers	some
`VALIGN=`*`alignment`*	Vertical position of text in cell	some
`WIDTH=`*`number`*`%`	Cell width as percentage of table	some
`WIDTH=`*`pixels`*	Cell width	some
`<TITLE>`	Sets page title, displayed in title bar	all
`<TR>`	Table row	some
`ALIGN=`*`alignment`*	Horizontal position of text in cells	some
`VALIGN=`*`alignment`*	Vertical position of text in cells	some
`<TT>`	Teletype format (fixed width font)	all
`<UL>`	Unnumbered list	all
`TYPE=CIRCLE`	Use open circle bullets on list	none
`TYPE=DISC`	Use dot bullets on list	none
`TYPE=SQUARE`	Use square bullets on list	none
`<VAR>`	Text format for program variables	all
`<WBR>`	Allows a break even in `<NOBR>` area	some
`<XMP>`	Example text format	all

Glossary

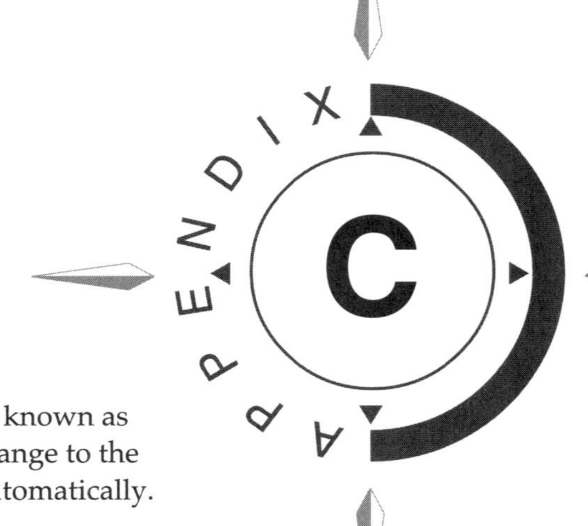

alias   A copy of an e-mail address is known as an alias because when you make a change to the original entry, the copy is changed automatically.

anchor   The part of a link that causes the mouse pointer to turn into a pointing finger. See also *links*.

anonymous login   The process of connecting to a system incognito. Many FTP sites (places where you can get files) allow users to connect anonymously and access public areas. Anonymous login privileges usually do not allow you to place files on the server or change anything.

applet   A small, single-purpose application, such as a loan calculator or a tic-tac-toe game. Java applets, which are found on Web pages, cannot run by themselves; they run in conjunction with a compatible Web browser (such as Navigator).

Archie   An Internet search tool that helps you find files on FTP sites. In most cases, you need to know the exact name of the file or a partial file name. See also *Jughead* and *Veronica*.

associate   To establish a connection between a given file type and the helper application needed to view or play that file type. In Navigator, you must create file associations so Navigator will know which application to run when you choose to view, watch, or listen to a file. For example, you might associate movie files that end in .mpg with an MPEG movie helper application.

attribute   A parameter that further defines an HTML command, giving such specific information as the size or color, for example.

BBS (bulletin board system)   A computer to which multiple users can send messages for the purpose of conversing or exchanging files and information. Special interest groups, professional organizations, and software companies often set up BBSs.

bookmark   A Navigator tool that lets you mark your favorite Web pages so you can quickly return to them later.

Boolean operators   Conjunctions including "and" and "or" that are used to separate search terms. For example, if you search for "Clinton and Whitewater," you get a list of all resources that relate to both "Clinton" and "Whitewater." If you use "or," the search is much broader, finding anything that relates to either "Clinton" or "Whitewater."

bps   Short for *bits per second*, this is a unit used to measure the speed of data being transferred between two computers. Most transfers on the Web take place at 14,400bps or higher.

browser   See *Web browser*.

bullet   A small graphic used to highlight each item within a list.

cache   A temporary storage area that Navigator creates both in RAM and on your hard disk. Navigator stores Web pages in the cache so that it can quickly load these pages if you decide to return to them. In other words, because Netscape saves the Web pages you've visited recently in this cache, the pages don't have to be transferred over the phone lines again.

channel   The equivalent of a conference room. When you chat on the Internet, you first connect to a chat server, and then you tune in to a channel. Each channel is supposed to deal with a different topic, but some are open for general conversation about the weather and where people are from. See also *chat room*.

chat   To "talk" to another person by typing at your computer. What you type appears on the other person's screen, and what the other person types appears on your screen. You can't chat with Navigator; you need another program such as Netscape Conference if you want to get chatty.

chat room   You enter into a conversation on a chat server by opening a channel, called a chat room. Conversations carried on within a room are copied to everyone else on that channel (in the same room).

client   Of two computers, the computer that's being served. Whenever you connect to a Web site, the computer at that site is the *server*, and your computer is the client or customer.

compressed file   A file that has been condensed so that it takes up less disk space and travels faster through network and modem connections. Before you can use a compressed file, you must decompress (or expand) it using a special program.

cyberspace   The universe created by the connection of thousands of computers. Computer users can use modems to enter cyberspace and converse with other users. This term was first used by William Gibson in his novel *Neuromancer*. In the novel, people plugged their brains into cyberspace. If you've ever seen the glazed look people get when they're wired to the Web, you know that Gibson's notion is not too far from the truth.

decompress   To expand a compressed file and make it usable. Popular decompression programs include PKUNZIP (for DOS) and WinZip (for Windows).

Dial-Up Networking   A program that comes with Windows 95 that establishes the Internet connection you need in order to run Navigator and access the World Wide Web.

document   On the Web, this can be anything: an index of topics, several screens full of text, or even a page full of pictures. See also *Web page.*

document source   The coded document that controls the way Web pages look. See also *HTML.*

domain name   A unique identification for an Internet site; also known as *host name.* Each computer on the Internet has a domain name that distinguishes it from other computers on the Internet. Domain names usually provide some vague indication of the establishment that runs the server. For example, the domain name of the White House server is www.whitehouse.gov. The .gov at the end stands for "government." Other popular extensions are .mil (military), .edu (education), .com (commercial), .net (network), and .org (nonprofit organization).

domain name server (DNS)   A computer that matches a site's name to a number that identifies that site. All servers on the Internet have a domain name, such as ncsa.uiuc.edu. Each server also has a unique IP (Internet Protocol) number, such as 128.252.135.4. Your Internet service provider has an electronic database called a DNS (Domain Name Server) that matches the domain to the IP number to find the server that has the data you've requested. As you innocently click links, the DNS is matching domain names and IP numbers to make sure you get where you're supposed to go.

download   To copy a file from another computer (usually an FTP server) to your computer. See also *upload*.

EDI (electronic data interchange)   A protocol through which information sent between two designated parties is encrypted so that it can be sent over the Internet in a secure manner.

e-mail   A system by which people can send and receive messages through their computers, either on a network or by using modems. Each person has a designated mailbox that stores messages sent by other users. He can then retrieve and read messages from the mailbox.

FAQ (frequently asked questions, pronounced "fak")   A list of answers to the most often-asked questions at a particular Internet site. Good Internet etiquette demands that you read the FAQ at a site before you post any questions.

finger   A special UNIX command that pokes around through a directory of users and finds information about them, including e-mail addresses, and whether or not people have read their mail recently or even logged in.

flame   To verbally abuse another user during an online discussion, via e-mail or in a newsgroup. Common flaming techniques include name-calling, abusive innuendoes about one's parents, and other puerile gems of wit.

form   A fill-in-the-blank Web document. Sites commonly use forms to take credit card orders, ask for your password, register downloaded software, or request search instructions.

frame   A Navigator feature that allows two parts of the same Web document to appear in the same window. For example, one frame might contain an outline of the document, and if you click a heading in that outline, the other frame shows the contents under that heading.

FTP (File Transfer Protocol)   A set of rules that governs the transfer of files between computers. You can download files off the Internet with an FTP program or with Netscape.

GIF file (Graphic Interchange Format, pronounced "giff file" or "jiff file")
A picture file that's often a photograph or painting. Also a format developed by CompuServe for transferring graphic files; this format is good for storing a lot of graphic information in very little space.

Gopher An indexing system that allows you to access various Internet services by selecting menu options. Whenever you connect to a Gopher site, it presents you with an opening menu. When you select a menu item, the server presents you with another submenu containing additional options and/or files. These options may kick you out to another Gopher server, an FTP server, a newsgroup, or other Internet servers. You proceed through the menus until you find the information you want… or until you reach a dead end.

handle A user's computerized nickname or ID number. When you look for a person using Whois, you might find the person's handle. You can often find out more about a person by performing the search again using the person's handle.

helper application A program that performs a specialized job that Navigator is unable to manage. Whenever you click a link to a file that Navigator can't play, Navigator loads the file to disk and then starts the helper application associated with that file. The helper application loads the file and plays it in a separate window. See also *in-line plug-in*.

hexadecimal The notation for a base-16 numeral, which uses the letters A–F as replacements for the numbers 10, 11, 12, and so on. Hexadecimal notation is used in the designation of color values in HTML.

history list A directory of all the Web sites you have visited since you connected. You can view the history list in Navigator by opening the Window menu and clicking History.

hits In a WAIS search, the number of times a search word was found in an article. The higher the number, the more likely it is that the article contains the information you're looking for. See also *score*.

home page The page that greets you when you first start Navigator or first connect to a Web site.

host The host is the computer that has the information. Your computer is the client, requesting information from the host.

host name See *domain name*.

HTML (HyperText Markup Language) The code used to create Web documents. These codes tell Navigator how to display the text (titles, headings, lists, and so on), insert anchors that link this document to other documents, and control character formatting (by making it bold or italic).

HTTP (HyperText Transport Protocol)   A set of rules that govern the exchange of data between a Web host and a client (your computer). The address for every Web server starts with **http**. If you see an address that starts with different letters (such as "ftp" or "gopher"), the address is for a different type of server. Gopher addresses start with "gopher," FTP with "ftp," WAIS with "wais," UseNet with "news," and Telnet with "telnet."

hyperdocument   A Web page that contains links connecting it to other pages. On the Web, a hyperdocument might contain links to other text, graphics, sounds, or movies.

hyperlinks   Icons, pictures, or highlighted chunks of text that connect two documents. For example, a document about pork might contain a link for sausage. If you click the link, Navigator displays a document about how to make sausage.

hypermedia   A dynamic computerized "soup" that contains movie clips, graphics, sound files, text, and anything else that can be stored in a digitized form. That's the "media" part, anyway. The "hyper" part deals with the fact that these ingredients are interlinked, so you can jump quickly from one to another.

hypertext   Specially formatted text that provides a link to another document, or another part of the same document. You'll find hypertext in most Help systems. When you click a hypertext word such as "save," you're taken to the part of Help that tells you how to save your work. On the Internet, hypertext (more correctly called *hyperlinks*) provides a link to a particular Web document (Web page).

in-line image   A graphic that appears inside a Web document. You can tell Navigator not to display these images if you can't stand waiting for them to load.

in-line plug-in   A program that links itself to Netscape Navigator in order to provide Navigator with some capability it would otherwise not have, such as the capability to play MPEG video files. Unlike helper applications, in-line plug-ins display their work within the Navigator window. See also *helper application*.

interactive   A user-controlled program, document, or game. Interactive programs commonly display on-screen *prompts*, asking the user for input so he can decide how to carry out a particular task. These programs are popular in education, allowing children to follow their natural curiosity to solve problems and gather information.

Internet   The world's largest system of interconnected networks. The Internet was originally named ARPAnet after the Advanced Research Projects Agency in the Defense department. The agency developed the ARPAnet in the mid-1970s as an experimental project that would allow various university and military sources to continue to communicate in a state of national emergency. Now, the Internet is used mostly by private citizens for connecting to databases, exchanging electronic mail, and finding information.

IP address   A unique number assigned to each computer on the Internet. Most of the time, you work with domain names, such as nasa.uiuc.edu. Behind the scenes, whenever you enter a domain name, your service provider matches that name to the site's IP number (for example 128.252.135.4) and calls that site. The idea here is that it's easier for you to remember names and easier for computers to remember numbers. The domain name/IP number link makes everyone happy.

IRC (Internet Relay Chat)   A technology that allows users to type messages back and forth using their keyboards. It's sort of like talking on the phone, but it's less expensive and much slower.

Java   A relatively new technology that enables its users to create animations and other moving video clips and embed them in Web pages. All you need to know about Java is that if you click a link for a Java applet (application), Navigator will play it.

JavaScript   Developed by Netscape, JavaScript is a variation of pure Java, in which Java code is embedded directly within an HTML document. By contrast, a programmer using only Java creates and saves his program as a separate file. That program is then launched from the HTML page by a single command.

JPEG (Joint Photographic Experts Group)   A file-compression format used for storing graphic files. If you come across a file that ends in .JPG, you can view it in Netscape Navigator, or you can have one of your helper applications display it.

Jughead   An Internet search tool used to find resources at a Gopher site. Archie, Veronica, and Jughead (all Internet search tools) are related. Archie searches for FTP servers that contain the files you want to download. Veronica searches all Gopher sites to find the ones that store the various resources you specify. Jughead searches only the current Gopher site to find the specified resources.

links   Also known as *hyperlinks*, these are icons, pictures, or highlighted chunks of text that connect the current page to other pages, Internet sites, graphics, movies, or sounds.

logical codes   In a Web document, codes that provide general directions on how to display text. For example, <em> stands for emphasis, which might mean bold or italic. Physical codes give more precise instructions. For example, <b> means bold. See also *physical codes* and *tags*.

login   To connect to another computer on a network or on the Internet so you can use that computer's resources. The login procedure usually requires you to enter your user name (or user ID) and a password.

logout   To disconnect from another computer on a network or on the Internet.

lurk   To read newsgroup messages posted by other people but not respond to them or post any messages of your own. That way, you can see what's going on before you decide to participate in a particular discussion.

map   A graphical navigational tool used on many Web pages. Think of it as one of those mall maps with the **YOU ARE HERE** arrow on it, but with a Web map, you can actually go places by clicking different areas of the map.

MIDI (Musical Instrument Digital Interface)   Some Web pages contain links to files that can play music on MIDI instruments or on MIDI-compatible sound cards within your PC.

MIME (Multipurpose Internet Mail Extensions)   A protocol that controls all file transfers on the Web. Navigator uses MIME to recognize different file types. If an HTML document arrives, Navigator "knows" to play that file. If an MPG file arrives, Navigator calls the associated helper application. MIME was originally developed to attach different types of files (usually multimedia files) to e-mail messages.

mirror site   A server that contains the same files as the original site. Mirror sites are very useful because some sites are so busy that users might have trouble connecting during peak hours. The mirror sites offer an alternative location that helps users avoid Internet traffic jams.

modem   Short for *modulator-demodulator*, a modem is a device that translates computer information into sound and transmits those sounds over conventional telephone lines or that receives such sounds and translates them into computer data.

monospace   In typesetting, a typeface in which all characters have the same width.

MPEG (Moving Pictures Expert Group)   A video-compression and movie presentation standard used for most video clips stored on the Web. The only thing that matters is that if you encounter a file that ends in MPG, you need an MPG or MPEG player to watch it.

Netscape Navigator   Popular Web browser. Netscape Navigator transforms Web documents (which consist of boring codes) into exciting multimedia documents complete with sounds, pictures, and movies.

newbie   Derogatory term for a new user on the Internet.

newsgroup   An Internet bulletin board for users who share common interests. There are thousands of newsgroups ranging from body art to pets. News-groups let you post messages and read messages from other users.

pane   A portion of a window. Netscape Mail uses panes to divide its window into logical areas. See also *frame*.

physical codes   In a Web document, codes that provide specific directions on how to display text. For example, <bold> stands for bold. Logical codes give less precise instructions. For example, <em> means emphasis, which might mean bold or italic.

plan   A text file that a user might attach to his finger file to include more information. A plan might include the person's address, phone number, job interests, or anything else that person wants to make publicly accessible.

port   1) The hardware connection through which a computer sends and/or receives data.   2) An application that's set up on a server. When you specify the server's port, you're actually telling it to run one of its applications.

post   To send a message to a bulletin board or newsgroup for all to see.

postmaster   The person at a given site who is in charge of assigning users their e-mail addresses. You can usually send a message to the postmaster by address-ing it to **postmaster@***sitename* or **webmaster@***sitename*.

PPP (Point-to-Point Protocol)   A type of Internet connection. What's important is that when you choose an Internet service provider, you get the right connection: SLIP or PPP; otherwise, you won't be able to use Navigator.

protocol   A set of rules that govern the transfer of data between two computers.

proxy   A special connection that allows two incompatible networks to communicate. For example, say you're on the Web with Navigator and you decide to use WAIS to search for a list of articles. You can't use WAIS directly from Navigator, so you have to work through a Web/WAIS proxy. The proxy acts as a middleman, ensuring that the data transfer goes smoothly.

relative reference   In a Web document, a link that refers to the location of another page or file in relation to the address of the current page. For example, if the page is in the /PUB directory, and a linked page is in /PUB/HOME, a relative reference might specify /HOME. An absolute reference would have to give the complete path (/PUB/HOME).

score   In WAIS searches, a number that indicates the relative likelihood that an article will contain the information you need. The topmost article gets a score of 1000. Subsequent scores are relative to 1000, so 500 would mean that the article had half as many occurrences of the search term as did the top article.

search tool   A searchable index of Web pages. Popular Web search tools include AltaVista, Yahoo!, InfoSeek, and Lycos.

server   In the politically incorrect world of the Internet, the computer that serves up all the data. The other computer, the client, acts as a customer, demanding specific information.

service provider   The company that you pay for permission to connect to its computer and get on the Internet.

shareware   Computer programs you can use for free and then pay for if you decide to continue using them. Many programmers use the Internet to distribute their programs, relying on the honesty and goodwill of Internet users for their income.

signature file   A text file that usually includes your name and some kind of logo or picture, created by using spaces and other characters such as x, |, and - to form a particular pattern (such as a bird).

SLIP (Serial Line Internet Protocol)   A type of Internet connection that allows you to connect directly to the Internet without having to run programs off your Internet service provider's computer.

SSL (Secure Sockets Layer)   Netscape's security technology. Web pages protected with SSL prevent misanthropic hackers from nabbing personal information that you might enter on the page (including your credit card number).

status bar   The area at the bottom of the Navigator window that shows you what's going on as you work. The little key in the status bar indicates whether a document is secure; if the key looks broken, the document is not secure.

stop word   In a search, any word that is excluded from the search. For example, if you are searching a computer database, the database may refuse to look for such common words as "and" and "computer."

subscribe   The process by which you gain access to the messages in a newsgroup. After subscribing to a newsgroup, its messages are downloaded to your PC so that you can access them.

tags   HTML codes that work behind the scenes to tell Navigator how to display a document and how to open other linked documents. Tags can control the look of text (as in titles and headings), insert anchors that link this document to other documents, and control character formatting (by making it bold or italic).

TCP/IP (Transmission Control Protocol/Internet Protocol)   The preferred method of data transfer over the Internet. With TCP/IP, the sending computer stuffs data into packets and sends it. The receiving computer unstuffs the packets and assembles them into some meaningful and useful form. The most popular TCP/IP program is Winsock.

telnet   To connect to a server and use it to run programs as if you were sitting at its keyboard (or sitting at the keyboard of a terminal that's connected to the server). Think of it as using the computerized card catalog at the local library.

terminal connection   The type of connection you don't want to have if you're using Navigator. A terminal connection makes your computer act like one of your service provider's workstations. You run programs on the service provider's computer and connect to the Internet indirectly through that computer. With a SLIP or PPP connection, you connect through the service provider's computer, but you use software on your computer to do all your work.

terminal emulation   A technique used to make one computer act like another so the two computers can carry on a conversation. Some mainframe computers will interact with only a specific type of terminal. If you want to connect to that mainframe computer using your personal computer, you must make your computer act like the required terminal.

texture mapping   A technique in which a three-dimensional object is rendered by a computer with a surface taken from a two-dimensional picture, giving that object an apparent "texture" or "feel."

thread   In newsgroups and e-mail, a way of grouping messages so you can quickly tell that they belong to the same topic of conversation.

tiled   Repeating a graphic on a Web page both horizontally and vertically.

UNIX shell   The equivalent of a DOS prompt for computers that are running the UNIX operating system. You type commands at the prompt as if you were using a PC.

upload   To copy a file from your computer to another computer. You usually upload files to share them with other users. See also *download*.

URL (Uniform Resource Locator)   An address for an Internet site. The Web uses URLs to specify the addresses of the various servers on the Internet and the documents on each server. For example, the URL for the White House server is http://www.whitehouse.gov. The "http" stands for HyperText Transfer Protocol, which means this is a Web document. "www" stands for World Wide Web; "whitehouse" represents the server or company name; "gov" stands for government.

UseNet   Short for *user's network*, UseNet sets the standards by which the various newsgroups swap information. See also *newsgroup*.

Veronica   One of many Internet search tools, this one finds Gopher sites that have what you're looking for. For a comparison of popular search tools, see also *Jughead*.

viewer   A program that Navigator uses to play movie clips, sound clips, PostScript files, graphics, and any other file Navigator cannot handle. See also *helper application* and *in-line plug-in*.

virus A computer virus is a program that hides itself inside another file. If you use the file, the virus attaches itself to your system, often destroying data and rendering your system inoperable. Although some viruses are simple pranks, many are extremely dangerous to your data. A virus can enter your system only from within an outside file; typically, you copy the diseased file from a floppy disk, or leave an infected floppy disk in its drive during startup. But you can also infect your system by downloading an infected file from the Internet, an online service, or a BBS.

VRML (Virtual Reality Modeling Language) A method that enables Netscape to bring a seemingly three-dimensional world to life on your PC's two-dimensional screen.

W3 Another name for the World Wide Web.

WAIS (Wide Area Information Server, pronounced "ways") A system that allows you to search various databases on the Internet for specific articles and other resources.

wave table In a sound card, a wave table contains a set of prerecorded sound patches that allows a MIDI device to simulate a musical instrument.

Web browser Any of several programs you can use to navigate the World Wide Web. The Web browser controls the look of the Web documents and provides additional tools for jumping from one Web document to another. Netscape Navigator is a Web browser.

Web page A document on a server that is viewed with a Web browser.

Web server A specialized computer on the Internet that's devoted to storing and serving up Web documents.

Webmaster The person who created and maintains a Web document. If you find an error in a Web document, you should notify the Webmaster (in a nice way).

Whois A UNIX command that you can use to find out a person's e-mail address, mailing address, phone number, or other information, if you know the person's last name and the location of the server that person logs in to.

World Wide Web   A collection of interconnected documents stored on computers all over the world. These documents can contain text, pictures, movie clips, sounds, and links to other documents. You move from one document to another by clicking links.

WWW   See *World Wide Web*.

WYSIWYG (What-You-See-Is-What-You-Get)   A feature that enables programs to display documents on-screen so they look exactly as they will when printed.

zip   To compress a file so that it takes up less space and transfers more quickly. If you have a zipped file, you must unzip it before you can use it.

Index

507

X - Y - Z

Check out Que® Books on the World Wide Web
http://www.quecorp.com

As the biggest software release in computer history, Windows 95 continues to redefine the computer industry. Click here for the latest info on our Windows 95 books

Make computing quick and easy with these products designed exclusively for new and casual users

Examine the latest releases in word processing, spreadsheets, operating systems, and suites

The Internet, The World Wide Web, CompuServe®, America Online®, Prodigy®—it's a world of ever-changing information. Don't get left behind!

Find out about new additions to our site, new bestsellers, and hot topics

In-depth information on high-end topics: find the best reference books for databases, programming, networking, and client/server technologies

A recent addition to Que, Ziff-Davis Press publishes the highly successful *How It Works* and *How to Use* series of books, as well as *PC Learning Labs Teaches* and *PC Magazine* series of book/disc packages

Stay on the cutting edge of Macintosh® technologies and visual communications

Find out which titles are making headlines

With six separate publishing groups, Que develops products for many specific market segments and areas of computer technology. Explore our Web Site and you'll find information on best-selling titles, newly published titles, upcoming products, authors, and much more.

- Stay informed on the latest industry trends and products available
- Visit our online bookstore for the latest information and editions
- Download software from Que's library of the best shareware and freeware

Complete and Return This Card for a *FREE* Computer Book Catalog

Thank you for purchasing this book! You have purchased a superior computer book written expressly for your needs. To continue to provide the kind of up-to-date, pertinent coverage you've come to expect from us, we need to hear from you. Please take a minute to complete and return this self-addressed, postage-paid form. In return, we'll send you a free catalog of all our computer books on topics ranging from word processing to programming and the Internet.

Mr. ☐ Mrs. ☐ Ms. ☐ Dr. ☐

Name (first) ⬚ (M.I.) ☐ (last) ⬚

Address ⬚

City ⬚ State ☐ Zip ⬚

Phone ⬚ Fax ⬚

Company Name ⬚

E-mail address ⬚

Please check at least three (3) influencing factors for purchasing this book.

Front or back cover information on book ☐
Special approach to the content ☐
Completeness of content ☐
Author's reputation ☐
Publisher's reputation ☐
Book cover design or layout ☐
Index or table of contents of book ☐
Price of book ☐
Special effects, graphics, illustrations ☐
Other (Please specify): _______ ☐

2. How did you first learn about this book?

Saw in Macmillan Computer Publishing catalog ☐
Recommended by store personnel ☐
Saw the book on bookshelf at store ☐
Recommended by a friend ☐
Received advertisement in the mail ☐
Saw an advertisement in: _______ ☐
Read book review in: _______ ☐
Other (Please specify): _______ ☐

3. How many computer books have you purchased in the last six months?

This book only ☐   3 to 5 books ☐
2 books ☐   More than 5 ☐

4. Where did you purchase this book?

Bookstore ☐
Computer Store ☐
Consumer Electronics Store ☐
Department Store ☐
Office Club ☐
Warehouse Club ☐
Mail Order ☐
Direct from Publisher ☐
Internet site ☐
Other (Please specify): _______ ☐

5. How long have you been using a computer?

☐ Less than 6 months   ☐ 6 months to a year
☐ 1 to 3 years   ☐ More than 3 years

6. What is your level of experience with personal computers and with the subject of this book?

	With PCs	With subject of book
New	☐	☐
Casual	☐	☐
Accomplished	☐	☐
Expert	☐	☐

Source Code ISBN: 0-7897-1065-x

7. Which of the following best describes your job title?

Administrative Assistant ☐
Coordinator ☐
Manager/Supervisor ☐
Director ☐
Vice President ☐
President/CEO/COO ☐
Lawyer/Doctor/Medical Professional ☐
Teacher/Educator/Trainer ☐
Engineer/Technician ☐
Consultant ☐
Not employed/Student/Retired ☐
Other (Please specify): _______________ ☐

8. Which of the following best describes the area of the company your job title falls under?

Accounting ☐
Engineering ☐
Manufacturing ☐
Operations ☐
Marketing ☐
Sales ☐
Other (Please specify): _______________ ☐

9. What is your age?

Under 20 ☐
21-29 ☐
30-39 ☐
40-49 ☐
50-59 ☐
60-over ☐

10. Are you:

Male ☐
Female ☐

11. Which computer publications do you read regularly? (Please list)

____
____
____
____
____
____
____
____
____
____

Comments: _______________________________
____
____

Fold here and tape to mail